THE ANALYTICAL ENGINE

Books by Rick Decker and Stuart Hirshfield:

The Analytical Engine: An Introduction to Computer Science Using HyperCard 2.1, Second Edition

The Analytical Engine: An Introduction to Computer Science Using HyperCard 1.0

The Analytical Engine: An Introduction to Computer Science Using Toolbook

Pascal's Triangle: Reading, Writing, and Reasoning About Programs

The Object Concept: An Introduction to Computer Programming Using C++

THE ANALYTICAL ENGINE

AN INTRODUCTION TO COMPUTER SCIENCE
USING HYPERCARD 2.1

RICK DECKER
STUART HIRSHFIELD

Hamilton College

PWS PUBLISHING COMPANY
BOSTON

PWS Publishing Company
20 Park Plaza, Boston, MA 02116-4324

PWS Publishing Company is a division of Wadsworth, Inc.

 ™

International Thomson Publishing
The trademark ITP is used under license.

 This book is printed
on recycled, acid-free paper.

Apple, the Apple logo, ImageWriter, LaserWriter, and MacPaint are registered trademarks of Apple Computer, Inc. HyperCard, HyperTalk, Macintosh, MultiFinder, and Stackware are trademarks of Apple Computer, Inc.

Some of the icons in this book were derived from other sources. The authors wish to thank the original creators for granting permission for their use:
   © 1989 by Bryan McCormick, Pleasant Hill, CA, all rights reserved; PrintDoc XCMD © 1988 by Ignatz Software;
      Flame Icons © 1989 by Radical Sheep Inc.; Files XFCN © by Guy de Picciotto.
   © 1989 by Marc Harrison, Pleasant Hill, CA, all rights reserved.
   © 1987 Heizer Software, Pleasant Hill, CA, all rights reserved.
   Seventh Wave Technologies, Newport News, VA.
   Some screens © Apple Computer, Inc. Used with permission.

Library of Congress Cataloging-in-Publication Data

Decker, Rick.
   The analytical engine: an introduction to computer science using Hypercard 2.1 / Rick Decker, Stuart Hirshfield—2nd ed.
      p. cm.
   Includes bibliographical references and index.
   ISBN 0-534-93696-2
   1. Electronic digital computers.   2. Macintosh (Computer)—Programming.   3. Hypercard (Computer file).   I. Hirshfield,
Stuart. II. Title.
QA76.5.D37   1994
004—dc20

93-25430
CIP

Sponsoring Editor: Michael J. Sugarman
Associate Developmental Editor: Susan M. Gay
Editorial Assistant: Ken Morton
Production Editor: Abigail M. Heim
Manufacturing Coordinator: Ruth Graham
Interior Designer: Abigail M. Heim
Cover Designer: Sally Bindari, Books by Design
Compositor: Pure Imaging
Cover Printer: John P. Pow Co., Inc.
Text Printer and Binder: Courier/Westford

Printed and bound in the United States of America
94 95 96 97 98—9 8 7 6 5 4 3 2 1

CONTENTS

PREFACE

THE Æ COURSE

What you have in your hands represents a departure from the traditional introduction to computer science textbooks. Indeed, we have coined the term "CS 0" to describe the course that this text/disk package embodies. Because this package is different, a few words of introduction and encouragement are in order.

We wrote the text and prepared the lab disks for the same reason we suspect many other authors do: We simply couldn't find an existing package that suited our needs. As at many other schools, our introductory course was a programming course that served two audiences: those who wanted an introduction to the subject and those who intended to major in computer science (or at least take some courses beyond the introductory level). And, as at many other schools, this approach simply didn't work well. Because of the wide range of talents and backgrounds of the students we were constantly performing a balancing act, trying to move slowly enough not to lose the bottom half of the class and quickly enough not to bore the students with some prior experience. The bimodal nature of the course was difficult to deal with, both for us and the students. Even more problematic was our perception that students were finishing the introductory course with the firm impression that computer science was nothing but programming. This attitude did a disservice to those wanting a taste of the discipline and frequently left our majors in shock when they later discovered that being a programming whiz counted for little in their subsequent courses.

"You get too soon old and too late smart," the saying goes. Having taught a programming introductory course for seven years, we finally realized that something had to be done and, more importantly, we realized that what had to be done was something that hadn't been done before, at least not in computer science. Consider introductory courses in other disciplines—English 101 does not consist solely of having the students complete writing exercises; of course, the students typically have a number of essays to write, but they are also exposed to the broad historical trends in literature, they are introduced to the forms of literature, and they are given the critical apparatus necessary to make sense of the material they read. The students enrolled in Physics 101 are likewise learning to manipulate laboratory equipment while being exposed to the material in context—perhaps learning about Galileo, Maxwell, and Einstein, certainly exploring the major divisions of the subject, and being exposed to the social, political, and moral implications of the use and misuse of physical discoveries.

Introductory courses in computer science, on the other hand, typically tend to suffer from one or more major shortcomings:

- *Equating computer science with programming.* One of the things we hear again and again from our students is the mistaken idea that computer science is programming. Of course, computer professionals do write programs from time to time. Computer science, though, steps back from programming and, like physics, seeks to formulate and understand the general principles that govern the objects of its study, which for us are computers and their programs. The study of computer science is related to writing programs in somewhat the same way that the study of music is related to the production of songs. The product is important, but the study of the principles behind the product is vastly more so: It is nearly impossible to produce the product without some understanding of the principles.

- *Confusing training with education.* Another popular form of the introductory course is what we might call "Getting Acquainted With 4th Dimension, WriteNow, and Excel." A slightly more elevated version of this course also exists in the form "So You Want a Career in MIS?" Neither version has much to do with the discipline of computer science, and, given the rapid advances in the field, both run the risk of providing specific training in technologies that will be out of date by the time the students graduate.

- *Concentrating on effects at the expense of causes.* In an attempt to avoid alienating their audience by introducing technical material, some introductory courses sidestep computer science almost entirely, stressing instead the social consequences of the computerization of society. Done poorly, such a course can become what one of our colleagues calls the "*People* Magazine Goes to MIT" approach. Done well, though, this approach can be valuable. We feel that it is important for every citizen to be aware of the possible consequences of the use of technology, but we also feel that to understand the implications of technology it is necessary to understand the technology itself. We believe that along with questions of what computers should and should not do, our students should also be aware of what they *can* and *cannot* do, both by virtue of the current state of the art and theoretical limitations.

We set out to design a true survey course, presenting a serious disciplinary point of view, firmly grounded in a liberal arts tradition. The collective experience of the authors (we have taught this course for five years now), our students, and our many faithful adopters seems to indicate that this approach—the Æ approach to CS 0—overcomes the aforementioned shortcomings while serving all of the course's constituencies.

THE TEXT

This second edition retains the basic organization and outline of the first. The arrangement of the topics proceeds first downward, to increasingly concrete points of view, and then up, returning to increasingly more general levels of abstraction—a kind of *Divine Comedy* itinerary.

Module 1 provides a historical orientation, describing the technological history of computers in the context of increasing use of technology, beginning with the Industrial Revolution. The lab portion of this module is devoted to an introduction to the Macintosh and HyperCard. **Module 2** discusses some computer applications—the familiar (calculators, word processors, and spreadsheets) as well as some more specialized and less familiar ones in medicine, the sciences, and education. This module concludes with an introduction to some social implications of computer use, a theme that is continued in Module 9. The lab part of this module provides the students with hands-on experience with HyperCard implementations of a simple word processor, a spreadsheet, a graphing calculator, a DNA pattern-matching stack, and arithmetic flash cards.

Modules 3 through 6 lead the students deeper into the inner circles of the abyss. **Module 3** discusses system design, using the example of the user interface. At this level the focus is on combining components with fully developed functionalities into a smoothly functioning system: A program begins to become less of a "black box" and the details begin to be apparent. The lab part of Module 3 is devoted to the authoring level of HyperCard; the students have a practice stack that provides a tutorial on stack design, fields, and buttons. The lab concludes with a restaurant guide stack that the students are asked to customize.

In **Module 4** the gray box becomes a clear box: Students are introduced to programming by inspecting scripts of existing stacks and writing scripts of their own. We discuss most of the canonical programming constructs as well as algorithm design, and we take students through a simple software life cycle, using the lab stack as an example. The lab portion of this module provides an accounting application with sorting and searching capabilities. The students are directed to modify and expand this stack.

Module 5 deals with program translation. The important idea here, of course, is that since a computer can only execute programs in its own machine language, a source program in HyperTalk must be translated into machine language to be executed. We discuss the problem of representing text in binary form and provide an assembler for a hypothetical computer. The labs for this module follow the pattern of all subsequent labs: Now that the students have been introduced to programming, they not only can run the labs to reinforce the text material, but they can also inspect and modify the scripts of the lab stacks. The first lab stack is a text-to-ASCII-to-binary converter, and the second is an assembler for the simulated computer.

Module 6 concludes the progress toward the concrete by describing how the hardware of a computer works. Starting with switches, we construct gates, which we combine to construct logic, arithmetic, and memory circuits. Finally, we use the circuits to build the small computer that was only hypothetical in Module 5. The lab stack for this module is a simulated breadboard that the students can use to design and test circuits of their own.

Modules 7, 8, and 9 ascend from the most concrete, physical level to the most abstract and general. In **Module 7** we make two points: First, that before there were physical realizations of computers, there were abstract, mathematical ones; second, that the physical machine is in some sense nonessential when thinking about the nature of programs and computation. We introduce the Turing Machine, discuss the ideas of encoding strings and programs, and show that there are infinitely many tasks that computers cannot do, not only because there are uncountably many input-output matchings and only countably many programs, but also because there are tasks (like the Halting Problem) that seem natural candidates for computer solution but are simply impossible to program. The lab for Module 7 is a Turing Machine simulator.

Module 8 is a segue, via Turing, from questions of what computers cannot do to what they might do. We use Arthur C. Clarke's HAL 9000 computer as a standard against which we view the current state of affairs in artificial intelligence research. The lab stacks include a poetry generator and a simulated optical character recognizer.

Finally, in **Module 9** we look at things to come. We identify the major trends in computer use and try to see what the implications of these trends might be, guided at all times by a knowledge of how difficult it is to predict the future. The lab stack, an ATM simulation, serves to demonstrate the basic concepts of security, privacy, and maintenance as they apply to computer systems and networks.

NEW TEXT FEATURES FOR THE SECOND EDITION

While the topical organization of the text has remained intact from the first edition, this second edition is indeed "new and improved" in a number of important ways. The changes we chose to incorporate reflect the expressed preferences of our "users"—that is, the students and faculty who have used the package in the classroom. In a nutshell, the new features of the text include:

- *Lab exercises that are "folded into" the text material for each module:* The first edition had this feature in only two of its nine modules.

It worked so well in those modules to better integrate the lab and the text (and also to break up long blocks of text) that we decided to do it throughout the book.

- *More detailed lab exercises, many involving writing:* One by-product of "folded-in" lab exercises is that many of the exercises could be rewritten to concentrate on particular sections of the text. As a result, the exercises are much more thorough and relevant to the text. Also, a number of new exercises have been written that ask students to write out English comments about particular lab experiences.

- *A textual version of balloon help:* In the dual interests of highlighting points made in the text and making it easier to find subsections of the text, we have added marginal notes (in the form of "balloon help," à la System 7).

- *No presumptions about computing environment:* The primary motivation for including a System Folder and HyperCard with the first edition software was to provide students with a "turnkey" environment. We now recognize (thanks to our adopters!) that this was a mistake. Every user of the package operates in an ever-so-slightly different environment with a complex combination of machine models, disk drives, system folders, and network connectivity. The new edition of the text is, as a result, decidedly less prescriptive about such matters. For example, the Quit button that appears on all Æ stacks no longer shuts the machine (and potentially your network!) down, but rather politely quits HyperCard and returns to the Mac desktop.

SUPPLEMENTARY MATERIALS

The *Instructor's Manual* includes transparency masters, and may be ordered (by instructors only) separately or with a *Sample Student Program Disk,* which contains stacks created by student users of the text.

THE Æ STACKS

This is a lab-based course. It might be possible to offer this course without a lab component, but we think it would be a serious mistake to do so. Computer science, like the other physical sciences, is a lab science. It is also a contact, rather than a spectator, sport. The disk that comes with the text contains all of the HyperCard stacks referenced in the text and lab modules. As long as you have access to HyperCard (version 2.0 or higher), and a Macintosh that will run it, you are in business.

The lab-based nature of the course was dictated by our experience with computer labs in an introductory computer science course at Hamilton College over the past ten years. We could talk forever about our discipline, but the best way for you to understand what we're talking about is to have hands-on experience, the more the better.

Interwoven with every text module, in addition to a variety of pencil and paper (keyboard and screen?) exercises, is a collection of directed lab exercises. These exercises are based on the disk materials that accompany the text and are central to the course. In the process of accomplishing the exercises, students will experience first-hand a word processor, a spreadsheet, a database system, a logic breadboard, an assembler, a Turing Machine simulator, a poetry generator, and more. All of these programs were designed to support the text directly, and all were written using Hyper-Card.

> **Note:** See the Appendix for a detailed description of the Analytical Engine disks, its setup and use.

Why HyperCard, you ask? In our opinion, HyperCard is the first commercially available program to offer software capable of supporting a true survey course. First and foremost is the fact that HyperCard provides a medium in which students can use the computer in interesting and creative ways *without being programmers*. Simply by learning how to navigate through and edit HyperCard stacks, one can develop an appreciation for how computer applications and languages work, how they are designed, and how they interact to form computer systems. The applications that the students use, design, and edit can then be examined from the perspective of programming by clicking the Macintosh mouse to examine the underlying programs. This approach is in marked contrast to the heretofore standard model that required students to spend an entire semester learning to write a program to perform a calculation that they could have solved in a few minutes using paper and pencil.

Programming a computer provides students with many valuable insights into how a computer works and how a computer scientist thinks. After all, if computer science is concerned in part with the study of programs, as we've said, what better way to begin than by having our students write some programs on their own? Our experience has been that for the audience of a survey course, where we assume no prior programming experience, the programming process itself is tough enough without having to master the mass of syntactic details of a language. Along with its many other capabilities, HyperCard includes a programming language, HyperTalk, which is distinguished by its very natural syntax. HyperTalk programs read almost like collections of English statements, enough so that if you leave out a word, HyperCard has at least a fighting chance of figuring out what you meant and instructing the Mac to do it.

NEW SOFTWARE FEATURES FOR THE SECOND EDITION

Almost by definition, software becomes outdated as soon as it is released, and the collection of Æ stacks that accompanied the first edition was no exception. While we were (and remain) quite pleased with the original text, we knew that the first edition of the software could be improved. The fact that the original software won an award from EDUCOM for curricular innovation has not stopped us from making significant revisions and improvements, as follows:

- *All Æ stacks (and associated lab exercises) have been rewritten from scratch to take advantage of HyperCard version 2.1* (but can be used with version 2.0).
- *Functionality and error-checking have been improved for many of the original stacks.* For example, spreadsheets and Logg-O circuits can now be saved to and retrieved from disk, Logg-O now accommodates combinational circuits, and all stacks that create data files also now create file signatures that ensure that only appropriate data can be opened.
- *The less inspired of the original stacks have been eliminated and replaced with more motivating, better-implemented ones.* Gone are Æpplications, Calendar, Practice, Little Mac Book, DR, and DR No!. Newly created, and supported by lab exercises, are GraphiCalc (a graphing calculator), Fitted Genes (the aforementioned DNA pattern-matcher), Flasher! (the aforementioned flash cards), Bill's Diner (a restaurant guide), Æ Workbook (an updated version of the original Practice stack), HyperChars (an OCR simulation), and ÆTM (a banking machine).
- *New utility-like stacks have been written.* These introduce and provide students with the ability to incorporate animation (Ært Show) and Macintosh resources (sounds, icons, and cursors, in stack Very Resourceful) into their stacks.

SCOPE AND ORDER OF TOPICS

We have made some very deliberate choices in choosing material for and organizing this text. Even a casual review of the table of contents gives the impression that the text covers a great deal of material. It does! One of our early decisions was to commit errors of commission, as opposed to those of omission. To be sure, there is more material in our text than can be covered in a semester course at most schools—including our own. (As indicated by the sample syllabus below, our version of the course pays only casual attention to many of the topics [Module 7, for example] and ignores others altogether [the Pip material in Modules 5 and 6]. This reflects both the interests of our audience and our curriculum.) On the other hand, we have not devoted entire modules to specific "hot" computer applications (except, of course, HyperCard). We have included what we regard as the core material of the discipline—material that is principled and resistant to change—and there is a lot of it.

The order of presentation of the topics reflects the lab orientation of the course. We want students to learn by doing, as well as by reading and thinking. The progression in Modules 2 to 6 from a black box, to a gray box, to a microscopic clear box, gives the students experience with a computer at a particular level of abstraction before taking them down to the next level. Having just used application stacks, students can customize them, evaluate user interfaces, and design their own. Having just designed a stack, they can click on a button and see the programs that underlay it. After using HyperTalk, students wonder how it is that the computer understands such a high-level language. The "language" that the machine understands is logic, and the Module 6 lab convinces most students that logical devices can be built to accomplish a number of interesting tasks. Having seen how the machine does what it does, and with a base of practical experience, it is then appropriate to question, as we do in Modules 7 to 9, the machine's theoretical limitations, the current boundaries of the discipline, and the social implications of the technology.

Also as a result of the lab orientation, this text is more tightly structured than many others. Using "depends on the material from" as a relation on the set of modules in this text, we find that the text is linearly ordered. We know that our order of presentation is not the one everyone would use, and we make no apologies about that. You can teach program translation after hardware or reverse the order of presentation of the entire text, if you wish, but be aware that in doing so you run the risk of dangling forward references. If you have good luck with a different order, let us know.

Hamilton College has 14-week semesters. Our syllabus for this course looks like this:

Module 1:	2 lectures, 1 lab	include a Mac tour for novices
Module 2:	2 lectures, 1 lab	demonstrate a variety of Mac applications
Module 3:	4 lectures, 2 labs	use the lab stacks to discuss design
Module 4:	4 lectures, 2 labs	review scripts of familiar stacks
Module 5:	3 lectures, 2 labs	(Pip material is not covered)
Module 6:	3 lectures, 2 labs	
Module 7:	2 lectures, 1 lab	use lab stack in casual, high-level coverage
Module 8:	3 lectures, 1 lab	show *2001: A Space Odyssey*
Module 9:	2 lectures, 1 lab	

This syllabus provides 38 class meetings, leaving the rest for exams, additional lab sessions, and supplemental material (including scores of relevant films and tapes). Of special note is the series of video tapes entitled "The

Machine That Changed the World," aired on PBS and produced in part by the ACM. The five tapes in the series (available as a set at a very reasonable cost) fit almost perfectly with our modules 1, 2, 3, 8, and 9, respectively, and help to bring the associated topics alive for our students.

PERORATION

Although this project was in many ways our creation, it would not exist in its present form without the contributions of many talented and dedicated people, each of whom influenced the final product in some significant and positive way. Our thanks go out to the following people for their insightful reviews of the original manuscript: Professors Dwight Barnette, Virginia Polytechnic Institute; Lee Bryant, SUNY, Geneseo; Scott Drysdale, Dartmouth College; Jim Gips, Boston College; Gordon Goodman, Rochester Institute of Technology; Will Goodwin, University of Oregon; Dan Kimura, George Washington University; Joan Krone, Ohio State University; Curt Lauckner, Eastern Michigan University; Henry Leitner, Harvard University; Jeff Naughton, Princeton University; Jeff Parker, Boston College; Ellie Quinlan, Ohio State University; Allen Tucker, Bowdoin College; and Henry Walker, Grinnell College; and also to the reviewers of the second edition:

Anselm Blumer
Tufts University

Bill Chen
University of Hawaii at Hilo

Matthew Dickerson
Middlebury College

Batya Friedman
Colby College

Otto Hernandez
Atlantic Community College

Jacquelyn Jarboe
Boise State University

Lawrence S. Kroll
San Francisco State University

Kenneth L. Modesitt
Western Kentucky University

Joseph O'Rourke
Smith College

Barbara Boucher Owens
St. Edward's University

Jane M. Ritter
University of Oregon

Robert Roos
Smith College

Scott Smith
SUNY, Plattsburg

Peter Wegner
Brown University

Robert J. Wernick
San Francisco State University

The changes made to produce this second edition result in a package that is, we believe, significantly improved. The second edition is more contemporary, cleaner, better tuned to our students, and even more empowering for them than was the first. For these improvements, we are also deeply indebted to those instructors who have shared their Æ experiences with us, to our students of the past five years, and to Frank Ruggirello, Mike Sugarman, Susan Gay, J. P. Lenney, Nathan Wilbur, Helen Walden, Abby Heim, Liz Clayton, Ken Morton, and Ed Murphy for trusting us.

Rick Decker
Stuart Hirshfield

A HISTORY OF COMPUTING

1.1 INTRODUCTION

If you look at the table of contents, you'll see that we've divided this course into nine modules. Each module corresponds to a level of abstraction (with its own metaphor) and will take a week or two to cover. Each module has a disk component and a text component, and in both text and disk parts we begin with a map of the territory we'll cover in the module.

TEXT OBJECTIVES

In this module, we will:

- Discuss some of the historical currents that led to the development of modern computers
- Learn about the machine, designed over a hundred years ago, that could be considered the first true computer
- Learn about the data-processing machines first developed around the end of the nineteenth century, which paved the way for commercial use of computers
- Trace the development of electrical computers during the period around World War II
- Describe the explosive growth of computers during the past three decades

THE MIRACULOUS MACHINE

In the text part of this module, we will first orient ourselves historically. We will look at the development of the computer, the machine itself, and the parallel notion of processing information. We will discuss the progress of these two ideas in the context of the historical forces at work in the past three centuries. In this overview of where we are and how we

This is a help balloon. Balloons like this contain definitions, key terms, comments, and other useful information.

got there, we will touch on most of the modules you'll see throughout this course.

On a more mundane level, we will also help you become comfortable with the Macintosh. We expect that many of you have never used a computer, and we'll show you that there is less there than meets the eye. The computer can be viewed as just another appliance—more complicated than a toaster, to be sure, but not forbiddingly so. Once you understand how to use the Macintosh, you'll be ready to start the lab part of this module.

METAPHOR: THE ANALYTICAL ENGINE

The metaphor for this first module shares the title of the book—the Analytical Engine, obviously a quaint name for a computer. What you might not realize is that the term *computer* originally applied exclusively to human beings—specifically, humans engaged in the task of arithmetic calculations. Arithmetic, particularly the arithmetic necessary to solve "real world" problems, has been with us for a long time—at least 5000 years—and has always been difficult, tedious, time-consuming, but necessary. Precisely because arithmetic is difficult, tedious, time-consuming, and necessary, mechanical aids to calculation have also been with us for a long time. The origin of the abacus, which uses beads strung on wires to serve as a substitute for human memory and to increase the accuracy of calculations, is lost in antiquity, but as early as 1642 Blaise Pascal (after whom the programming language Pascal was named) invented a mechanical adder that used a collection of rotating numbered wheels, much like the odometers in today's cars. The Analytical Engine was another mechanical aid to calculation, one that could properly be called the first nonhuman computer, in the sense that we use the word *computer* today.

We tend to think of computers as electrical devices, but you will see that a computer depends on electricity only by happenstance. We have a considerable amount of experience with electronic technology, so it is convenient today to build computers out of electronic components. When Charles Babbage designed the Analytical Engine in the middle of the nineteenth century, the technology of choice was mechanical, so his Analytical Engine used gears and shafts, like a gigantic clock, to store and process information. The Analytical Engine was never completed, partly because of engineering problems but mostly because Babbage ran out of money. A model of the Analytical Engine languished in pieces in the British Museum for more than a century.

As is often the case, however, ideas may prove to be more important than objects. We have in the writings of Babbage and his chronicler Augusta Ada, Countess Lovelace, the seeds of modern computer science. What Babbage intended was a mechanical device to process information, but more important than that, he envisioned a *general purpose* information processor, which stored the instructions that it was intended to execute. In essence, instead of performing one task, like Pascal's adding machine, the Analytical Engine would be given a list of tasks to perform—a recipe, if you will—and would perform those tasks in sequence. Rather than having to stop and rebuild the machine for each operation, the Analytical Engine would be capable of performing any number of operations, governed by the program stored in its memory.

In this respect, the Analytical Engine is no different from the computers of today. It is in homage to Babbage and his machine that we choose our first metaphor—a physical device capable of processing information in the most general and flexible way possible.

Æ STACKS: THE STARTER STACK IS JUST THE BEGINNING

Accompanying this text, you have a Macintosh disk containing Hyper-Card programs that illustrate material covered in this text. The programs for this module will continue where the text leaves off—you'll practice using the Macintosh and begin exploring the features of HyperCard. In very short order, you will learn everything you need to know in order to begin the first series of lab exercises. From then on—and throughout the remainder of this course—you will learn by doing.

LAB OBJECTIVES

In the lab part of this module, you will

- Be introduced to the HyperCard system
- See how HyperCard programs ("stacks"), and your Æ stacks in particular, are organized
- Become an adept HyperCard "browser"—that is, you will learn how to use the mouse, keyboard, and menus to navigate through and between stacks
- Investigate a variety of stacks that demonstrate the breadth, look, and feel of HyperCard

---

1.2   ORIGINS

A continuing theme that runs through Western intellectual history over the past 400 years is the steady displacement of humanity from the central role in creation. In 1543, Nicholas Copernicus moved the earth from the center of creation. He hypothesized a vast universe with all humankind inhabiting an insignificant planet rotating about what we now know to be a perfectly ordinary star in the hinterlands of a perfectly ordinary galaxy consisting of millions upon millions of other stars, spread so widely in the heavens that light itself takes a hundred thousand years to cross from one end of the galaxy to another.

Not only did we lose our central role in space, but we lost our central role in time as well. As the eighteenth and nineteenth centuries passed, growing evidence demonstrated that we humans were very recent arrivals on a planet whose history extended more than four billion years into the past (unimaginably earlier than October 24, 4004 B.C., which was established as the date of Creation by Bishop Ussher in 1611). While geologists were assigning to us an insignificant slice of the Earth's history, Charles Darwin and those who followed in his footsteps dealt what many considered the final blow by removing us from our special role in creation and showing that we, as all other living things, are part of a natural process of evolution, extending in an unbroken chain of changes heaped upon changes over thousands of millennia. Each change in humanity's role was (and continues to be) resisted fiercely, of course. It is always hard to leave center stage and become one among many members of the cast in a vast and often frightening, confusing play.

Still, throughout history, we could always take comfort in our unique nature as thinking beings. The horse may be faster and stronger, birds may take to the air while we can only imagine what flight must be, dogs may hear and smell more acutely than we can, but, as far as we knew, humans alone among all living things had the unique gifts of thought, language, and creativity. Throughout history, horses, birds, and dogs have served humanity, augmenting our limited abilities with theirs, because we can think and learn to domesticate at least some of the beasts of land, sea, and air.

The Industrial Revolution extended our mastery to machines, as well as to animals, increasing our power even further. Through the eighteenth and nineteenth centuries the engine—powerful, tireless, self-regulating, and completely under humanity's control—became one of the central metaphors of society. The steam engine, and later the internal combustion engine, replaced the horse and the ox as primary sources of power. This itself was an important step, but the Industrial Revolution marked the beginning of a much more important trend, the replacement of human skills by the machine.

SKILLED MACHINES

The mill and the factory consumed the work force at a prodigious rate, and produced goods even more rapidly. This production was made possible by building the skill of the worker into the machine. For example, weaving a fabric with an intricate pattern was a complex task that for centuries had been the sole province of master weavers. Typically, the pattern in a woven cloth was made by stretching many threads in parallel on a loom and attaching these *warp* threads to several harnesses that could be raised by the weaver. In the simplest fabric, the structure of the cloth is produced by weaving the crossways *weft* thread over and under alternating warp threads. This was achieved on a loom by attaching warp threads 1, 3, 5, and so on to one harness, and the remaining even-numbered threads to another harness. Then, by raising one harness, the weaver raised half of the warp threads so that the weft thread could be passed between the two warp layers, in effect passing the weft *under* half of the warp and *over* the other half. The weft was then beaten into place, the first harness was lowered, and the other harness raised so the weft could be passed between the layers again, locking the previous row in place. In this way, the cloth was formed.

By increasing the number of harnesses, weavers could make more complex patterns. This was the way weaving had been done for 3000 years or more, and for all that time it was the master weaver alone who knew how to thread the loom's many harnesses and raise them in just the right way to produce complex brocades with intricate floral patterns. The master weaver took decades to learn this skill and he was the only one who could do this work. In essence, then, the production of complex fabrics was limited to the amount that the master weavers could produce. In other words, production was limited by the knowledge bound in the heads of a small number of people. That began to change as the eighteenth century gave way to the nineteenth.

In 1801, the Frenchman Joseph Jacquard invented a loom in which the raising of the warp threads was controlled by punched cards. Each harness was replaced by a collection of hooks linked to the warp threads, and each collection of hooks could be raised or lowered as a group. This in itself was nothing new—such *draw looms* had existed for hundreds of years. Typically, such looms had two operators: the master weaver who sat at the front of the loom, and the drawboy who was an apprentice weaver and sat within the loom itself, raising the hooks at the command of the master weaver. What Jacquard did, though, was to mechanize not only the physical power of the drawboy but also the skill of the master. Instead of the drawboy raising and lowering the groups of hooks, this process was controlled by cards of wood or paper with holes punched in them. Each card in turn passed into a box containing many small wires that were connected to the hooks. The tips of the wires were pressed onto the punched card, and where there was a hole for a wire to pass through the card, the corresponding warp thread would be raised, thus forming the pattern, row by row—and card by card.

The Jacquard loom was a genius stroke, removing the bottleneck of productivity by storing in the machine itself the knowledge of the master weaver. Having made the cards, the weaver was no longer necessary. The drawboy, or anyone else with a minimum of training, could produce cloth on the Jacquard loom faster than the most skilled master. In much the same way as a book can be regarded as a machine that stores knowledge, the cards and the loom stored the expertise of the master weaver. Just as the invention of printing allowed a vast increase in the amount of available knowledge, the Jacquard loom allowed a vast increase in the production of fine fabrics. Not only could the new loom weave faster and more accurately than any human, but this information could be spread by simply making more looms and more cards.

The implications of this new information technology were not lost on the French people, and they quickly enacted strict laws in an attempt to halt the spread of the secrets of this new machine to competing countries. Of course, the attempt was doomed to failure. As has been the case throughout history, even if such secrets could not be bought or stolen, the knowledge that such a device could be built was sufficient in itself, and within a few years the technology had spread throughout the world, carrying with it the seeds of social change.

The notion of storing expertise in a machine was not confined to the weaving industry. An automatic lathe could make flawless chair legs by the thousands by duplicating a single pattern made by a master woodworker. Again, such a machine could be tended by an inexperienced factory worker who had received a day or two of training. In Europe at the time there was an abundance of unskilled labor. A simple fact was obvious to factory owners from the outset—unskilled labor, merely by virtue of its abundance, was far less expensive than skilled. As a result, thousands of skilled craftsmen found themselves without work and with the prospect that their expertise would never be valuable again. In 1811, these people took action. Angered and frightened by this change in their lives, many of them banded together, calling themselves Luddites,* and reacted by breaking into their former factories and mills, destroying any of these new machines they could lay their hands on.

Technological progress, however, had then, as now, a nearly irresistible momentum, especially when the march of progress benefited the wealthy and powerful. Within two years, the Luddites were broken, their leaders either hanged or imprisoned. This was neither the first nor the last time that technological change brought with it social change. We will have much more to say about the social implications of technology in later modules.

THE WEAVER OF ALGEBRA

Although little note was made of the fact at the time, the Industrial Revolution planted the seeds of the Information Revolution. We can now see that not only could the new skilled machines produce and manipulate ob-

---

* Named after Edward "Ned" Ludd, who may or may not have been a real person. The term *luddite* is used today to refer to someone with a hostility toward technology.

jects, but also there was the possibility that machines could produce and manipulate information. Machines could augment the powers of the human brain, as well as the powers of arm and leg.

Calculating machines were in existence long before the Industrial Revolution. The abacus and Pascal's calculator had been developed years before and mechanical calculators were in widespread use by the early part of the nineteenth century. The increasingly complex worlds of science and commerce demanded increasingly complex calculations, and by the early 1800s the time was ripe for a new, more powerful machine.

Charles Babbage, a gifted British inventor and mathematician, was born in 1792. As a mathematician, he was well acquainted with the drudgery that many human calculators endured in their jobs of producing tables of logs and solving equations. Babbage had both the funds and the talent to do something about this problem, and he bent his skills and much of his inherited wealth to devising a machine that would automate the tedious tasks of calculation. In 1821 he proposed his *Difference Engine,* and in 1822 he demonstrated a pilot model to the Royal Astronomical Society. In its individual parts, the Difference Engine was similar to mechanical calculators of the time, representing numbers by the positions of wheels connected by shafts, cogs, and ratchets. This clockwork technology was well developed by then, and indeed had produced not only clocks, but also mechanical birds and dancing mannequins of astonishing complexity, largely as toys for the very rich.

The Difference Engine was to be vastly more complex than any calculator or automaton yet built, but it was still a special-purpose machine. To find the solutions of a polynomial equation, such as $3.56x^7 - 7.6x^3 + 2.39x - 8.94 = 0$, a human calculator of the time would perform a long series of additions, subtractions, and multiplications, and so on, dictated by his or her knowledge of the steps needed to find the solutions. These individual calculations could be performed with the help of existing mechanical calculators, but the important part of the process was the human calculator's knowledge of which steps to perform, in which order. Babbage, in designing the Difference Engine, built his mathematician's knowledge of the steps to be performed directly into his machine, in effect eliminating the need for the skills of a mathematician by the way he connected his cams and shafts. In the pilot model, the operator had only to set the wheels to correspond to the equation to be solved and turn a crank until the answer appeared.

The idea of the Difference Engine was received enthusiastically, and Babbage immediately built a workshop on his property, hired machinists, and set to work. Eleven years later, after having spent tens of thousands of pounds of his own money and grants from the British government, Babbage had still not completed the Difference Engine. The fault lay not in Babbage's plans, but rather in the technology with which he was forced to implement his plans. The inescapable fact is that gears, shafts, and other mechanical parts require energy to turn them, and this energy must be

Just recently a working model based on Babbage's original plans was built and successfully demonstrated.

smoothly transmitted from each part to the next. This presents few problems in a watch (or in Babbage's pilot model), since any slight binding or failure to mesh smoothly would be unnoticed in the overall working of the machine. Such small irregularities, however, tend to accumulate, to be passed from one part to the next, and in a machine with thousands of parts these irregularities grew to such a degree that the machine would invariably jam or break during operation. In short, Babbage's conception was doomed to failure by what we today call the *problem of scale:* An idea that works perfectly well at one size may fail in entirely unpredicted ways at a size ten or a hundred times larger.

> The recently built Difference Engine demonstrates that Babbage's technical problems, while difficult, could have been solved. Unfortunately, Babbage was by all accounts a notoriously difficult person to work for and wound up alienating not only his chief engineer but also his sources of funding.

Babbage's vision, clearly far beyond the production of windup finches that could sing and hop about their cages, went further still beyond the capabilities of his uncompleted Difference Engine. Just as the Jacquard loom contained in its cards the knowledge of the master weaver and contained in its structure the ability to perform the instructions on any series of cards, Babbage envisioned a much grander machine, capable of performing any series of mathematical instructions given to it. This *Analytical Engine* would be composed of several smaller devices—one to receive the list of instructions (on punched cards, as it happened), one to perform the instructions coded on the cards, one to store the results of intermediate calculations, and one to print out the information on paper. The entire device was to be powered by a steam engine, much as the power looms of the time were. As Lady Ada was to remark in her writings about Babbage, "The Analytical Engine weaves algebraical patterns just as the Jacquard loom weaves flowers and leaves."

There must certainly be other instances of an idea being a hundred years ahead of its time but probably none so compelling. The organization of the Analytical Engine is in its broad outlines virtually identical to that of modern computers. Almost universally, the architecture of a computer today consists of an *input* section, a *central processor* that performs arithmetic and logical operations dictated by a program of instructions, a *memory* unit to store information, and an *output* section to make the results available to the user, exactly as described by Babbage a century ago. It is poignant to imagine the completed Analytical Engine as Babbage must have, this vast and certainly deafening machine with its thousands of gears and levers turning smoothly, glistening with machine oil in the light streaming through the windows of a large brick building, the punched cards clacking through the receiver one by one, the paper rolling out of the printing press at one side, all against the background of a chugging steam engine—a perfectly fitting Victorian vision of a machine that we all consider a quintessential part of the late twentieth century.

REVIEW QUESTIONS

1. What were the roles played in our story by Nicholas Copernicus, Charles Darwin, Charles Babbage, and Augusta Ada?

2. What were the differences between the Difference Engine and the Analytical Engine?

3. Why was the Analytical Engine never completed?

4. Why do we call the Analytical Engine the first true computer?

LAB EXERCISE 1

An automobile is approximately as complicated as a small computer. In fact, if you just count the number of parts in each, a car, with about 10,000 parts, is quite a bit more complicated than a computer. (We're cheating a little for effect here, since the tiny integrated circuit chip that does the real work in a computer may have 100,000 transistors embedded in it, but we're counting it as a single part.) One thing that most of us take for granted today is that a car is simple to operate—if you learned to drive a Buick, you can step into a Mercedes and drive away without ever looking at the operator's manual. It wasn't always that way, however.

In the early days of automobiles, there was no standardization of what we might call the "user interface"—if you knew how to operate a Winton, you would very likely be at a complete loss in the driver's seat of a Stanley Steamer. In that sense, computers today are at roughly the same stage as automobiles were at the beginning of this century. Knowing how to use manufacturer X's line of computers won't always guarantee that you'll be able to operate a machine from manufacturer Y. Apple Computer, Inc., devoted a considerable effort toward making the Macintosh simple to use, as you'll see, but you will still need some direction if you've never used a Macintosh before. If you are already familiar with the basics of using a Mac, and are comfortable using a mouse, menus, windows, and the Macintosh desktop, proceed to Exercise 1.2, below. In either case, all subsequent exercises require such a basic familiarity.

1.1 Ask your instructor to help you obtain a floppy disk containing a "Tour of the Macintosh." Get whatever help you need to turn on a Mac and to start the tour. Then, you're on your own.

A brief note is in order to prepare you for entering the HyperCard world. In this day of personal computers with sophisticated graphics capabilities, many computer programs project an image that reflects how the program is to be used. For example, word processors often appear as pages of paper on the user's screen, spreadsheet programs appear as an accountant's ledger, and graphics programs are portrayed as an artist's palette. The HyperCard program is conceived of as a tool for organizing and presenting information (we will see that it does this and much more!). In this light, the image HyperCard projects to its users is that of an *ordered stack of index cards*. Once you start the HyperCard program the first card of HyperCard's Home stack (see Figure 1.1) will appear on the screen. This card is a visual directory of some of the programs, called *stacks,* that can be used from within HyperCard. More about the Home stack will follow shortly. For now, take a close look at the screen.

Notice that much of the information on the screen (including the cursor) is presented in graphic fashion. The pictures are intended to help describe the information being presented. Some of the pictures have a special property: When you "click" the mouse when the cursor is near that picture, something happens. For example, a different card may be presented on the screen. Such pictures are called *buttons.* The button we are presently interested in is the one that looks like a lock with a key inserted and is labeled "HyperCard Tour." On our Home stack it appears near the upper lefthand corner of the card.

FIGURE 1.1   HyperCard's Home Stack

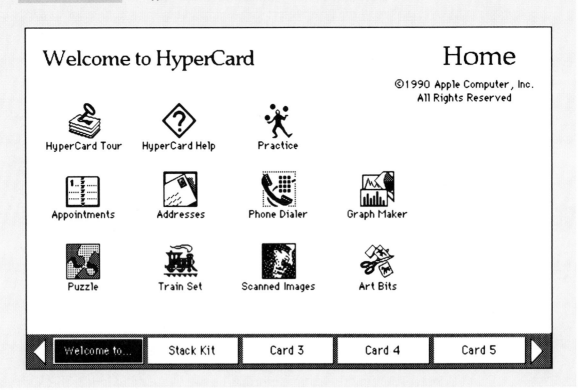

1.2   Turn on a Mac and locate the HyperCard icon on your desktop. Double-click the HyperCard icon to start HyperCard. The screen should look something like that pictured in Figure 1.1.

1.3   Click the HyperCard Tour button (one click will do it!), and take the tour to enter the world of HyperCard.

1.3   HANDLING THE INFORMATION EXPLOSION

Charles Babbage died in 1871 and his work passed into obscurity. Mechanical calculators were gradually improved over the following years, but the idea of the computer had died, temporarily. In 1887, Verdi's *Otello* premiered in Milan, Sir Arthur Conan Doyle wrote the first Sherlock Holmes story, the telephone was 11 years old, the phonograph 10, and the 1880 U.S. census was seven years behind schedule. This latter was a serious problem, since the census is mandated by law—Article 1, Section 2 of the United States Constitution states that, for the purposes of assigning congressional districts:

> The actual Enumeration [of the population] shall be made within three Years after the first meeting of the Congress of the United States, and within every subsequent Term of ten Years, in such Manner as [the House of Representatives] shall by Law direct.

When the Constitution was written, the population of the new United States stood at slightly under four million, a figure well within the abilities of statisticians of the day to tabulate. A century later, in 1887, the U.S. population, as near as anyone could figure, numbered about 57,217,000, and it was clear to the officials at the Census Bureau that, at the rate things were going, the 1890 census could not be completed by the end of the century. Fortunately, Herman Hollerith, a young mathematician-inventor in the spirit of Babbage, combined the old technology of punched cards with the new electrical technology to produce a sorting and tabulating machine. With the help of his machine, the 1890 census was completed in six weeks. Hollerith founded the Tabulating Machine Company to produce and sell his machines, and his company did remarkably well. The machines his company produced kept time records and were used for sorting, tabulating, and collating information. They were not computers in the sense we know them, but they were ideal servants in an age that increasingly felt the need for accurate and timely management of large quantities of data. If time travel were possible, it would be worth the price of a trip to go back a hundred years or so and invest in Hollerith's fledgling venture, which today is known as IBM.

Given recent news about IBM, it might be better to use the time machine for other purposes.

THE BIRTH OF COMPUTERS, FROM A TO Z

Beginning in the 1930s, events began to move much more rapidly than before, not only in the world in general, but particularly in the world of information processing. In 1932, Franklin Roosevelt was elected President by a landslide, Adolf Hitler refused an offer to become Vice Chancellor of Germany, Aldous Huxley wrote *Brave New World,* Amelia Earhart became the first woman to make a solo flight across the Atlantic, and at the Massachusetts Institute of Technology, Vannevar Bush completed a mechanical calculator called the Differential Analyzer, which solved calculus problems. Like the Difference Engine, the Differential Analyzer was a purely mechanical device with essentially a single purpose. The promise of the Analytical Engine remained unfulfilled, though not for much longer.

John V. Atanasoff received his doctorate in physics from the University of Wisconsin in 1930. Part of the research for his dissertation involved months of laborious calculations on a mechanical desk calculator. Like Babbage, he became interested in finding a way to eliminate the drudgery of computation. Unlike Babbage, Atanasoff lived in a world with a well-developed electronics technology, and that made all the difference. In 1939 Atanasoff began work on a machine that used currents of electricity to represent information.

The idea of encoding information electrically was not new in 1939. Indeed, Samuel F. B. Morse had demonstrated the practicality of the idea with his telegraph in 1838, only five years after Babbage began research on the Analytical Engine, and Hollerith's card-reading machine used electrical signals as well. By 1939, though, the technology of controlling, switching, and amplifying electrical signals had reached a level comparable to the technology of mechanical devices in Babbage's time. Atanasoff and his assistant Clifford Berry were as comfortable with their technology as Babbage had been with his.

As far as we need to be concerned, the chief difference between the two technologies is that electrons are very light and easy to shove around, moving through wires at about a billion feet per second, well over a million times faster than most mechanical devices can move. A vacuum tube that Atanasoff could buy off the shelf for a few dollars could switch a signal on or off thousands of times faster, far more reliably, and at far less cost than it would take to perform the same function with rods, gears, and levers.

Like the Difference Engine and the Differential Analyzer, the Atanasoff-Berry Computer (ABC, for short) was a single-purpose machine, designed to find solutions to systems of linear equations. An example of such a problem is to find values of x and y that satisfy both $2x - 3y = 1$ and $x + 5y = 20$. You may recall enough algebra to find that $x = 5$ and $y = 3$ is a solution (and, indeed, is the only solution). Whether or not you know how to solve such a system, you can imagine that solving a system of 29 such equations, each with 29 unknowns, would be a horrifying task to do by hand. The

ABC was built for just such a task, and Atanasoff estimated it would produce the answer five times faster than a person could, even with the aid of a desk calculator.

Meanwhile, at about the same time, Konrad Zuse, a German engineer, and his assistant, Helmut Schreyer, were working on a machine similar in principle to the ABC, though grander in conception. It is here, almost exactly a century after the conception of the Analytical Engine, that we see the notion of a *general-purpose* computer reborn. The machines of Zuse and Schreyer—Z1, and later versions Z2, Z3, and Z4—used electrical signals to represent information, just as in the ABC, but while Atanasoff's machine could do only one thing, Zuse's, from the beginning, was intended to perform its tasks under control of a program of instructions. Zuse, in other words, had become the intellectual heir of Babbage.

> The airplane and the telegraph are other examples of this. The Wright brothers and Morse weren't the only ones working on these inventions—they just got there first.

This simultaneous and independent development of electronic calculation by Atanasoff and Zuse, including Zuse's rediscovery of Babbage's ideas, is an example of a recurrent theme in the history of technology. Often the time just seems right for an idea, the necessary technology and the right way to look at a problem providing fertile ground for independent discoveries of the same principle or device. Sadly, though, the time was also wrong for both Atanasoff and Zuse. Their governments were locked in a deadly war and called for their efforts elsewhere. Neither Atanasoff nor Zuse was able to complete his machine, and by the end of World War II, the march of progress had passed them by, fueled by the same war that interrupted their separate projects.

MILITARY COMPUTERS

At about the same time Atanasoff and Zuse were working on their machines, a third such project was going on, independently of the others, under the direction of Howard Aiken, an applied mathematician and physicist at Harvard University. While Atanasoff and Zuse were struggling with extremely limited funds, Aiken went to IBM with his idea for a computer and returned to Harvard with a million dollars. Unlike Atanasoff's ABC, Aiken's machine, like Zuse's, was an *electromechanical* device, a hybrid of electrical and mechanical components. Switching in the ABC was controlled by vacuum tubes, while the other two devices relied on relays, components much like contemporary light switches, except that the switch arm was moved by a magnet controlled by another electrical circuit. Although about a thousand times slower than vacuum tubes, relays were reliable (vacuum tubes burn out, much like light bulbs), used very little power (vacuum tubes have a filament that must be kept glowing at all times), and were cheap (the telephone company used relays by the hundreds of thousands).

Far from being halted by the war, Aiken's project was encouraged by the U.S. Navy, which quickly clamped a lid of secrecy on the entire operation. By 1944, the International Business Machines' Automatic Sequence

Controlled Calculator, also known as the Harvard Mark I (certainly a more euphonious name than the corporate version), was completed, the first true working computer. Babbage's dream was finally a reality, a fact that was not lost on Aiken, since he alone of the three pioneers had read the reports on the Analytical Engine (albeit three years after he had begun thinking about the Mark I).

A useful point of view of the history of computers is to place them against the background of a world that needed to handle increasingly large and complex sets of information. Warfare, throughout history, has always demanded accurate and timely information. The global war of the 1930s and 1940s, with its huge armies and new machinery, demanded computational power on a scale undreamed of before. This insistent demand for powerful computing was met, again independently, by two machines, the British Colossus and the American ENIAC.

Sending military information via coded messages has been a common practice since Caesar's time and was indispensable during World War II when radio messages could be heard by anyone with the proper equipment. The German military relied on a machine called Enigma, a mechanical device that looked like a large typewriter. By setting the dials of the Enigma machine, the code could be changed daily. Through Polish secret agents, the British managed to obtain an Enigma, but while that told the British the principles behind the German encoding schemes, the coded messages still could not be deciphered without the correct dial settings. In theory, of course, all one had to do was run the coded message through the captured Enigma while trying all possible dial settings—much as one would open a safe by trying all possible combinations. The number of different settings was so large, though, that the information would be cold and useless long before the right combination was found. What was needed was a way to *simulate* the action of the Enigma on a much faster device.

The British were fortunate to have the services of Alan Turing, a mathematician who, in 1936, published a paper with the forbidding title "On Computable Numbers with an Application to the Entscheidungsproblem." In this remarkable work, written *before* there was a working computer of any kind, Turing laid the theoretical groundwork for all of modern computer science. We will return to Turing's contribution in a later module; for now, he is of interest to us for his wartime work in code breaking. Turing and a group of British scientists, mathematicians, and engineers, working in the tightest possible secrecy at a country estate known as Bletchley Park, managed by 1943 to build a completely electronic computer, like Atanasoff's ABC but vastly more powerful. Colossus was designed for code-breaking, and it worked spectacularly well. It is not too farfetched to suggest that the efforts of the Bletchley Park group in breaking the Enigma codes won the war for the Allies. It is chilling to speculate what the result would have been if Zuse, who had considered using tubes but discarded the idea because of their expense, had been allowed to complete a similar machine for the Axis.

Meanwhile, on the other side of the Atlantic, John Mauchley and J. Presper Eckert were working on a similar machine, the Electronic Numerical Integrator and Computer, or ENIAC. Mauchley and Atanasoff had communicated extensively during 1941 about the possibilities of electronic computation, and many of the principles of ENIAC are similar to those of the ABC. ENIAC was designed to produce ballistic firing tables for artillery, a forbiddingly complex computational task, and was completely operational by the end of the war. Along the way, the ENIAC project was lucky enough to acquire the considerable talents of John Von Neumann, who first proposed the idea of storing the program of a computer in the computer's memory, along with the data. The importance of this idea cannot be overestimated, since it led to the eventual practical use of the new technology. Without a stored program, ENIAC could still be "instructed" to perform different tasks, but the instruction took the form of essentially rewiring most of the machine. The scene was set for an explosion of computers that dwarfed anything seen during the Industrial Revolution.

REVIEW QUESTIONS

1. Arrange the following machines in chronological order, and associate them with the names below:
   ABC, Colossus, Differential Analyzer, ENIAC, Mark I, Z1
   Aiken, Atanasoff, Bush, Eckert, Mauchley, Turing, Zuse

2. What did Hollerith's tabulating machine and the Jacquard loom have in common?

3. What advantage does electrical technology have over mechanical?

4. What advantages do tubes have over relays? relays over tubes?

5. In what ways did World War II spur the development of computers?

Æ LAB

LAB EXERCISE 2

You are now ready to start using the stacks that we have developed specifically to support the laboratory component of our version of the Analytical Engine. We refer to these stacks collectively as the "Æ stacks." The floppy disk that accompanies your text contains copies of all of the Æ stacks. The place to begin investigating them is with the stack named "Æ Home" (see Figure 1.2).

The Æ Home stack, like its HyperCard counterpart, provides a visual directory of all of the Æ stacks. Each Æ stack is represented by a button that, when clicked, will open that stack directly. As you will also see, each of the Æ stacks contains a button like that in the upper left corner of Æ Home (a small house with the "Æ" logo on it) that will return you to Æ Home with a single click of the mouse. Typically, a lab exercise begins with instructions to open the particular Æ stack that supports the exercises to follow. The Æ stack for the following exercises is named, appropriately enough, the "Starter Stack."

The Starter Stack is a collection of cards that provides you with further instruction on and experience with using the Macintosh and HyperCard, as well as some general information about the organization of the Æ stacks. To open the Starter Stack, click on its button on Æ Home. Having done so, your screen should look like Figure 1.3.

2.1   Open stack Æ Home now. This can be accomplished directly from the Macintosh desktop (double-click on the Æ Home icon to start HyperCard and open Æ Home) or from within HyperCard (start HyperCard, and then use the Open Stack... command from the File menu).

FIGURE 1.2   The Æ Home Stack

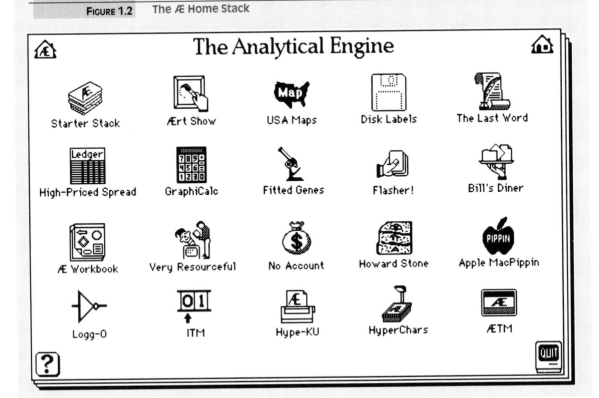

FIGURE 1.3   The First Card of the Starter Stack

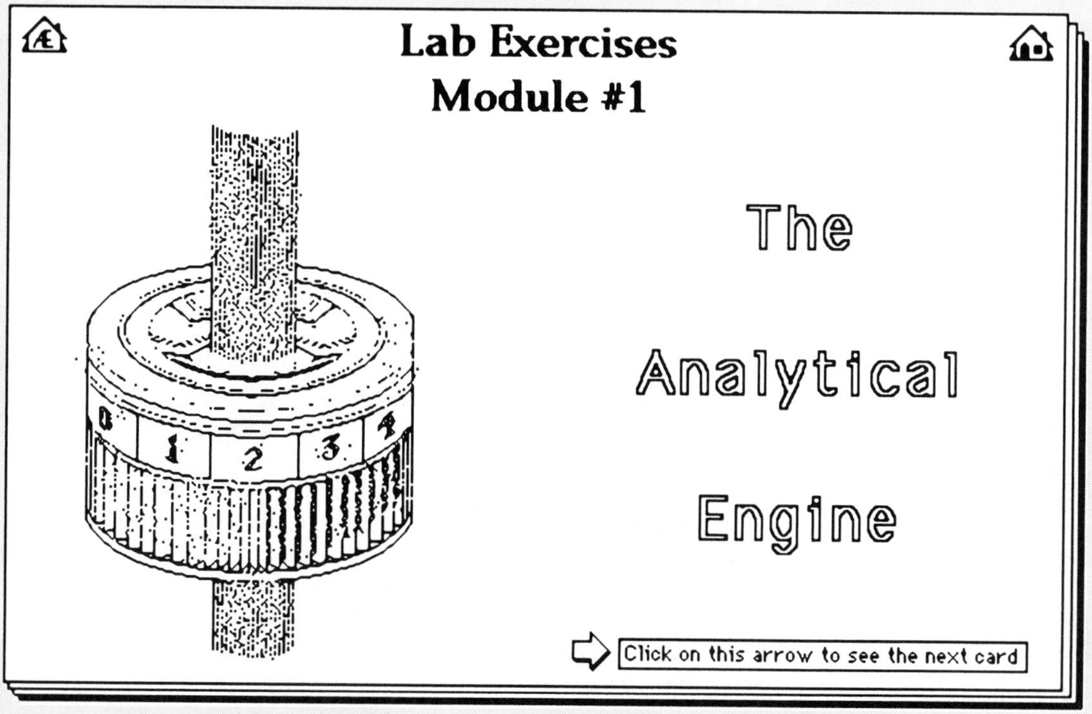

Lab Exercises
Module #1

The Analytical Engine

Click on this arrow to see the next card

2.2 Open the Starter Stack by clicking (once!) on its button from Æ Home.

2.3 Follow the instructions in the Starter Stack and perform all of the suggested exercises up to and including those on card number 14. (All of the Starter Stack's cards—except the first one—are numbered on their bottom center.)

2.4 When you finish with card number 14, choose Quit HyperCard from the File menu to return to the Mac desktop.

1.4   GENERATIONS

Colossus was aptly named—the first computers were physically titanic by today's standards. The Mark I was over 50 feet long, and ENIAC completely filled a 30- by 50-foot room with its 18,000 vacuum tubes and miles of wiring. The technical side of the rest of computer science history takes us from the "giant brains" of the postwar years to the microcomputer on which this text was written, and can be summarized in one word—*size*. Without the invention of a simple device made largely from common sand, there would be no Information Revolution, and the world would be profoundly different from the one we know.

The computers of the 1950s were huge machines, requiring enormous power to heat their thousands of tubes—a typical computer of the time used as much power as an entire block of single-family homes. Vacuum tubes could switch electrical signals quickly (the electronic ENIAC was a thousand times faster than the electromechanical Mark I), but most of the energy to run a tube goes to make heat, which is useless to the function of the computer and in fact must be disposed by air conditioning systems lest the computer bake itself into scrap. While they were large, expensive (typically costing a million dollars or more), and required an extensive maintenance staff, the early commercial computers found a ready market in large corporations, research institutes, the military, and the government. The impact of the computer, though, was not felt by the average citizen, and analysts of the time estimated that the computing needs of the entire world could easily be met by a few dozen large machines. All this was changed by a very small but important device.

> First Generation computers used vacuum tubes.

The transistor was invented at Bell Telephone Labs in 1947. The transistor, like the vacuum tube, is essentially an electric switch, made of a bit of silicon with small impurities added. The first transistor was a can about the size of your thumbnail with three wires running into it. In simple terms, a current applied to one wire determined whether or not another current could pass between the other two wires. The transistor used much less power than a tube and could be switched much more quickly. More important, though, was that transistors could be made very small, much smaller than a tube. The First Generation vacuum tube computers gave way in 1957 to the Second Generation—transistorized machines that were faster, smaller, more reliable, and cheaper than their ancestors.

> Second Generation computers were based on transistors.

In the late 1950s and the 1960s small businesses could for the first time afford computing power previously available only to those with a spare million dollars or two. From another point of view, for prices similar to those of their old machines, large companies could purchase ten times the computing power they could before. As was the case with earlier emergent technologies, uses were found for computers that had not been dreamed of by their inventors. Airline reservations were automated, billing and inventory were done by machines, and complex tasks such as air defense were computerized.

New programming techniques eased the job of instructing the machines to perform their tasks, and new programming languages were developed: FORTRAN, for scientific calculation; COBOL, tailored for business use; and BASIC, for teaching programming. No longer was it necessary to write programs in the forbidding binary language of the computer—these new languages were closer to human languages than to the dialect of the machine.

Third Generation computers used integrated circuits.

While computer companies were riding an exponential sales curve, scientists and engineers were developing circuits of a completely new design. In these *integrated circuits,* the transistors, wires, and other components of the computer were all fabricated on a single chip of silicon. In much the same way as a color print is made by photographically depositing layers of dye, integrated circuits can be made by "printing" a picture of the circuit on a silicon base, adding one chemical layer after another. Because it is easy to photographically reduce such a circuit, such a typical Third Generation computer might pack a thousand transistors into the same space occupied by a single transistor a decade before. Also, just as the printing press allowed many books to be made from the same master type, dozens of integrated circuits could be made simultaneously out of a single wafer of silicon a few inches across. Again, computers became cheaper, smaller, and faster (largely because the signals had less distance to travel—electrons move quickly, but not instantaneously). More power was available for the same price; the same power cost less than it did before. At this time, we began to see the first *embedded computers,* small, special-purpose computers that could run traffic signals, elevators, and pocket calculators—miniature descendants of the Difference Engine. To give you an idea of the progress made in 30 years, in the mid 1970s, one could purchase a handheld programmable calculator, weighing perhaps half a pound, that was faster than the room-sized ENIAC, at about one ten-thousandth the cost.

Fourth Generation computers rely on large-scale integrated circuits.

The pace of progress showed no sign of slackening; indeed, it continued to accelerate. In 1971, the Vietnam war was grinding to its conclusion, Erich Segal published *Love Story,* the Baltimore Colts defeated Dallas, 16–3, to win the Super Bowl, and the first microprocessor went on sale. The *microprocessor* is an entire computer on a single chip, a Fourth Generation machine based on the technology of *large-scale integration*—a Third Generation machine with many more circuit elements, on a much smaller scale. For $300 (the price today is under $3, in quantity), you could buy a single chip and program it for your needs, as a calculator, a traffic control mechanism, an ignition control in a car, or a general-purpose computer. When your computer broke down, all you had to do was throw it out and buy another. The Analytical Engine had shrunk to a size that Babbage could have used as a shirt button, and was similarly disposable.

Within a few years, microcomputers based on these new chips were available to everyone with a few hundred dollars. At first, the computer giants—such as IBM, Digital Equipment, and Hewlett-Packard—had no interest in this new "micro" market, not imagining that any money was to be made by selling small computers for people to use at home. Dozens of new microcomputer companies sprang up, competing for spaces in this new ecological niche.

Steve Jobs and Steve Wozniak were not the first to produce microcomputers, but they are certainly among the most successful. Beginning in

1976 with 50 machines assembled in Jobs's parents' garage in Los Altos, California, the two began their own computer company. In the next six years, their sales were $2.5 million, then $15 million, $70 million, $117 million, $335 million, and $583 million. By 1982, their company, Apple Computer, Inc., was listed among the largest 500 companies in the United States. If you can't afford the price of a time machine ticket to invest in Herman Hollerith's company, you might consider two shorter trips—one to 1978 to invest in Apple at nine cents a share, and one to late 1980, when the stock was first offered to the general public at $22 per share, a tidy return of 24,444 percent on your investment in just two years.

TODAY

There has never been a technology in the history of the world that has progressed as fast as computer technology. We could, for instance, compare advances in computer technology with those in the automotive industry: If automotive technology had progressed as fast as computer technology between 1960 and today, the car of today would have an engine less than one tenth of an inch across; the car would get 120,000 miles to a gallon of gas, have a top speed of 240,000 miles per hour, and would cost $4. This is the stuff of fantasy, not science fiction.

While we're on the subject, science fiction authors have a reputation for accurate prognostication (the first description of the atomic bomb appeared before the first bomb was even tested) but the computer revolution took them completely by surprise. You can search the literature of the 1940s and 1950s in vain looking for any mention of a society that has computational powers in every household appliance. In computer science in particular, we see reason to believe what we might call the First Law of Futurology: *Any reasonable prediction of future technology is almost certain to be too conservative.*

In the lab part of this course, you have the opportunity to deal with one aspect of this fantastic progress—the Macintosh computer. As you use the Mac, try to bear in mind that this soon-to-be-familiar appliance has powers beyond the imagination of Atanasoff, Zuse, Aiken, Turing, Von Neumann, Mauchley, Eckert, and the rest of the pioneers. As for how father Babbage would have viewed the Macintosh, we can only recall the dictum of Arthur C. Clarke, whom we'll meet again in Module 8: "Any sufficiently advanced technology is indistinguishable from magic."

REVIEW QUESTIONS

1. Define First, Second, Third, and Fourth Generation computer technology.
2. In simple terms, what is a transistor?
3. What advantages do transistors have over tubes?

4. What is an integrated circuit, and why is it important to computer technology?

5. What theme best describes the advances in computer technology over the past 40 years?

LAB EXERCISE 3

Before we leave this module, we'll return to the Starter Stack and use it as a launching pad for exploring some other interesting stacks, Æ and otherwise. When you complete the exercises below you will have finished the lab portion of Module 1.

Although we have covered a lot of territory in this lab, don't be intimidated. We have intentionally attempted to immerse you quickly and with relatively little explicit direction into the Mac/HyperCard "world." This world was meant to be experienced firsthand, and that is what we are encouraging you to do through these and subsequent lab modules. Welcome to Computer Science.

3.1 Open the Starter Stack now, by whatever means you choose.

3.2 Proceed as directly as you can to card number 15 of the Starter Stack, and complete the exercises described in the remainder of the stack.

3.3 Instead of quitting HyperCard when you are done with the Starter Stack, return to stack Æ Home.

3.4 Use the Æ Contents menu in Æ Home to review the material covered in Module 1, and to preview the topics we will cover and the stacks we will use in future modules.

1.5   EXERCISES

1. There is a chance that there could have been a working computer by 1850, if Babbage had employed Morse's electrical technology. Assuming he had done so, speculate on how pervasive the computer would have been and its likely uses between 1850 and 1900.

2. What were some of the social consequences of the widespread use of the automobile? You might want to investigate the traction industry (interurban trolleys, streetcars, and the like) in the period 1900–1920, or the effects of the automobile on dating patterns, mobility, urban growth, and so on.

3. List three professions that are likely to become obsolete (or nearly so) as a result of the spread of computers, and explain your answer.

4. Report on the background of the October 19, 1973, court decision that the ENIAC patent was invalid.

5. Find three good John Von Neumann anecdotes. This is an easy question, once you find a contemporary account of Von Neumann's life.

6. An *analog computer,* such as the Differential Analyzer, stores information by representing it as the continuous position of an object. The number 17.56, for example, might have been represented in the Differential Analyzer by a shaft that was rotated 17.56° from its starting position. A *digital computer,* such as the abacus, represents each digit (ones, tens, hundreds, and so on) by a separate wire. What are the limiting factors to the accuracy of an analog computer, and how does this differ from the accuracy of a digital computer? In particular, is it easier to increase the accuracy of an analog or a digital computer?

7. Think of a new use for embedded computers. Let us know, care of the publisher. A good enough idea might make us very wealthy.

8. Why does making an integrated circuit smaller make it cheaper? Speculate on whether a desire for small computers or economic reasons led to smaller chips.

9. Bearing in mind the First Law of Futurology, speculate on one use of computers in the year 2010.

10. There are connections between Charles Babbage and his legacy and Victor Frankenstein and his. Both concern man's creations run wild, but there is also a literary connection, through Countess Lovelace. Write on both.

11. In the period since 1900, which has increased more—humankind's computing power or destructive power? Provide figures to support your answer, and be careful to explain what you mean by "power."

12. What is a computer? Are you a computer by your definition? Be careful in using the words *inorganic* or *living,* especially in light of recent speculations about building very small computers from organic molecules.

13. Take one more trip in our time machine, and give a Macintosh (and disks) to Atanasoff or Zuse, with no explanation, manuals, or supporting information. What would scientists of the time have been able to discover about its workings? Needless to say, you'll have to read up on the science of the 1930s.

1.6 ADDITIONAL READINGS

Bernstein, J. *The Analytical Engine.* New York: Random House, 1963.

Bowden, B. V. *Faster Than Thought.* London: Sir Isaac Pitman, 1953.

Engelbourg, S. *International Business Machines: A Business History.* Salem, N.H.: Ayer, 1976.

Evans, C. *The Micro Millennium.* New York: Washington Square Press, 1979.

Gassée, J.-L. *The Third Apple.* New York: Harcourt Brace Jovanovich, 1987.

Goldstein, H. *The Computer from Pascal to Von Neumann.* Princeton, N.J.: Princeton University Press, 1972.

Kranzberg, M., and Pursell, C. W., Jr., eds. *Technology in Western Civilization.* New York: Oxford University Press, 1967.

Mackintosh, A. R. "Dr. Atanasoff's Computer." *Scientific American* 258, no. 2 (Aug. 1988): 90–96.

Martin, J. D. *Inside Big Blue: Will the Real IBM Please Stand Up?* New York: Vantage, 1988.

Moritz, M. *The Little Kingdom: The Private Story of Apple Computer.* New York: William Morrow, 1984.

Morrison, P., and Morrison, E. *Charles Babbage and His Calculating Engines.* New York: Dover Publications, Inc., 1961.

Singer, C. J., et al. *A History of Technology.* 7 vols. Oxford: Clarendon Press, 1954–1978.

Stein, D. *Ada: A Life and Legacy.* Cambridge, Mass.: MIT Press, 1987.

———. *Ada Lovelace and the Thinking Machine.* Cambridge, Mass.: MIT Press, 1985.

Turing, S. *Alan Turing.* Cambridge: W. Heffer and Sons, 1959.

Winterbotham, F. W. *The Ultra Secret.* New York: Harper and Row, 1974.

APPLICATIONS AND IMPLICATIONS

2.1 INTRODUCTION

You've seen that microelectronic technology—computer technology in particular—has undergone a rate of growth that can, without fear of contradiction or exaggeration, be called explosive. In terms of both production and technical sophistication, there has never been anything in the history of technology that can match the growth of computers. In this module, we will explore this growth in more detail, focusing mainly on the past decade and looking at the reasons for the pervasive influence of the computer in today's world.

TEXT OBJECTIVES

In this module, we will

- Concentrate on the combination of computer and program that is visible to the user of computer applications
- Discuss a small but important part of the history of computers in detail, by focusing on the extraordinary growth of microelectronic technology that made the electronic calculator possible
- Discuss two common personal computer applications, word processors and spreadsheets
- Present an inventory of some computer applications in business, technology, the professions, and entertainment
- Consider some social implications of widespread computer use

THE COMPUTER AS A TOOL

In Module 1 we concentrated almost entirely on the computer itself, that collection of microcircuitry and wires that you can pick up and hold in your hand. We'll come back to the hardware in Module 6; in this module we will adopt a point of view that is at the same time more abstract and more personal—namely, the user's view of computers and their programs. In our efforts to peel away the layers of mystery that surround the computer, we will begin with the "black box" approach, by discussing computers with their programs. Computer hardware is versatile, in that it can perform a virtually unlimited collection of tasks, given the right programs. We could call a computer by itself a *data processor,* manipulating electrical signals that we think of as zeros and ones. People generally have little use for data, however; the real power of the computer appears when, combined with a program, it acts as an *information processor.* Consider, for example, the number 102.7. As a rational number—as data, that is—102.7 has little intrinsic meaning and is of little interest to us. A program, however, can invest that number with meaning: either innocent as the frequency of an FM radio station, enviable as an hourly wage in dollars, deplorable as an hourly wage in lire, worrisome as a child's temperature in degrees Fahrenheit, or impossible as a child's temperature in degrees Celsius, depending upon the intentions of the programmer. In this module, we will concentrate on the combination of computer *cum* program as a single machine, a powerful black box.

The natural question to ask here is, "Now that we have all this power, what can we do with it?" The answer, as we will see here and in Modules 3 and 4, is, "(Almost) anything that we can write a program to do." We will see in later modules that there *are* limits to the power of computers— some tasks are inappropriate for computers because of purely physical limitations on speed and storage, and there are logical limitations in the sense that some tasks can be proven impossible to perform by their very nature. However, within the boundaries set by these limitations, we have an immense field in which to work.

Computer applications are commonplace today and likely will be ubiquitous tomorrow. Why are there so many uses for computers? One answer is that computers, properly programmed, can perform tasks that would be either infeasible or downright impossible otherwise. This, in turn, stems from the fact that the computer is, first, fast enough to do otherwise impossible tasks in a reasonable amount of time and, second, flexible enough to be applied to a wide variety of problems.

The most visible computer applications today are those for personal computers. Even restricting our attention just to programs written for microcomputers, we can comb through popular computing magazines and easily come up with several thousand programs, ranging from those for serious word processing and file management to those that perform astrological readings. Using microcomputer applications as our starting point, we will begin by exploring some of the most popular programs, then go on to look at some commercial and industrial applications generally written for larger machines. Along the way, we will lay the groundwork for Module 9 by beginning our discussion of the social and personal implications of the computerization of the modern world.

METAPHOR: THE CALCULATOR

The portable electronic calculator is a program and computer in a box; it serves as the fundamental paradigm of a computer application, as well as the guiding example of this module. Unlike what we generally call a computer, you cannot get inside the box and change the program that controls the calculator. The "+" key will always perform an addition, no matter what you do. In many cases, modern calculators do indeed contain fully functional, programmable microcomputers, but the programming to make the computer act as a calculator is done once and for all at the factory. From the user's point of view, a calculator is like all the other computer/program combinations we will discuss here—a black box designed to perform one complex and open-ended task, the internal workings of which need be of no concern to the user.

The calculator and the digital watch were the first major commercial and practical successes of microelectronic, integrated circuit technology. Of course, calculating devices existed long before the development of electronic technology. Mechanical calculating devices consisting of gears and wheels had been around for centuries. A bronze astronomical calculator dating from the first century B.C. was discovered by sponge divers in a shipwreck off the Greek island of Antikythera, for example. By the 1930s, a century after the Analytical Engine, it was possible to buy for about $1000 a hand-powered desktop calculator that could add, subtract, multiply, and divide ten-digit numbers much faster and more accurately than is possible with pencil and paper (see Figure 2.1).

Despite the speed and accuracy of mechanical calculators, their sales were sparse, constrained by their cost and limited capabilities. Of course, other options were available. Until very recently, most scientific calculations were performed with the aid of slide rules and mathematical tables (see Figure 2.2). We might be inclined to dismiss these calculating aids as hopelessly neolithic, but we should also keep in mind that the atom bomb, the most ambitious engineering project in history at the time, was developed almost entirely without the aid of electronic computers. Still, it is a measure of the astonishing success of electronic calculators that the slide rule, once standard equipment of every college student in a science course, has almost completely vanished from the scene. Indeed, we can claim confidently that scarcely any of today's students have ever seen a slide rule, much less used one. We take the calculator so much for granted today that it is worth our time to consider briefly its rise to prominence.

There are conflicting claims as to the origin of the first electronic calculator; suffice it to say that the first such device was developed in about 1963. Texas Instruments marketed an electronic calculator in 1967, with-

FIGURE 2.1 **A Mechanical Calculator.** (© Devaney Stock Photos, Inc.)

out much commercial success at first. The calculator market blossomed in the late 1960s and early 1970s, however—annual sales went from zero to millions of units in less than a decade, and the price of a typical calculator dropped from $100 to $5 in less than five years. The industry was stunned at first; analysts who had projected demands for integrated circuits in the tens of thousands found that their predictions were a thousandfold too low. Almost overnight, the microelectronics industry changed from a producer of scientific specialty items to a major producer of consumer goods. Now, of course, electronic calculators are cheap enough to be given away as premiums, and there are about 190 million calculators in the United States alone, according to an estimate by Texas Instruments. One might wonder how many people actually need to compute square roots, but including this extra functionality adds effectively nothing to the cost of a calculator. We thus have a technology in the unprecedented position of being able to provide consumers with more than they need at no increase in price.

If we think of the calculator as a microworld, as a model of one aspect of the world, it's clear that the calculator is based on the model of a person performing numeric calculations. Indeed, the design of most calculators is a direct reflection of this model: To add 345 and 720, one presses, in order, the "3," "4," "5," "+," "7," "2," "0" keys, and then presses the "=" key to display the result. If we extend the model slightly, we can consider the calculator as an electronic assistant, capable of performing not just a single operation, but a *series* of calculations at blinding speed. For instance, one way to compute the square root of a positive number, *n*, is to perform the following steps:

1. Begin with a guess, say 1, for the square root of *n*.
2. Repeat the following process until you are as close to the square root as you wish to be:

   Replace the original guess by $(n + guess^2)/(2 \cdot guess)$.

   For example, to compute $\sqrt{5}$, we have the following guesses:

$$1.000000000 \rightarrow (5 + 1.000000000^2)/(2 \cdot 1.000000000) = 3.000000000$$
$$3.000000000 \rightarrow (5 + 3.000000000^2)/(2 \cdot 3.000000000) = 2.333333333$$

FIGURE 2.2   **A Slide Rule.** (© Devaney Stock Photos, Inc.)

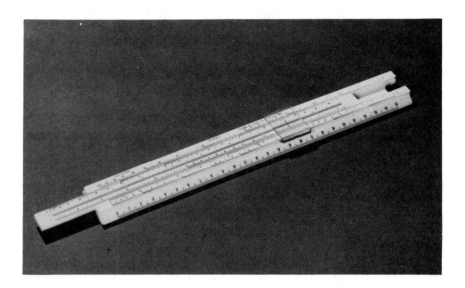

$$2.333333333 \rightarrow (5 + 2.333333333^2)/(2 \cdot 2.333333333) = 2.238095238$$
$$2.238095238 \rightarrow (5 + 2.238095238^2)/(2 \cdot 2.238095238) = 2.236068896$$
$$2.236068896 \rightarrow (5 + 2.236068896^2)/(2 \cdot 2.236068896) = 2.236067977$$

The last guess, after only five steps, is correct to nine decimal places. This technique, known as *Newton's Method*, is our first example of an *algorithm,* a finite collection of simple instructions that can be performed by a computer and is guaranteed to halt in a finite amount of time. We've all used algorithms before, perhaps without knowing the name—think, for instance, of the elementary-school algorithms for multiplication or long division.

At any rate, if we wanted our hypothetical calculator to be able to compute square roots, we would only need to include a small program, activated by the square root key, to perform the algorithm above until, say, the guesses didn't change. Notice, by the way, that the only operations required by the square root program are addition, multiplication, division, and moving and storing numbers. This is a common feature to almost all areas of computer science, where, as we will see over and over again, complex objects with sophisticated behavior are built by combining simpler parts.

The historical contribution of the electronic calculator is that it is the direct ancestor of today's microcomputer. The first computer on a single chip was designed in 1971 by Ted Hoff for the Intel Corporation in response to a request from the Busicom Company of Japan, which wanted to develop a calculator of its own. At the time, a typical calculator consisted of several chips wired together on a printed circuit board. The resulting circuit was a single-purpose machine, designed with the sole purpose of driving the calculator. To design a different calculator, one would have to replace the chips with others, in effect rebuilding the entire circuit. Hoff's brilliant idea was to design a single chip that could be programmed by the manufacturer, so that changing the design of the calculator required no hardware changes at all. It didn't take Hoff and others long to realize that this chip, the Intel 4004, could be put to many uses beyond mere numeric calculations, and thus was born the microcomputer.

> Hoff is said to have had a great deal of difficulty explaining that although the small size of the microprocessor would indeed make it difficult to repair, that wasn't the right question to ask. "When it breaks, just throw it away!" brought the computer to the level of the ballpoint pen.

Æ STACKS: ÆPPLICATIONS GALORE

At the end of Module 1's Lab Exercises 2 and 3 you experimented with some interesting HyperCard stacks. Still, those stacks did little more than present material to you (in an admittedly stylish fashion). Other stacks, like the ones you will see in this lab module, actually provide you with tools that you can control in a certain sense and use to accomplish some generally useful tasks. Such stacks are examples of computer applications.

The two distinguishing features of applications, as we have seen, are their interactivity (the user of a stack typically plays an active role in what the stack does) and their black box nature. As long as a user knows what an application is capable of and how to interact with it, the stack will work. We have reached the point that you don't even need to know much about how computers work in order to use them effectively. The Macintosh and HyperCard have combined to extend the domain of useful applications dramatically, as you will see in the Module 2 lab exercises.

LAB OBJECTIVES

In the lab part of this module, you will

- Gain hands-on experience with HyperCard implementations of some standard and some more specialized computer applications
- Learn about HyperCard's "user level" and how to set it
- Develop the essential keyboard, menu, and mouse skills for processing text in HyperCard—that is, you will become a HyperCard "typer"

2.2   FAMILIAR MICROWORLDS

You have already seen that the modern computer owes its existence to electronic technology. That's true enough, but in a sense it is not particularly relevant to the nature of the computer, particularly when viewed as a black box. Although we cannot do it yet, it is at least theoretically possible to build a computer using photonic technology, in which information is transferred by light rather than electricity. As another example, it is not only theoretically possible to construct an information processor using carbon, rather than silicon, chemistry, it is also eminently practical today—one only has to look at our own brains and those of our pets. What a computer is made of and how it works is just an *enabling technology;* the important notion is what J. David Bolter calls a *defining technology.* Just as the steam engine could be viewed as the defining technology of the Industrial Revolution—the technology of power, of manipulating the physical world—Bolter views the computer as a defining technology of our time—the technology of information, of manipulating the world of ideas.

Revolutionary technologies never spring forth from a social vacuum. New devices always owe their existence to older ideas, and the computer is no exception. In particular, the computer and its programs are a natural step in an evolutionary process that began more than 5000 years ago with what are the most important of all technological innovations to date—

writing and (much later in history) mechanical printing. Both of these technologies can be viewed as the representation of ideas in physical form: "petrified truth," as Mark Twain said. In the case of this book, for instance, when we wrote down our ideas about Module 2, we could put the pages away and come back to them years later, and they would still be there, unchanged, for us to read again. We could give the pages to others, for them to read at their leisure, even if we were no longer around to communicate the ideas contained therein. You are holding a printed copy of our ideas, one of many identical copies owned by many other people, yet we can speak to you through these pages just as if you were sitting in a class listening to us—better, in some ways, since the book is not constrained by time. You can read the same passage again and again—a book never cuts you off because it is impatient or its feet hurt. Also, you can write your own additions to our ideas in the margins, thereby customizing our ideas to suit your own purposes.

What you now hold in your hands or your lap, though, is a comfortable old technology. The subject matter might be new, but the idea of a physical embodiment of ideas on paper would be familiar to a scribe in the time of the Pharaohs. The disk portion of this module, however, represents a new way of thinking about information in physical form. Except for the comments you add in the margin, the information in this text, like all written and printed matter, is essentially static. The programs on the disk, however, contain not only representations of information, but also instructions to the computer to manipulate this information. The computer can perform arithmetic calculations, sort lists of numbers, solve algebraic equations, and, by treating the data as characters rather than numbers, handle mailing lists of names and addresses. Furthermore, if the bits of data are considered to be graphical rather than textual, the computer can use these data to display pictures on the screen.

In all of these examples, the computer and its program together take on the nature of an active metaphor, a *microworld,* if you will, having its own natural laws to govern its behavior. These microworlds are frequently models of a portion of the real world, either in an attempt to imitate the physical world or to create the environment of the job to be done. As we will see shortly, computer microworlds may begin by modeling familiar tasks, but often they evolve to include behavior far beyond the ranges of the tasks they originally imitated.

THE WORD PROCESSOR

At first, people thought of the computer solely as the apotheosis of the adding machine, a glorified supercalculator. It didn't take long to realize, though, that any information that could be expressed in numeric code could be grist for the computer's mill. By assigning a code number to each letter, digit, and punctuation mark, for instance, a text document could be stored in a computer's memory, and hence manipulated by a program. This, in simplest form, is all that a word processor really does.

Word processors began as models of typewriters. Indeed, one of the first word processors, the IBM magnetic tape Selectric of 1964, actually was a typewriter, with a way of storing electrically a coded version of what had been typed. In these early, paper-based word processors, the typist used special code sequences or keys to type a chosen range of lines and to enter or modify text in those lines. To produce a perfectly typed document, then, the typist made a draft copy that was stored electrically, then edited the paper copy, returned to the tape to make the corrections, and finally printed the finished version. A master copy of a commonly used letter, for example, could be made and slightly modified for each name and address, so it was no longer necessary to retype the entire letter to make just a few changes.

As useful as early word processors were, they were of limited commercial impact until they were combined with display screens in the 1970s. Still, they didn't really take off until personal computers became popular in the late 1970s and early 1980s. With these WYSIWYG (for "What You See Is What You Get," pronounced *whizzy-wig*) word processors, the user didn't have to insert special *control characters* while typing to produce special printed effects. Instead of having a document that looked like this:

```
{\bf 1.} Some of the {\it invisible benefits} of
    this plan include: \cr
\tab \bullet Reduced {\ul downtime} for the \Sigma
    -7 units \cr
```

The user could see on the screen exactly what the finished document would look like:

1. Some of the *invisible benefits* of this plan include:
    • Reduced <u>downtime</u> for the Σ-7 Units

On the Macintosh and similar computers, for example, control of the typefaces, styles, and special characters is achieved by pressing certain key combinations or making selections from the menu. These are translated in turn into invisible control characters that are translated by the word-processing program into instructions to the screen display. The internal representation of the document in the computer's memory still looks very much like the first example above—the difference is that the screen display on the Mac is sophisticated enough to show the letters in many forms, when instructed by the word processor to do so.

Notice that by this time the microworld that began as a model of the typewriter had evolved to include features that were difficult or even impossible to achieve with the typewriter, such as the mixing of fonts and typestyles in the example above. This evolution beyond the original model also included such features as the ability to cut a selection of text and paste it elsewhere in the document (something which would have to be accomplished with scissors and tape in the typewriter world, hence the terms *cut* and *paste*), as well as the ability to replace every occurrence in a document of a nonword such as *alot* with the correct version *a lot* at the stroke of a key (or click of a mouse). A program that instructed the computer to perform simple "reading" of a text file also led to features that were undreamed of in the typewriter model, such as automatic spelling checkers.

While we are discussing enhancements of the typewriter model, we should make note of a new idea, still in its infancy at present. We remarked before that the computer allows us to link actions with data, producing what might be called "smart documents." One example of this is known as *hypertext*. In a hypertext document, the invisible control characters are extended beyond instructions to the screen, allowing parts of a document to be linked together. In such a document, you might read text on a screen as in a conventional word processor, and then by clicking on a word, get a definition, a picture, or a more detailed background. In effect, a hypertext document could have "active footnotes" that could be called up and explored by the user, mirroring the way we might browse through a book, looking in the index, then in the text, then following a reference to a later section, then turning to the illustrations.

We have noted before that paper and ink provide a physical embodiment of the world of ideas. Still, you can pick up a paper and smudge the ink with greasy fingers. In a sense, the word processor is even closer to the world of ideas than the typewriter or pen, since the words cannot be touched. They are fleeting electrical currents internally, and patterns of light and dark dots on a screen externally. This "light writing," to use the words of Jack Harris, provides a flexibility impossible with paper and ink, by dispensing (at least from the user's point of view) with the need to produce and manipulate physical objects.

Æ LAB

LAB EXERCISE 1

Most of the sample stacks we described in Module 1 could be controlled and explored by means of a single input device—the Mac's mouse. In order to use many other interesting applications from within HyperCard, we must use the keyboard as an additional input device, and to do that we must notify HyperCard that we intend to do some typing. Hyper-Card has five different "user levels"; each successive level has associated with it increasingly sophisticated and complex operations. To this point, you have been operating as a "browser," one who can view stacks and

Setting the user level.

navigate through them with the mouse. If we want also to be able to enter information from the keyboard, we must identify ourselves to Hyper-Card as "typers."

There are three ways to accomplish this (we told you HyperCard is big on providing alternative ways to accomplish most tasks). One method is to return to HyperCard's Home stack and select Preferences from the Home menu. Having done so, your Mac's screen will display the card shown in Figure 2.3. By clicking on any of the five user levels, you alert HyperCard of your intentions, and it adjusts the operations it automatically makes available to you.

You can perform most HyperCard operations this way, by typing them into the Message box and pressing the Return key.

A second method is to use the Message... command in the Go menu. Remember that choosing the Message... command causes the message box to appear at the bottom of the screen. You may also recall we said that most HyperCard commands can be invoked by typing them into the message box. Typing "set userLevel to 2" into the message box, followed by pressing the Return key, has the identical effect of going to the User Level card and clicking on the Typing button (the second button from the bottom). You can set the user level from the message box, to anything from 1 (Browsing) to 5 (Scripting).

There will most certainly be times when you want to control your user level. In practice, though, we have done our best to anticipate your needs

FIGURE 2.3   Setting the User Level

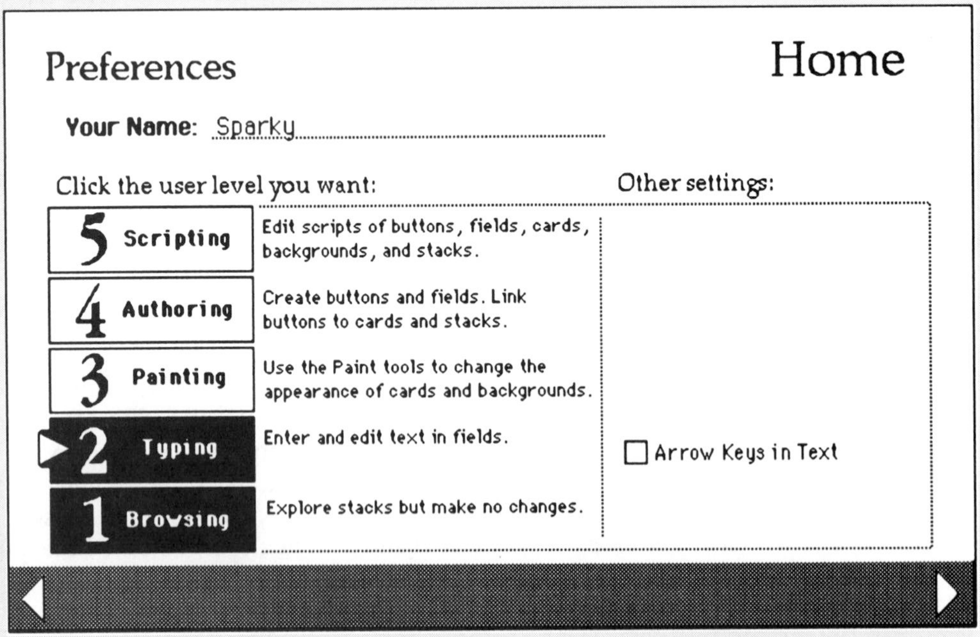

Preferences   Home

Your Name: Sparky

Click the user level you want: Other settings:

5 Scripting   Edit scripts of buttons, fields, cards, backgrounds, and stacks.

4 Authoring   Create buttons and fields. Link buttons to cards and stacks.

3 Painting   Use the Paint tools to change the appearance of cards and backgrounds.

2 Typing   Enter and edit text in fields.   □ Arrow Keys in Text

1 Browsing   Explore stacks but make no changes.

FIGURE 2.4 The Last Word Processor

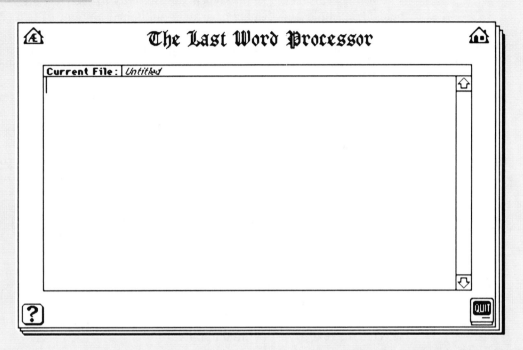

and have preset most of the Æ stacks to be used at one of the five levels. That is, we have included a "set userLevel..." command directly into each of the stacks and, thus, instructed HyperCard to set your user level for you. This third method for controlling which operations are available to a user of a stack—by programming—will be discussed in detail in later modules.

1.1 Start HyperCard now and, if necessary, navigate your way to Hyper-Card's Home stack.

1.2 Use the Go menu to open the Message box.

1.3 Type "set userLevel to 2" into the Message box, and hit the return key.

1.4 Select Preferences from the Home menu, and verify that your user level has been properly set.

Now that you are a HyperCard typer, you can appreciate (if you don't already) the power of one of the most pervasive computer applications, the word processor. (*Note:* If you are already familiar with standard Macintosh text-editing techniques, you may skip the remainder of Lab Exercise 1, and continue your reading with the next section, "The Spreadsheet.") In fact, HyperCard provides you with many of the standard features normally associated with word processors. The first Æ stack for this lab module, named The Last Word Processor (see Figure 2.4), presents a simple rectangle on the screen with an unusual vertical bar along its right side. This rectangle (in HyperCard, we refer to such rectangles as "fields") can hold and display a virtually unlimited amount of text. By clicking on the up- and down-facing arrows in the vertical bar we can "scroll" the field to make different lines of text visible. The vertical bar is referred to as the "scroll bar," and fields with a scroll bar are called "scrolling fields."

> A field is a container for textual information. If you can type it, you can store it in a field.

This and all HyperCard fields are designed to let you manipulate text within them in a number of interesting and useful ways. Simply clicking in the field changes the cursor from a pointing finger to an "insertion bar," which marks the spot where typed characters will be inserted into the field. You need not concern yourself with "carriage returns" as you type, unless you want text broken at specific points. HyperCard knows the size of the field and adjusts your text to fit into it. For the moment, you can use the Delete or Backspace key to erase individual characters. Note, too, that you can reposition the insertion bar within the field by moving and clicking the mouse. Subsequent insertions and deletions are made relative to the new spot.

> To enter text in a field, you must first click in the field.

If inserting and deleting text were the only operations available, word processors would be little more than automated typewriters. Most, though, offer a wide range of editing features. Before reviewing the operations offered for HyperCard fields, we must first describe how one "selects" the text to be operated upon.

The pattern for describing a text-editing operation (in fact, for most Macintosh operations) is to first select the thing to be operated upon and then to choose an operation from the appropriate menu. Selecting text is the process whereby you specify which part of the text is to be edited (moved, removed, revised, and so on). To select a point for inserting text or for removing text using the Backspace or Delete key, simply click the mouse at any point within the field. To choose a group of characters, click at the start of the group (immediately before the first character desired) and drag the mouse (with the button held down) until the entire group is highlighted. Dragging the mouse down or up within the field selects entire lines. The operation chosen (even typing and pressing Backspace or Delete) then applies to the entire selection.

The menu in Figure 2.5 shows the editing commands available to HyperCard typers. Each command applies to whatever text has been selected when the menu item is chosen.

> Using the undo command.

The Undo command undoes the most recent editing operation. If, for example, you inadvertently delete some text, choosing Undo immediately after doing so will restore it. Note that this operation works only for the operation immediately preceding it. Choosing Undo many times in a row accomplishes nothing more.

FIGURE 2.5   HyperCard's Edit Menu

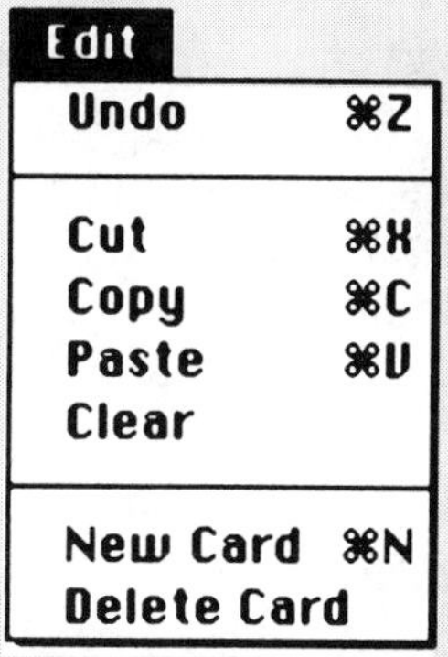

```
┌─────────────┐
│ Edit        │
├─────────────┤
│ Undo    ⌘Z  │
├─────────────┤
│ Cut     ⌘X  │
│ Copy    ⌘C  │
│ Paste   ⌘V  │
│ Clear       │
├─────────────┤
│ New Card ⌘N │
│ Delete Card │
└─────────────┘
```

> Cutting, copying, and pasting all use the Clipboard, a temporary storage location the Mac provides.

The Macintosh Clipboard is a special place used to save information from the immediately preceding operation. Cutting a portion of text removes it from the field and saves it (temporarily!) on the Clipboard. The cut text can then be pasted into another location within the same or even another field. Copying text works just like cutting text—the copied text is saved on the Clipboard so that it can be pasted—except that the selected text is not removed from the original field. Once copied to the Clipboard, text can be pasted into any field. Pasting inserts the current contents of the Clipboard at the current insertion point in a field. The Clipboard remains unchanged by pasting. The normal method for moving text from one location to another (even across cards and stacks) is to cut or copy the text to be moved, clicking where it is to be inserted, and choosing Paste from the Edit menu.

Clear removes the current selection from its field. It is equivalent to hitting the Delete or Backspace key. Note that clearing a portion of text does not place it on the Clipboard and cannot be "undone."

1.5   Open the Last Word Processor stack now.

1.6   Enter the memo below into the stack's scrolling field.

```
Friday, January 13, 1993
To: Professor Decker
From: Ben Realbusy Re: Homework
I regret to report that do to an extremely full
calendar these past two weaks (my new car broke
down, I've been trying to maintain my tan, and I
have had to prepare for an outrageous Super Bowl
party-you're invited!), I will not be handing
in assignment #1 on thyme. I amsurethatyou appreciate
```

```
the pressure I have been under and, since you have
nothing to do but sit in your office anyway, I feel
certain that you will except my assignemtn whenever
I get around to handing it in.

If there is any problema, please leave a massage
on my answering machine.

        Chow,

Ben
```

1.7 Use the keyboard and the Edit menu to

  a. Correct all misspelled words
  b. Fix the spacing in the memo (use the space bar and the Return key to add spaces, the Backspace or Delete keys to remove them)
  c. Customize the memo to include your name and that of your favorite instructor

> The file operations New, Open, Save, and Save As... .

Another essential ingredient of today's word processors is their ability to save and retrieve documents as "files" on disks. This allows not only for documents to be revised at any time after they have been created, but also for them to be revised as often as necessary (which, in the case of our memo, may be often indeed). The file-handling capabilities of our Last Word Processor are embodied in the Words menu at the top of the screen. The commands therein use standard Macintosh parlance for describing common storage and retrieval operations.

Selecting New from the Words menu, appropriately enough, creates a new document named (in the small rectangle above the text field) "Untitled." If a document already appears in the text field when New is selected, you are asked if you want to save it before creating a new—and blank—document.

The Open... command allows you to retrieve an existing document from a disk file and to have it appear in the text window. The ellipses following the word "Open" in the Words menu are significant according to Macintosh naming convention. Ellipses are commonly used in command names (whether on buttons or in menus) to indicate that there is more to invoking the command than a single click of the mouse. In this case, after selecting Open... we must specify which file is to be opened. We do so by means of a dialog box like the one we saw when we opened stacks in the Module 1 Starter Stack. (If you want to review the dialog box format, open the Starter Stack by choosing Open Stack... from the File menu now. Return to the Last Word Processor before continuing.)

Selecting the Save command stores the contents of the text field using the file name that appears in the Current File: field above the document. The Save As... command also stores the text field, but first presents you with a dialog box (as indicated by the ellipses) that asks you to name the file and to specify which disk the file is to be saved on.

1.8 Edit your memo so that it is a generic excuse letter. That is, fix it so that it can be used for any instructor, any assignment, and any excuses.

THE SPREADSHEET

A spreadsheet combines the attributes of a calculator and a word processor. Represented as a rectangular array of "cells," the spreadsheet is modeled after an accountant's ledger sheet. Figure 2.6 illustrates a typical spreadsheet with six columns—one for the row title, one for each quarter of the year, plus one for the year to date—and four rows, representing the column titles, and the sales, costs, and profits for each quarter.

Each cell of the spreadsheet contains not only visible information, but also codes representing how the information is to be displayed—the numeric information is displayed with two decimal places of accuracy, right justified, with any negative values enclosed in parentheses, while the textual information in each cell of column 1 and row 1 is centered. In this sense, the spreadsheet is very much like a modern word processor. The display of information (which can be regarded simply as a collection of strings of characters) can be edited by typing, cutting, copying, and pasting, while each piece of information carries with it a hidden collection of formatting information, as specified by the user. In a modern spreadsheet, this format information can be spread to each row or column. For example, to change the format of a column from integers to decimal numbers with two-place accuracy requires only changing the format of a single cell and issuing a command to extend the characteristics of that cell to its entire column, in much the same way that the margins of a paragraph could be made to apply to an entire document in a word processor.

This by itself would be useful to accountants, saving the trouble of having to redo a ledger sheet to adapt to a client's wishes, but the true power of the spreadsheet goes much further than mere "prettyprinting." When Daniel Bricklin and Robert Frankston designed VisiCalc, the first spreadsheet, they began with a microworld that was dynamic rather than static. Along with numeric or textual data and display format information, each

FIGURE 2.6   A Sample Spreadsheet

	1	2	3	4	5	6
1		Spring	Summer	Fall	Winter	YTD
2	Sales	2275.91	1120.65			3396.56
3	Cost	1480.03	1289.98			2770.01
4	Profit	795.88	(169.33)			626.55

FIGURE 2.7   Spreadsheet Formulas

	1	2	3	4	5	6
1		Spring	Summer	Fall	Winter	YTD
2	Sales	2275.91	1120.65			3396.56
3	Cost	1480.03	1289.98			2770.01
4	Profit	795.88	(169.33)			626.55

row 2 - row 3 of this column   sum of (column 2 to column of this row)

cell of a spreadsheet can communicate with every other via a user-defined rule that describes the information to be stored in the cell. Look at the YTD (for Year To Date) column in Figure 2.7, for example. We know that the total cost to date is the sum of the costs that have been entered so far, and the spreadsheet allows us to specify that the value in row 3 of column 6 will be the sum of the values in columns 2 through 5 of that row. When setting up the spreadsheet, then, the user enters a rule in row 2, column 6, and then enters the command to make that rule apply to all the cells in column 6. After all the formulas have been properly entered (including the "profit = sales – cost" rule for the cells in row 4), the user need only enter the numbers to be operated upon. As each number is entered in a cell, any other cell that uses that number is immediately recalculated. Of course, some cells, such as the title cells in the first row and column, may have "empty rules" that say, in effect, "just display the information in this cell."

In a manner similar to the way that the word processor quickly evolved beyond its original typewriter model, the spreadsheet was from the first recognized by its users as not only a powerful and efficient tool for managing existing data, but also as a simulator, a "what if" tool. Every faculty member, for instance, has had a student who comes in with the plaintive cry, "What grade do I need on the final to pass this course?" If the course records have been kept in an electronic spreadsheet, the instructor can use the spreadsheet, saying "Well, let's see . . . suppose you got a 65 on the final [types in "65" in the column for final exam and the spreadsheet recalculates the course grade]. That'll give you a 59 average in the course, so maybe we'll try a 75 on the final . . . ," and so on, until the student is satisfied. In a similar vein, the cells in a spreadsheet could be programmed with the rules for computing income tax, and the operator could use the spreadsheet to answer questions such as, "Assuming that my gross income next year is $45,788, how large should my charitable deductions be to make my tax liability no larger than it is this year?"

REVIEW QUESTIONS

1. Explain the distinction we make between *data* and *information*.
2. What is an algorithm? Give an example other than those mentioned in the text. What is the difference between an algorithm and a program?
3. List at least four ways in which the word processor has transcended the model of a typewriter.
4. What are the three kinds of information that are stored in a cell of a spreadsheet?

LAB EXERCISE 2

Although our HyperCard version of a spreadsheet, as implemented in the Æ stack High-Priced Spread (see Figure 2.8), is nowhere near as powerful as are full-blown, commercial spreadsheet applications, it is generally useful for a wide variety of calculations. Like its commercial

FIGURE 2.8   **The High-Priced Spread Stack**

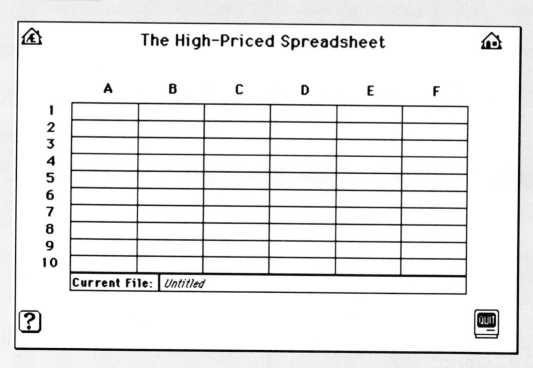

counterparts, it is essentially an unformatted ledger sheet. In order to use it, one must decide what and how information is to be entered, and then describe for the program what calculations are to be performed.

The ledger sheet provides us with 60 cells into which either numbers or formulas can be entered. The cells are named by the column and row headings. For example, the cell in the upper left corner of the ledger is named A1, and the cell in the lower right corner is named F10.

To enter either a value or a formula into a cell, one must first select the cell. A cell is selected by clicking the mouse inside of it. Once a cell is selected, a dialog box will appear soliciting an entry for that cell. To enter a value (either a number or a piece of text), simply type the desired value into the dialog box. The value can be edited using the Backspace or Delete key, or any commands for HyperCard's Edit menu (for example, values can be cut, copied, and pasted). Clicking OK in the dialog box (or hitting the Return or Enter key on the keyboard) records the value in the selected cell.

We signal to High-Priced Spread that we are entering a formula into a selected cell by typing an equal sign ("=") as the first character of an entry. Formulas are composed of cell names (A1–F10), arithmetic operators (+, –, *, /), and left and right parentheses. For example, if we wanted to calculate the average of the values in cells A1, B1, and C1, and to store the formula for the calculation in cell D1, we would type `= (A1+B1+C1)/3` into the dialog box for cell D1, and click OK (see Figure 2.9). In this case, whenever the values in cells A1, B1, or C1 change, the value of D1 (the average) changes automatically.

High-Priced Spread also comes with its own menu, named "Spreads," which provides you with the equivalent of the four Macintosh standard file operations, customized to spreadsheets. Selecting New from the Spreads menu clears the current ledger. The Open... command clears the current ledger and reads into it a previously saved spreadsheet, formulas and all. The two commands for saving a spreadsheet, Save and Save as..., write the current ledger to a disk file using either the name of the current file (as indicated below the ledger sheet) or a new name you provide in a standard file dialog box, respectively.

> Note for non-bowlers: Scores are whole numbers from 0 (lousy) to 300 (perfect).

2.1   Open the High-Priced Spread stack now.

2.2   Follow the steps below to define a ledger to keep track of a bowling team's weekly scores on High-Priced Spread. Imagine a team of five players, each of whom bowls three games per week.

    a. Enter three scores for player 1 into cells A1, B1, and C1.

    b. Enter a formula for player 1's total score (A1 + B1 + C1) into cell D1.

    c. Enter the formula for player 1's average score (D1/3) into cell E1.

    d. Change one of player 1's scores and verify that the total and average values change correspondingly.

    e. Enter the scores for players 2–5 into columns A, B, and C of rows 2–5, respectively.

    f. Enter appropriate formulas for each player's total and average scores into columns D and E. (*Note:* You may want to copy and paste formulas from player 1.)

    g. Enter formulas that calculate the team's total score for all games in cell D6 and the team's overall average in cell E6.

2.3 Change some of the players' scores. Once you are convinced that the totals and averages are being calculated correctly, use the Save as... command from the Spreads menu to save the spreadsheet in its current form. A dialog box will appear on the screen that will allow you to name the file and to decide which disk it should be stored on.

2.4 Clear the ledger by selecting New from the Spreads menu.

2.5 Use High-Priced Spread to define a ledger that acts as a grade book for a class of seven students. Each student is to complete two homework assignments (each receiving a numeric grade out of 25 points), one midterm exam (50 points), and one final exam (100 points). The spreadsheet should calculate the numeric class average for each assignment and exam. Each student's weighted average is also to be calculated, given that the homework constitutes 50 percent of the grade, the midterm 15 percent, and the final exam 35 percent.

FIGURE 2.9   **Entering a Formula into the High-Priced Spreadsheet**

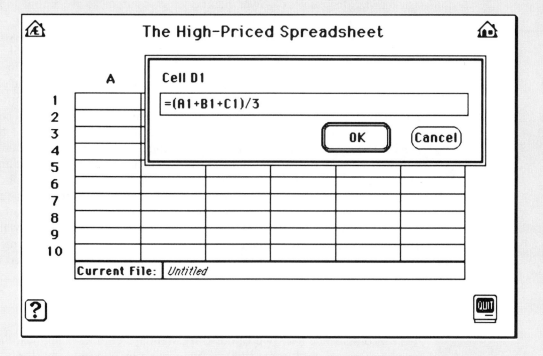

2.3   THE STATE OF THE ART

Calculators, word processors, and spreadsheets are among the most visible computer applications today. This is due in large part to their accessibility and their general utility. Each is applicable to a variety of common tasks in a wide range of settings. Most important, these programs have evolved to the point that they are genuinely useful to nonspecialists. Indeed, that explains their appeal. One need no longer be a whiz at arithmetic (or even, as we shall see, mathematics) to solve numeric problems. Neither does one have to be an expert typist to produce polished-looking documents. Whereas standard high-school graduation gifts were once typewriters and slide rules, today's graduates come to college with calculators and, in increasing numbers, word processors and spreadsheets in hand.

These applications, though, represent the tip of the iceberg. Far more numerous and pervasive are the highly specialized programs that solve domain-dependent problems, or help humans to do so, in virtually every profession. The number of such off-the-shelf, task-specific applications grows daily as software developers respond to acknowledged professional needs. Still, this market goes largely unnoticed by most of us, who have little use for or appreciation of, say, a program that helps to determine the best mix of components to be used in the casings of an oil well. This is not to say that such specialized applications don't affect us in our everyday lives. On the contrary, it is safe to say that there would be no telephone service, space program, nuclear power plants, or computers as we know them without applications programs used by specialists in related fields.

> It's been estimated that to provide today's level of phone service without computers would require every man, woman, and child in the country to be hired as an operator.

The fields that rely heavily on applications software are not limited to the highly technical ones you might expect. Programs are now available at your local computer store and through the mail (electronic or the more conventional postal service variety) to assist specialists in business, the sciences, industry, the professions, the arts, entertainment, and education. The following pages review applications programs in use today. The list is by no means comprehensive, and provides no details about most of the specific programs. We do not even mention "embedded applications" (those that are an indistinguishable part of some larger system or machine, such as a car or a microwave oven), and we similarly disregard applications related directly to computer science (for example, programs that control touch-sensitive screens or produce computer "speech"). Rather, we provide the list to expose you to the breadth of applications software. The common thread relating all of these programs is that, despite the magnitude of the problem the application addresses, each can be regarded by those who use it as a black box.

BUSINESS APPLICATIONS

It is no coincidence that two of our three standard computer applications, word processors and spreadsheets, grew essentially out of the business world. Business or "data-processing" needs that exploit the computer's facility for storing and processing vast amounts of information were among the first addressed by commercial computers. The general accounting processes of governments, insurance companies, banks, and other businesses have long since been implemented as computer applications, which are now available and affordable for small businesses using personal (Macintosh-like) computers. Individual and integrated applications can be purchased off the shelf for, among others, general ledger, accounts receivable, accounts payable, payroll, inventory, and tracking and billing of professional services. These programs typically provide word-processing-like features for recording information, spreadsheet-like features for accomplishing standard calculations, and database-like functions for storing, retrieving, sorting, and organizing information. Many allow their users to print standard forms such as checks and W-2 forms, and some even allow users to design their own forms and reports.

Similar programs have been developed for personal use and customized for use in specific businesses. There are programs for maintaining checkbooks, for home budgeting, for individual tax preparation (complete with printable federal and state tax forms), and for portfolio management. Small and large businesses, ranging from restaurants to pharmacies and publishing houses, similarly benefit from applications programs that take into account the specifics of those businesses. For example, inventory programs of restaurant management applications incorporate food spoilage rates into their algorithms for ordering food stock. Programs that print labels on prescription drugs typically check a patient's chart to make sure that a newly prescribed medication will not interact in harmful ways with any other of the patient's prescribed medicines. Desktop publishing systems provide full text and graphic layout facilities that go far beyond conventional word processors.

Perhaps the most common business application is the *database* program, used to organize and classify information for convenient access. In a common form of database, information is classified as a *relation,* which may be regarded as a table describing the attributes possessed by the elements in the database. Figure 2.10 illustrates a sample relation for a database consisting of student information.

The relation of Figure 2.10 consists of five records, each of which has five attributes or fields identified by the names "Name," "Year," "GPA," "FinancialAid," and "MealPlan." The information stored in the fields may be strings of characters, integers, real numbers, logical values, and so on. Viewing a computer application as a model of a real-world situation, it would be appropriate to think of a database program as a fast, efficient, and tireless records clerk or inventory manager.

The advantage of a database program is that it allows one to *query* the program to search and manipulate the database. In the example of Figure 2.10, for instance, we could enter the query

```
LIST Year = 2 AND FinancialAid > 1000
```

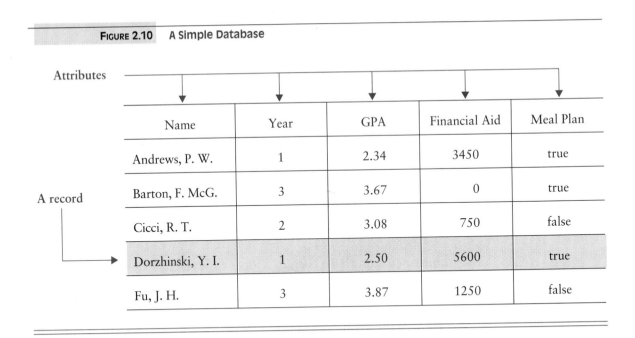

FIGURE 2.10   A Simple Database

Attributes

Name	Year	GPA	Financial Aid	Meal Plan
Andrews, P. W.	1	2.34	3450	true
Barton, F. McG.	3	3.67	0	true
Cicci, R. T.	2	3.08	750	false
Dorzhinski, Y. I.	1	2.50	5600	true
Fu, J. H.	3	3.87	1250	false

A record

to obtain a list of all student records for the sophomores whose financial aid is larger than $1000. The query language might also have commands such as

```
SORT FinancialAid
```

to sort the relation in order of increasing financial aid amounts. Other commands add new fields or new records, or format reports for printing or screen display, as follows:

```
EXPAND TABLE Student ADD FIELD Id (INTEGER 9)

DEFINE VIEW StudentFinancialView AS
  SELECT Name, Id, FinancialAid
  FROM Student
```

The tabular nature of our sample database makes it look very much like a spreadsheet, and indeed there are considerable overlaps between the two types of programs. The principal differences are not between what they can and cannot do, but rather between what they can and cannot do easily. A typical database lacks some of the simple "what if" features of a spreadsheet, but includes the ability to store large numbers of records for fast access, and allows complicated interdependencies between the records.

NUMERICAL APPLICATIONS

Historically, the main beneficiary of the computer's numerical prowess has been the sciences. Scientists and engineers use applications programs based on numerical techniques to design aircraft and space vehicles; to design and test camera lenses and other optical systems; to launch and track vehicles in space; to enhance photographs taken from space; to analyze aerial and satellite images for weather prediction, pollution patterns, crop assessment, and military recognizance; and to simulate the formation of galaxies. As other disciplines become increasingly quantitative, they too benefit from similar applications. Economists and social psychologists, for example, make use of programs that allow them to describe models and test their theories. Image-processing programs are used in archaeological studies to restore and analyze blurred pictures, and by geographers in developing maps. Linguists use programs that record and analyze speech and text. As tools for writers and literary critics, certain programs even help to analyze text for stylistic tendencies. Anthropologists and historians use statistical programs to analyze cultural data in an effort to better understand our past.

Our first standard application, the calculator, embodies the computer's facility in performing efficient numerical calculations. As useful numerical techniques were implemented on computers, they were incorporated, first, into the computer's circuits (we'll see how this is accomplished in Module 6), then into programming languages, and subsequently into software "libraries" that can be used conveniently by programmers. These techniques are now incorporated into stand-alone applications that can solve a remarkable variety of mathematical problems.

How remarkable? Suffice it to say that many—if not most—of the calculations one encounters in college courses in algebra, calculus, linear algebra, numerical analysis, and differential equations can be solved by typing them into a program and pushing a "button." Results can be expressed numerically and graphically (in two or three dimensions) with equal facility. The programs that solve such problems have been written, encapsulated, made accessible to nonprogrammers, and, thanks to advances in hardware technology, they can now run on personal computers. Consider, for example, the Mathematica program, designed by Stephen Wolfram. Mathematica is a recent example of a class of programs that act as intelligent mathematical assistants. In this program, the operative metaphor is a notebook of the kind mathematicians use to keep the results of their investigations, but the notebook is unlike the conventional type in that it is active, like a word-processing document or a spreadsheet.

To illustrate some of the simplest features of Mathematica, consider a session one of us had with the program recently. In analyzing the running time of a program we had written to sort lists of numbers in increasing order, we had accumulated data on the time the program took to sort lists of 250, 500, 750 . . . , 2000 numbers. Entering the running times and identifying them by name required only the line

```
bData  =  [0.45, 1.85, 4.18, 7.45, 11.67, 16.8, 23.06,
29.99]
```

Then, the command

    Plot [%]

displayed a plot of the data, as follows:

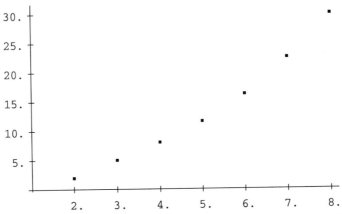

At this stage, we had good reason to believe that the data could be modeled as a quadratic curve, so we requested Mathematica to find the quadratic curve that best fitted the data by the command

    bCurve = Fit[bData, (1, x, x^2), x]

which yielded the approximation

    $0.0119643 - 0.031131 \ x + 0.472917 \ x^2$

which we could then plot along with the data, to obtain the following graph:

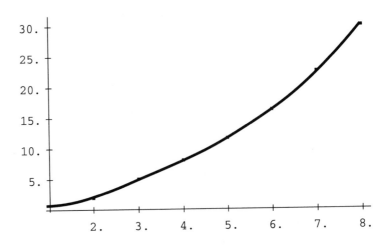

This is a *very* simple Mathematica exercise, one that hardly begins to draw upon its full functionality. Except for fitting the data to a quadratic curve, it is not hard to imagine how Mathematica must have worked in the example. Far more sophisticated, however, is the ability of programs such as Mathematica to perform *symbolic algebra*, as, for instance, when it factors

$$x^2 - y^2 + x^3\ y - x^2\ y^2 - x\ y^3 + y^4$$

into

$$(x\ +\ y)\ \ (x\ -\ y)\ \ (1\ +\ x\ y\ -\ y^2)$$

The point, however, is that even in this simple example Mathematica can do in seconds the data plotting, curve fitting, and graphing that would have taken the better part of an hour to do manually. As with all applications, Mathematica and its cousins are not intended to substitute for the working knowledge of the user they are designed to assist. Let's look at a simple example: the equations $x + y = 3$, $2x + 2.0001y = 6.2$ have the common solution $x = -1997$, $y = 2000$, as you could verify by substituting these values into each of the equations. If a mathematics assistant program stored numbers to only four digits of accuracy, however, the two equations would be represented internally as $x + y = 3$, $2x + 2y = 6.2$, and these equations have *no* common solutions at all. The moral, of course, is that any computer application is an assistant to human experience and judgment, not a replacement. Like any other tool, applications must be used wisely.

Æ LAB

LAB EXERCISE 3

We began this text module by recounting the explosive development of the hand-held calculator. The fact that many of us now carry calculators in our briefcases, back packs, and checkbooks does not mean that the market for these devices has become saturated, nor does it imply that this prototypical computer application has been unaffected by subsequent developments in technology. On the contrary, state-of-the-art calculators are more powerful by almost any measure (except, of course, size, power consumption, and cost) than were the giant electronic "brains" of the 1940s. Many of today's calculators are not only programmable (they come equipped with the equivalent of their own programming languages), but are also equipped with miniature screens that allow them to display the results of their calculations in graphical form.

The Æ stack for this set of lab exercises is a HyperCard implementation of such a graphing calculator, named "GraphiCalc" (see Figure 2.11). At one level, GraphiCalc can be used as a conventional calculator, with the minor exception that you must click the mouse to activate the calculator's keys. GraphiCalc's keyboard allows you to enter numerical values to compute some basic mathematical functions, and to save and recall a single value from the calculator's modest memory. The C key clears the numeric display (the horizontal window directly above the numeric keys) and sets the display to zero.

3.1   Open the GraphiCalc stack now.

3.2   Click on the numeric keys (ignore the Graph and Clear Graph keys for now) to perform some basic computations.

3.3   Use the memory keys to store a value in the calculator's memory, to add and subtract values for memory, and to recall a value from memory.

FIGURE 2.11   The GraphiCalc Stack

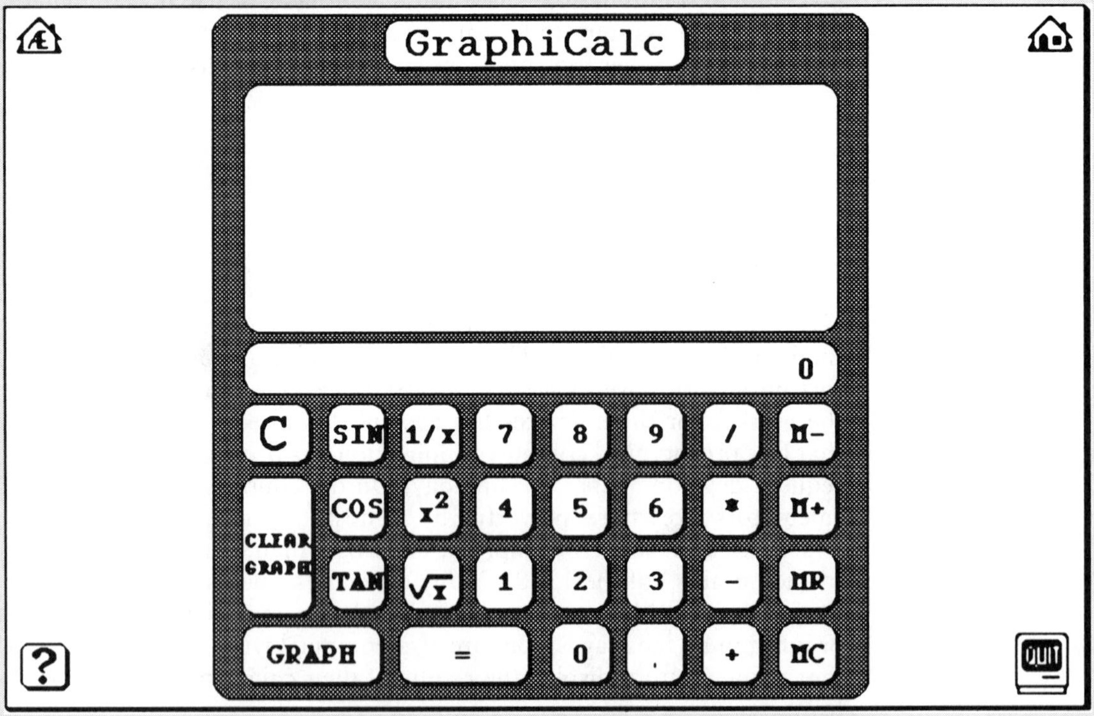

The larger rectangular window at the top of GraphiCalc is the one in which the stack displays its graphical output. To produce a graph, we click on the GRAPH button. After doing so, the calculator displays a dialog box in which it solicits values to describe a graph (see Figure 2.12). It is up to you to enter an equation (involving variable x and using HyperCard notation for arithmetic expressions) and the other parameters necessary to define which portion of the graph is to be displayed. These other parameters include: minimum values for the x and y axes (these can differ), maximum values for the x and y axes (so can these), increment values for the x and y axes, and labels to appear along each of the axes. You can click directly in any of the rectangles and use your text-editing skills and your Mac's keyboard to enter values (or, hit the Mac's Tab key to move from field to field). Once your graph has been fully defined, hitting the Draw button will close GraphiCalc's dialog box and display in its graphical window your graph as described. Clicking the CLEAR GRAPH button, as you would expect, clears the stack's graphical window.

FIGURE 2.12   Graphing with GraphiCalc

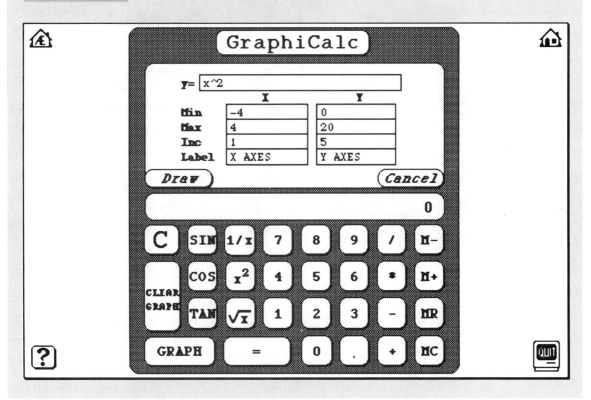

3.4   Click GraphiCalc's GRAPH button, and provide the following information to describe a graph. Type the underlined characters into the corresponding positions of GraphiCalc's dialog box

$$y=\underline{x\wedge 2}$$

	x	y
Min	-3	0
Max	3	10
Incr	1	2
Label	MY X	MY Y

When all information has been entered correctly, click the Draw button and examine the resulting graph.

3.5   Click the CLEAR GRAPH button. Now, enter the information below to draw and examine another graph.

$$y=\underline{(2*(x\wedge 2)) + (5*x) + 3}$$

	x	y
Min	-1	0
Max	3	40
Incr	1	10
Label	MY X	MY Y

3.6   Do the same for one final graph, as described below.

$$y=\underline{sin(x)}$$

	x	y
Min	-4	-1
Max	4	1
Incr	1	1
Label	MY X	MY Y

APPLICATIONS TO THE PROFESSIONS

Many of the professions suffer equally from information overload and make extensive use of specialized application software. Doctors have for years relied on imaging equipment (such as X rays and sonograms) that is controlled by software. Now, medical consultation programs can advise doctors on pulmonary dysfunction, infectious diseases, glaucoma, renal disease, internal medicine, Hodgkin's disease, and psychopharmacology. Other programs monitor patients being treated by experimental drugs. There are even programs that run on personal computers and serve as family health care consultants. A variety of programs have similarly been developed for the offices of lawyers (for preparing and analyzing contracts, doing literature searches, and preparing briefs), law enforcement agencies (for maintaining driving records and automatic fingerprint matching), and architects (for producing drawings and three-dimensional renderings).

The programs used by architects and industrial designers exploit the computer's relatively newfound facility with pictures. While computers have been used to print graphs and tables for many years, only recently have they become sophisticated enough to display arbitrary shapes on their screens. Indeed, just as we saw a proliferation of word-processing software a few years ago, we are now seeing picture-processing programs—applications that let a user create, edit, refine, and print graphics at the computer. These stand-alone graphics applications have already evolved to the extent that they produce colored, three-dimensional pictures with shadings and perspectives that are controlled by the user: Light sources can be varied and the picture changes accordingly, and the picture can be moved, rotated, or translated in any dimension. Equally fascinating are the ways in which graphics programs are being incorporated into other specialized applications. Desktop publishing systems, which operate on pictures as well as text, would not exist today without graphics applications programs. Spreadsheet programs can now represent tabular data in a variety of graphical forms at the click of a mouse, thanks to graphics programs.

The medical CAT scan (for Computerized Axial Tomography) is a good example of an application used in the professions. While X rays allow a physician to obtain information about the internal structure of a patient—to find tumors, for example—traditional X-ray images are difficult to interpret. Consider the example in Figure 2.13. In a conventional X-ray picture, the X rays pass through the body much like light rays to make a photograph, one slice of which we illustrate in the figure.

In the figure, the tumor is obscured by the large dark mass in front of it (a bone, perhaps). To find the tumor, several pictures might be necessary from different directions, but the images would still be difficult to interpret, not to mention that excessive exposure to X rays can injure the patient.

In a CAT scan, however, the scanning X ray is a single thin beam that is rotated to pass through a section of the patient in many different directions, as shown in Figure 2.14. For each direction, the computer stores the intensity of the beam after the beam has passed through the patient, and a program uses that information to reconstruct the internal structure of the patient. The process of reconstructing the cross-section from the data re-

FIGURE 2.13   Constructing a Conventional X-Ray Image

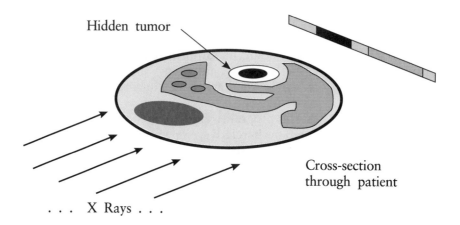

quires prodigious computing resources, as you might well imagine; it would be quite impossible to generate the resulting image without the aid of a computer. The result of a CAT scan is a much clearer image than could be achieved by conventional means, an image that also requires less exposure to the potentially damaging X rays.

FIGURE 2.14   A CAT Scan

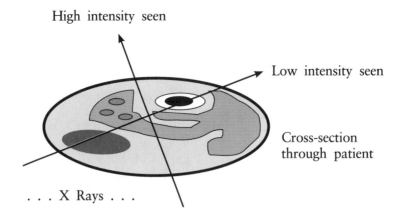

LAB EXERCISE 4

The final two sets of lab exercises for this module are based on simplified HyperCard versions of highly specialized applications. The first, named "Fitted Genes," is a stack for evaluating sequences of DNA genes, as described by strings of characters. Geneticists often are called upon to search gene sequences for particular patterns and to compare distinct sequences with one another, looking for common patterns. Such analyses may be required for code sequences that are many thousands of characters in length, a horribly tedious and error-prone task for even the most dedicated scientist. Conversely, this is a task for which the computer is ideally suited, as evidenced by the ease with which the Fitted Genes stack accomplishes its analyses.

On Fitted Gene's single card (see Figure 2.15) are two fields for holding gene sequences. Each sequence has three descriptive parts: In the left-

FIGURE 2.15   The Fitted Genes Stack

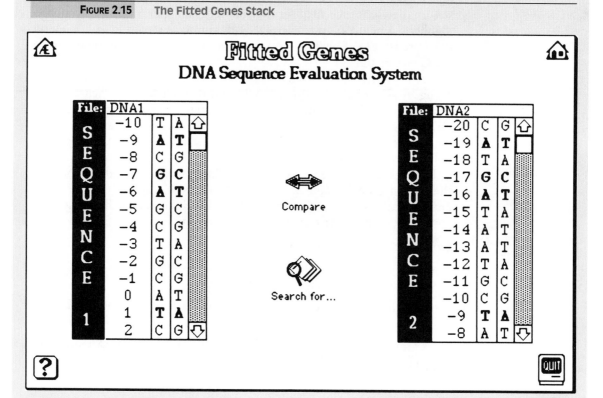

most part of the field are sequence numbers used to identify portions of the sequences. The rightmost section of each sequence field holds the string of characters describing the sequence itself. In the center section of each sequence field, Fitted Genes calculates and presents the "antisense" (or gene complement) of the sequence entered.

Sequences can be entered manually from the keyboard (you tell the stack where to begin numbering the sequence and then type the sequence in; it produces the antisense). For the purposes of this lab exercise, it is far easier to have Fitted Genes read in DNA data from files we have prepared for you. You may have noticed that this stack comes with its own menu, named "Genes," containing the basic Mac file operations of New, Open..., Save, and Save as.... It should not surprise you that the Open... command will let you read a DNA file into a sequence field.

Before invoking any of Fitted Genes commands we must indicate which of its two sequence fields we intend to make use of. For example, to open and read in a DNA file, we must first select one of the sequence fields to hold the incoming data. We do this by (you guessed it) simply clicking on the sequence field. Clicking on the words "SEQUENCE 1" or "SEQUENCE 2" as they appear vertically on the card highlights and selects that sequence field so that subsequent operations apply to the highlighted field. So, to read in DNA data into sequence field 1, click on the words "SEQUENCE 1" and then choose the Open... command from the Genes menu.

Similarly, you can search a sequence field for a particular character string by selecting the sequence field and then clicking the Search for... button. You will be prompted for a character string, and when you click OK, Fitted Genes will search the current field for the string you entered. All occurrences in the DNA data of your string will be highlighted, as will the corresponding antisenses.

In order to compare two sequences, data must be entered into both of the sequence fields. You can then click on the Compare button (which automatically selects both sequence fields) and the stack will highlight all common character strings in each of the two fields.

4.1 Open stack Fitted Genes now.

4.2 Select sequence field 1, and choose Open... from the Genes menu.

4.3 Open file "DNA1" from folder DNA Sequences.

4.4 Click the Search for... button to search DNA1 for the string ATG.

4.5 Open file "DNA2" into sequence field 2.

4.6 Click Compare to look for common patterns in the two DNA sequences.

4.7 Quit HyperCard.

APPLICATIONS IN EDUCATION

Applications have been developed to meet the needs of educators as well. Programs to assist in course scheduling, generating and grading exams, and maintaining computerized grade books are available for many computers. "Authoring" systems, programs that help instructors to develop interactive lessons for use by students on the computer (your lab modules, for example), are becoming commonplace. Intelligent tutoring systems designed to diagnose and respond to student errors as a teacher would can help students learn the alphabet, U.S. geography, the principles of running a small business, and even HyperTalk, the programming language that is part of the HyperCard system.

A typical authoring system is DISCUSS, used to help an instructor develop computerized lessons. Not too long ago, an instructor needed to know his or her own discipline as well as be an expert programmer to produce a package of computer-assisted instruction. As a result, most CAI (as computer-assisted instruction is known) was simplistic, boring to use, and time consuming to construct. Recent applications, such as DISCUSS, however, embody a high-level approach in which the authoring program does the work of producing the end product seen by the student, freeing the instructor from the need to know how to write a program.

In DISCUSS, the student sees a screen like the one in Figure 2.16, with two independently scrollable panels, the top one for the question text and the bottom one for the student's response. The student user reads the question, types a response, and then clicks on a button in the lower bar to move to the next question or to review an earlier question.

There are several different forms for student screens—multiple choice, a look at other students' responses to questions, and so on—providing a flexible environment for the student sessions. The best part of the DISCUSS system, though, is that—like other courseware packages—the mechanics of building a lesson are made relatively easy for the author. The *design* of the lesson—the difficult and important part—now becomes the primary issue rather than the programming.

The author creates a lesson by manipulating schematic representations of the screens the student will see, adding text in a separate panel, as shown in Figure 2.17. The authoring program then uses this schematic representation, along with the text, and constructs the lessons for the student.

You don't have to look any further than HyperCard to find a state-of-the-art computer application. It is not a specialized program like many of the applications noted earlier. Rather, it is more of a general-purpose program that combines the powers of a word processor, a graphics program, a database system, and a programming language. Because of its generality and utility, it is spawning a new generation of computer applications—"stackware"—that accomplish what old applications did yet in a better, easier-to-use way, and that tackle heretofore unautomated information management tasks. Because it is so powerful and easy to use, HyperCard gives applications users, for the first time, a tool for creating and customizing their own applications. HyperCard does, though, share one essential characteristic with other significant computer applications: It has the capacity to change how we think about and accomplish certain tasks. This text is based on the premise that HyperCard can change for the better how students learn about computer science.

REVIEW QUESTIONS

1. Describe two uses that an automobile manufacturer might have for a database program.
2. Consider a database program, a program such as Mathematica, a CAT scanner, and a program such as DISCUSS. For each of these, would it be better described as a faster and more efficient way of performing a traditional task, or as a way to perform a task that was not possible prior to the development of computers?
3. In what ways is an application such as Mathematica significantly different from a high-powered calculator?
4. DISCUSS and similar programs may be regarded as "intelligent assistants." List some other programs that may also be so regarded.

FIGURE 2.16   What the Student Sees in DISCUSS

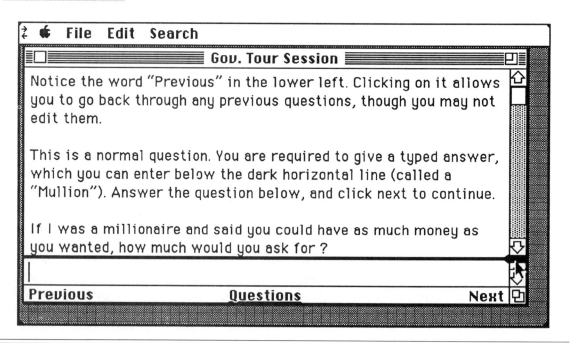

FIGURE 2.17   What the Author Sees in DISCUSS

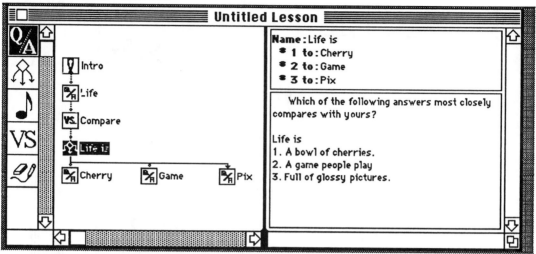

LAB EXERCISE 5

We conclude this lab module with a HyperCard implementation of one of the most basic and time-honored educational tools—the arithmetic flash card. Once opened, the Flasher! stack (see Figure 2.18) allows you to choose the level of difficulty for the problems to be presented (1 being the easiest, and 3 the most difficult). Once a level is chosen and the Level OK button is clicked, you will be presented with a series of problems (as many as you want, click the Quit button to stop). For each problem, the answer you enter is evaluated and the bunny will correct you, if necessary.

5.1   Open the Flasher! stack now.

5.2   Select Level 1, and click the Level OK button.

5.3   Answer a few questions.

5.4   Do the same for levels 2 and 3.

FIGURE 2.18   The Flasher! Stack

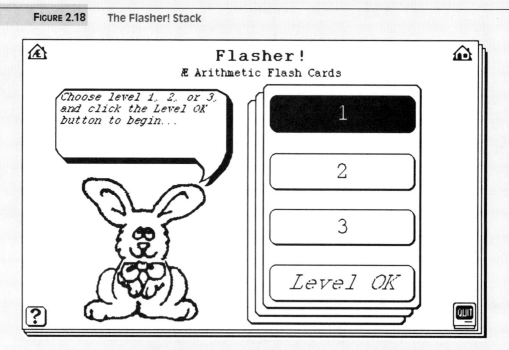

5.5   On a separate sheet of paper, write a paragraph describing what you see as the advantages of computer-controlled flash cards (à la Flasher!) over the old-fashioned, unautomated kind.

5.6   Write a paragraph describing any disadvantages you can see with automated versions of flash cards.

2.4   IMPLICATIONS

Will the calculator destroy the ability of the next generation's children to do even the most elementary arithmetic? What will the word processor do to the skill of handwriting? These are just two of the more obvious questions about the impact of the computer on our way of life. We mentioned earlier that new technologies do not develop in a vacuum; neither do they exist in one. The history of technology is inextricably bound to the historical forces that shape human society. A machine may be value-neutral, but the uses to which the machine is put are most emphatically not. Being able to do something does not necessarily mean that we *should* do it— that was the point made by the Luddites as they destroyed factory machines. Of course, the Luddites failed to halt the mechanization of factory work; in many cases, the introduction of a new technology simply proves to be irresistible. We will talk about the computerization of society in more detail in Module 9. In this section, we will merely pave the way by discussing some of the obvious consequences of this tidal wave of computerization.

DIMINISHING SKILLS

We probably do not need to concern ourselves overly with the decline of arithmetic and handwriting skills. In the large scale, social forces tend to maintain the level of skills deemed necessary for the functioning of society. We may deplore the deemphasis of certain skills for nostalgic reasons, but there is little evidence that today's world has suffered from a lack of skilled drivers who can handle a team of mules or people who know how to cut a quill so that it can be used as a pen.

As long as arithmetic is a valued skill, it will continue to be part of the primary school curriculum. If, somehow, calculators become as common as pencils, we might then see an actual decline of arithmetic skills. True, someone who forgets to bring a calculator to the store may then be unable to decide whether it is better to buy the three-for-a-dollar items rather than those selling for thirty-five cents apiece, but then many people today are in the same predicament. Most people have few qualms about asking a stranger if they may borrow a pen; the same would probably hold for calculators in our hypothetical future.

A similar argument holds for other simple skills, such as handwriting. As long as there is a need for a skill, as long as there is no universal replacement for that skill, it will not be allowed to vanish. Most of us could not live off the land unassisted for an extended period of time, a complex collection of skills quite common (and vitally necessary) 10,000 years ago, and society is, arguably, none the worse for the loss.

PRODUCTIVITY

The computer and its applications are often touted as means of enhancing productivity, of accomplishing more in less time. This is unquestionably true in some cases, particularly in those tasks involving massive calculations or massive amounts of information. We have seen that mechanized information processing arrived just in time to save the census from being hopelessly delayed, and it is certainly true that many large corporations and government agencies could not operate as they do today without the aid of computers. We see the computer as an agent of social change, as it indeed is, but to view the computer solely as an agent of change is to ignore the subtler view of the computer as an agent of stabilization. In *Computer Power and Human Reason*, Joseph Weizenbaum argues compellingly the opposing view:

Yes, the computer did arrive "just in time." But in time for what? In time to save—and save very nearly intact, indeed, to entrench and stabilize—social and political structures that otherwise might have been either radically renovated or allowed to totter under the demands that were sure to be made on them. The computer, then, was allowed to conserve America's social and political institutions. It buttressed them and immunized them, at least temporarily, against enormous pressures for change. Its influence has been substantially the same in other societies that have allowed the computer to make substantial inroads upon their institutions: Japan and Germany come immediately to mind. [p. 31. See additional readings at the end of this chapter.]

Weizenbaum's point, that the computer is often just another tool for doing the same things that were done before, holds equally well in the small as in the large. The word processor, for instance, has from its inception been touted as a device that can lead to great increases in office productivity. The processes of proofreading, editing, and revising a document are certainly easier and faster with a word processor than with a typewriter. With a word processor, multiple copies of a form letter can easily be customized for its recipients, and it is increasingly common that a disk containing a document produced on a word processor is used directly by a mechanical typesetter, saving weeks or months of time in publishing books and articles. We must keep in mind, though, that it is often easier to change technology than it is to adapt the new technology smoothly into the workspace.

The production of the text you are holding is a good example of the impact—or lack thereof—of the word processor on productivity. Prior to the word processor, we would have written this text by hand (or dictated it), then given it to a secretary to type. After editing it, cutting sections out with a pair of scissors and taping them elsewhere, we might have had the secretary make a clean—but not necessarily perfect—copy, perhaps retyping some of the pages. Finally, we would have gone through the manuscript, underlining the words to be italicized, putting wavy underlines under the words to be boldface, and so on. The publisher would have been perfectly content with a few handwritten corrections, a necessary compromise in a time when changing a single letter would otherwise involve 15 minutes to retype the entire page.

The word processor allows us to send a manuscript to the publisher that could almost be copied directly and bound between covers. Running heads and page numbers are handled automatically, italicized and bold words are displayed rather than indicated, paragraphs are left and right justified, and headings and subheadings are displayed in a typeface that is different from that of the body of the text. The manuscript, we admit with justifiable pride, is lovely, almost as nice-looking as what you're holding, but at what cost? To begin, our secretary is out of the loop, free to work on other projects for the department. That's a benefit, but the downside is that we have to do the typing ourselves, and neither of us can even come close to her speed at the keyboard. By doing the typing ourselves, we can make the manuscript look pretty and not have to worry about conflicting demands on secretarial time, but the time required to produce the manuscript is at least as long as it would have been without the word processor. Finally, for good reason or not, our time costs our college much more than a secretary's, not to mention the fact that we have to arrange typing sessions so that they don't conflict with classes, office hours, faculty and committee meetings, and all the other duties of a faculty member.

The bottom line is that using a word processor to produce this text is not significantly better than the old-fashioned way, and may be less cost-effective, all things considered. Why, then, did we produce the manuscript that way? Because it looks so darned good, that's why. Designed originally to fill a need for efficient editing, the word processor evolved so many attractive features that instead of filling a need, it created one. Because it can do so many things, we use an application to the hilt and take time doing things we wouldn't have even considered doing before. We might call this the "power user's syndrome" and note that it appears with many applications.

In fairness to an emerging technology, we should close by mentioning that the overall situation is not as bleak as it might appear. If we imagine writing a book of this size a few years in the future, the picture is considerably rosier. We would still type the manuscript ourselves, if only because we have a better idea of the format we want than does our secretary, but after having produced the manuscript we could then send the disks to the publisher (or transmit the document directly over the phone lines) and receive in turn an edited copy that when we loaded it into our computers, would appear on our screens exactly as it would when typeset between covers. Major changes in format at this stage could be made by a few keystrokes, rather than resetting the entire book in type. In short, the publication time could be reduced to a small fraction of its present amount.

In presenting our personal example of the use of word processors, we have been harder on this new technology than many authors would be. We are certainly not Luddites—we would never want to go back to the typewriter and we realize that there certainly are applications in other areas that would simply be impossible without computers. We took as long on this example as we did, however, because it is important to underscore the point that *new* is not necessarily a synonym for *better,* and that a new technology often requires changes in the patterns of its use.

INFORMATION TECHNOLOGY

Mozart was said to produce his manuscripts complete on the first draft, without corrections. Robert Frost said that "Stopping by Woods on a Snowy Evening" came to him all of a piece, without any preliminary versions. Most authors don't work that way, though. Any major library has collections of manuscripts with authors' corrections liberally sprinkled throughout. Indeed, scholars of literature can often gain valuable insights into the creative process by studying these steps along the way to the finished product. Even in the highly unlikely event that scholars of the future would be interested in the collected works of Decker and Hirshfield, there will be no preliminary versions of this text for them to study. It is so easy to make corrections on the disk that the final version of this text, or any work made with a word processor, will be the only version available. Of course, as information storage technology improves, we might be able to store a complete transcript of all work on a document, from the first keystroke to the last change, but at least for the immediate future we see that the new technology has introduced a change that may not be for the better.

Libraries are the repositories of our written culture. Often the information we need to answer a particular question is available, but only to those who know exactly where to look. Automated search and retrieval programs promise to make finding information far easier than it has been in the past. It seems that here, as in the detailed study of the works of an author, we are in a difficult period of transition. A computerized database allows the user to select a topic and browse through all of the references stored in the database in much less time than it would take to track down the citations in thousands of indices and bibliographies. We mentioned earlier, for example, that there are 190 million electronic calculators in the United States. That information took a reference librarian the better part of two days to track down. How much more efficient it would have been to have a program to search for such data in the mountains of reference guides available. The problem, though, is that until such time—if ever—when the entire written output of society is available for computer search, there will be problems of omission. These problems will not become pressing until computerized searches become the primary way of doing research. Then we will be faced with the real danger of assuming, incorrectly, that information that is not on-line does not exist. To take another example, the work of anthropologists today is considerably simplified by a standard database of 186 cultures, broken down by categories such as methods of food distribution, social structure, attitudes toward conflict resolution, and so on. As useful as this database is, it would obviously be very risky for an anthropologist to use it as the only source of information about human culture. The point is that new technologies are often almost irresistibly seductive, leading us to assume that the new way of doing things is better, and, eventually, to believe that the new way is the only way.

HyperCard stacks are nothing if not seductive. They are, in most cases, both easier to use and more pleasing to view and work with than were earlier computer applications that accomplished similar tasks. Note, though, the subtle shift in perspective that many of the currently available stacks imply. Stacks that maintain daily—even hourly—calendars, look up and

> Even if a library could store our word processing disks for archival purposes, computer technology changes so fast that the library would likely be placed in the uncomfortable position of having to store a collection of ancient computers, as well.

dial phone numbers, or retrieve recipes are all designed to provide more efficient access to personal, everyday information. It is one thing to turn on a calculator to use in balancing your checkbook, or to sit down at a word processor to prepare a term paper. It is quite another to assume that your Macintosh is always on, constantly at the ready to provide you with (nearly) any information you need, as these stacks imply. Such computer applications—those that assume the computer is always on—have the potential for impacting our daily lives in ways we can barely imagine. They might even render "personal" computers truly personal.

REVIEW QUESTIONS

1. Should we worry about a decline in arithmetic skills due to increasing use of computers and calculators? Explain.

2. Give an example of an area where introduction of computers has led to significant increases in productivity, and one where significant gains in productivity have yet to be felt.

3. Give two reasons for concern about the near-term effects of computerized information storage. Explain whether you expect these concerns to be important in the distant future.

2.5   EXERCISES

1. What contributes to making a computer application "successful"? That is, what are the common ingredients in calculators, word processors, and spreadsheet programs?

2. In your opinion, are computers really labor-saving or time-saving devices? If you think they are, how do you explain the fact that we still seem to be working as hard as ever? If you think they aren't, then why are computer applications so popular?

3. Spreadsheet programs, word processors, the Mathematica program, and HyperCard can all be viewed as active extensions of former static entities, where the computerization of a task allows a document to act on its data. Think of a currently static entity and speculate on the effects of making it active through computerization.

4. Which computer application do you use most often, and for what task? How has the application affected how you would otherwise have accomplished the task?

5. If you were designing a spreadsheet program, what operations would you like cells to be able to perform? If you can, find a spreadsheet program such as Microsoft's Excel and see if your list of operations agrees with its list.

6. In the course of your normal activities, how might you make use of a spreadsheet's "what if" capabilities?

7. If you have used a word processor, are there any features that it does not have that you would like included?

8. Two of the classic three Rs of education—wRiting and aRithmetic—have been addressed quite successfully by computer applications. What about the third R, Reading? Can computers help us to read?

9. Choose a business, a profession, or an industry that you are interested in or know something about. Find three specialized applications for it.

10. List some of the commands that should be in the query language of a database program.

11. How does Mathematica factor algebraic expressions? Describe at least two specific problems that must be solved for a program to be able to factor (for example, reading the input and keeping track of what the variables are).

12. To give you an idea of how much computational effort a CAT scan requires, consider a simple problem of determining the composition of a two by two grid, in which each cell can be filled or empty. The 16 possibilities are:

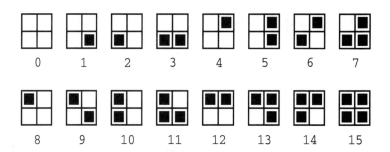

Your scanner can send a beam through the grid in one of six ways (along the bottom row, the top row, the left column, the right column, or either of the two diagonals) and record the number of filled cells. Scanning just the bottom row and the top row is not sufficient to distinguish all possible patterns, since those two scans cannot tell the difference between patterns 1 and 2, or among patterns 5, 6, 9, and 10.

a. Show that no two scans can distinguish all possible patterns. *Hint:* Compare the number of possible values for the two scans with the number of possible patterns.

b. Find a collection of four scans that will suffice.

c. Prove or disprove: There is a collection of three scans that will distinguish all patterns.

13. Is the introduction of a new technology really irresistible? Why are certain societies relatively immune to technological advances whereas others (such as ours) tend to embrace them all?

14. It has been said that the value of any tool lies in its ability to change how we think about certain tasks. Which computer application has had the most dramatic impact on your way of thinking? Why?

2.6   ADDITIONAL READINGS

Bell, D. *Using Applications Software.* New York: McGraw-Hill, 1986.

Bylinsky, G. "Here Comes the Second Computer Revolution." In *The Microelectronics Revolution,* edited by Tom Forester. Cambridge, Mass.: MIT Press, 1982.

"Computer Software." Theme issue, *Scientific American* 251, no. 3 (Sept. 1984).

Marx, L. *Machine in the Garden.* New York: Oxford University Press, 1964.

Miller, R. K., and Walker, T. *Artificial Intelligence Applications in Manufacturing.* Madison, Ga.: SEAI Technical Publishers, 1988.

O'Shea, T., Self, J., and Thomas, G., eds. *Intelligent Knowledge-Based Systems: An Introduction.* London: Harper and Row, 1987.

Price, D. J. de S. "An Ancient Greek Computer." *Scientific American* 201, no. 6 (June 1959): 60–67.

Rogers, E. M., and Larsen, J. *Silicon Valley Fever.* New York: Basic Books, 1984.

Sanders, D. H. *Computers in Society.* New York: McGraw-Hill, 1977.

Weizenbaum, J. *Computer Power and Human Reason.* San Francisco: W. H. Freeman, 1976

DESIGNING FOR USE

3.1 INTRODUCTION

So far, you have seen a brief technological history of computers and some state-of-the-art applications, but you probably have almost no idea how to construct such applications. Your HyperCard experience up to now has been limited to typing text and using the mouse to navigate through stacks. We have designed these modules, both the text and the lab exercises, so that your HyperCard experience and your knowledge of computer science will increase together—in parallel, if you will. In a sense, we are using HyperCard itself as a metaphor for computer science.

Up to this point, the computer, its programs, and HyperCard have been "black boxes"—perhaps fascinating, probably complicated, and certainly incomprehensible in their details. In this module, we will explore the design process, showing you how complicated systems are constructed. By the end of this module, the black box will have become a gray box, and you will be ready for the next module, on programming, in which we make the box transparent, exposing all its inner workings.

TEXT OBJECTIVES

In this module, we will

- Examine the evolution of the user interface
- Discuss the desirable features of a user interface
- Explore the composition of a HyperCard stack
- Demonstrate how to use the authoring tools of HyperCard to create stacks of our own

THE USER INTERFACE

This module will introduce you to the principles of system design. We will concentrate on an important part of the design of any system, the *user interface*. The user interface is the aspect of a program or machine that is visible to the user—the look and feel of the beast, if you will. We will explore some of the desirable features of a user interface and speculate on the ways in which people might interact with computers in the future.

Along the way, we will use the *authoring* and *painting* levels of Hyper-Card to demonstrate the principles of system design, showing how you can build stacks by combining and modifying existing stacks, cards, buttons, and fields. By the end of this module, you will be ready to apply what you've learned when you go to the lab and modify an existing stack to suit your own purposes.

Although we will pay particular attention to the look of a system, bear in mind that the principles we discuss apply to other aspects of a computer system as well. Just remember that at the system level, we are interested mainly in the smooth interaction of the major pieces, not the details of how they work.

METAPHOR: THE HIPPOGRYPH

We have mentioned before—and will do so again—the importance of *levels of abstraction* when viewing a subject as complex as computer science. The notion of concentrating on the "big picture," to avoid being bogged down by details, is important in all disciplines, but especially so in computer science. At the system design level, we think of combining parts, each of which already has a complicated functionality. At this level, we don't concern ourselves with the details of the parts. We just put them together into a functioning whole, leaving the details until later.

Our guiding metaphor in this module is the hippogryph—a mythical beast having the hind parts of a horse and the fore parts of a gryphon, which is itself an admixture of a lion and an eagle. In much the same way as a mythical animal can be constructed by combining the parts of known animals, a computer system—either hardware (which we will discuss in Module 6) or software (which we discuss here and in Module 4)—can be viewed as a combination of pieces, each with its own complex structure. This way of thinking is not new. In Greek mythology, Prometheus was given the task of creating the human race, while his brother Epimetheus was to make the animals. Unfortunately, Epimetheus used up all the good parts, leaving Prometheus to create furless, clawless, wingless, fangless, trunkless humans.* A tale with a related theme, of course, is that of Victor Frankenstein, who built his monster from parts of human bodies. Although Mary Shelley's story is necessarily vague on technical details, it seems that Herr Frankenstein didn't create the monster's eyes, brain, and limbs. Rather, like a system designer of today, he took available "components" and fashioned his creation from them.

---

* Prometheus' attempts to redress this imbalance make a marvelous—albeit grim—story, which, unfortunately, we cannot explore here.

Æ STACKS: A WORKBOOK, AN EXAMPLE, AND SOME EXTRA TOOLS

In the Module 2 lab exercises we used a variety of simple stacks to demonstrate some salient features of standard computer applications. In your role as "user" you could control how each application was used, but you had little control over much else. Through its Authoring tools, HyperCard allows you to build stacks and, without being a programmer, control to a great degree both what they look like and their functionality.

The first Æ stack of the three that we will refer to in this lab, named "Æ Workbook" (see Figure 3.1), has two related functions. First, it provides you with a set of blank cards on which you can experiment with the Authoring tools we describe in the text portion of this module. The Æ Workbook also contains three help-like segments, one each for fields, buttons, and painting, which can be browsed as needed to review how to accomplish common authoring tasks. We will direct you through a series of exercises to make sure that you cover the basics, and you will be encouraged to practice on your own.

FIGURE 3.1   The Æ Workbook Stack

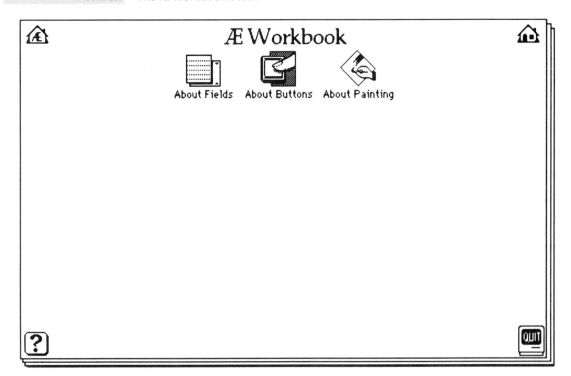

 FIGURE 3.2 Bill's Diner Stack

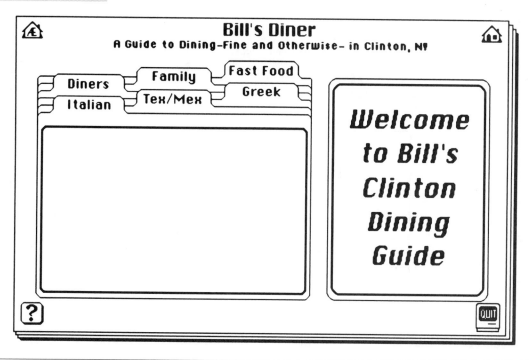

Later, some of your authoring efforts will be directed toward another Æ stack, named "Bill's Diner" (Figure 3.2). We will describe in full detail how Bill's Diner was built in HyperCard, and you will customize it to our specifications. Finally, we provide you with a stack, named "Very Resourceful" (see Figure 3.3), that illustrates how Macintosh "resources"—for example, sounds, icons, and cursors—can be incorporated into your stacks to enhance the user interface.

LAB OBJECTIVES

In the disk part of this module, you will

- Learn to use HyperCard's Tools and Objects menus
- Learn to use the Button, Field, and Painting tools
- Gain experience editing an existing stack
- Become a competent HyperCard Author
- See how to use Macintosh "resources" to enhance HyperCard stacks

FIGURE 3.3   The Very Resourceful Stack

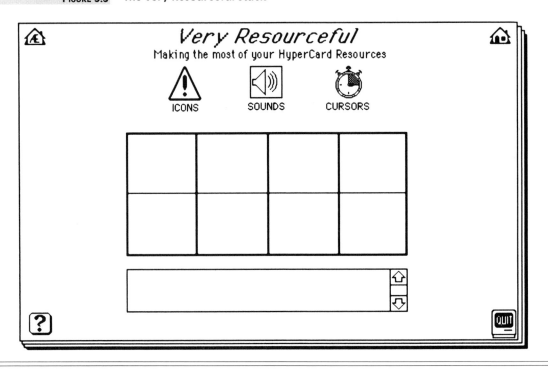

3.2 ## 3.2   PEOPLE AND MACHINES

We will begin by talking about the good old days. You will see that the old days weren't so long ago and weren't always good. In the very early days of computers, the only users were the specialists—the programmers who had written the programs and who were intimately acquainted with their quirks and foibles. The very first user interface was wires and plugs: To change ENIAC's program, the operator literally had to rebuild the computer, by reconnecting the components.

EVOLUTION OF THE USER INTERFACE

It didn't take long for the programmers/designers/engineers of computers (often the same person held all three titles) to realize that rebuilding the computer for each new task took entirely too much time. Even the earliest efforts of Atanasoff, Zuse, and Mauchley and Eckert soon came equipped with a device (switches or a keyboard) to control the connection between the functional units of the computer. How these devices controlled the action of these computers is a subject we will cover later; for now it is enough to assert that they did indeed allow the operator to instruct the machine, so that the computer carried out the instructions with a minimum of supervision. One turned on the machine, set the right switches or pushed the right key, and "let 'er rip." Although the Analytical Engine was never completed, Babbage had much the same idea a century before, when he envisioned storing the sequence of instructions on Jacquard-like cards, to be executed one after another. Even the first hobby computers of the 1970s, some 30 or more years after the pioneer computers and almost a century after Babbage, had to be programmed by setting switches on the front panel.

When the user of a computer was the designer, or a programmer, the user interface wasn't too important. Suppose, for instance, you had an intimate knowledge of the workings of a computer, and the only way of communicating with the computer was at the very lowest machine level. First, you might never consider that there could be a more user-efficient way to get the machine to do what you wanted. In fact, while many of the earliest programs were computationally complex, the demands they placed on the user were very simple, requiring little more than a mass of numeric input, along with a command to run the program on that input. Second, you might prefer to program at the machine level. After all, whether one believes or disbelieves that the accepted way of doing things is the best way, there is still a heady feeling of superiority that comes from being privy to great mysteries—the secrets of Egyptian hieroglyphics were the sole province of a handful of scribes for nearly 2000 years for what we suspect was partly this reason.

This increasing distance between the user and the hardware is a continuing theme in the history of computers.

The computer scribes quickly lost their exclusive claims to the machine, largely for economic reasons. As computers made their way into commercial applications, it became clear that their hunger for data could not be appeased by having the operators set switches. To speed input, data was stored on paper tape or punched cards, prepared on a machine much like a typewriter and read mechanically. The user was in effect being separated from the machine. A typical session consisted of entering a program and its input on cards, carrying the completed deck of cards to the operator, who would place the cards in a mechanical card reader, wait for the computer to run the program, and, five minutes to several hours later, return the cards and the printed output to the user.

This *batch mode* of operation was slow at best. The computer operator controlled scheduling of jobs, running job 1 until completion, then running job 2, then job 3, and so on. In effect, the user interface was the counter at the operator's window, with an in basket for the user to place his or her cards and an out basket where the user would find the results. Not only was this process slow, it was anything but user-friendly. In addition to the program and the data, the user had to include in the deck certain cards that told the computer how to handle the job, so that the full deck of cards for a job might look like the following (taken from G. Struble, *Assembler Language Programming: The IBM System/360*, Reading, Mass.: Addison-Wesley, 1969):

```
//QUESTNAR        JOB  204121,MARCO.POLO,MSGLEVEL=1
//               EXEC  ASMFCLG
//ASM.SYSIN       DD  *
```

(Some of your program cards would go here.)

```
/*
//LKED.SYSLIB     DD  DSNAME=USERLIB,DISP=OLD
//LKED.SYSIN      DD  *
```

(Some more of your program cards would go here.)

```
/*
//GO.SYSPRINT     DD  SYSOUT=A,DCB=(BLKSIZE=133)
//GO.INDATA       DD  DISP=OLD,UNIT=TAPE9,DSNAME
                      QUEST215,VOLUME=SER=102139
//GO.SYSIN        DD  *
```

(Your data cards would go here.)

```
/*
```

With the advent of *time-sharing* in the late 1960s, control was returned to the user, or at least the illusion of control. In such an arrangement, a computer would be connected to several terminals, each of which looked like an electric typewriter with a roll of paper attached (called a *TTY*, in the jargon, for "teletype"). Unlike batch mode, the computer would divide its attention among the terminals, running each job for a fraction of a second in turn. Since the computer could perform its operations vastly faster than either the user could type or the TTY could print, each user could act as if he or she had complete control of the computer.

Time-sharing was a considerable improvement in the user interface. Not only could the user see what he or she had typed without having to leaf through a deck of punched cards, but the interaction with the machine was in "real time," so that the interval between making an error and being informed of the error could be measured in seconds, rather than hours. One could run a program, find an error, edit the program to fix the error, and try again, all in the space of a few minutes. Of course, editing a program—or any text, for that matter—was still somewhat cumbersome. Text editors of the time were generally *line oriented*, meaning that the basic unit of text was a single line. Lines were identified by number, and a typical session might consist of typing the following editing commands:

p 125:450	*print lines 125 through 450*
i 220	*insert a new line before line 220*
d 245:350	*delete lines 245 through 350*

`stotal$sum$340:#`   *substitute "sum" for every instance of "total" in all*
lines from 340 to the end

The *video display terminal* (VDT for short, or "glass TTY" to insiders) replaced the roll of paper with a video screen. This user interface should be familiar to you if you have ever looked behind the scenes at an airline ticket counter or the Department of Motor Vehicles. With such an arrangement, the user can move to any location on the screen by pressing the right combination of keys (the up arrow might move the *cursor*—such as the blinking text insertion bar on the Mac—up one line, for instance) and modify the text at that location by typing. For example, in a simple system to handle airline reservations, the screen might contain several lines of text. To make a reservation, the clerk would first type a code for the departure airport, then press the tab key, type the code for the destination airport, tab once more to move to the flight number field, and enter the flight number. At that time, the screen would display the available seats on that flight, and the clerk could enter the chosen seat number. The rest of the process, such as payment method and so on, would be handled similarly.

While this process is a smoother version of what would happen with a typewriter terminal, it is still text oriented and essentially line based. Using the Macintosh or any similar modern computer as an example, we can imagine what the reservation system would look like on a computer that supports graphics and has a mouse attached. A simple improvement, for instance, would be to display a picture of the aircraft for the selected flight with available seats highlighted, perhaps in a different color. Instead of requiring the reservation clerk to memorize the seating arrangement of each plane the airline used, the picture would provide instant verification that there was a forward aisle seat available on the starboard side of the aircraft. Then, a move of the mouse and a click on that seat would instantly reserve seat 8C for the customer. The reservation process would likely be no faster, but it would probably make the system easier for the clerk to use, and the ease of use is what we have been aiming for throughout the evolution of the user interface.

We should make the point here that there is a considerable chronological overlap among the varieties of user interface we have described. All the types we have mentioned, with the possible exception of rewiring, are in use today and will almost certainly continue into the future. After all, the horse wasn't replaced overnight by the automobile, and for a variety of reasons it will never be completely eliminated.

GUIDELINES FOR SYSTEM DESIGN

We have presented the user interface as a model of system design. It might seem that the user interface was driven by changes in technology, and while this is partly true, it ignores a parallel theme in the evolution of computer systems. As computers became more pervasive, they were used increasingly by operators with little or no computer experience. It seems reasonable that one way to increase sales of a piece of hardware or software is to make it simpler and more pleasant to use, assuming that its functionality is roughly the same as that of competing products. We have already mentioned the parallel between computer and automotive technologies, and we can see another example here. The exotic sports cars of the 1950s and early 1960s (which would include almost all sports cars of the time) were exciting and fun to drive, especially compared to the conventional products then available. However, since they were quirky, not particularly reliable, and notoriously difficult to maintain (facts to which both your authors can attest, based on bitter experience), their sales were limited to a few aficionados.

What, then, do we mean by "easy to use," in the case of hardware and software? What are some of the desirable features that a system designer should use as guidelines? These questions are examples of the engineering aspect of computer science, where there isn't a single "right" answer, but rather there are "better" answers. Drawing on years of experience observing and questioning users, we have identified three general guidelines for user-friendly systems.

> 1. A system should be *transparent,* in that the technology should not intrude excessively between the user and the task. In other words, the operator should be able to use a program or a computer, at least at the novice level, without having to master the entire user's manual.

This is an area in which computer technology lags behind automotive technology. We have to learn how to drive a car first, but having mastered that task, we can sit behind the wheel of an unfamiliar vehicle and drive to Buffalo without ever looking at the manual. At the very least, a transparent system should be easy to use—the commands should be as simple and logical as possible. For example, saving a document should be the result of choosing Save from the File menu, rather than having to type something like `V$=SYS(CHR$(6%) + CHR$(F0%) + 0$)`.

In this respect, computer technology is still at the stage where the machine drives the user's behavior, rather than the user's expectations driving the design of the machine. The situation is somewhat better for software, since knowing how to use one word processor for an IBM PC, for instance, will prepare you fairly well to use another for the same machine. Apple Computer, in particular, has made diligent efforts to specify user interface guidelines for Macintosh software developers (as we will see later), so that, for example, the keystroke combination "⌘-X" will cut the current selection, whether one is using a word processor, a painting program, or HyperCard.

2. In addition, a system should be *forgiving,* so that there is usually a way to avoid or recover from potentially disastrous actions. Avoidance might take the form of *alerts* for some actions, like this somewhat frivolous example:

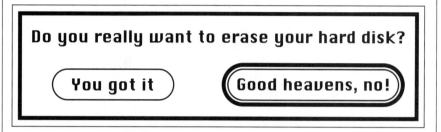

Do you really want to erase your hard disk?

You got it   **Good heavens, no!**

On a more mundane level, a forgiving program will not crash if the user enters numbers that would entail division by zero, but rather will either alert the user to the fact or handle the error without intervention, perhaps by printing "Division by zero!" where the answer might have gone.

Recovery means the ability to return to a previous state after taking one or more actions. Some programs, for instance, have a File menu item such as Revert to Saved, which changes the current document back to the state it was in the last time it was saved. An Apple-recommended part of each program's Edit menu is the Undo command, which undoes the effects of the most recent editing action.

3. A system should be *visually oriented,* since most people are. It's for good reason that we say "a picture is worth a thousand words." The Macintosh—along with its relatives from Xerox, Sun, Next, and for that matter, any computer that runs Microsoft Windows—has a highly visual interface, with icons representing files, disks, and the trash, and visual controls such as scroll bars and buttons. In technical terms, visual data has a higher *bandwidth* than textual, meaning that you can pack more information in a similar space.

This visual versus textual orientation is a source of some controversy today, primarily because there is a large installed base of computers and programs that still use what is essentially a TTY mode of operation. It is natural for people to resist the new, especially if they have become accustomed to the old ways, and, to be honest, it is also much easier to design a text-based program than it is to design one that must deal with mice, menus, windows, and icons. In spite of this, we are convinced that this difference of opinion will largely vanish in the near future.

DATA AND PROGRAMS

Until fairly recently, most computer applications presented a clear conceptual boundary between data and programs. In the conventional way of thinking, data was purely raw material: inert stuff that was acted upon by programs. A text file, in this view, was like a lump of clay with a word-processing program serving as a potter's wheel. As we saw in Module 2, this paradigm was broken by the invention of the spreadsheet. A document produced by a spreadsheet program contained raw data, of course, but could also contain within itself formulas for manipulating the data. The spreadsheet program was still controlling the action of any spreadsheet, but in the background, as it were. To the user, it appeared as if the spreadsheet was acting on itself, so that entering or changing the value of a cell could cause recalculation of the average of all the cells in that row, for example, with no further intervention on the part of the user.

The spreadsheet is a *user-configurable* object, whose functionality can be designed to suit its purpose. When we use a spreadsheet to design a gradebook for one of our classes, we can construct a column of cells, each one of which will compute and display the weighted average of the exam scores in its row. Having built the spreadsheet, we need only to enter the scores as they arrive, and the spreadsheet itself calculates the averages for us. Not only does this save us the trouble of calculating the averages anew for each entry, but, even better, if we need a similar average for another class, we can copy the formulas from the existing spreadsheet to a new one or even duplicate the entire spreadsheet for use in the other course. The spreadsheet contains not only data, but mini-programs to manipulate the data, and the mini-programs can be cut, copied, pasted, and edited just as the data can be. We might call such a document *smart data;* in its most advanced form, computer scientists call the marriage of data and methods to manipulate the data *object-oriented programming.*

HyperCard is a powerful extension of the idea of combining data and data manipulators in single units. A HyperCard stack is a document that can be designed to be a spreadsheet, a calculator, a database along with a database management system, or any of a multitude of other forms, all wrapped up in a sophisticated graphics package. In the following sections, we will investigate the structures and objects used in HyperCard to organize and manipulate data, and will show you how to customize a Hyper-Card stack to suit your own purposes.

REVIEW QUESTIONS

1. Trace the evolution of the user interface.
2. What are three guidelines for good system design? Can you think of any other desirable features for an easy-to-use system?
3. Give some examples of good and not-so-good system design in the lab stacks you've seen so far.
4. What do we mean by "smart data"?

LAB EXERCISE 1

1.1 Open Bill's Diner stack now.
1.2 Read the help message on the first card, and then browse through (in any order you want) the remaining cards of the stack.
1.3 On a separate piece of paper, write a paragraph that describes and evaluates the stack's user interface.

3.3   ANATOMY OF A STACK

A stack, like a spreadsheet, has two primary aspects: what you see and what it does. This section will be devoted largely to the visual aspect; we will discuss the functional aspects in the next section and again in Module 4. Both visually and functionally, a *stack* is an object consisting of *cards* (only one of which is visible at any time and which may share a common *background*) containing *fields* where data may be entered and stored and *buttons* that may be used to control the actions of the stack. A common use for buttons, for example, is to cause the next card to be displayed.

Stacks are collections of cards. Cards can contain graphics, buttons, and fields.

Each object in a stack, including the stack itself, can have a mini-program, called a *script,* associated with it. In the example of Figure 3.4, for instance, one of the buttons may have a script that says, roughly, "When the mouse is clicked in me, put this card away and display the next card in the stack." The other button might have a script that says, "When the mouse is clicked in me, add the contents of fields 1 through 3 and display the sum in field 4." HyperCard's ability to generate the more common scripts automatically frees us from worrying too much about scripts, and allows us to concentrate instead on the design of a stack.

The objects that comprise a stack can be treated as units, as we will see, allowing you to copy, paste, or move them within a stack or across differ-

---

FIGURE 3.4   A Stack

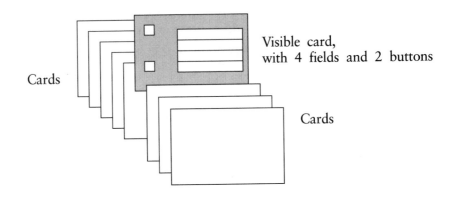

Cards

Visible card,
with 4 fields and 2 buttons

Cards

---

ent stacks. You will appreciate this feature when you design your own stacks: You can, for example, look in other stacks to find a card you want to use, copy that card, and move it—scripts, graphics, and all—into your own stack.

CARDS AND BACKGROUNDS

Think of each card as a transparent sheet of plastic. HyperCard contains a powerful graphics program that allows you to paint a picture on each card or customize the picture on a card that you have copied from another stack. You can make each card look like an open book, a file folder, an index card, or anything else you can imagine. If you want, you can paint text for titles or explanatory messages on the card, include fancy borders for fields, or put a picture of yourself on the card.

Even with the ability to copy an existing card, it is a waste of both your time and the computer's memory to paint the same picture on each card. With this in mind, HyperCard provides *backgrounds* that can be shared by as many cards as you wish. Each card has a background, but there may be many more cards than backgrounds (and never more backgrounds than cards). Generally, the basic look of a related group of cards is controlled by a single background, while differences between cards are controlled by painting on the cards themselves, as shown in Figure 3.5.

The basic concept *background* + *card* = *apparent card* carries over to the objects that appear on cards and backgrounds—namely, fields and buttons—as we will now see.

FIGURE 3.5   Cards Act Like Overlays on Backgrounds

Background   + Card   = Apparent card

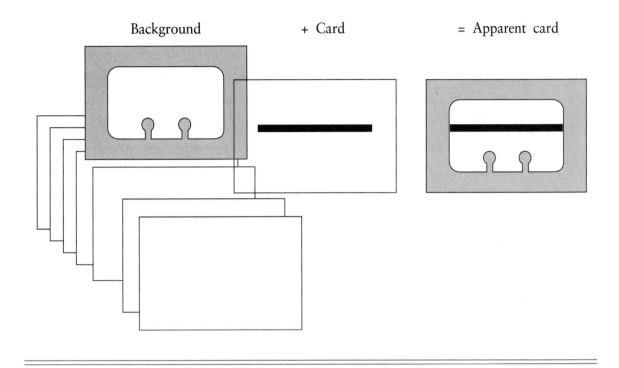

FIELDS

Fields are the basic "containers" for data in HyperCard. Unlike many other programming environments, HyperCard makes its data directly accessible to the user. You can enter or modify data in a field just by typing, or you can define a HyperCard stack so that it modifies the contents of a field in response to some other action.

Fields are customarily associated with backgrounds, so a single field on a background may serve as a template for storing data on many cards—all the cards having that background. While the field "resides" in the background, the information in the field resides on the cards. In other words, if you enter data in a field by typing, that data is associated with the card that was visible when you began typing. This may seem confusing at first, until you think of a background as a master plan for all its cards, containing pictures and places to enter information. A background field can be explained by thinking, "Here is where data can go on each card," as shown in Figure 3.6.

FIGURE 3.6   Information in Background Fields Resides on Cards

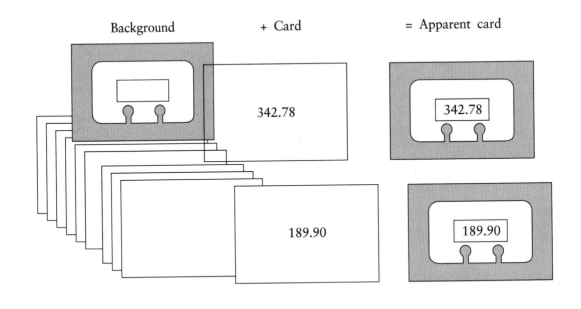

You need not place fields only on backgrounds, however. If you need a field on only one card, it is quite simple to attach a field to that card, as we will see later. In fact, since the visible, active part of a card is made by overlaying the card on its background, you can "hide" a background field by covering it with a card field. In this case, the card field will effectively obscure the background field, since objects in front have precedence over those to the rear. You will have a chance to explore this idea in the lab exercises of this module.

BUTTONS

If we think of fields as essentially passive (although we will see later that they too may have associated scripts), then buttons are the action objects of a HyperCard stack. With buttons, we can link one card to another, causing the current card to be replaced by another in the same stack or a different stack. Anyone who has used a HyperCard stack has seen the three most common buttons: the left-pointing arrow, which sends you to the previous card; the right-pointing arrow, which goes to the next card; and the picture of a house, used to close the stack and return to Hyper-

Card's Home stack. Unlike fields, the standard residence for buttons is on a card. Like fields, buttons can be placed anywhere, including on backgrounds. Since the Previous card and Next card buttons almost invariably appear on each card in a stack, these are generally placed on backgrounds.

REVIEW QUESTIONS

1. In the hierarchy defined by "is made of or contains," arrange the following objects: backgrounds, buttons, cards, fields, stacks.

2. What is a background? What do we mean by "background + card = apparent card"?

3. Both fields and buttons can be associated with either cards or backgrounds. Where do fields and buttons most commonly reside?

4. What is the difference between a field and the data contained in that field?

3.4   AUTHORING

One of the outstanding virtues of HyperCard (and one of the reasons we adopted it for this text) is that it allows us to build stacks and, to a great degree, control both what they look like and how they function—all without being programmers, at least in the conventional sense of that term. *Authoring* in HyperCard is the process of building or modifying stacks by manipulating backgrounds, cards, buttons, and fields as objects.

Before you can begin your career as an author, however, you must obtain HyperCard's permission. HyperCard has five *user levels*. From lowest to highest they are:

- browsing
- typing
- painting
- authoring
- scripting

At each level you are allowed to do everything you could at a lower level, along with some new things previously denied. At the *browsing* level, all you can do is move through the stack by clicking the mouse. At the *typing* level, you can enter and edit text in fields, as well as click the mouse. A stack in which the user was restricted to the browsing and typing levels would be useful for tutorials, for example, since you wouldn't want the user to disturb the organization or look of the stack. This, in fact, applies to all of the Æ stacks you have seen so far. At the *painting* level, the user has access to HyperCard's graphic tools to modify the look, but not the function, of a stack. At the *authoring* level, the user has all the features available in the three lower levels, and can add, delete, or modify objects—adding new cards and moving or deleting fields, for example. The *scripting* level allows the user to modify all parts of a stack, including the programs that are associated with every object in the stack. In this module, we will restrict ourselves to discussing operations available at the authoring level.

> To get to the Home stack, select Home from the Go menu, or type ⌘-H.

You have already seen the User Preferences card in HyperCard's Home stack, which looks like Figure 3.7. Clicking the Authoring button will set your user level appropriately for this module.

FIGURE 3.7   Setting the User Level

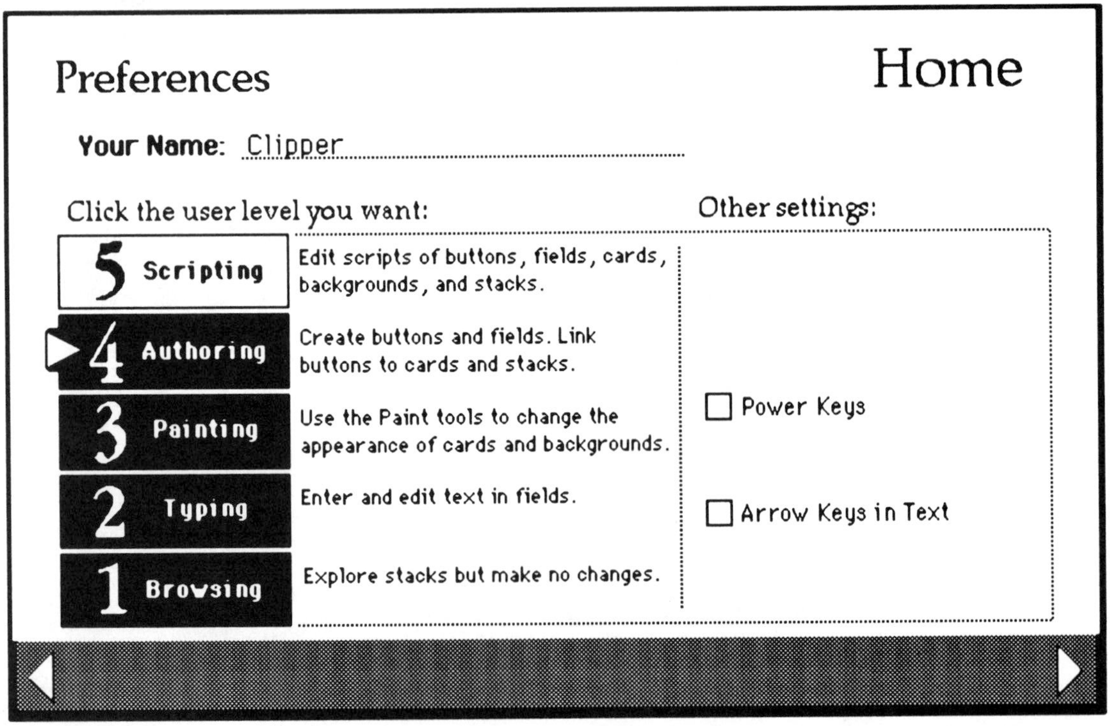

Home

Preferences

Your Name: Clipper

Click the user level you want:

5 Scripting	Edit scripts of buttons, fields, cards, backgrounds, and stacks.	
4 Authoring	Create buttons and fields. Link buttons to cards and stacks.	
3 Painting	Use the Paint tools to change the appearance of cards and backgrounds.	☐ Power Keys
2 Typing	Enter and edit text in fields.	☐ Arrow Keys in Text
1 Browsing	Explore stacks but make no changes.	

Other settings:

MENUS

Much of the power you have just inherited resides in the menus at the top of the screen. At the browsing and typing levels, you had access to the Apple, File, Edit, and Go menus; the painting level gives you access to a new Tools menu, and the authoring level provides an Objects menu as well. In addition, some of the existing menus have more commands. The Edit menu, for instance, now includes editing operations on the stack objects, as you can see by comparing the browsing-level and the authoring-level Edit menus in Figure 3.8.

While we're on the subject of menus, it's worth mentioning that the Tools menu has a couple of features that are not shared by most of the other menus. First, it looks different. The Tools menu, as shown in Figure 3.9, controls all of the operations available to you in HyperCard and takes the form of a *palette* rather than being text oriented. By selecting the tools menu and dragging the mouse to one of the icons in the menu, you change both the action of the mouse and, in some cases, the operations that will appear in the other menus. The second difference between

---

FIGURE 3.8   **The Edit Menu at Browsing Level (left) and at Authoring Level (right)**

Edit	
Undo	⌘Z
Cut Text	⌘X
Copy Text	⌘C
Paste	⌘U
Clear Text	
New Card	⌘N
Delete Card	

Edit	
Undo	⌘Z
Cut Text	⌘X
Copy Text	⌘C
Paste	⌘U
Clear Text	
New Card	⌘N
Delete Card	
Cut Card	
Copy Card	
Text Style...	⌘T
Background	⌘B
Icon...	⌘I

FIGURE 3.9   **The Tools Menu**

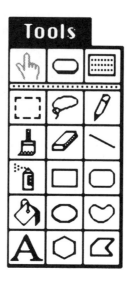

the Tools menu and the others is that the Tools menu is a *tear-off menu,* which means that it doesn't have to reside exclusively at the top of the screen. If you select the Tools menu and keep the mouse button down while you drag the pointer off the menu, you'll see that the entire palette follows the pointer. In other words, you can select the Tools menu once and keep it visible while you're performing any HyperCard operation, dragging it elsewhere if it gets in your way.

This tear-off feature is particularly useful because of the critical nature of the Tools menu. It is the one that controls which menu operations are available to you as an author, depending upon which tool is currently chosen. The top three tools are, from left to right:

The *browse* tool, used to click buttons and fields as a browsing or typing user would

The *button* tool, used to manipulate buttons while authoring

The *field* tool, used to inspect and modify fields

The browse tool is the one you have already used to move through a stack, so we don't need to explain it further. The other two tools turn off the stack's actions and provide access to its objects, so that, for instance, clicking on a button with the button tool does not cause that button's actions to take place, but rather selects that button. Once the button has been selected, the Edit menu changes to allow cutting, copying, pasting, and clearing of the selected button, along with all its properties, and the Objects menu can be used to get information about the button. The field tool acts in very much the same way as the button tool, allowing you to manipulate fields. We will discuss the bottom fifteen "painting" tools in the next section.

> While using the button (or field) tool, double-clicking on a button (or field) will also bring up the Button (or Field) Info dialog, without your having to go to the menu.

If you do authoring beyond the most elementary, you will find yourself switching among these tools frequently, using the button tool to lay out buttons, going back to the browse tool to test the changes you have made, switching to the field tool and back to the browse tool, and so on.

> HyperCard will switch from the button or field tools back to the browse tool whenever you press the Tab key, again eliminating a trip to the menu bar.

MANIPULATING OBJECTS: THE HEART OF AUTHORING

How to make a new stack.

Building a new stack is easy. All you do is select the New Stack... item from the File menu. When you do this, a dialog box will appear, as in Figure 3.10, asking what you want to call your stack and where you want to save it. If the "Copy current background" box is checked, your new stack will have the background of the currently open card as its sole background. If you click in the box, turning off the check, the background in your new stack will be completely white. Similarly, you can "Open [a] stack in [a] new window" on the screen (leaving the current stack also open) by checking the box with that name. If the box is unchecked, the current stack will be closed before creating your new one.

Each new stack consists of a single blank card and its background, either the background you copied or a blank background. If you have elected to copy the current background, you will also get all the buttons and fields (but not the text in the fields!) on that background.

Adding cards to a stack.

Now that you have a one-card stack, you can add as many new cards as you wish by repeatedly selecting New Card from the Edit menu (or, equivalently, holding down the command key, ⌘, while you press "n"). Each new card you add will share the current background. If your new stack does not yet have any navigation buttons to take you from card to card,

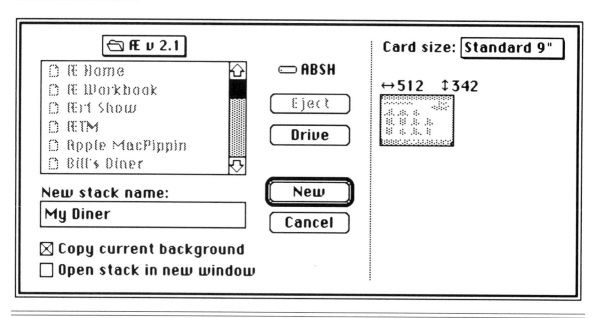

FIGURE 3.10   The New Stack Dialog Box

you will have to use the Go menu to move from one card to another while you are building your stack.

> Typing ⌘-B, or selecting Background from the Edit menu, will toggle you between the current card and the background for that card. You can tell where you are at any time, since the menu bar at the top of the screen will be outlined with hash marks when you are looking at the background.

The Objects menu.

You will find that you use the Objects menu, shown in Figure 3.11, quite often while authoring. The items in this menu allow you to get information about any object in the current stack, including the stack itself, and to construct new objects. Selecting Stack Info..., for instance, will bring up an information box like the one illustrated in Figure 3.12, telling you the name of the stack, how many cards and backgrounds it has, and so on.

If you look at the typical Card Info dialog box in Figure 3.13, you will see that a card has two identifying numbers: a card number and a card ID. The card number tells where in the stack the card is and changes as you add or delete cards in the stack. The card ID, however, is unique for each card, and doesn't change during the life of the stack. You also have the option, as indicated by the flashing cursor, of naming the card.

FIGURE 3.11   The Objects Menu

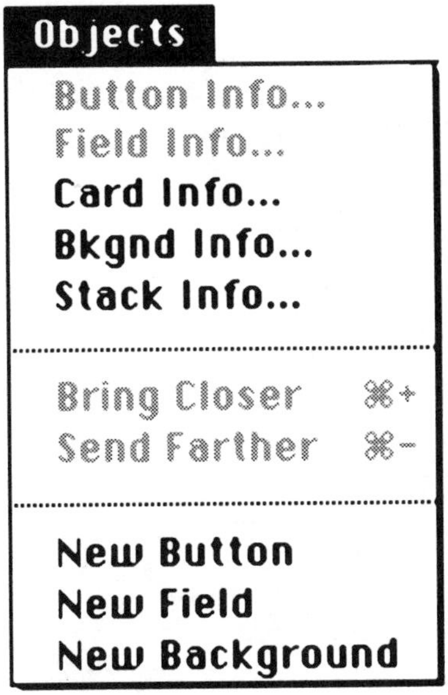

Objects

Button Info...
Field Info...
Card Info...
Bkgnd Info...
Stack Info...

Bring Closer   ⌘+
Send Farther   ⌘−

New Button
New Field
New Background

FIGURE 3.12   The Stack Info Dialog Box

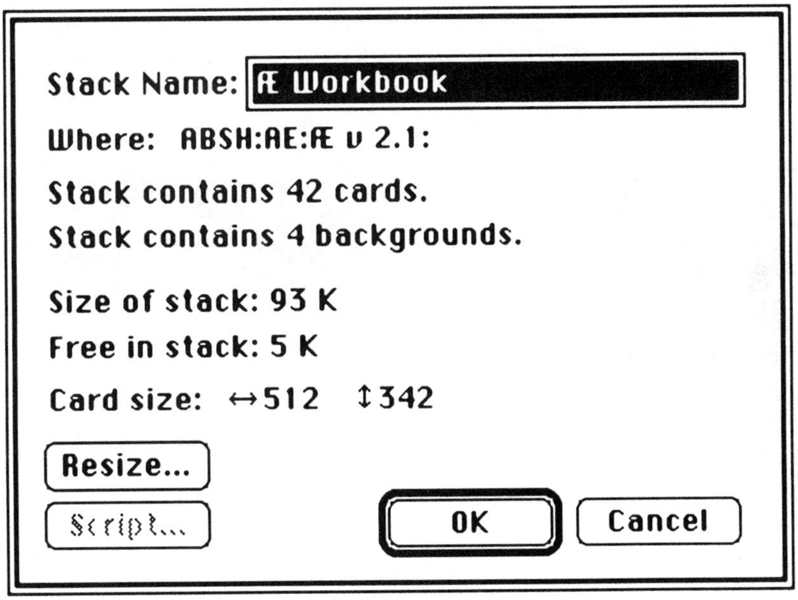

Stack Name: Æ Workbook

Where: ABSH:AE:Æ v 2.1:

Stack contains 42 cards.
Stack contains 4 backgrounds.

Size of stack: 93 K
Free in stack: 5 K
Card size: ↔512   ↕342

Resize...

Script...   OK   Cancel

FIGURE 3.13   The Card Info Dialog Box

The Card Info Dialog Box

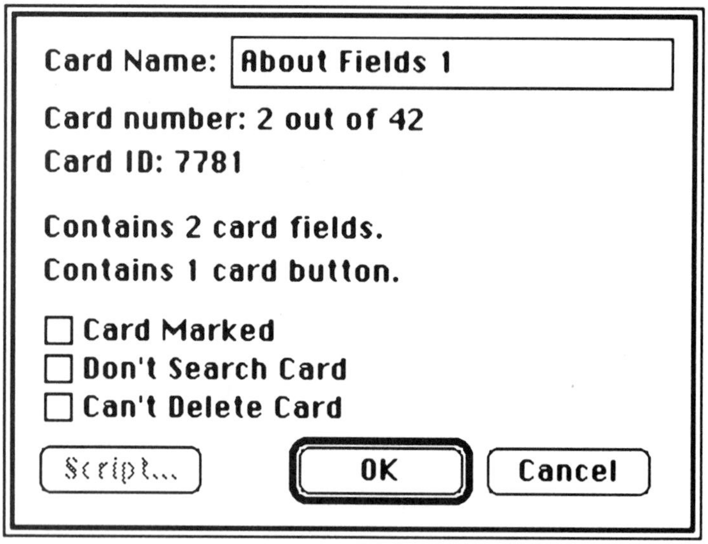

The New Card command adds a new card after the current card, sharing the background of the current card. If you are looking at the second card in the stack when you invoke the New Card command, a new card is created with the same background as card 2 and is inserted immediately after it. The old first and second cards will still be first and second in the stack, but the old third and fourth cards will be numbers four and five after the insertion, to make room for the new (third) card. Note that when you use the First, Prev, Next, and Last commands from the Go menu, navigation is based on card numbers rather than card IDs. Card IDs and names are used for navigation by the stack's programs (scripts), as we will see later. If you have a button that takes you from one card to another in a stack, for instance, you would not want to be forced to change the description of the button's destination card each time you added or deleted a card in the stack.

> The Edit menu's functions are modal, in that they change according to the tool you have currently selected.

The Edit menu can be used in the customary way to cut, copy, and paste cards. This is particularly useful when there is a card in another stack that you would like to include in the current stack. The only feature that is not obvious about these functions is that they act not only on a card, but also on its associated background. This is in keeping with the HyperCard design philosophy that a card cannot exist on its own, but must have a background as well.

> Inserting new backgrounds.

The New Background command inserts a new card and background on top of the currently visible card, without disturbing the connection between any existing cards and backgrounds. It is easy to suppose, mistakenly, that the new background should somehow apply to all subsequent cards in the stack, especially if you think in terms of transparent overlays. This, though, is not the case. In Figure 3.14 we show what would happen in a stack if card 3 were visible and the author selected New Background, followed by New Card. New Background inserted a new card and its new background in front of card 3, thereby bumping old card 4 into position 5. New Card, invoked while the newly added card 4 was visible, placed a new card (with card 4's background) in front of card 4, again bumping the last card in the old stack up one more position, to number 6. Card 6 retains the original background.

One of the interesting features of HyperCard is that changes made to a stack (like those you are about to make to the Æ Workbook and Bill's Diner) are both instant and permanent. That is, every change you make to a stack is immediately recorded and saved as part of that stack. The good news is that this feature frees you from having to remember to regularly "save" your work. The bad news is that the original version of a stack is lost as soon as that stack is edited.

FIGURE 3.14   **Modifying a Stack by New Background, Then New Card**

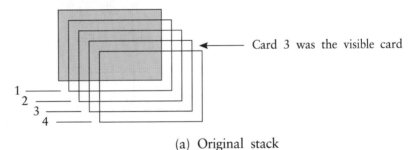

(a) Original stack

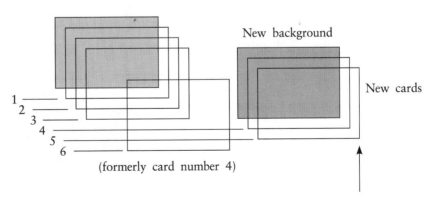

(b) New stack

This latter news is particularly noteworthy in light of your newfound authoring capabilities. As a HyperCard author you have facilities available to you that, at the click of a mouse, allow you to delete buttons, fields, and entire cards and backgrounds from a stack. In stacks like Æ Workbook, little damage can be done because there is not much there to begin with. The Bill's Diner stack, on the other hand, could easily be rendered useless by a few misguided authoring commands.

To protect against just such an occurrence, HyperCard provides us with a menu command that allows us to make a copy of a stack. The Save a Copy... command in the File menu creates a complete copy of the current stack. Before doing so, HyperCard presents you with a dialog box like that pictured in Figure 3.15 that allows you both to name the copy (if you don't change it, the name "Copy of"-stack name will be used) and to determine which disk the copy will be saved on (you can change the disk by clicking the Drive button). Clicking the Save button creates the copy as named on the disk specified.

Beware: Saving a copy of a stack does not open the newly created stack. After saving a copy, the current stack is still the original from which the copy was made. To make the copy become the current stack, you must

> **Making copies of a stack.**

FIGURE 3.15   The Save a Copy Dialog Box

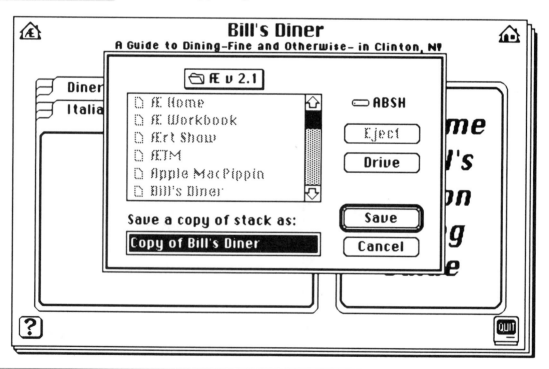

open the copy using the Open Stack... command from the File menu. You can always tell which stack is the current one by choosing Stack Info... from the Objects menu. A dialog box like the one in Figure 3.12 will appear on the screen, displaying, among other things, the current stack's name and where (on what disk, in what folders) it resides.

LAB EXERCISE 2

2.1 Open the Æ Workbook stack now.

2.2 Check out the menus in HyperCard's menu bar to verify that your user level has been set to Authoring. If it has not, return to the Home stack and set your user level appropriately.

2.3 Click on the About Fields button near the top of the Æ Workbook. Then, choose Card Info... from the Objects menu and review the descriptive properties of this card.

2.4 Choose Background Info... from the Objects menu and review the descriptive properties of this card's background.

2.5 Choose Background from the Edit menu to view just the current background. Choose Background again (or hit ⌘-b on the keyboard) to view the entire card.

2.6 Open Bill's Diner stack now, and save a copy of it using the Save a Copy... command from the File menu.

2.7 Open your copy of Bill's Diner now.

2.8 Use the Stack Info... command from the Objects menu to verify that your copy is the one that opened.

2.9 Add a new card to Bill's Diner to follow the card for "Tony's." Leave the new card blank for now.

FIELDS

Much of the power of HyperCard authors derives from the Tools menu, which affords us access to HyperCard's four basic tools. You already have considerable experience using the Browsing tool. We will concentrate now on developing a similar base of experience with the Field, Button, and Painting tools.

Making new fields.

You can place fields on either a card or a background by selecting the New Field... item from the Objects menu. Selecting Field Info... will bring up the Field Info dialog box, illustrated in Figure 3.16. In this dialog box you can select the style of the field to be any of five types: *transparent,* in which the card and background graphics are visible in the field; *opaque,* in which they are not; *rectangle,* in which an opaque field is bounded by a rectangle; *shadow,* in which the bounding rectangle has a drop shadow; and *scrolling,* in which the field has a scroll bar on the right side, allowing the user to see more of the field than can fit in the bounding rectangle.

Additionally, clicking the Font... button brings up the Text Style dialog (see Figure 3.17), allowing you to set the default characteristics of the text in the field. Text entered into a field will automatically appear in the font and style specified in the field's Text Style dialog box. Any portion of the text in a field (individual characters, words, lines, or combinations thereof) can be set to different fonts and styles using the Browsing tool. To do so, select the text to be changed (the field will have to be "unlocked" to do this), and then use HyperCard's Font and Style menus to reset these properties for the selected text only.

Once you have set the field's characteristics and clicked the OK button (or pressed the Return key—the equivalent to clicking on any thick-bordered button) the field will be highlighted on the card or background. As long as the field is highlighted, you can move it by dragging from its center or change its size by dragging one of its corners.

FIGURE 3.16   The Field Info Dialog Box

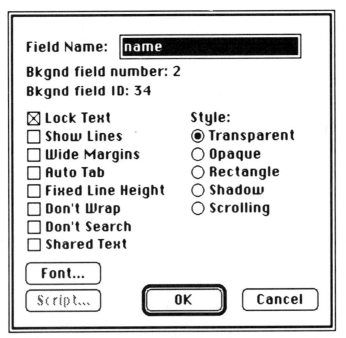

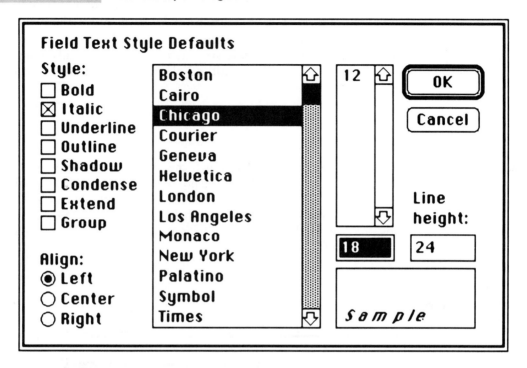

FIGURE 3.17   The Text Style Dialog Box

LAB EXERCISE 3

3.1 Open the Æ Workbook stack.

3.2 Review carefully the material in the "About Fields" section of the stack.

3.3 Use the practice cards at the beginning of the workbook to experiment with creating and setting the properties of fields. The Workbook menu provides commands for clearing the current card and for creating additional cards for practice.

3.4 Now, open your copy of Bill's Diner in a new window.

3.5 Go to the new restaurant card that you created in Lab Exercise 2, and select the Field tool to see what fields are on the card and its background.

3.6 Make up a restaurant name and a description, and enter this information into the existing fields of your new card.

3.7 Return to the first card of the Diner stack. Set the font and style of the restaurant name to something distinctive for each card of the stack.

3.8 Now, add a field to every card in the stack to hold the restaurant's phone number. Feel free to move or re-size any of the existing fields to accommodate your new one. Enter fictitious phone numbers into this field on every card.

BUTTONS

Making new buttons.

Buttons can be constructed in much the same way as fields by selecting New Button... from the Objects menu. Selecting Button Info... will bring up the Button Info dialog box, allowing you to set the button's characteristics in much the same way as with fields (see Figure 3.18). Also as with fields, the size and location of a button may be controlled by dragging its corners or center, respectively.

FIGURE 3.18   The Button Info Dialog Box

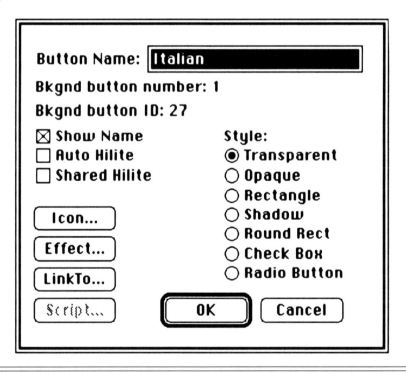

Button Name: |Italian|

Bkgnd button number: 1

Bkgnd button ID: 27

☒ Show Name   Style:
☐ Auto Hilite   ⦿ Transparent
☐ Shared Hilite ○ Opaque
                 ○ Rectangle
[Icon...]   ○ Shadow
                 ○ Round Rect
[Effect...]   ○ Check Box
[LinkTo...]   ○ Radio Button
[Script...]   [OK]   [Cancel]

FIGURE 3.19   The "Link To..." Dialog Box

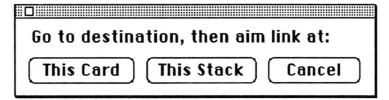

Unlike fields, buttons necessarily have some "action" associated with them: When we click on a button, we want something to happen. Most often what we want is to move from one card to another. That's exactly the purpose of the LinkTo... button in the Button Info dialog. To define a button so that clicking on it causes one to go to another card, click the LinkTo... button; a small window, as shown in Figure 3.19, will come up and will stay on the screen while you navigate to the card where you want the button to take the user. Clicking on This Card will instruct the button that the next time it is clicked, that card should be brought to the front. You can instruct the button being linked to display the first card of the stack you are now in by clicking This Stack.

Making a button link to another card.

Æ LAB   LAB EXERCISE 4

4.1   Open your Æ Workbook.

4.2   Review carefully the material in the "About Buttons" section of the stack.

4.3 Use the workbook's practice cards to experiment with creating, setting the properties of, and linking buttons.

4.4 Create a new button on the first card of the Æ Workbook that links you directly to your copy of Bill's Diner.

4.5 Set your new button's other properties, including its visual effect, using the Button Info... dialog box.

4.6 Use your new button to open your copy of Bill's Diner.

4.7 Add a new button to every card of the Diner stack that takes you directly to the first card of the Æ Workbook.

4.8 Set this button's other distinguishing properties using the Button Info... dialog box.

4.9 Return to browsing mode, and check to see if your new button performs as expected.

> Like the Edit menu, the painting tools are modal in that they change the action of the pointer.

PAINTING

You saw in Figure 3.9 what the Tools menu looks like; now let's discuss what you can do with the 15 painting tools in the bottom five rows. These tools control the *drawing mode;* selecting any of the 15 icons will change the action of the pointer on the screen, allowing you to perform different graphics functions. In fact, all of the cards, buttons, and icons that you use to create your own stacks were originally drawn on the screen with the painting tools. We will briefly describe each tool here, and later give you time to try them out in the lab.

The image on the screen is composed of small dots, which can be either black or white, very much like a halftone picture in a newspaper. These dots are called *pixels* (short for "picture elements"), and it is these dots that are modified when you paint in HyperCard. Keep this in mind while you read the descriptions of the painting tools—it may help.

When you select the pencil tool, the pointer changes to a picture of a pencil, allowing you to draw freehand on the visible card or background. The pencil draws a fine line as long as you hold down the mouse button. The "color" of the pencil line is opposite that of whatever color was underneath the pencil when the mouse was first clicked, so if you begin sketching on a white area you will draw black lines, and if you begin in a black area the lines will be white.

The paintbrush acts much like the pencil, except that you can change the shape of the line it leaves as well as the patten it draws in. To change the shape of the brush, select Brush Shape... from the Options menu (see Figure 3.20). To change the pattern with which the brush

---

FIGURE 3.20   **The Brush Shape Dialog Box**

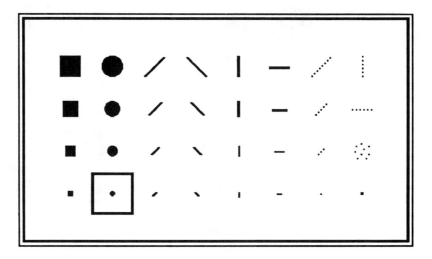

---

paints, select from the 40 patterns in the "Patterns" tear-off menu, or use Edit Pattern... from the Options menu to create a pattern of your own (Figure 3.21).

╲ The line tool, as you would expect, draws straight lines. Clicking once anchors one end of the line, which stretches on the screen like a rubber band as you move the mouse, until the mouse is clicked again, anchoring the other end. The width of the line can be changed by the Line Size... item of the Options menu (Figure 3.22).

The spraypaint tool, like the paintbrush, draws the currently selected pattern, but it "spatters" the pattern, only drawing some of the pixels. By holding the mouse button down and moving the spraypaint tool over an area, you can make as much of the pattern appear as you wish.

The paint can is used to fill areas with the currently selected pattern. The area filled is the selected region on the card or background that is completely bounded by black pixels. You have to be careful with the paint can—if there is the smallest hold in the boundary of the region you are painting, even as small as a single white pixel, the paint pattern will "leak out" all over the card. Fortunately, HyperCard is a forgiving environment, and you can select Undo from the Edit menu to revert to the picture you had before the paint spilled all over everything.

FIGURE 3.21   The Options Menu and the Patterns Menu

FIGURE 3.22   The Line Size Dialog Box

The eraser tool, when selected, turns the pointer into a small white square. When the mouse button is held down in this mode, all pixels beneath the square will be erased, as if you had never painted them in the first place. Be careful about double-clicking on the eraser—it will erase everything on the current card or background. If that happens, Undo can rescue your painting.

The rectangle and rounded rectangle tools draw rectangles of the indicated type on the screen.To draw, click and hold the mouse button while moving the mouse. The points where you first clicked and where you released the mouse button will form opposite corners of the rectangle. The size of the border lines can be changed by using the Line Size... dialog from the Options menu. If you want the rectangle to be filled with a pattern, you can either use the paint can or select Draw Filled from the Options menu, in which case all bounded objects will be filled automatically when drawn.

The oval tool acts almost exactly like the rectangle tool, except that it draws ovals that are bounded by an invisible rectangle you specify by clicking the mouse button on one corner and releasing it on the opposite corner. As with rectangles, you can modify the width of the border or the fill pattern.

The regular polygon tool draws symmetric polygons with either three, four, five, six, or eight sides. It can also draw circles. You have to play with the polygon tool to appreciate it. To draw a polygon, select the number of sides using the Polygon Sides... dialog from the Options menu, as shown in Figure 3.23 (the polygon will have four sides if you don't make a selection). Then click where you want the center of the polygon to be, hold down the mouse button, and drag the pointer away from the center to draw the polygon. As long as you hold the mouse button down, you can also rotate the polygon about its center. As with rectangles and ovals, you can change the border width or the fill pattern of regular polygons.

FIGURE 3.23   **The Polygon Sides Dialog Box**

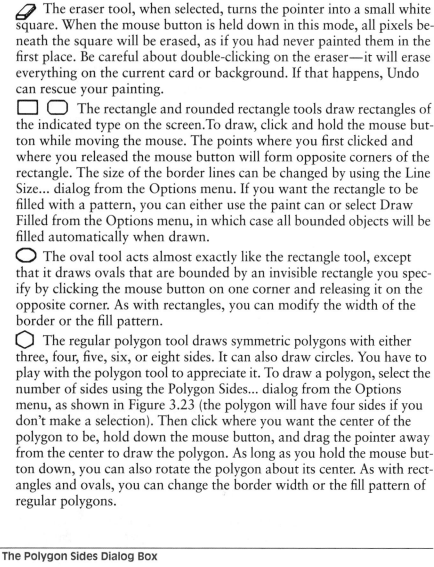

◿ The irregular polygon tool acts almost like a number of line tools strung together. Clicking once with this tool makes a "rubber-band" straight line, clicking again anchors the first edge and starts a new edge at the end of the one you've just drawn, and so on, until you double-click to complete the polygon. When you double-click, the polygon will be completed with a line from the current position to where you began the polygon. You can change the border widths and fill patterns just as with the other geometric figure tools.

♡ The curve tool combines some features of the pencil and some of the geometric figures tools. Like the pencil, you begin drawing by clicking on the screen and holding the mouse to draw a curve. When you release the mouse, the curve is completed. This is exactly the way the pencil works, but the curve tool allows you to fill the region bounded by the curve and a straight line between its starting and ending points. If you have selected Draw Filled from the Options menu, a straight line will be drawn between the starting and ending points as soon as you release the mouse button, and the resulting region will then be filled with the current pattern. In addition, you have the option of setting the border width (which does not include the line between the starting and ending points), as with the rectangle tool.

A The text tool allows you to paint text on the screen by typing. Clicking with the mouse selects the place on the screen where the text will begin. As long as you haven't clicked the mouse again, you can do simple editing of what you've typed by backspacing and retyping. None of the other text-editing features work in this mode, however, so don't try to select a word by dragging over it, for instance.

You can change the style of the text you are about to type by selecting the Text Style... item from the Edit menu. Altering the text style also works while you are typing, but before you click the mouse again within the card or background. Once you have clicked the mouse after typing, the text becomes nothing more than a collection of pixels on the screen and can no longer be modified (except by erasing or drawing over it, of course). In general, you "paint" text when the text is simple and fixed—that is, when there is no need for extensive editing.

⌞⌝ The selection tool has a number of uses, the most common of which is to move graphics from one place to another. With this tool, clicking and dragging the mouse creates a rectangular region on the screen, just as the rectangle tool does. This rectangle, sometimes called a *marquee*, has a dashed border that "crawls" around the rectangle (some people call this effect "marching ants") to make it clearly visible. Once a part of a picture has been selected, clicking and holding the mouse button within the marquee allows you to drag the selection, both black and white pixels, anywhere you wish on the card or background.

Along with dragging a selection, you can also use the features of the Edit menu with a selection. Choosing Cut from the Edit menu removes the selected rectangle and stores it in an area of memory called the Clipboard; Copy leaves the selection intact, storing a copy of it on the Clipboard. Both Cut and Copy destroy anything that was in the Clipboard before. Selecting Paste places a copy of the contents of the Clipboard in the same location it was in originally. Cutting, copying, and pasting are particularly useful for moving images from one card to another. The Clear command removes the selection, without modifying the contents of the Clipboard.

As with most of the rest of the painting tools, there are enhancements available that change the behavior of the selection tool. Once a selection has been made and the marching ants are hard at work, dragging the mouse with the Option key held down will drag a copy of the selection, leaving the original in place, thereby allowing you to make copies of painted objects. Holding down the Shift key while dragging the selection will constrain the dragging motion to a horizontal or vertical direction, depending on the initial dragging motion. Finally, holding down both the Shift and Option keys will drag a copy of the selection in a horizontal or vertical direction.

Many of the paint tools do different things if you hold down the Shift or the Option keys (individually or together) while clicking or dragging. Try it!

The lasso tool also selects an object, but includes as little of the exterior as possible. To select an object with the lasso tool, hold down the mouse while you use the lasso to draw a curve around the object. Like the curve tool, when you release the mouse button, the curve is finished with a straight line between its starting and ending points, but then the curve "shrink-wraps" the object enclosed, selecting only the black pixels within the curve, along with any white pixels totally enclosed by black. The lasso tool is particularly useful for selecting an object in tight quarters, where a rectangular selection simply wouldn't fit.

Once a collection of pixels has been selected, you can drag or clone it just as you can with the selection tool. The Edit menu commands work on lasso selections just as they do on those made by the selection tool. The lasso also has Option, Shift, and Shift-Option enhancements that act like those for the selection tool.

Along with the painting tools themselves, you have seen several menus that control the painting process. The Paint menu, shown in Figure 3.24, contains a number of features, most of which you can discover on your own in the lab exercises, but two of which—Opaque and Transparent—deserve special mention here.

Opaque and transparent paints.

We have already mentioned that you can draw on the currently visible card or on its background. We also mentioned that you can paint each pixel black or white, but when we said that, we were obscuring part of the truth—until now, that is. It is true that white and black are the only "colors" available for painting on the background, but since, conceptually, cards overlay their backgrounds, HyperCard allows graphics on cards to

FIGURE 3.24   The Paint Menu

```
┌─────────────────────────────┐
│ Paint                       │
├─────────────────────────────┤
│   Select          ⌘S        │
│   Select All      ⌘A        │
│ ............................│
│   Fill                      │
│   Invert                    │
│   Pickup                    │
│   Darken                    │
│   Lighten                   │
│   Trace Edges               │
│   Rotate Left               │
│   Rotate Right              │
│   Flip Vertical             │
│   Flip Horizontal           │
│ ............................│
│   Opaque                    │
│   Transparent               │
│ ............................│
│   Keep            ⌘K        │
│   Revert                    │
└─────────────────────────────┘
```

be transparent, as well as opaque white or black. This feature permits you, for example, to "paint out" part of the background by covering it with an opaque graphic on the card layer, or to enhance the background graphic by allowing it to show through a transparent picture on the card.

The default mode for painting on a card is with transparent paint. In this mode, all card pixels that are not black are transparent, allowing the background picture to show through in those areas. If you draw an un-filled rectangle on a card, for example, the black border will cover any background pixels, but the background will show through the unpainted interior. To obscure the background, you must fill the rectangle with the white pattern. A word of warning: The default mode for figures that have been cut or copied and then pasted onto the card is opaque, rather than transparent. If you want a pasted selection to be transparent, select Transparent from the Paint menu while the pasted picture is still selected. The eraser, by the way, will erase card pixels to transparent, showing the underlying background, unless you hold down the Command key while erasing, in which case the erasure will be made with opaque white.

Another way to change the transparency of the card layer is to select a portion of the card with the selection or lasso tool and select either Opaque or Transparent from the Paint menu. Selecting Opaque will change all nonblack pixels in the selected region to white, hiding any background pixels beneath. Selecting Transparent will allow the Background to show through the nonblack pixels in the selected region on the card. In Figure 3.25 we show some of the possible ways of combining images on a card and its background, keeping in mind our equation *background + card = apparent card.*

Finally, we have talked about painting the background or a card. The default object for painting is the visible card, but it is easy to get to the background of a card—all you have to do is choose Background from the Edit menu. The Background command is a *toggle*—to get out of the background and back to the card, you only need to select the Background command again.

If all of this information about painting seems confusing, take heart: You'll have time to practice painting in the lab. The best way to master these new tools is to try them out—once you have had time to play with painting, you'll probably wonder why it seemed so complicated while reading the text.

A stack may have a large collection of buttons and fields, placed on cards and backgrounds, each with its own graphics. How does HyperCard decide what to show and what to obscure? In terms of visibility to the user, fields visually overlap buttons, and buttons overlap graphics, subject to the rule we already know—namely, that cards overlap backgrounds (and all background objects). These rules about overlaps apply only to functional objects, so that even if a card's graphics obscure a background

> Remember, ⌘-B toggles you to and from the background.

> Visibility rules for objects.

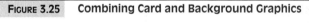

FIGURE 3.25   Combining Card and Background Graphics

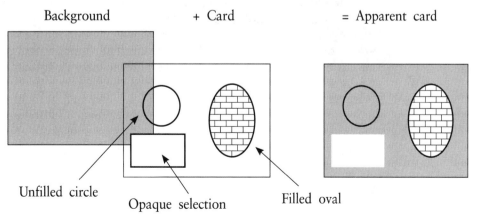

Background   + Card   = Apparent card

Unfilled circle   Opaque selection   Filled oval

FIGURE 3.26   **The Visible Arrangement of Objects on Cards and Backgrounds**

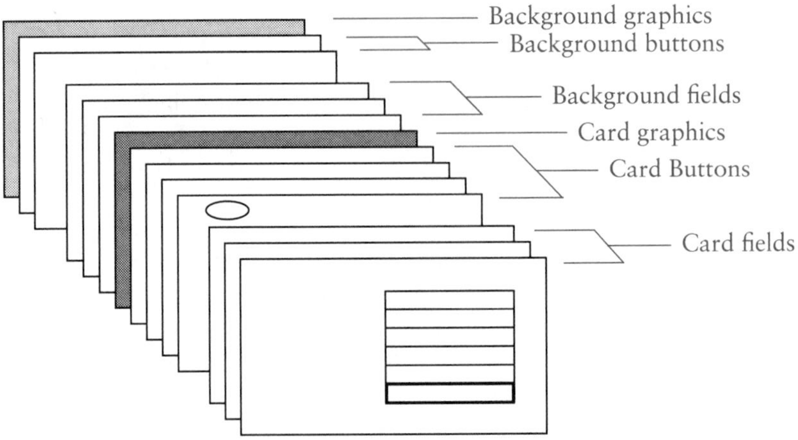

button completely, the button is still active—that is, a click where the background button is located will cause the button to take action even if it can't be seen. In Figure 3.26 we illustrate the visual hierarchy of objects on cards and backgrounds.

Congratulations! You are well on the road to being an author. You know how to build a system—a stack, in this case—by combining functional units—backgrounds, cards, fields, and buttons. In spite of the length of this section, there is a considerable amount of information we have left out. After all, the standard reference for HyperCard, Danny Goodman's *The Complete HyperCard Handbook* (New York: Bantam Books, 1987), is 720 pages long, 253 pages of which are devoted to authoring alone. Some of the omissions will be covered in the lab exercises, but we make no apologies for the rest. It was not our purpose here to make you HyperCard experts. HyperCard's user-friendly interface helps you to do that on your own. Rather, our intention was to use HyperCard's authoring capabilities to make points about system design, which was where we began this module and where we'll end.

REVIEW QUESTIONS

1. What must you do first in order to be able to use any of the painting tools?
2. Describe the steps necessary to create a stack with one background and two cards.

3. What menus are accessible in the authoring level? Which menu would you use to obtain information about a card?

4. Give two ways you could get information about a button.

5. If there was a button on a card's background, what could you do to make that button invisible on the card?

LAB EXERCISE 5

5.1 Open your Æ Workbook, and review the material in the "About Painting" section of the stack.

5.2 Use the practice cards in the Workbook to experiment with creating and editing graphic objects.

5.3 Open your copy of Bill's Diner.

5.4 Add a picture of a telephone to every card of the stack. Place the picture (it should be the same for every card!) near the field you created to hold the telephone number. You may draw your own phone, or copy one from another stack.

5.5 Add a distinctive picture to each card of the Diner Stack that conveys the type of restaurant it is. For example, draw (or copy and paste) a pizza onto the card of any of the Italian restaurants, or a hamburger on a fast-food restaurant's card.

3.5   DOING IT RIGHT

We return now to our mythological metaphor, continuing to investigate the problems of system design. In this design process, it's not enough to know how to put the parts together; we must be able to put the parts together to produce an elegant whole. We want to design the computer equivalent of a thoroughbred, rather than a hodgepodge of unrelated pieces.

We have already mentioned some of the desiderata of a good system: It should be transparent, forgiving, visually oriented, and user-configurable. If you put yourself in the position of a frequent user of computers (which you may become after going through this text), it would probably not be too difficult to come up with a wish list of other features.

For instance, an application should be *fully functional* for its intended purpose. This text, for instance, was produced on a contemporary word processor with the ability to include graphics along with text. This means that we didn't have to estimate the amount of space the pictures would take, leave blank spaces, and cut and glue the graphics in later. (We're guilty of exaggerating the state of the publisher's art somewhat here. The typesetter actually did manually combine text and art, but that's a situation that should be quaintly anachronistic within a few years.)

A good application should be *seamless*. In an ideal publishing application, we should not have to switch between a word processor and a graphics program to produce a manuscript for a textbook such as this. At the very least, we should be able to take a document from one application and import it into another application, and we should expect that at least some of the standard commands function in an analogous way across applications. Further, as we mentioned before, we should be able to start a new application and run it at the novice level without having to master an intimidating manual of unfamiliar commands.

The Mac scores fairly well in this category, primarily because of a set of guidelines published by Apple Computer that help software developers ensure that their products will be familiar to experienced Macintosh users and compatible with those of other manufacturers. To give you a feel for what these guidelines entail, we have excerpted below some portions of "The Macintosh User Interface Guide" from *Inside Macintosh,* volume 1 (New York: Addison-Wesley, 1985).

> The user should feel in control of the computer, not the other way around. This is achieved in applications that embody three qualities: responsiveness, permissiveness, and consistency.
>
> Responsiveness means that the user's actions tend to have direct results. The user should be able to accomplish what needs to be done spontaneously and intuitively, rather than having to think: "Let's see; to do C, first I have to do A and B and then. . .". For example, with pull-down menus, the user can choose the desired command directly and instantaneously.
>
> Permissiveness means that the application tends to allow the user to do anything reasonable. The user, not the system, decides what to do next. Also, error messages tend to come up infrequently. If the user is constantly subjected to a barrage of error messages, something is wrong somewhere.
>
>   *   *   *
>
> The third and most important principle is consistency. Since Macintosh users usually divide their time among several applications, they would be confused and irritated if they had to learn a completely new interface for each application.
>
>   *   *   *
>
> A fundamental object in Macintosh software is the **icon**, a small graphic object that's usually symbolic of an operation or of a larger entity such as a document.

Icons can contribute greatly to the clarity and attractiveness of an application. . . . Whenever an explanation or label is needed, consider using an icon, instead of text.

*   *   *

To choose a command, the user positions the pointer over the menu title and presses the mouse button. . . . Nothing actually happens until the user chooses the command; the user can look at any of the menus without making a commitment to do anything.

*   *   *

The most frequently used commands should be at the top of a menu; research shows that the easiest item for the user to choose is the second from the top. The most dangerous commands should be at the bottom of the menu, preferably isolated from the frequently used commands.

*   *   *

Some characters that can be typed along with the Command key are reserved for special purposes, but there are different degrees of stringency. Since almost every application has an Edit and a File menu, the keyboard equivalents of those menus are strongly reserved, and should never be used for any other purpose:

Character	Command
C	Copy (Edit menu)
Q	Quit (File menu)
V	Paste (Edit menu)
X	Cut (Edit menu)
Z	Undo (Edit menu)

Note: The keyboard equivalent for the Quit command is useful in case there's a mouse malfunction, so the user will still be able to leave the application in an orderly way (with the opportunity to save any changes to documents that haven't yet been saved).

*   *   *

One of the strongest ways in which Macintosh applications can take advantage of the consistency of the user interface is by using standard menus. The operations controlled by these menus occur so frequently that it saves considerable time for users if they always match exactly. Three of these menus, the Apple, File, and Edit menus, appear in almost every application.

*   *   *

Every user of every application is liable to do something that the application won't understand or can't cope with in a normal manner. Alerts [like the

"Do you really want to erase your hard disk" box we illustrated earlier] give applications a way to respond to errors not only in a consistent manner, but in stages according to the severity of the error, the user's level of expertise, and the particular history of the error.

*   *   *

The preferred (safest) button to use in the current situation is boldly outlined. This is the alert's default button; its effect occurs if the user presses Return or Enter.

It's important to phrase messages in alert boxes so that users aren't left guessing the real meaning. Avoid computer jargon.

*   *   *

Under no circumstances should an alert message refer the user to external documentation for further clarification. It should provide an adequate description of the information needed by the user to take appropriate action.

If much of this seems to be common sense applied to computer programs, that's because it is. The most important thing about user interface guidelines such as these is that they are there at all. For the Macintosh, at least, these guidelines not only let system designers know what users expect across applications, they also relieve the designers of the burden of designing the interface from the ground up for every application.

The Macintosh user interface is certainly not the only one available, nor would we make any claims that it is perfect. Computers like the Mac, with a sophisticated graphical interface, have been commercially available only for a decade or so, and there is certainly much yet to be learned. We doubt that there will ever be an externally imposed set of standards for user interfaces; rather we suspect that as computers become more pervasive, user expectations will converge on a loose collection of features that will become a *de facto* standard, as has been the case in the automotive industry over the past three quarters of a century.

We will close this module by discussing user interface guidelines as they apply specifically to HyperCard. Again, we offer some excerpts, this time by Katie Withey of the Human Interface Group of Apple Computer, Inc. The following excerpts are from *HyperCard Stack Design Guidelines* (New York: Addison-Wesley, 1988).

The nature of the information in a HyperCard stack has a lot to do with the structure of the stack. There are many sorts of structures that a stack can have; for example:

- A stack can be primarily linear, encouraging users to move through it in a "straight line"—there's a logical path through the information that you want them to follow. . . .

- A stack can be tree-structured, letting users choose between several branches at each point to follow the path they are interested in. . . .

- A stack can be nonlinear, with no specific order—users can explore in many different ways. Buttons may lead to other cards or other stacks, or may have other actions. An adventure game is a nonlinear stack.

* * *

Multiple backgrounds within a stack let you make subgroups of information that serve the same purpose as separate stacks—fields in different positions or with different text styles, for example—but with the convenience of a single stack. Don't use a different background for every slight change of information, though, or you may end up confusing users instead of helping them.

* * *

You can think of a stack as an ordered list of cards that use an unordered list of backgrounds. It's similar to a book that has different page styles: The first page of each chapter may have the same page style, which is different from the style of the main body of the book. . . . Decide what elements should be common to all cards—pictures, buttons, and text fields—and put those in the background.

* * *

Keep it simple. When you design the background for a stack, it may look very bare. This is okay—when you add the information to a stack, it will look much more intricate. If the background itself is very complicated, it may disrupt the user from the information.

* * *

The fundamental rule in dividing your information into cards is *one idea per card.* If each card contains only one basic idea or topic, there is probably room for both text and a picture, with a title, without getting cramped. . . . Even in stacks that are explaining or describing something, don't fill up your cards with text. Long passages of text can become tiresome on the screen, and users get frustrated if cards contain run-on text. If you have a lot of text, try to break it up—put less important information in pop-up fields or off the screen in a scrolling field. If you really can display your information only in large blocks of text, it may be better suited to a different medium.

* * *

In HyperCard (or any large database), maps are useful for helping users find their way through "information space." You probably have a picture in your mind of how your stacks are arranged—you may be able to turn this picture into a map that will present the same model of the system to users.

REVIEW QUESTIONS

1. Suppose that the menu bar in the Mac user interface had never been considered. In what ways might the HyperCard interface be different?

2. Why is the ⌘-Q command key equivalent a useful substitute for the File menu Quit command?

3. Invent a different-looking scroll bar, and discuss the advantages or disadvantages of your design over the Mac's scroll bars.

4. Why are user interface guidelines useful?

5. In the context of HyperCard, what is a "map," and why is it useful?

Æ LAB

LAB EXERCISE 6

We mentioned at the beginning of this module that we would be making use of three Æ stacks in these lab exercises. The one we have yet to see (except for its picture in Figure 3.3) is named "Very Resourceful." The stack derives its name from the fact that Macintosh "resources" (files containing descriptions of sounds, icons, cursors, and the like) can be used within HyperCard for adding some finishing touches to the user interface of any stack.*

Clicking on any of the three resource types at the top of the Very Resourceful cover card provides you with eight simple examples of each type of resource (for example, the icons displayed in Figure 3.27). Once a particular resource is selected (by clicking on it), it becomes highlighted and an instance of it appears to the left of the selection. (Ignore, for now, the field below the selections. It will become meaningful and useful to you after you complete Module 4.)

In order for a HyperCard stack to make use of a resource, the resource must first be accessible to the stack. The surest way to make a resource accessible is to "attach" it directly to the stack. Attaching a resource to a stack requires some special HyperCard scripting—which, of course, we haven't discussed yet. So, we have included in Very Resourceful the Attach to... button. When clicked, it asks you (via a standard "open file" dialog box) which stack the selected resource should be attached to, and does the attaching for you.

Once you attach one of the Very Resourceful icons, for example, to one of your stacks, the newly attached icon will appear among this list of those available for defining a new button. Better still, as a HyperCard author, you can copy and paste the New Button that appears to the left of your icon selection into your stack and use the icon directly. Similarly, if you attach one of Very Resourceful's sounds to your stack and then copy and paste the Play It! button into your stack, your stack will then be able to sound off.

---

* It is also a direct quote from the Wizard of Oz, in the film of the same name.

FIGURE 3.27   **Very Resourceful's Icons**

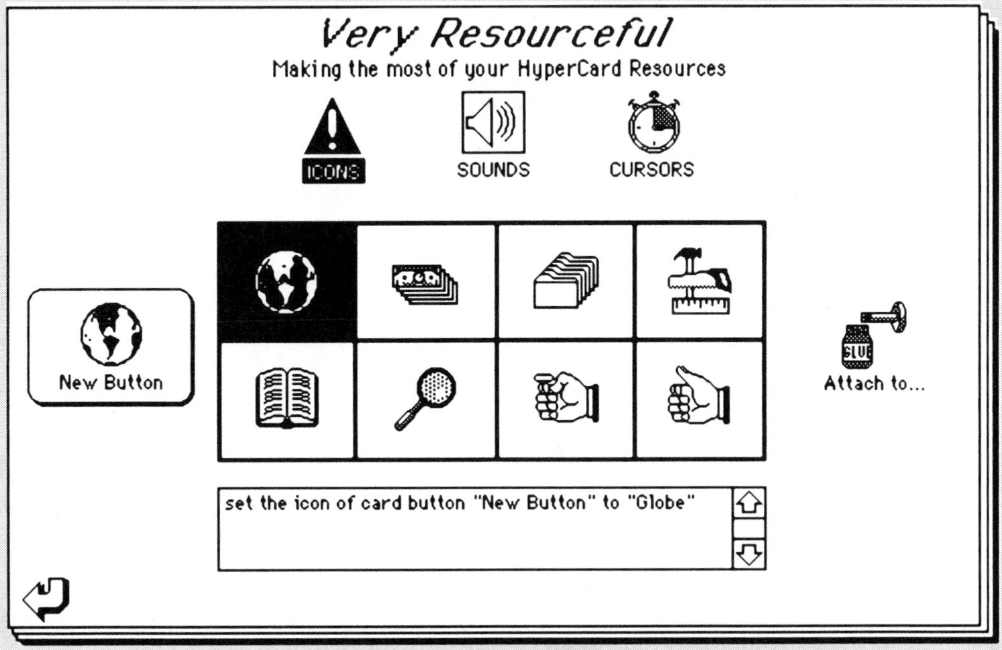

6.1 Use Very Resourceful to attach an icon to your copy of Bill's Diner.

6.2 Copy the New Button displaying your selected icon and paste it onto the first card of your copy of Bill's Diner.

6.3 Link the new button to the first card of the Very Resourceful stack.

6.4 Attach a sound resource and copy and paste its Play It! button onto the first card of your Æ Workbook.

6.5 Select the Browse tool and click on the Play It! button that now exists in the Æ Workbook. You have completed the Module 3 lab exercises—let's hear it!

3.6   EXERCISES

1. List three ways that advances in computer hardware—that is, the machines themselves—have influenced the evolution of the user interface.

2. In what ways do you think computers of the future will be easier to use?

3. We described well-designed systems as being, among other things, transparent, forgiving, and visually oriented. Describe situations that you have encountered using HyperCard that demonstrate these three properties.

4. What do computerized spreadsheets look like on the screen to their users? Why? What about word processors? Is it important that programs present familiar images to their users?

5. Can you think of a reason for distinguishing between a HyperCard field and the information in it? That is, if a field is placed in a background, why aren't its contents also regarded as part of the background?

6. How does HyperCard's user level represent an advance in user interface?

7. Look at the Starter stack from the lab in Module 1. Briefly describe each background used in that stack.

8. For each of the following cards from the Starter stack (the cards with these numbers showing at their bottom center), identify all objects on the card and describe briefly how each might have been created:

   a. card labelled number 3
   b. card labelled number 8
   c. card labelled number 12

9. Pick some machine that you have access to (a digital watch, a microwave oven), and compare it to the Macintosh in terms of its responsiveness and permissiveness.

10. It has been said that there is no such thing as a completely new Macintosh program. What do you think this means? Is this a compliment or a complaint?

3.7   ADDITIONAL READINGS

Apple Computer, Inc. *Inside Macintosh*. Vol. 1. Reading, Mass.: Addison-Wesley, 1985.

Badre, A., and Schneiderman, B., eds. *Directions in Human/Computer Interaction*. Human/Computer Interaction Series, vol. 1. Norwood, N.J.: Ablex, 1982.

Card, S. K.; Moran, T. P.; and Newell, A. *The Psychology of Human-Computer Interaction*. Hillsdale, N.J.: Lawrence Earlbaum Associates, 1983.

Dumas, J. *Designing User Interfaces for Software*. Englewood Cliffs, N.J.: Prentice-Hall, 1988.

Goodman, D. *The Complete HyperCard Handbook*. New York: Bantam Books, 1987.

———. *HyperCard Developer's Guide*. New York: Bantam Books, 1988.

Ledgard, H.; Singer, A.; and Whiteside, J. *Directions in Human Factors for Interactive Software*. Lecture Notes in Computer Science, vol. 103. Berlin: Springer-Verlag, 1981.

Sanders, W. B. *HyperCard Made Easy.* Glenview, Ill.: Scott, Foresman, 1988.

Schneiderman, B. *Designing the User Interface.* New York: Addison-Wesley, 1986.

Schneiderman, B., ed. *Human/Computer Interface Design Guidelines.* Human/ Computer Interaction Series, vol. 5. Norwood, N.J.: Ablex, 1986.

MODULE 4

PROGRAMMING: *CORDON BLEU* COMPUTER SCIENCE

4.1 INTRODUCTION

In the previous module you saw how to produce a HyperCard application by combining buttons and fields on cards and then combining cards to produce a stack. The exceptional utility of HyperCard comes in part from this very high level of abstraction, where the objects that make up a stack are available to you as distinct entities, to be copied from one application and used in another. In much the same way as a word processor allows you to cut, copy, and move words, sentences, and paragraphs from one document to another, HyperCard can be viewed as a program processor, designed so that a button or card that performs some function in one application will perform the same function when pasted into another.

What happens, though, when you need a button to perform a task and can't find one with the desired function in any of your sample stacks? How were the buttons, fields, and cards designed in the first place, and how do they do what they do? In this module you will see that every HyperCard object can have a *script* associated with it—that is, a list of instructions to the computer. You will see how these scripts are designed and integrated to form a computer program.

TEXT OBJECTIVES

In this module, we will

- Learn about the simple and structured types of information available in the HyperTalk programming language
- Discuss the statements that are used to manipulate information
- See how HyperTalk allows us to control the order of execution of statements
- Discover how to make a program modular by using procedures and functions, and discover how messages are passed from one unit of a program to another

116

- Investigate the activities involved in the programming process, and learn how to manage these activities efficiently

THE ALGORITHM MACHINE

HyperTalk is the language used to write HyperCard scripts. Scripts describe the actions associated with HyperCard objects. In the pages to come, we will teach you the fundamentals of HyperTalk programming. Along the way, we will discuss the similarities between HyperTalk and other programming languages, pointing out HyperTalk's comparative strengths and weaknesses. Finally, we will discuss some programming principles. Programming a computer is similar in many ways to any other large cognitive task, such as writing an essay. We will see that the precepts of efficient programming are nothing more than commonsense rules applied to the task of designing a collection of instructions to the computer.

You don't learn programming by reading a book, however, any more than you become an author by reading books on literary criticism. Computer programming is most emphatically not a spectator sport—it is a contact sport. You learn to program by programming, which you will do in the lab portion of this module.

METAPHOR: THE ELECTRONIC KITCHEN

In Module 2 we explored the world of computer applications. Using the stacks designed for the Module 2 exercises was similar to being a guest at a dinner party—the sequence of courses and their contents had been chosen for you, and all you had to do was sample them. In Module 3, when you designed stacks of your own by combining objects from other stacks, you were the host of the dinner party, choosing the courses for the meal from a menu so they would blend together in a pleasing evening's experience.

In this module we will take you into the kitchen and show you how to combine the raw ingredients to produce each dish. Just as in a cooking school, we will begin by discussing the ingredients themselves, then instruct you in the fundamentals of combining these ingredients—the computer equivalent of a basic white sauce—and finally discuss how to blend all the individual components into a pleasing (and functional) whole. At the end, you will have more than a cookbook knowledge of programming and will be on your way to creating your own recipes with taste and elegance. Although we won't be able to transform you into a master of the electronic kitchen in a single module, we hope that these first steps will be enjoyable and enlightening, providing the "flavor" of the programming process itself.

Æ STACKS: NO ACCOUNT

Whereas HyperCard authors have a great deal of control over what a stack looks like, they are constrained to build stacks from components with predefined functionality. Authors cannot control the details of what a stack does. For example, we can copy a button that sorts cards of an existing stack and paste it into a new stack. We can control where the button will appear in our new stack and what it will look like. We cannot, though, customize its behavior. If the button sorted the stack it was copied from by "last name", "last name" had better be meaningful in the context of our new stack.

To attain the necessary level of control to customize the behavior of a stack, we must become HyperCard programmers. This lab module will provide you with a hands-on introduction to the HyperTalk language. HyperTalk is a rich and expressive programming language with a flexible vocabulary and a wide repertoire of commands. As you have seen, stacks—and thus scripts—can be and have been written to address many complex information processing needs. In this module, we will just scratch the surface of HyperTalk, restricting ourselves to the scripts of the No Account stack on your Æ Stacks disk. It is not our intention to provide you with an in-depth discussion of either HyperTalk or computer programming. Indeed, the former is described in some detail in the Appendix (and in complete detail in suggested additional readings; see Apple Computer, Inc., and Shafer), and the latter demands a separate course (or two!) of its own. Rather, our goal is to expose you to the algorithms and the language that underlies the behavior of HyperCard stacks. You will see how scripts can be customized to given tasks and how they can be developed from scratch to accomplish new ones. You will, at last, be able to see through to the inner workings of HyperCard stacks: They will become "clear boxes."

LAB OBJECTIVES

In the lab part of this module, you will

- Learn to use the HyperTalk programming language—that is, you will become a HyperCard "scriptor"
- Experiment with a stack and examine its scripts
- Understand how HyperCard uses messages, message handlers, and the object hierarchy to process HyperTalk scripts
- Learn about the "conditions" and "properties" that are attributed to HyperCard objects and how they can be referenced from within HyperTalk scripts
- See some of the additional features of HyperCard that come with being a "scriptor"

4.2   SCRIPTING WITH NO ACCOUNT

Every stack that you have seen has scripts associated with it. Despite the fact that we haven't discussed them explicitly, you have already manipulated and even created scripts. Every time you copy a button and paste it into one of your stacks, you copy not only the button's appearance, but also its functionality—in other words, its script. That is why a copied button performs as did the original. Similarly, when creating your own buttons (using the New Button command), you have used the LinkTo... operation to prescribe the action to be associated with clicking the button. What you have done (actually, HyperCard did it for you) is write a script that tells HyperCard which card to display when the button is clicked.

Look at the scripts of some of the standard buttons we have used (see if you can guess which script corresponds to which icon). They illustrate both the language and the format of all HyperCard scripts. Each script tells HyperCard two things.

```
on mouseUp          on mouseUp          on mouseUp          on mouseUp
   go to prev card     go to next card      go Home             go to stack "Æ Home"
end mouseUp         end mouseUp         end mouseUp         end mouseUp
```

The line (or lines—there may be many) between the "on" and "end" tell HyperCard which actions to perform. Each action line begins with a HyperCard command that describes the effect of that particular command. For example, "go" tells HyperCard to move to and display another card, which is then to be regarded as the current card. The word appearing after "on" and "end" ("mouseUp" in each of these cases) tells Hypercard when—in response to which event or condition—the actions should be performed. Thus, each of our standard buttons tells HyperCard—by means of its associated script—to go to a different card when the mouse is clicked on it.

"Next", "prev", and "card" are special HyperTalk words. You can also refer to the "first" and "last" cards of the current stack, and to the "recent" card—the last card viewed from any stack. Cards can also be referred to by name, number, or ID number. If a card was named "Directory", you could tell HyperCard to go to card "Directory", as long as that card was in the current stack. To transfer control to another stack, use the HyperTalk word "stack." Clicking on our Æ Home button, HyperCard will move to the first card of that stack. To transfer to a particular card (with ID 6547) in another stack (named "TestStack"), tell HyperCard to "go to card ID 6547 of stack TestStack."

If simple navigation commands were all that could be accomplished in HyperTalk, programming would not extend the repertoire of HyperCard at all. In fact, HyperTalk has a catalog of conditions and actions that can be used in composing very sophisticated scripts and that form the bulk of the language. The parts of the language that we will describe in this module are illustrated in the stack No Account (see Figure 4.1) on your disk.

FIGURE 4.1   The No Account Stack

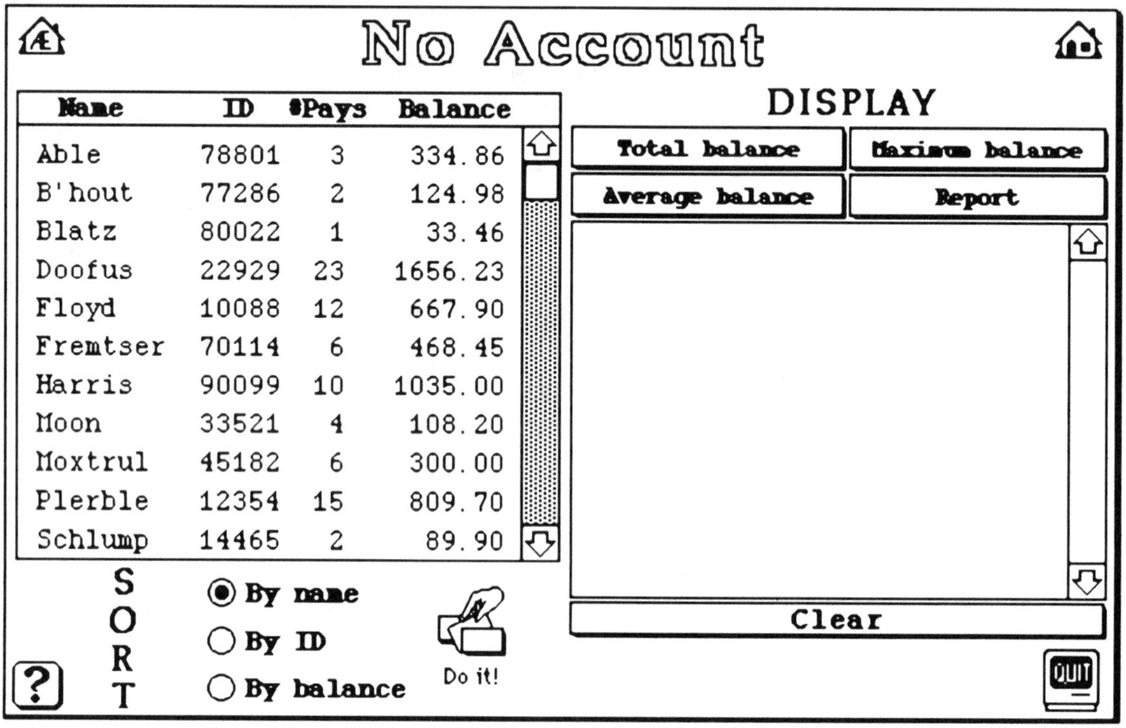

The No Account stack contains one card with two fields. The leftmost field, named "Data," contains a series of lines providing account information. Each line contains four values—a customer name, an account ID, an integer indicating the number of remaining payments, and a balance. Values on a line are necessarily separated by blanks (you'll see why shortly), and lines end with a return. The field to the right is named "Results" because this is where the results of calculations are displayed. Three of the four Display buttons (Total, Average, and Maximum balance) perform the calculations described. Clicking Report issues a brief report of the number of accounts currently in the Data field and lists explicitly those accounts with large outstanding balances (over $1000). Sorting can be performed by name, ID, or balance, as indicated by the radio buttons on the left, and is accomplished by clicking the Do it! button. The Clear button empties the Results field. The standard Æ buttons are provided for help, going to Æ or HyperCard Home, and for quitting HyperCard.

Your job is to explore all the scripts in the No Account stack. In order to do so, your user level must be set to Scripting. As usual, we have fixed No Account so that it assumes its users are scriptors. The only—but significant—difference between user levels 4 (authoring) and 5 (scripting) is that as scriptors we are privy to the scripts that underlie the HyperCard objects we define as authors.

We will review the scripts for each of No Account's buttons, beginning with the simpler ones and building to the more complex (which do you think is which?). To view these, you must first choose the Button tool. Then, select the button you want to look at. Choose Button Info... from the Objects menu, and click on the Script button, which is now highlighted and available for selection. Alternatively, you can double-click a button to get its information box immediately. Better still, if you hold the shift key down while double-clicking a button (with the button tool chosen), you get directly to the button's script.

LAB EXERCISE 1

1.1 Open stack No Account.

1.2 Save a copy of No Account that you can use for the remainder of these exercises.

1.3 Open your copy of No Account and test out each button, recording in English what happens when the mouse is clicked on it.

1.4 Look at the script for each button to see how and why it performs as it does.

1.5 Familiarize yourself with the section of the Appendix that is devoted to the HyperTalk programming language. In it are descriptions of every HyperTalk command that you will encounter in the No Account stack, or any of the Æ stacks that you will use in subsequent lab modules.

Whereas the scripts for the Home buttons contain standard navigation-type commands, those for the Clear and Quit buttons have nothing to do with changing the current card or stack. Rather, they perform tasks of interest to No Account.

```
--script for button "Quitter"
on mouseUp
    answer "Quit HyperCard now?" with "Yes" or "Cancel"
    if it is "Yes" then
        send closeStack to this stack
```

```
      visual effect iris close
         doMenu Quit HyperCard
      end if
   end mouseUp

   --script for button "Clear" on mouseUp
      --clears and scrolls to the top of field "Results"
      put empty into card field "Results"
      set the scroll of card field "Results" to 0
   end mouseUp
```

> The doMenu command, followed by the name of a menu item (in quotes), causes that menu item's action to be performed.

The script of the Quit button is interesting in that it demonstrates one of HyperTalk's more distinctive features—the ability to invoke menu commands from within a script. The doMenu command can be used to make any HyperCard object perform as if it had somehow reached up and chosen one of HyperCard's menu commands. In this case, clicking on the Quit button has the identical effect of choosing Quit HyperCard from the File menu. (Notice that because all menu commands are identified by unique names, there is no need to specify which menu is being referenced.) The doMenu command can be followed by any HyperCard menu item (exactly as it appears on the menu) to initiate the menu command from within a script.

The Clear button is more directly related to the mission of the No Account stack than any other button. Clicking on it causes nothing (empty) to appear in the "Results" field. The put command accomplishes this operation directly. Note that since put is followed by into (as opposed to before or after, which are also legal), the contents of "Results", in this case, are completely replaced by empty.

Buttons are distinct among stack objects in that—in order for them to serve any purpose—they must have scripts that tell HyperCard which actions to perform when they are clicked. Other stack objects can, and often do, have scripts of their own.

Look, for example, at the script associated with the No Account stack itself (to view this from within No Account, click on Script... in the Stack Info... dialog box). Notice that it contains two sets of instructions*—one to respond to the stack being opened, the other responding to the stack being closed. Upon being closed, the stack automatically compacts itself using the menu command Compact Stack. (This is done in the interest of conserving disk space.)

```
on openStack
   global oldUserLevel
   --save the previous user level
   put the user level into oldUserLevel
   hide the message box
```

---

* These are called "message handlers," for reasons that will become clear by the end of this module.

```
      set the user level to 5
      reset menuBar
      show menuBar
      go first
   end openStack

   on closeStack
      global oldUserLevel
      reset menuBar
      if (freesize of this stack) > (0.1*(size of this stack)) then set user level to 5
         doMenu Compact Stack
      end if
      --reset user level to what it was upon opening stack
      set the user level to oldUserLevel
   end closeStack
```

> The hide command, followed by the name of an object, makes that object invisible. The show command makes the object visible.

Upon opening, the Message box is hidden (hide causes the object in question to be invisible—but still there!), and the menu bar is shown so that you will have access to the menus (-show does the opposite of hide).

Also, you can see how we have managed in this and other stacks to set your user level for you, using the set command within a script. Any object property (such as its location, visibility, name, and style) can be set in this manner.

Cards, too, can have scripts. It is common, for example, to have actions performed automatically when a card is opened (becomes the current card) or closed (is no longer current). The script for the one and only card of stack No Account reflects this. When that card is opened, the "helper" field is made invisible using the hide command.

```
   on openCard
      hide card field "helper"
   end openCard
```

> Otherwise HyperCard couldn't tell whether a mouse click was supposed to activate the field's script or position the text insertion pointer.

Even fields can have scripts. Fields can respond to being opened (clicked within) or closed (clicked outside of after being open) using, respectively, openField and closeField conditions. Also, fields can be made to act like buttons—they can be programmed to be responsive to mouse clicks within their boundaries. To do so requires two steps: (1) the script for the field must contain an "on mouseUp" clause, like the one displayed below, and (2) the field must be defined so that its text is locked—that is, it can be read, but not changed by a user. A field's text can be locked by clicking in the Lock Text button of its Field Info... dialog box or can be locked directly from within a script by setting its lockText property to true. Both operations accomplish the identical effect.

```
   on mouseUp
      hide card field "helper"
   end mouseUp
```

Performing a Hyper-
Talk command from
within the Message
box.

A brief note about the Message box: We have had little occasion to use it so far, but the Message box is particularly useful to HyperCard programmers. Any HyperTalk command can be typed directly into the message box and, once the Enter key is hit, HyperCard will execute the command immediately. Similarly, conditions can be entered to see how stack objects respond to them. For example, if you want to test how your program will respond to an openStack message, just type openStack followed by the enter key into the Message box.

Note that all of HyperCard's basic text editing features can be used to enter and modify scripts. Indeed, the menus that are available to you when a script window is open provide you with commands to cut, copy, paste, search, and print scripts.

Æ LAB

LAB EXERCISE 2

2.1 Open your copy of No Account.

2.2 Modify it so that every time the stack is opened, the help message associated with button Help is displayed.

2.3 Test out your modifications using the Message box.

4.3   INFORMATION: APPLES, HONEY, AND FLOUR

One need only look at the recipe in Figure 4.2 and then back at the scripts above to see the similarity between programming and cooking. So striking is the analogy that programs have been described in many contexts as recipes that the computer follows to accomplish its processing. Just as there is a notation for describing culinary recipes (accepted abbreviations, terminology for units of measure), there are notations (programming languages) for describing programs. Each type of notation relies on a predefined set of operations to express the desired processing. Each allows for operations to be controlled in the sense that they can be performed in a prescribed order, under certain conditions, or repeatedly. Further, each notation, as we shall see, provides a means for defining and referencing higher-level operations.

Prior to performing the operations described in either a program or a recipe, one needs to know the "ingredients" to be used. In most recipes (and, in fact, in many programming languages—though not HyperTalk), the ingredients are listed explicitly and in great detail at the head of the

| FIGURE 4.2 | Rick and Stu's Deep Dish Apple Pie |

Ingredients

1-1/2 c. quartered apples, peeled and cored
1/2 c. honey
1-1/2 tsp. lemon juice
1/4 cup unbleached white flour
1-1/2 tsp. cinnamon
1-1/2 tbsp. butter

Place apples in bowl.
Toss with flour and cinnamon until covered.
Follow procedure for Rick and Stu's Flaky Pie Crust.
Place bottom portion of crust into 2-inch deep baking dish (either 8-inch round or 6-inch × 10-inch rectangle).
Arrange apple mixture in baking dish.
Blend honey and lemon juice in a cup.
Dribble cup contents over apple mixture.
Dot with butter.
Cover apple mixture with top portion of crust.
Bake at 425 degrees for 40 minutes, or until top is golden brown.

recipe. All operations make reference to and use these ingredients. At various points in the cooking process, ingredients are stored in containers and combined with other ingredients for intermediate combinations, which can then be referred to collectively in subsequent steps.

The basic ingredients of a program are the pieces of information it processes. Information can be simple, like numbers, characters, or words (or, even more abstractly, names, account IDs, and balances). Like the contents of a kitchen pantry, simple information can be saved in containers (called fields and variables), combined, and referenced collectively as a unit or as individual constituents.

SIMPLE INFORMATION

The simplest types of information that can be represented in a programming language dictate to a great degree the types of programs that can be written. Since computers began as calculating machines, it comes as no surprise that virtually all programming languages* include the ability to represent nu-

---

* We say *virtually* all only out of a sense of caution. In fact, we can't think of any programming language that doesn't include numbers of some form or another. Given the scores of languages that have been invented, though, there might be some nonnumeric language lurking out there that we haven't heard of (though we doubt it).

Representing numbers in HyperTalk.

meric information. HyperTalk is no exception: We can use *integers* such as 0, 13, −67, and *5625514324444423332898400099999*, and *real numbers* such as 0.3, 13.0, and *4555243.0000000087771092882887326625533*. Numbers in HyperTalk must be represented without spaces, commas, or any other nondigits except an optional minus sign at the left and a single decimal point anywhere in the string of digits. The programming metaphor enters here, in that the numbers available in a programming language are not precisely what we think of when we think of numbers. HyperTalk is more flexible than many languages, in that a number may have as many as 73 digits (72 for negative numbers, to allow for the minus sign), while many other popular languages limit numbers to five digits or so. However, since computers are finite machines, there will always be numbers such as the square root of 2 that, because they would require infinitely many digits to be represented precisely in memory, can only be represented approximately in any programming language.

Another difference between HyperTalk and many other programming languages is that HyperTalk makes little distinction between integers and real numbers. Languages such as Pascal and C, in contrast, consider integers and reals as separate *types* and permit only limited mixing of objects of different types (in arithmetic expressions, for instance). While this "strong typing" of information reduces the chance of a programmer requesting something impossible (like referring to the third-and-a-half-th item in a list), it also reduces the flexibility of the language. There are other types of numeric information besides integers and reals, as you may know. For instance, FORTRAN, a programming language designed to facilitate scientific and engineering computation, can represent and manipulate *complex* numbers such as $5.8 + 45.6\sqrt{-1}$.

Many of the common uses of computers stem from the ability of programming languages to represent *strings* of characters, such as "Hi there!"

Representing strings of characters.

and "THIS IS A VERY LONG STRING, CONSISTING OF MANY CAPITAL LETTERS AND BLANKS, SEPARATED BY COMMAS," and even "•~∂→ÇΩ°...æ¿Ù§‰!á≫." Strings in HyperTalk consist of any collection of characters enclosed in quotation marks (so that HyperTalk can distinguish between strings and other objects in a script). Again, HyperTalk is more flexible here than are many other languages, since HyperTalk strings have an effective maximum length of 32,767 characters. A string in HyperTalk can consist of any characters whatsoever, except quotation marks (do you see why?).*

---

* Some characters, such as the return character (which you generate by pressing the Return key on the keyboard), cannot simply be typed into a string, but rather require a somewhat complicated series of steps to be included. This distinction will not concern us here, since we'll simply avoid typing return characters as part of strings.

As do many other languages, HyperTalk also recognizes the *boolean* values *true* and *false* and can manipulate them in logical expressions, in much the same way as we will see numeric information can be manipulated in arithmetic expressions.

> The boolean values true **and** false.

The script of the Total balance button from our No Account stack contains examples of HyperTalk integers (0,1, and 4) and character strings ("OK, I will" and "Total balance = $").

```
on mouseUp

    --first, check to make sure there is data
    if card field "Data" is empty then answer "Enter data before calculating or
    sorting" with "OK, I will"

    else

        --initialize a counter variable
        put 0 into totalSoFar

        --go line-by-line through the data field, adding up balances
        repeat with count = 1 to number of lines of card field "Data"
            add word 4 of line count of card field "Data" to totalSoFar
        end repeat

        --display the result
        put "Total balance = $" & totalSoFar into card field "Results"
        set the scroll of card field "Results" to 0
    end if
end mouseUp
```

> Variables, like fields, are containers for information. Unlike fields, you can't see them on the screen.

An important feature of HyperTalk and other high-level programming languages is that, in addition to representing information explicitly, information can also be represented symbolically, by name. If, for instance, we want to add a collection of numbers, we might decide to keep the running sum in a variable named totalSoFar. A variable—a name used to reference information—can be as long as you wish in HyperTalk, as long as (1) it begins with a letter that is (2) optionally followed by any combination of letters, digits, or the underscore character (the underscore is generated by the shift-hyphen combination), and (3) it cannot be the same as HyperTalk *reserved words*—words such as get and repeat, which have special meanings in HyperTalk. Thus, x, line_count, word3, and Convert2decimal are legal HyperTalk variable names, but line count, word3+, and 2decimal are not. Finally, variables in HyperTalk are *case insensitive*—for example, HyperTalk considers MYSUM, MySum, and mysum to refer to the same variable.

STRUCTURED INFORMATION

Variables are typically used to store one value at a time. In fact, if variables were our only means for referencing information, it would be awkward, if not downright impossible, to write many conceptually simple recipes and programs. What, for example, would our recipe look like if we could not refer to the "apple mixture," but instead had to reiterate its basic ingredients every time we wished to refer to the collection? Worse still, imagine the recipe if we could not simply refer to the "crust."

We encounter similar problems in trying to write a program to add a list of 100 numbers; one approach would be to store each number in a separate variable and to write the program in terms of the 100 names chosen for the variables. Imagine that we had chosen the names numberList1, numberList2, . . . , numberList100 to refer to our numbers. Try writing down, in English, a sequence of steps that would accomplish the adding of those numbers. Go ahead, we'll wait. . . .

*   *   *

Even thinking about the adding task in these terms is unnatural. If you went to the trouble of describing a method of adding, you probably resorted to using phrases like "the first number in the list," "the next number in the list," and "the start of the list"—that is, you referred to the values to be added as parts of a composite structure.

Most programming languages afford programmers some means for describing and referencing collections of information. Many allow programmers to define *arrays* (fixed-size lists of a single type of value, with individual elements referenced by their position in the list—for example, numberList[1], numberList[100]) and *records* (collections of different types of values, such as a customer's account record, containing a person's name in string format, an account ID in integer form, and a real number indicating an account balance). *Pointers* are often provided to create lists of arbitrary length and organization.

These facilities can be combined to describe a full range of complex structures. For example, one can define an array with records as its elements (such as a list of account records). Similarly, a record can have as one of its values an array (add to our account record a list of the last ten transactions on the account). Records can contain pointers to other records to indicate logical connections between them or just to organize a collection or records. Also, elements of arrays can themselves be arrays, thus creating multidimensional tables of information. We will have much more to say about these structured types of information in Module 5, when we discuss their use in programming languages other than HyperTalk.

> HyperCard fields can contain many simple data values, separated by returns, spaces, or tabs.

One of the notational advantages of HyperTalk is that HyperCard fields can be used to represent any of these composite structures. Fields are composed of *lines,* which end with return characters. Lines, in turn, can be defined to contain *items* (any string of characters between commas), *words* (which are separated by blanks), or *characters*. A single field can be accessed using any of these units in any sensible combination.

Imagine that (this should be easy) field "Data" of a particular card is used for storing some account records. Field "Data" could look like that pictured in Figure 4.3. This field can be *chunked*—that is, described in terms of its component pieces (chunks) of information—to retrieve almost any combination of its values. The following table shows how we could use HyperTalk to reference different chunks of card field "Data."

CHUNK	HYPERTALK DESCRIPTION
all of Able's account	line 1 of card field "Data"
the name of the fourth account	word 1 of line 4 of card field "Data"
Floyd's account ID	word 2 of line 5 of card field "Data"
the first character of the name of the eighth account	char 1 of word 1 of line 8 of card field "Data"
the first two accounts	line 1 to 2 of card field "Data"
the last three digits of Blatz's account ID	char 3 to 5 of word 2 of line 3 of card field "Data"
all balances in the field	word 4 of line i of card field "Data", where i varies from 1 to 13

> Chunks of information in a field.

Notice how, in general, chunks are described from small to large. That is, the description begins with the smallest unit involved in the chunk and proceeds to the largest. (For example, to reference the last three digits of Blatz's account ID, the HyperTalk description begins with the characters in-

FIGURE 4.3   A Sample HyperCard Field

Able	78801	3	334.86
B'hout	77286	2	124.98
Blatz	80022	1	33.46
Doofus	22929	23	1656.23
Floyd	10088	12	667.90
Fremtser	70114	6	468.45
Harris	90099	10	1035.00
Moon	33521	4	108.20
Moxtrul	45182	6	300.00
Plerble	12354	15	809.70
Schlump	14465	2	89.90
Smortz	30287	7	770.84
Zogg	45632	3	342.87

volved and then lists the word, line, and field, in that order.) This example also demonstrates how chunks can be described as arbitrary ranges of characters, words, or lines. Notice, too, how variables can be used, as in the last example of the table, to help in specifying any value in any chunk. Finally, note that this fine control in accessing elements of fields does not cost us anything (aside from a slightly verbose notation). That is, we can still refer to and perform operations on the field as a whole. Also, fields have the flexibility of being of arbitrary length. That is, no matter what a field's size is on the screen, you can always add information to any line, or you can add lines to the field. Even if this new information is not visible on the screen, it is part of the field and can be used by and referenced from within scripts.

REVIEW QUESTIONS

1. What are the simple (that is, nonstructured) types of information available within HyperTalk?

2. Which of the following are legal HyperTalk variable names? For those that are illegal, tell which rule they violate.

   AVariable, the sum, C3PO, 4ScoreAnd7, line, twenty_two, dollar$_and_ ¢ents.

3. Define the following: char, item, line, word.

4. Refer to the definitions of *line* and *item*. Can a word be divided into items? That is, is it legal to refer to "item 2 of word 3" of a field? Can an item be divided into words?

4.4   INFORMATION PROCESSING: TOSS, BLEND, AND DRIBBLE

> A command is an instruction for HyperCard to perform some action.

> put *source* into *destination* places a copy of the *source* information into the *destination* location.

Implicit in every recipe is the assumption that the person doing the cooking is familiar with a somewhat standard repertoire of actions (or commands) that can be carried out. These commands define the cook's ability to manipulate ingredients. Notice that every line of the instruction section of our recipe begins with such a command. HyperTalk provides a particularly rich set of commands that allows programmers to describe virtually any kind of information processing.

MOVING INFORMATION

The put command is HyperTalk's basic means for moving information. This command takes a *source* expression and a *destination* location, and copies the source into the destination. For example,

```
put 0 into totalSoFar
```

will place the number 0 in the variable totalSoFar, replacing whatever was stored in totalSoFar. In a similar way,

> put empty into card field "Results"

will replace the contents of card field "Results" with empty, destroying what was previously stored there. Look at the other instances of the put command that occur in the No Account button scripts. Notice that the source in each case can be any expression that yields a value, while the destination must be a *container*—somewhere information can reside. In other words, put totalSoFar into 0 would be an illegal command, since 0 is a constant rather than a place where information can be stored. Notice, too, that we refer to a *card* field in our example. Since the usual location for a field in HyperCard is on the background, we must specify those fields that are associated with cards.

> HyperTalk assumes that *field* refers to a background field, unless prefaced with the word *card*. Similarly, HyperTalk assumes that *button* refers to a card button, unless prefaced with the word *background*.

A simple variant of the put command, one in which no destination is specified, can be used to place values into HyperCard's Message box. For example,

> put line 1 of card field "Data"
> put totalSoFar

These commands, like most HyperTalk commands, can be issued either directly from the Message box itself or from within a script, and will prove very useful in the lab exercises to follow.

> A put command with no destination specified puts the value of its source expression into the Message box.

MANIPULATING INFORMATION

Numeric commands and operators.

HyperTalk provides many commands for manipulating numeric, boolean, and string types of information. The numeric commands include the common arithmetic commands add, subtract, multiply, and divide, as well as their operator forms +, -, *, and /. Complicated arithmetic expressions can be built using parentheses to group subexpressions. These arithmetic commands and operators act just as you would expect and can be combined with other commands as well. Here are some sample arithmetic expressions, the last two of which come from the No Account scripts:

```
add 1 to sum
--increase sum by 1

put x + 3 into field "holder"
--background field "holder" gets value of x plus 3

subtract sum from sum
--silly command; sets sum to 0

multiply sum by 1.1
--replace sum's value by 1.1 times old value

put 3.6* (sum + 5/(x + 2)) into field "holder"
--arithmetic expressions can be as complex as you want

add (word 4 of line count of card field "Data") to totalSoFar
--chunks of information can be used in calculations

put sum/num into average
divide sum by num
--two ways to calculate the average balance
```

> **Comments in a script begin with two hyphens and are ignored by Hyper-Card.**

We have written these statements as they would appear in HyperTalk scripts. Notice the double hyphens: They mark the beginning of *comments*. Comments serve no HyperTalk purpose; they are provided solely for the convenience of the people reading the script. So, paradoxically, they are the most useful and common parts of HyperTalk scripts, in spite of the fact that HyperTalk ignores them.

> **Continuing a line in a script.**

While we're on the subject of how HyperTalk programs look, one more feature must be mentioned. As you may have noticed by now, HyperTalk statements tend to be wordy. If a statement is too long to fit on a single line, you can break it by including the ¬ *line continuation symbol* (Option-Return key combination) before the break to produce a statement like this, for example:

```
answer "Enter data before calculating or sorting" ¬
    with "OK, I will"
```

The only restriction on the use of line continuations is that you cannot break meaningful HyperTalk units across a line, as would happen if you tried to continue the line between the *n* and *t* characters of the word *into* or if you tried to introduce a continuation within a string.

The Option-Return key combination breaks a statement over one or more lines.

In addition to the arithmetic commands and operators, HyperTalk includes a wealth of arithmetic functions. A *function* in HyperTalk is represented by a name that instructs HyperTalk to go to the function's script (which, for each of the functions HyperTalk provides us, is already written), do whatever it says, and return a value to be placed where the original name was found. Examples of HyperTalk arithmetic functions include round (for rounding a number to the closest whole), random (for producing a random number in a specified range), and sqrt (for calculating square roots). We'll talk more about HyperTalk functions in the next section. For now, it's enough to think of functions as being replaced by whatever value they compute. Other HyperTalk functions are described in the Appendix.

> **Operating on strings.**

HyperTalk also includes several operators and functions on string type values (including chunks, because HyperTalk stores information in fields as strings of characters). The & operator *concatenates* strings, attaching the end of the first to the beginning of the second to produce another string. For example, if the variable totalSoFar had the value 4094.76, the command

    put "Total balance = $" & totalSoFar into card field "Results"

would result in the string "Total balance = $4094.76" being stored in the "Result" field. There is a variant of the concatenation operator, &&, which concatenates with a blank between, so

    put "Max balance = S" & value && "For" && word 1 of line where ¬
    of card field "Data" into card field "Results"

would result in storing a string like "Max balance = $1656.30 for Doofus" in the field "Results".

> **The number function.**

HyperTalk includes string functions as well, such as length (*string*), which returns the number of characters, including spaces, tabs, and return characters, in the variable *string*. Another function that has already proven useful to us is number of *chunks* in *source*. This counts the number of chunks of the kind specified in the text *source*, so when we say, in the Avg. balance script,

    put number of lines of card field "Data" into num

the variable num assumes the value 13. Note, by the way, that the words *in* and *of* are interchangeable in chunk descriptions.

In addition to numeric and string operations, HyperTalk can operate on the boolean values *true* and *false*. HyperTalk includes boolean operators =, ≠, <, ≤, >, and ≥, which can be used to compare expressions of the same type for equality, inequality, or size, and operators and, or, and not to combine boolean expressions as follows:

OPERATOR	ACTION
$op1 = op2$	*true* when $op1$ and $op2$ have the same value
$op1 \neq op2$	*true* when $op1$ and $op2$ have different values ($\neq$ is Option-=; can also be written < >)
$op1 < op2$	*true* when $op1$ is less than $op2$

continues

OPERATOR	ACTION
$op1 \leq op2$	*true* when $op1$ is less than or equal to $op2$ ($\leq$ is Option-<; can also be written < =)
$op1 > op2$	*true* when $op1$ is greater than $op2$
$op1 \geq op2$	*true* when $op1$ is greater than or equal to $op2$ ($\geq$ is option->; can also be written >=)

(These last three require $op1$ and $op2$ to be boolean.)

$op1$ and $op2$	*true* when $op1$ and $op2$ are *true*
$op1$ or $op2$	*true* when either $op1$ or $op2$ or both are *true*
not $op1$	*true* when $op1$ is *false*

These boolean operators can be combined to any complexity you wish. Note that none of the expressions below are HyperTalk statements themselves—they would appear as *parts* of commands in the scripts of No Account.

```
word 4 of line theLine of card field "Data"  > maximumValue
   --from Maximum balance
word 4 of thisLine > 1000   --from Report
buttonNum = counter   --from No Account's background script
not (the visible of card field "helper")   --from button Helper
```

This last example of a boolean operation is particularly interesting for a couple of reasons. First, notice the use of parentheses. Parentheses can be included in any HyperTalk expression. In the above case, they are included merely for clarification—they make explicit what the logical operator not applies to. In other instances, parentheses are used to resolve ambiguities in complex expressions. For example, 3 + 4*5 could be interpreted as either 35 (add first, then multiply), or 23 (multiply first). HyperTalk has its own *precedence rules* that specify how to evaluate such expressions (it would produce 23), which it resorts to when complex expressions are left unparenthesized. If you, as a programmer, want to dictate the order of evaluation (say, to produce 35), include parentheses, like (3 + 4)*5.

The not expression from the helper script also illustrates HyperTalk's **set** command, which we mentioned briefly earlier in this module (see No Account's stack script). All Hyper Card objects (stacks, backgrounds, cards, buttons, and fields) have properties associated with them. You saw and experimented with many properties in Module 3 when you defined cards, buttons, and fields of your own. For example, buttons have name, ID, location, style, showName, and autoHilite properties that we set when we create a button and we modify when we change the button in some way. Many of these properties can be set from within the Button Info... dialog

Object properties and the set command.

box. Similarly, some of a field's properties (its name, style, font, and so on) can be defined via a Field Info... dialog. All properties of all objects can be accessed (using the HyperTalk get command) and set (using the set command) from within scripts.

Visibility is in fact a boolean property of every button and field. That is, every button and field has a visible property that is either true or false, dictating whether or not the object can be seen on the screen. The hide command is just a shorthand notation for setting the visible property of an object to false. The two commands

```
hide card field "helper"
set visible of card field "helper" to false
```

have the identical effect.

In the case of our "helper" button, each time it is clicked we want it to reverse the visibility of the helper field. If the field is visible, it should become invisible when the button is clicked, and vice versa. The logical not operation used in conjunction with the set command accomplishes exactly this behavior. The button's script sets the field's visible property to the logical inverse of the field's visible property.

REVIEW QUESTIONS

1. In the statement put sum into field "Holder" where does the field reside?
2. Evaluate the following expressions. You may assume angle contains 17.9, limit contains 3, and result contains *true*.
   ```
   limit + 4 * angle
   1.1* average(limit, sum, sum - 2 * limit)
   sqrt(round(abs(7.7 - angle)))
   (result or (limit > 3)) and (not(exp2(limit + 1) ≤ angle))
   ```
3. What is the difference between + and add?
4. For the field illustrated in Figure 4.3, what expression would you use to find the number of letters in the name of the person on line 3?
5. How do you extend a HyperTalk statement over more than one line?

LAB EXERCISE 3

3.1 Open stack No Account.

3.2 Open the Message box.

3.3 For each of the following expressions, write down how you think HyperCard will evaluate the expression. Then, enter put commands into the

Message box, which cause HyperCard to evaluate them and compare the results with your predictions:

line 5 of card field "Data"
word 1 of line 7 of card field "Data"
char 4 to 5 of word 2 of line 1 of card field "Data"
word 2 of line 2 of card field "Data"
item 2 of line 2 of card field "Data"
word 5 of line 2 of card field "Data"

3.4 Define HyperTalk expressions corresponding to the following pieces of information from field "Data". Use the Message box to see if your expressions retrieve the expected information.

Able's balance
Doofus's account ID
the name of the holder of account ID 45182
the first 2 characters of Schlump's account ID

3.5 Record your evaluations of the following expressions. Then, see how HyperCard's evaluations compare to yours.

8 + 4 * 7
(8 + 4) * 7
8 + 4 * 7/7
((8 + 4) * 7)/7
the number of lines of card field "Data"
the length of word 1 of line 2 of card field "Data"
the visible of card field "Results"
the visible of card field "helper"
the name of card button 1

4.5   LOCAL CONTROL: UNTIL GOLDEN BROWN

Does it matter in our recipe if one dots the apple mixture with butter before arranging the apples in the baking dish? What if you dribble the cup contents over the apple mixture before blending the honey and lemon in the cup? Of course, the linear order of the operations is important; that's why we write them down that way! Similarly, we write commands within each part of a script in the order that we want them carried out. This type of implicit control works well in both contexts partly because it reflects how cooks and computers assume they are to carry out instructions—linearly. When there is a need to perform operations in nonlinear ways, we must resort to explicit indications of control.

This is the role of the phrases "until covered," "either . . . or," or "until golden brown" in our recipe. They are not operations themselves. Nor are they ingredients. Rather, they indicate that the operations to which they refer are being conditionally qualified. The scripts we have seen contain similar phrases (like "repeat," "until," and "if . . . then"), which control the logical flow of the commands in a script. When combined with linear ordering, these *control structures* help us to express a full range of complex processing tasks.

Consider, for example, the processing to be accomplished by the Total balance button of stack No Account. What we need is a script that will add the balances (word 4) of each line. Knowing what we do now about Hyper-Talk, we could approach the problem as follows. We can use a variable (count), initially containing 1, to keep track of which line in field "Data" we are about to add to the running sum of balances (also a variable, totalSoFar). If you think about the problem a bit, you'll see that we could attach a list of instructions to the button that will do the following whenever the button is pressed:

1. Add the fourth word (the balance) of the current line of field 1 to the running sum in field 2.

2. Increment the invisible field 3 by one to obtain the number of the line we'll get when the Add button is next pressed.

That's not hard—the HyperTalk commands would look like this:

```
put card field 3 into num
--get the current line number, stored in field 3
--(num is used just to save typing time)
add item 3 of line num of card field 1 to card field 2
--get the balance from the current line and add it
--to the running sum in field 2
add 1 to card field 3
 --add 1 to line number to prepare for next button press
```

That wasn't too bad, was it? Well, it wasn't too good either. Thinking of this card as an application, as we did in Module 3, we can see that there are a number of shortcomings as far as the user is concerned. First, the routine requires the user to know the number of lines in field 1. Set up as it was in the example, that's not too hard—a quick count shows that there are thirteen lines—but this would be a real bother if field "Data" had several hundred lines. Also, the user must not only keep track of the current line, but must press the button once for each line. Surely there must be a way to automate this process, letting HyperTalk keep track of the lines and do the addition without any intervention on the user's part.

Unfortunately, there isn't any easy way, knowing just what we do now. We could write a script that would look in part like this:

```
put word 4 of line 1 of card field "Data" into totalSoFar
--totalSoFar must have a value before we can add something to it!
add word 4 of line 2 of card field "Data" to totalSoFar
add word 4 of line 3 of card field "Data" to totalSoFar
```

add word 4 of line 4 of card field "Data" to totalSoFar

.

.

.

add word 4 of line 12 of card field "Data" to totalSoFar
add word 4 of line 13 of card field "Data" to totalSoFar

But that would be rather tedious, not to mention the fact that we would have to rewrite our script every time we changed the number of lines in card field "Data". What we need is the ability to execute *conditionally* some parts of our script, like this:

1. Find out how many lines there are in card field "Data."
2. Set the current line number to 1 and the running sum to 0.
3. If the current line number is less than or equal to the total number of lines in card field 1, do steps a–c below; otherwise do step 4.
   a. Add item 3 in the current line to the running sum.
   b. Increase the current line number by 1.
   c. Go back to step 3.
4. Display the running sum, and stop.

With the addition of conditional and repetitive execution, we gain enormous flexibility in what our scripts can do. Programs also become much simpler to write and more general. No longer are we restricted to programs that look like this:

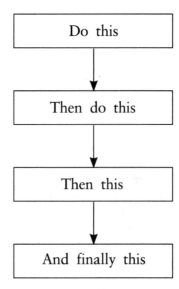

Rather, we can write programs like this:

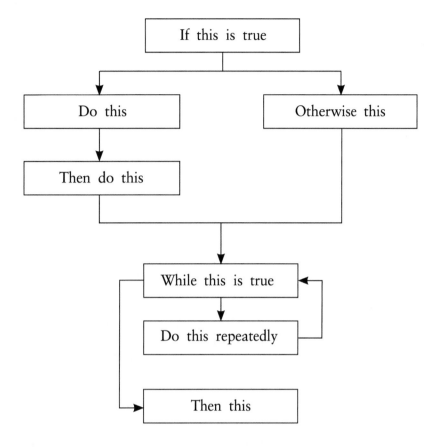

Indeed, this is very nearly the structure of our Total balance script. We begin by checking to see if there are any entries in field "Data" to be added. If there are not (the field is empty), an answer command* is executed that prompts the user of the stack to enter data. If there is account information to be processed, the balances are added repetitively to variable totalSoFar, and the resulting total is displayed in field "Results".

---

* HyperTalk's **answer** command acts like a control structure. The general form of the command is: **answer displayString with choice1 or choice2 or choice3**. When the command is executed, the value of displayString is presented in a standard Macintosh dialog box with buttons labelled as choice1, choice2, and choice3 (there may be from 1 to 3 choices; we need only one in the above example). The user must then click on one of the choice buttons for the program to continue.

Conditional execution using if.

The first control structure, wherein a condition is evaluated and different statements are executed based on the truth value of the condition, is represented in HyperTalk by the if structure. The if structure takes one of the following forms:

```
if boolean expression then
    statements
end if
```

or

```
if boolean expression then
    statements
else
    statements
end if
```

where *statements* can be any one or more HyperTalk statements. In the first form, the *boolean expression* is evaluated according to the rules described previously for determining the value of a boolean expression. If the result is *true*, the *statements* are executed in order, after which execution continues with the command following end if. If the *boolean expression* is *false*, however, the *statements* are not performed, and control passes directly to the statement after end if. An example of if occurs in the reportLargeOnes segment of the Report button script. The condition checked determines if one of the balances (word 4 of a certain line) is greater than 1000. If it is, a line is added (that's what put...after does) to field "Results". If the balance is not greater than 1000, no action is taken, and processing continues with the line after end if.

```
if word 4 of thisLine > 1000 then
    put (word 1 of thisLine) && (word 4 of thisLine) & return ¬
    after card field "Results"
end if
```

The if...else structure, used in each of the calculation button scripts to ensure that the data field contains entries that can be processed in a meaningful way, is an extension of the if structure. The *boolean expression* is evaluated; if it is *true*, the first group of *statements* (the answer command) is executed, and if it is *false*, the second group of *statements* (which performs the desired calculation) is done instead. In either case, when the statement group is completed (one or the other will be executed), control passes to the command after end if.

Repetitive execution using (what else?) repeat.

The HyperTalk equivalent of "until golden brown" is the repeat command, which has analogs in many other programming languages. This structure comes in five versions, only one of which is used in No Account. In all versions a group of statements is executed repeatedly until some condition is achieved. The versions differ in how the condition for terminating the repetition is expressed (see the Appendix). The repeat with structure, used in many of No Account's scripts, has the general form:

```
repeat with variable = start expression to finish expression
    statements
end repeat
```

Unlike the other forms of repeat, the repeat with structure is used when we know precisely how many times a group of statements is to be repeated. A repeat with command acts as follows:

1. The *start expression* and the *finish expression* are each evaluated once at the start and not modified thereafter.
2. *Variable* is set to *start expression.*
3. If *variable* is less than or equal to *finish expression,* steps a and b are performed, otherwise step 4.
    a. The *statements* are performed.
    b. The *variable* is increased by one and control passes to step 3 again.
4. Control is passed to the statement following end repeat.

The repeat with structure also gives us the advantage of a built-in "counter"—the variable in the command itself—which can be used in the statement part of a loop. The body of the Total Balance script can now look like:

```
repeat with count = 1 to number of lines in card field "Data"
    add word 4 of line count of card field "Data" to totalSoFar
end repeat
```

This is *much* nicer than our first attempt, for several reasons: (1)Hyper-Talk automatically keeps track of the current line number in the variable count; (2) the user only needs to press the button once; and (3) we no longer need to worry about changing our program to accommodate a change in the number of lines in the field (our script uses the number function to adjust itself accordingly). This is what good programming is all about, folks.

The script for button Average balance, below, should now make sense, as it has essentially the same structure as that of Total balance. The if-else structure is used to check whether or not field "Data" is empty. Within the else branch, a repeat-with structure is used to add the balances of all accounts. After doing so, and prior to displaying the average in field "Results", division is performed to calculate the average.

```
on mouseUp

    --first, check to make sure there is data
    if card field "Data" is empty then
```

```
        answer "Enter data before calculating or sorting" ¬
        with "OK, I will"

    else

        --initialize a counter variable
        put 0 into totalSoFar

        --this is for our convenience, so we don't have to write
        --"number of lines of card field "Data"" twice later
        put number of lines of card field "Data" into num

        --go line-by-line through the data field, adding up balances
        repeat with count = 1 to num
            add word 4 of line count of card field "Data" to totalSoFar
        end repeat

        set numberFormat to "0.##"
        --so that average will be rounded to two decimal places
        put totalSoFar/num into average

        --display the result
        put "Total balance of $" & totalSoFar && "for" && num && "accounts" & ¬
            return & return into card field "Results"
        put "Average balance = $" & average after card field "Results"
        set the scroll of card field "Results" to 0
    end if


    end mouseUp
```

You may have noticed that some of the variables used in Average balance are different from those in Total balance. In the averaging script, x (not count) is used for counting which line of the data field we are processing. In fact, we could have named these variables Rick and Stu, as long as we replaced occurrences consistently. That is the essence of variables. They are simply names that we use to store information. The names themselves have no more inherent meaning than the information (which is to say none). Meaning is derived from _our_ interpretations of the names and the values stored.

Finally, let's look at the script of the Maximum balance button. Whereas the basic structure of the script is the same as for the other calculate buttons, the details of the processing are slightly more complex. Take a minute to think about how you would do this, without worrying about the HyperTalk syntax, before you go on. As a hint, you might consider saving the largest value seen so far.

*   *   *

One way to think about this problem goes like this: "I'll inspect every word 4 in turn. At each step, if I find one that is larger than any I've seen so far, I'll replace the old maximum value with the new one." What, though, can we use for our initial maximum? Any ideas? What about starting with the first word 4 value? When we begin, that will certainly be the largest value we've seen so far. Now we're ready to write the routine. You may want to try it yourself first, before looking at the next paragraphs. Go ahead—cover the following answer and try it on your own.

*   *   *

Here's the way we did it. It's certainly not the only way, and not even the best—it's *a* way, though.

```
on mouseUp

   --check to make sure there is data
   if card field "Data" is empty then
      answer "Enter data before calculating or sorting"¬
      with "OK, I will"

   else
      --assume that the balance in line 1 is the maximum so far
      put 1 into whichLine
      put word 4 of line 1 of card field "Data" into maximumValue

      --starting at line 2, check to see if any balances are
      --higher than the current maximumValue
      repeat with theLine = 2 to the number of lines of card field "Data"
         if word 4 of line theLine of card field "Data" > maximumValue then
            put word 4 of line theLine of card field "Data" into maximumValue
            put theLine into whichLine
         end if
      end repeat

      --display the result
      put "Maximum balance = $" & maximumValue & return && "for" && ¬
         word 1 of line whichLine of card field "Data"¬
         into card field "Results"
      set the scroll of card field "Results" to 0
   end if

end mouseUp
```

Notice that two variables are used to remember the maximum value seen so far: maximumValue stores the balance itself (initially the balance from line 1), and whichLine stores the line number in which the maximum balance was found (initially 1). This is done so that the final put command can display not only the maximum balance, but also the name of the customer (word 1 of line whichLine) with that balance. Both of these variables are updated in the if structure within the repeat-with structure. As we proceed line by line through field "Data", word 4 of each line is checked to see if it is greater than variable value (the current maximum). If the balance we are now looking at is indeed the largest so far, it is stored in variable maximumValue and the current line number (variable theLine in the repeat structure) is saved in whichLine. Subsequent comparisons will then be made in terms of the new, larger balance. Note also that, because we begin processing with the assumption that the balance in line 1 is the largest, the repeat structure initializes its counter (theLine) to 2. There is, after all, no need to compare the balance in line 1 to itself.

REVIEW QUESTIONS

You can consider yourself a HyperTalk *sous-chef,* well along the road to mastery, if you can answer the following questions about the preceding program:

1. Why did we use the variable whichLine?
2. In the repeat-with loop,
    a. Why did we begin with theLine = 2 rather than 1?
    b. What would have happened if we had begun with theLine = 1?
3. What would be the result of changing > to < in the if structure?
4. How would we modify this routine to display the number of the line where the maximum was found, as well as the maximum value?
5. Why did we say that our solution was not the best one? Think of the principles of good design discussed in Module 3, in particular, and describe what circumstances would cause our routine to fail.

LAB EXERCISE 4

4.1 Open your copy of stack No Account.
4.2 Create a new button that calculates and displays in field "Results" the name and account ID of the account with the minimum balance. Test the button. [*Hint:* You may want to start by copying and pasting button Maximum balance.]
4.3 Edit the script of button Average balance so that after calculating and displaying the average balance, it then determines and displays (a) the number of accounts with greater than average balances, and (b) the number of accounts with less than average balances.

4.6 UNIT-LEVEL CONTROL: RICK AND STU'S FLAKY PIE CRUST

You have already seen that the basic HyperCard objects are buttons, fields, cards, backgrounds, and stacks. *Every* HyperCard object has a script associated with it (although some scripts may be empty), and it is these scripts that describe the actions a HyperCard stack performs. So far, we have described some of the commands that can make up a script, but as yet we haven't explained what scripts are or how they work.

HyperCard is different from most applications, and this difference is a reflection of the way the Macintosh was designed. The Mac (and a typical program for the Mac, such as HyperCard) was designed from the beginning to subordinate itself to the user, rather than forcing the user to adapt his or her actions to a program. In the jargon, good Macintosh programs are *event driven,* in that a Mac program will wait for the user to initiate an "event," such as a mouse click or key press, and initiate its response according to the event. For example, a traditional program on a traditional computer might display the line

        ENTER AN INTEGER >

and do nothing (except perhaps sound an error beep) until an integer was entered. But a program that adheres to the Macintosh design philosophy is ready to handle a menu choice, selection of a desk accessory, or a click in another window, as well as reacting to the user typing in an integer.

MESSAGES AND HANDLERS

In keeping with the Mac's design philosophy, HyperCard stacks are not like programs in most other languages. The functionality of a HyperCard stack does not reside in a single list of instructions, but rather is spread among the various objects that comprise a stack. Each object has a separate program—its script—associated with it, and objects communicate with each other by *messages.* Messages can be initiated by a user-instigated event, such as a mouse click, or can be initiated by any HyperCard object. Each object's script may have a collection of *message handlers,* each designed to take action upon receipt of a particular message.

> A message is sent to an object, where the object's script may or may not have a handler to respond to the message.

Consider the simple example of a button that is designed to sound a beep when it is clicked. HyperCard constantly monitors events, and if nothing is happening, it sends an idle message. When the mouse is clicked within a button, HyperCard responds to this event by interrupting the stream of idle messages with two new messages: mouseDown, when the user presses the mouse button, and mouseUp, when the user releases the mouse button. These messages are sent to the object—the button, in this case—that was under the mouse pointer when the mouse click occurred. If we want our button to respond to a mouse click, we must include a handler for that event in the button's script, as follows:

```
on mouseUp
--when the button's script receives a mouseUp message
   beep 1
   --do a single beep
end mouseUp
```

If this is the only handler in the button's script, the button will ignore other messages and respond only to a mouseUp message, as indicated in Figure 4.4.

A handler for a message begins with the line on *event name,* followed by a list of commands, and ends with end *event name.* In this case, the button has a handler for the mouseUp message, but not for any other message, so it ignores all other messages and simply passes them on to other objects (about which we'll say more shortly). When the script receives a mouseUp message, it finds that it has a handler for such messages, so it intercepts the message and handles it, as a good handler should.

FIGURE 4.4   A Handler Responds to Messages

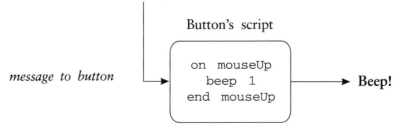

A script can have many handlers, though it can have at most one for each kind of message. For instance, we could make our button noisier by giving it the following script.

```
on mouseUp
    wait 1 second
    --you should be able to figure out what this command does
    beep 1
end mouseUp


on mouseDown
    beep 2
end mouseDown
```

We now have a button that responds to two messages: mouseUp and mouseDown. What happens when you point to the button on the screen, and then click and release the mouse?

1. Since the pointer (the browse tool's finger) is over the button, a mouseDown message is sent to the button's script. (If the pointer was over a different object at the time of the click, the message would be sent to that object.)

2. The button's script responds to the mouseDown message by sending a message to HyperCard to beep twice.

3. Nothing further will happen while the mouse button is held down, since we didn't build a handler for the mouseStillDown message.

4. If you lift your finger from the mouse while the pointer on the screen is in the button, a mouseUp message is sent to the button, and this message is handled by the button's script, telling HyperCard to wait a second and then beep once.

We have mentioned that HyperCard sends messages to objects, but a stack may have dozens or even hundreds of objects, including all its buttons, fields, and cards. Are messages such as mouseUp broadcast to all objects at once? Pretty clearly, they can't be—contemplating the chaos that could result from 20 objects responding simultaneously to a mouseUp message should convince you that there must be some sort of selection process involved. The rules HyperCard uses are actually quite simple:

1. Messages to which a button or field can respond are sent to the button or field where the mouse pointer is currently.

2. Messages that are appropriate for cards are sent to the currently displayed card.

3. Messages (such as mouseUp) that are appropriate for cards as well as buttons or fields are sent to the button or field if the pointer is

currently in one of those objects, or to the current card, if the pointer isn't in a button or field.

Some of the 36 HyperCard messages and their possible destinations are listed here:

DESTINATION	MESSAGE	SENT WHEN
Button or field	mouseUp	mouse button is released
	mouseDown	mouse button is pressed
	mouseStillDown	button still down, pointer still in object
	mouseEnter	pointer has entered object
	mouseLeave	pointer was in object, has left
	mouseWithin	pointer in object
Card	mouseUp	
	mouseDown	
	mouseStillDown	
	openCard	card becomes current (displayed)
	closeCard	another card becomes current
	openStack	stack with this card is opened
	closeStack	stack with this card is closed
	quit	quitting HyperCard
	idle	nothing is happening

THE OBJECT HIERARCHY

Suppose we want to design a card that would provide aural feedback, such as a beep, whenever a mouseDown event occurred anywhere in the card. We could provide a mouseDown handler in the script of every object on the card, as well as on the card itself, but this would become tedious if the card had a dozen buttons and eight fields. Along the same lines, what happens when a message is sent to a button that has no handler for that message? We probably don't want the message to die in the button, since there might be another object that could profitably react to the message. What we need, and what HyperCard provides, is an orderly plan for transmission of messages, called the *object hierarchy*. In simple terms, if a message is passed to an object and that object has no handler for that message, the message is passed on to the next higher level in the hierarchy, and so on, until it is intercepted by HyperCard itself, which will either handle the message or signal an error, indicating that the message is unrecognizable.

The HyperCard object hierarchy is simple enough:

button or field → card → background → stack → Home stack → HyperCard

In other words, if there is no handler for a message in the chosen button or field, the message is passed to the script of the card containing the button or field; if the card's script does not handle the message, it is passed to the card's background script; if the background script has no handler for the message, it is passed to the stack's script; if the stack script cannot handle the message, it is passed to the Home stack, and then to HyperCard itself, the final arbiter (see Figure 4.5). To use Danny Goodman's metaphor in *The Complete HyperCard Handbook*, it is as if you talked to a clerk in a store and received the response, "I can't handle that—you'd better talk to my supervisor."

To provide aural feedback to mouse clicks in every object in card 55, then, we would put the sole mouseDown handler in the script for card 55, and not in any of its buttons or fields. Then, when a mouseDown message was sent to field 1, button 1, or button 2 of card 55, they, being incapable of responding, would pass the message to the next higher object in the message hierarchy, card 55, which does have a handler for that message (see Figure 4.6).

FIGURE 4.5   **A Sample Object Hierarchy**

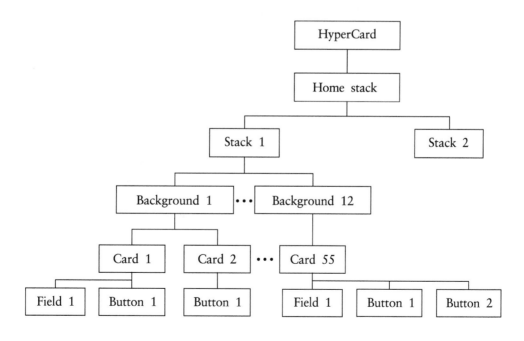

HyperTalk does provide a means for an object to intercept and respond to messages and then pass the same message to some other object higher up the hierarchy. This is accomplished by including a pass command in the lower object's script. For example, if we wanted a click on button 1 of card 55 to produce an extra beep, its script could include the handler

```
on mouseDown
   beep 1
   pass mouseDown
end mouseUp
```

Messages don't have to be generated by user events such as mouse clicks. In fact, every HyperTalk command can be thought of as a message generator. When a script executes the command put x into card field 1, for instance, the script doesn't actually cause the put command to be executed. Instead, what happens is that a put message is generated by the script, and that message is passed upward through the object hierarchy to HyperCard itself, which includes a put handler. You could even define a put handler of your own and associate it with some card or background. In this case, your put handler would get the first crack at intercepting and responding to the command and, unless your handler contained a pass put command, HyperCard would never see, let alone respond to, it. More typically, you will define your own messages and handlers for them using the HyperTalk commands as they have been defined by the developers of the language (see Figure 4.7).

FIGURE 4.6   Handling a mouseDown Message in Card 55

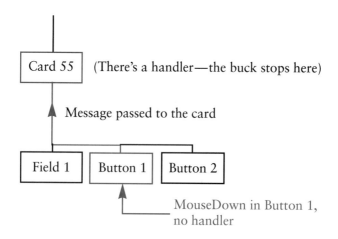

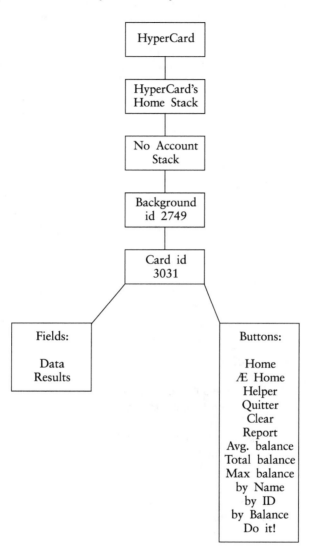

FIGURE 4.7   No Account's Object Hierarchy

SCRIPT-GENERATED MESSAGES

HyperCard encapsulates the code for the put command, so that you do not have to write the code for put each time you need it. When you write a handler for a message of your own, you are, in effect, encapsulating a collection of HyperTalk commands and structures under a distinct name, to be called upon when needed. This feature is included in almost all programming languages, in one form or another. In Pascal, for instance, such capsules of code are called *procedures*.

In our recipe, the instruction "Follow procedure for Rick and Stu's Flaky Pie Crust" is analogous to a procedure reference. The pie crust recipe is a separate collection of ingredients and instructions that, in the interests of clarity (why complicate the apple pie recipe with the details of making a crust?), brevity (why duplicate the crust recipe here?), and generality (we want to refer to it in other pie recipes as well), we have distinguished as such and named. The pie crust recipe is regarded as a single subtask of the larger task of making an apple pie.

The simplest example of a procedure in No Account is in the script for button Report. Notice, first, that the Report button script contains two message handlers, one to respond to a mouseUp event over the button, and the other to respond to a reportLargeOnes event. reportLargeOnes is not one of the events that HyperCard is programmed to respond to. Instead, it is an event we created and named for the sole purpose of clarifying Report's mouseUp handler. The last command of the mouseUp handler simply says reportLargeOnes. As are all first words of commands, this is regarded as a message. Before sending the message up the object hierarchy, the current script (the one where the message originated) is checked to see if it contains an appropriate handler. In this case it does, and the net effect is as if the reference to reportLargeOnes within the mouseUp handler was replaced by the statements of the reportLargeOnes handler.

```
on mouseUp

    --clear the results field
    send mouseUp to background button "Clear"

    put the number of lines of card field "Data" into numAccounts
    put "Total number of accounts:" && numAccounts & return & return ¬
    into card field "Results"

    --use a separate handler to produce one type of report
    reportLargeOnes
end mouseUp

on reportLargeOnes

    put "Accounts with Large Balances ( $1000):" & return ¬
    after card field "Results"

    --go line-by-line through field "Data" looking for large balances
    repeat with lineNumber = 1 to the number of lines of card field "Data"
        put line lineNumber of card field "Data" into thisline

        --check to see if the balance is  > $1000
```

```
            if word 4 of thisLine  > 1000 then

                --if it is, display the name and the balance
                put (word 1 of thisLine) && (word 4 of thisLine) & return ¬
                after card field "Results"
            end if
        end repeat

        set the scroll of card field "Results" to 0
    end reportLargeOnes
```

> **The send command sends a message to another object, not necessarily the next one in the hierarchy.**

One brief aside: The first command of Report's mouseUp handler, a send command, can be used to direct messages to specific objects in the hierarchy. In this example, the first step in producing a report is to clear the "Results" field. We have already defined a button (Clear) to accomplish this task. We could have duplicated that button's script in Report (which wouldn't have been much of a duplication), but chose to make the Clear button respond as if it had been clicked by "sending" it a mouseUp message. The send command is needed here because if we simply instigated a mouseUp event from within Report's mouseUp handler, the Report button itself would respond and the message would never be seen by button Clear. More generally, send is useful when the object hierarchy doesn't provide the necessary line of communications between objects. In this case, button Clear is on the same level of No Account's object hierarchy as is button Report, and Clear would not normally be given an opportunity to respond to any message sent by Report.

Another slightly more sophisticated example of a user-defined procedure is referenced from within No Account's By name, By ID, and By balance buttons. You no doubt noticed that every time one of these buttons is clicked, it becomes highlighted and the other two buttons are turned off. Once again, as opposed to duplicating the instructions needed to control the highlighting of the sort buttons in each of the sort button scripts, we have written a message handler, named TurnOn, which can be referenced from each script directly. We could, then, have used send commands to transmit TurnOn messages. In this case, though, there is an easier solution. Because all three of the scripts that require access to the TurnOn handler occur at the same level of the object hierarchy, we can simply attach TurnOn to an object, like the background of the card on which the sort buttons are found, which occurs above the sort buttons in the object hierarchy. So, if you want to see the commands which implement the TurnOn procedure, look at No Account's card script.

```
    --By name
    on mouseUp
        global whichWord
        --This button corresponds to the first data word in each line
        put 1 into whichWord
        --this is card button #1
```

```
      TurnOn 1
   end mouseUp

    --By ID
   on mouseUp
      global whichWord
      --This button corresponds to the second data word in each line
      put 2 into whichWord
      --this is card button #2
      TurnOn 2
   end mouseUp

    --By balance
   on mouseUp
      global whichWord
      --This button corresponds to the third data word in each line
      put 3 into whichWord
      --this is card button #3
      TurnOn 3
   end mouseUp

   on TurnOn buttonNum
      --Handles hiliting of a group of radio buttons.
      --Called by any of the three buttons when they receive a mouseUp.
      --Each button sends its own number to this handler.

      repeat with counter = 1 to the number of card buttons
         --i.e., do this for all three radio buttons
         if buttonNum = counter then
            --Turn on selected button
            set hilite of button counter to true
         else
            --Turn off any other button
            set hilite of button counter to false
         end if
      end repeat
   end TurnOn
```

Æ LAB

LAB EXERCISE 5

5.1   Edit the script of button Report so that in addition to its current report, it produces a listing of names and IDs of accounts that have fewer than six payments remaining.

5.2 Edit each of the sort button scripts (by name, ID, and balance) so that when it is clicked sorting occurs automatically, so that there is no need to explicitly click the Do it! button.

4.7 INFORMATION CONTROL: AT 425 DEGREES FOR 40 MINUTES

We have seen that encapsulating operations into distinct procedures can help to clarify scripts for human readers and saves us from having to duplicate identical groups of commands in many parts of a program. We will now see that procedures need not be invoked identically from all points of reference. In fact, procedures can be defined so that they can be "parameterized"—that is, made to operate across a range of specified parameters—and thus rendered even more general.

The analog for a parameterized procedure in our recipe is the command "Bake at 425 degrees for 40 minutes." The bake operation can be thought of as a procedure in the sense that it involves carrying out a number of more primitive commands (preheat the oven, set the oven controls, arrange the cooking racks inside the oven, and so on), and it is certainly generally useful in most recipes. Still, even the most experienced cooks need more direction from a recipe than to be told to "bake" something. In writing a recipe, we instruct the cook to bake something, for example, at 425 degrees for 40 minutes. These pieces of information—the temperature and the time—are the parameters of the bake command. If it were necessary to instruct someone on the details of "baking," the instructions would necessarily include entry lines "set the temperature control to the desired temperature" and "set the timer to the desired time." The phrases "desired temperature" and "desired time" can be thought of as placeholders in the general baking procedure that get filled in by the values provided in a particular recipe.

> Parameters are somewhat like variables in that they are named objects where information may reside.

You may have wondered, in looking at the sort button scripts above, what those numbers are that follow the references to TurnOn (1, 2, and 3). Now you know—they are the parameters needed to complete the TurnOn message. Just as it is not enough to tell a cook to bake, it is not enough to tell the No Account stack to "TurnOn"—it needs to know which button to highlight. In each reference to TurnOn, the number following TurnOn corresponds to the number of the button to be highlighted.

The TurnOn message handler itself begins by identifying which name is to serve as its placeholder. When we invoke the command TurnOn 3, for example, the name buttonNum in the TurnOn script is replaced by the number 3 throughout the handler, with the effect of highlighting button number 3 and unhighlighting (setting the hilite property to false) all other buttons. The only requirement in using parameters—and it's an important one—is that the parameters sent to a handler must correspond both in number and in type of information to that expected by the handler. If we were to include the statement TurnOn "Hello" in some script, the TurnOn handler would accomplish nothing, since "Hello" does not match any of the stack's button numbers. Similarly, if we leave the placeholder button-Num out of the first line of the TurnOn handler, TurnOn is not prepared to accept any additional information. Regardless, then, of how it was invoked, TurnOn would accomplish nothing since buttonNum would have no value within the TurnOn handler.*

Whereas procedures allow processing capabilities to be shared and accessed by stack objects, parameters are a means for sharing information. Parameters are particularly useful because variables in HyperTalk are inherently "local." That is, they only have meaning within a particular message handler. Whenever HyperTalk sees a word in a script that it doesn't recognize, it assumes that the word is a variable name and it associates the variable with the handler in which the name occurred. Thus, variable counter in TurnOn takes on values that it retains only in TurnOn. If we use counter in another handler (which we are perfectly free to do), it would be considered a different variable from the counter in TurnOn. The two variables share a name, but not a value. Indeed, that is the reason buttonNum has no value in TurnOn unless it is specified as a parameter. It is treated as a local variable, and nowhere in TurnOn is buttonNum given a value.

HyperTalk does afford us another means for sharing information, which is also illustrated in No Account's sort button scripts. Notice that each mouseUp handler begins with the statement global whichWord. This statement identifies explicitly variable whichWord as being "global" as opposed to local. A global variable can be shared in both name and value among any message handlers that designate it as global. In our sample stack, the variable whichWord in the By name script is the same whichWord that is in the By ID script, which is the same that is referenced from within By balance. These handlers have no good reason for sharing the value of whichWord between themselves, but each is vitally concerned with the mouseUp handler for button Do it! We will discuss the Do it! script in more detail in the next section. For now, suffice it to say that the sort buttons set the value of whichWord to indicate which word number of each line of the field "Data" is to be used in sorting the field. The mouseUp handler in Do it! uses the same whichWord (which is why it is designated as global) to accomplish the sort.

---

* Actually, if buttonNum was not specified as a parameter, referencing TurnOn would result in an error message indicating that HyperCard could not understand what follows the word "if" in the TurnOn handler.

```
on mouseUp
   --Here's where the actual sorting goes on.
   --Uses a "selection sort," by repeatedly selecting the least item,
   --and swapping its line into its proper place in the field.

   --The global "whichWord" is set by the radio button scripts
   --to tell this routine whether to sort by name, ID, or balance
   global whichWord

   if card field "Data" is empty then
      answer "Enter data before calculating or sorting" ¬
      with "OK, I will"

   else
      play "harpsichord" a3#e—just to provide some aural feedback

      --And this is the sorting algorithm
      repeat with current = 1 to ¬
         (number of lines of card field "Data") - 1
         put FindMin(current, whichWord) into found
         swap current, found
      end repeat
   end if
end mouseUp

function FindMin startingLine, whichWord
   --finds the location of the least element among all words "whichWord"
   --in card field "Data" beginning at line "start" in that field.

   --Initialization: As far as we know now, the smallest value is
   --the first one we are going to look at
   put startingLine into where
   --so we'll store its line number in "where"
   put word whichWord of line startingLine of card field "Data" into currentMin
   --and its value in "currentMin"

   --Here's where we look through each line from "start"
   --to the last line in the field, looking for the smallest item
   repeat with thisLine = startingLine to number of lines of card field "Data"
      if word whichWord of line thisLine of card field "Data" < currentMin then
         --We found a new smallest element, so save its value
         put word whichWord of line thisLine of card field "Data" into currentMin
         --and save the line number where we found it
         put thisLine into where
      end if
   end repeat
```

```
    --We're done checking lines, so we return the location
    --of the least item
    return where
end FindMin

on swap line1, line2
    --Interchanges line1 and line2 in card field "Data".
    put line line1 of card field "Data" into tempLine
    put line line2 of card field "Data" into line line1 of card field "Data"
    put tempLine into line line2 of card field "Data"
end swap
```

REVIEW QUESTIONS

1. What is a local variable?

2. Where can a mouseDown message be sent? Knowing what you do about HyperTalk, do you think that a mouseDown message could be sent to a stack?

3. What is a parameter, and what is its purpose?

4. What is a handler? In what ways do command and function handlers differ?

5. What is the difference between a script and a handler?

Æ LAB

LAB EXERCISE 6

6.1 Add a button and the necessary scripts to No Account to allow the stack to sort the lines of field "Data" in ascending order of number of remaining payments. [Note: You won't have to change the Do it! script at all.]

4.8   PROGRAM DESIGN: RECIPES OF YOUR OWN

Now that you know the rudiments of HyperTalk programming, you no longer have to rely on other buttons and cards designed by other people—you're ready to go out and develop an application on your own, right? Well, yes and no. You know how to design the objects in your proposed stack and probably could write their scripts as well. The question is, though, how efficient would you be? A HyperCard stack, even a small one, might have dozens of objects, each with its own script, and each script could have many handlers. It's not hard to imagine quickly becoming overwhelmed by a mass of detail, trying to keep track of every script and making sure that they mesh together smoothly.

In the best of all possible worlds, you could hire an expert, tell him or her what you want, and wait for the finished product. That won't work, though, for two reasons. First, you probably can't afford the services of an expert—the good software engineers are already being paid high salaries to work on other projects. Second and more importantly, in a global sense hiring another only postpones the problem. The experts can't hire experts whenever they need them—somewhere along the line the experts had to learn how to become experts, and that's what this section is all about.

We'd like to be able to tell you that there are 13 magical rules to follow, and that if you follow them you will always write functional and efficient software, but that's simply not the case. Software design is an art as well as a science. Essentially, though, designing an application in any programming language is nothing more than a large mental task—like designing a house or writing a book—and there are certain commonsense rules that make any such complex task less painful. In the pages that follow, we'll take you through a sample project—in fact, the very project one of us wrote as his first HyperCard application. We'll play Virgil to your Dante, taking you on a voyage through the software development Inferno, pointing out the landscape and the pitfalls along the way.

THE SOFTWARE LIFE CYCLE

We can regard the life of a software product as consisting of five rough phases:

- **Conception:** precise *specification* of the software
- **Incubation:** *design* of the software
- **Birth:** *coding,* according to the design, and debugging the code
- **Growth:** *testing,* to make sure the code performs as specified
- **Maturity:** *maintenance* of the software

In practice these phases are neither independent nor chronological. Indeed, they regularly overlap and influence one another so that the development process becomes an interactive one, as opposed to a linear one. For the sake of our discussion, we will address these activities individually and will show you how they apply to our sample stack.

SPECIFICATION

The specification phase is devoted to progressing from a fuzzily worded description of what the application should do to a precise and detailed set of descriptions. At the start I had in mind little more than "Design a fairly simple stack that I could use as an example in Module 4.* It should be a simple accounting program that will keep track of names, ID numbers, and unpaid balances." Acting as my own consultant, I decided on the following specifications:

1. The data will be stored in one scrollable card field, divided into lines with one line for each customer. Within each line the information will be divided into four items, separated by spaces.
2. There will be another field, used to display information.
3. There will be seven buttons, divided into two main groups.
   a. The first group will consist of three buttons, each of which will cause information to be displayed in the second field:
      i. A button to display the average balance
      ii. A button to display the total of all balances
      iii. A button to display the name and balance of the customer with the largest balance
   b. The second group of buttons will be devoted to sorting the lines in the "data" field, in increasing order:
      i. Three buttons, used to select whether to sort by name, ID, or balance
      ii. A button that will initiate the sorting process, according to the choice made by the sorting buttons
4. To keep things simple, only limited error checking will be performed.
   a. It will be the responsibility of the user to ensure that there are four words per line.
   b. I will, however, make sure that the program handles the case of no lines in the "data" field by doing nothing in such a case.

DESIGN

With these specifications, I could now sketch out the design. By "design" I mean both the graphic design of the single card, which reflects my interpretation of the design guidelines from Module 3, and also the *software blueprint,* describing the processing and information dependencies of the message handlers themselves, described in Figure 4.8.

Notice, first of all, how the blueprint reflects HyperCard's object hierarchy. This, of course, is no coincidence because the processing and data dependencies of the handlers must somehow be accomplished within the object hierarchy. Notice, too, that I haven't specified here *how* I wrote the

---

* It seems much more natural to use the first person singular here, rather than the plural. I hope the transition wasn't too abrupt for you. I'll let my co-author talk again when this section is finished.—RWD

handlers for the buttons. That's deliberate. In order to avoid having to think about the structure of the stack while at the same time worrying about the details of the scripts, I adopted a *top-down* design approach: I sketched the broadest outline I could of the application, deferring implementation details until later.

I actually wrote small scripts for each button, however—each button's handler consisted of a put command, such as put "This button will eventually average" into card field 2. Using such *stubs* instead of fully worked-out code has two advantages. First, at each step, I had a functioning stack, so I could test its actions while designing and (later) coding. That way, if something did go wrong, I could be fairly sure that the error was caused by the code I just entered, saving me the pain of having to look at every line of code in all the scripts. Second, I put off coding as long as possible. The most common temptation of beginning programmers is to jump right in

FIGURE 4.8   **Software Blueprint for the Sample Stack**

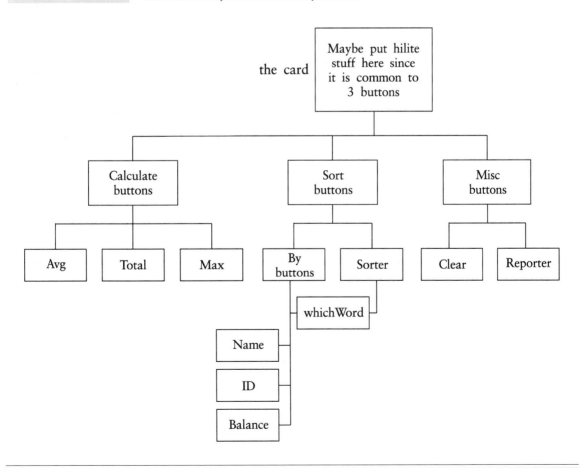

and write code, without thinking first. Henry Ledgard was right when he said, "The sooner you start coding your program, the longer it is going to take." As with any writing process, typing is no substitute for thinking.

Related to top-down design is what is known as *stepwise refinement*. Notice that I avoided thinking of how sorting was to be done. The other actions are fairly simple, but sorting is sufficiently complicated that it will likely need to be described in further detail. It was time to think seriously about the *algorithm* to use for sorting—again, before starting to code. A simple (though not particularly efficient) sorting technique is *selection sort:* Inspect the list of items and find the smallest; swap that line with the first line, and the list is partially sorted. Now look at the list from line 2 to the end, and find the smallest item there; swap that line with the second, and the list is sorted further, having the smallest and the next-to-smallest items in their proper positions. Continue this process until all the elements are where they belong. Presto! A sorted list. My sort handler looked like this, written *pseudocode,* which substitutes English phrases for the details of coding (again, keeping attention at a high level as long as possible):

```
on mouseUp
   repeat with lineNum = 1 to the end of the list
      find the smallest item in the line at or after lineNum
      swap that line with the line lineNum
   end repeat
end mouseUp
```

Now I could fill in the card part of the software blueprint. It makes sense to define separate handlers for the "find the smallest item" and "swap" routines for two reasons. First, look how easy the sort routine is to understand with the details omitted, and notice how it parallels our English description of the selection sort algorithm, above. Second, in writing the separate handlers for finding the minimum and for swapping, we are similarly freed from worrying about the more general problem of sorting. We can concentrate instead on the distinct, isolated, and simpler problems at hand.

CODING

After thinking about the problem at the conceptual and component levels, I found that I had almost no coding to do whatsoever and the code that had to be written followed quite directly from English descriptions of No Account's buttons and fields. The most complex code (and the most complex part of the problem) was the sorting routines, found in the script of button Do it!, above. The mouseUp handler looks suspiciously like our pseudocode description of the sorting algorithm (with an additional error check at the beginning). Global variable whichWord (set in the sort button routines) tells the routine which data line item is to be used in sorting and is passed as a parameter to a general FindMin routine.

In terms of its algorithm, FindMin looks quite similar to that of our Max balance button. The three differences are that (1) we are finding the minimum, rather than the maximum, (2) we are basing the sort on word theWord, which can vary each time we sort, as opposed to item 3 (the balance) uniformly, and (3) we begin our search for the minimum at line start, which varies each time FindMin is invoked, instead of the first line.

In terms of its structure and method of invocation, FindMin is different from any handler we have seen up to now. Notice that it begins with the word "function" instead of the conventional "on". Further, when in the mouseUp handler we want to refer to FindMin, we don't issue a FindMin command. Instead, we refer to FindMin in the context of a put command, such as put FindMin(current, whichWord) into found. Both of these traits are common to HyperCard functions, which we described briefly in the context of HyperTalk's built-in functions.

FindMin is a *user-defined* function handler. Functions are designed to calculate and return one and only one value to the calling routine. The returning of a calculated value is accomplished by a return command from within the function handler. In FindMin, the single return statement occurs after we have searched the prescribed lines of field "Data" to find the minimum value for the prescribed items (name, ID, or balance). The value returned as the value of the function (variable where) is the number of the line of field "Data" containing the minimum item. This line number is stored in variable found in the mouseUp handler of Do it! and is used in performing the swapping of lines. The swap handler is a conventional message handler that accepts as parameters the two line numbers of field "Data" to be interchanged.

TESTING

Once the coding was done, it was time to make sure everything worked as planned. I had been testing as I wrote, of course—every new piece of code was followed by tests to make sure that the stack still did what it was supposed to do. Most of the tests simply amounted to clicking on buttons and watching what happened. Others were instigated by typing a message into the Message box and observing the stack's behavior. When things went as expected, I was relieved (and sometimes, surprised!). When they didn't— when an error message appeared on the screen, or an incorrect result was produced—I had to *debug* the program.

Debugging is an inherent part of testing devoted to tracking down errors in a program. Many programming languages provide programmers with sophisticated debugging tools, and HyperTalk is no exception. In fact, HyperCard provides scriptors with a menu full of useful debugging commands that becomes available when a script window is open and active (see Figure 4.9). These commands allow you to set and clear "checkpoints" in a script (so that the program will stop when it hits a given instruction, "Set/

ClearCheckpoints"), to step through a script one instruction at a time ("Step", "Step Into"), to observe the values of local and global variables ("Variable Watcher"), and to see which messages are being generated and responded to by which scripts in a stack ("Message Watcher"). The good news is that by placing checkpoints at suspected trouble spots in a script, observing the values of relevant variables when the checkpoint is reached, and "stepping through" the script, one can—usually, and possibly after considerable confusion—deduce the sources of all detected errors. The bad news is that you can only fix an error if you know of its existence.

Once the last handler was complete, the time came for serious testing. When you enter this phase, you should try *everything*. Of course, you should test with the expected input data, but—particularly if you are writing programs for others—you should try the unexpected as well. It is very easy to become seduced by your own application and miss bizarre cases; after all, you have been using it extensively, and you may have gotten used to its quirks. You may have forgotten that it blows up when you press certain keys, and simply gotten into the habit of avoiding those actions. One of the best strategies at this point is to have someone else run your application for an extended period. Even if your program handles the pathological cases gracefully, don't relax. This is a good time to keep Dijkstra's maxim in mind, that testing reveals the presence of errors, but never their absence. There's probably not a programmer alive who hasn't produced

FIGURE 4.9   HyperCard's Debugger Menu

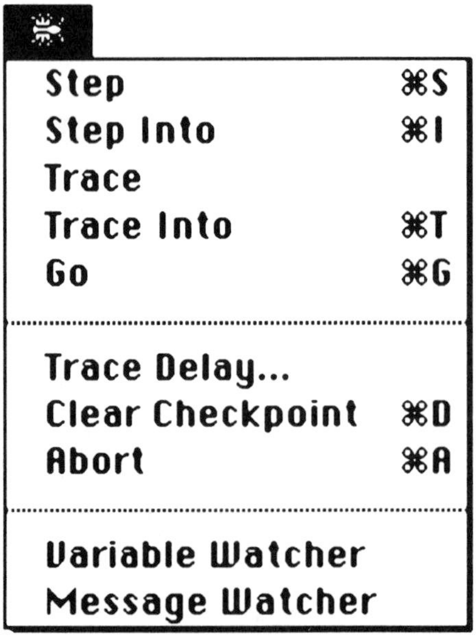

an apparently bulletproof software product, only to find a hitherto unexpected bug after months of uneventful use.

MAINTENANCE

At long last, the stack was complete and as reliable as the specifications warranted. Now I could think of future changes. The stack might grow as new features had to be added, or might shrink as I thought of more efficient ways to implement the specifications. After completing the sample stack, I decided to add a "next card" arrow, and a Home button, and an icon for the Sort button, all copied from HyperCard's Button Ideas stack. In a real product, the specifications might change, bugs might yet be found, or management might decide to introduce a new version to be more competitive in the market. This is where *documentation* becomes vitally important. You will notice that the scripts for the sample stacks are liberally larded with comments, for good reason. Unless you have ever read unfamiliar code (and that includes your own, after a week or two), you simply wouldn't believe how difficult it is to decipher a program without extensive documentation.

REVIEW QUESTIONS

1. Describe the software life cycle.
2. What is top-down design, and why is it a useful design strategy?
3. Reusing code, often called "self-plagiarization," can facilitate the development process. If you keep in mind the possibility that the code you write may be used in another script, how should this influence the way you write?
4. Why do we stress documentation of all code?

Æ LAB

LAB EXERCISE 7

7.1 Make function FindMin more general by editing it so that it accepts a third parameter indicating which field is to be searched. That is, the first line of the function handler could read function FinMin start, theItem, theField. Revise your mouseUp handler for button Do it! to use your new version of FindMin.

7.2 Write a new function handler that returns a boolean value (true or false) to indicate whether or not a particular line of field "Data" has four items, as required. This function could be invoked from within any of the calculation or sorting scripts before attempting to process any ill-defined data line. For example, the function could be named formatOK, and each calculation button could include a clause like if formatOK(thisLine) then.... If the function returned a value of true, the calculation would be performed as usual. If the function returned false, no calculation would be attempted, and an alert box could be displayed notifying the user of the error in the data.

ÆLAB   EXTENDED LAB EXERCISE

Design and write a stack that allows a user to enter a metric length value (in millimeters, centimeters, meters, or kilometers). The stack should then convert the value to its equivalent in inches. Extend the stack so that conversions can be made to feet, yards, and miles, in addition to inches, as specified by the user.

4.9   EXERCISES

1. Define the following terms:

    a. Message, handler, structure, object hierarchy
    b. Top-down design, stub, stepwise refinement

2. If you were designing a programming language that distinguished between real and integer types, how would you define the type of value returned by mixed expressions such as 3 + 4.76, 2.667*3, or 2/3?

3. Why can't a HyperTalk string include quotation marks?

4. What are the values of the following HyperTalk expressions?

    a. 3 + 4*5
    b. abs(4.2 - 7)
    c. true and (5≤ 4)
    d. (average(0,y) ≤ max(y,0)) and ((not (x = x)) or (1 ≥ 2))

5. If you were designing an inventory program for a pants store, any item in stock could be described by design number (1 = blue jeans, 2 = green jeans, 3 = baggy purple pants with narrow cuffs, and so on), waist dimension, and inseam length. A common data structure for such a job would be a three-

dimensional array *inventory*[design, waist, inseam], so that *inventory*[1, 32, 34] would represent the number of blue jeans in stock with a 32-inch waist and 34-inch inseam. How would you implement such an array in Hyper-Talk? (*Hint:* You may want to use multiple cards.)

6. A *global variable* in HyperTalk is a variable that can be shared by several handlers or scripts. A variable is declared to be global by including the line global *name* in a handler so that if the line global size appeared in one handler, the value of the variable size could be used in any other handler, as long as it also included a global size declaration. Think of a HyperTalk example that would be difficult to implement without using global variables.

7. What sort of task might HyperCard itself have for an idle handler? (*Hint:* Think about what happens to fields.)

8. Why does the if structure include an end if line? HyperTalk does not require an end if line if there is just one statement following the if clause, as in

```
if x < 3 then
    put "the variable is small" into field "Display"
```

Does this make sense in terms of your understanding of the purpose of end if?

9. For what possible values of x and y are statements A and B executed in the following two structures?

a.
```
if x = 3 then
    if y = 4 then
        (statement A)          Done when: _____
    else
        (statement B)          Done when: _____
    end if
end if
```

b.
```
if x = 3 then
    if y = 4 then
        (statement A)          Done when: _____
    end if
else
    (statement B)              Done when: _____
end if
```

10. Are either of the structures in exercise 9 equivalent to the following?

```
if (x = 3) and (y = 4) then
    (statement A)
else
    (statement B)
end if
```

11. The repeat with structure always increments the control variable by 1. How would you change the following structure to one in which the statement in the loop was provided with the values 13, 16, 19, 22, 25, . . . , 40?

    ```
    repeat with index = 1 to 10
        (some statements that used index)
    end repeat
    ```

12. Read the definition of repeat with carefully, and tell what the action of the following segment would be.

    ```
    repeat with index = 3 to 1
        put index into field "Display"
    end repeat
    ```

13. If you haven't already done so, answer the review questions at the end of Section 4.5.

14. In Figure 4.4, we simplified the message stream. What did we leave out?

15. Why are mouseEnter, mouseLeave, and mouseWithin commands not sent to cards?

16. For the card field of Figure 4.3,

    a. Write a mouseUp handler for a button that would display in card field 2 all customers with a balance greater than 100.
    b. Write a mouseUp handler for a button that would display in card field 2 the *median* balance, namely a value m for which an equal number of the balances were greater than m and less than m. In the example of Figure 4.3, for instance, the median balance is 100.00, since there are three balances less than 100.00 and three balances greater than that value.
    c. Would either handler for parts a and b be more appropriately written as a function handler? Explain.

17. Suppose we modified the *selection sort* algorithm to sort a list from smallest to largest, by only swapping elements in the list if the minimum element found at each stage was smaller than the current one being compared. In this modification,

    a. How many times would *swap* be called on the data 3, 2, 1, 5, 4?
    b. What arrangement of the numbers 1, 2, 3, 4, 5 requires the largest number of swaps?
    c. What arrangement of the numbers, 1, 2, . . . , n requires the largest number of swaps, and how many are required?

18. Illustrate the steps in the software life cycle, using the metaphor of designing and building a house.

4.10   ADDITIONAL READINGS

Apple Computer, Inc. *HyperCard Script Language* Guide. Reading, Mass.: Addison-Wesley, 1988.

Brooks, F. P. *The Mythical Man-Month*. Reading, Mass.: Addison-Wesley, 1975.

Dahl, O.-J.; Dijkstra, E.; and Hoare, C. A. R. *Structured Programming*. London: Academic Press, 1972.

Dijkstra, E. *A Discipline of Programming*. Englewood Cliffs, N.J.: Prentice-Hall, 1976.

Goodman, D. *The Complete HyperCard* Handbook. New York: Bantam Books, 1987.

Lamb, D. A. *Software Engineering*. Englewood Cliffs, N.J.: Prentice-Hall, 1988.

Parnas, D. L. "On the Criteria to Be Used in Decomposing Systems into Modules." *Communications of the ACM* 15, no. 2 (Dec. 1972): 1053–58.

Shafer, D. *HyperTalk Programming*. Indianapolis: Howard W. Sams, 1988.

PROGRAM TRANSLATION

5.1 INTRODUCTION

Countess Lovelace, in describing the principles of the Analytical Engine, said, "The Analytical Engine has no pretensions whatever to originate anything. It can do whatever we know how to order it to perform."* Substitute *computer* for *Analytical Engine,* and her statement is as true today as it was nearly a century and a half ago. You have seen that a computer is a general-purpose information processor, and that in order to use the speed and power of the computer, we must provide a program, a list of instructions, for the computer to execute. In this module, we ask, What is a program, and how is it that a computer can execute its instructions?

TEXT OBJECTIVES

In this module, we will move from the lowest hardware-level programming to the translation of high-level languages, such as HyperTalk. We will

- Introduce the binary representation of information used by modern computers
- Discuss *machine language,* the language that is used to instruct a computer's hardware at the level of binary representation
- See the advantages of *assembly language* over machine language, and discover how assembly language programs are translated into machine language
- Introduce several contemporary *high-level languages,* concentrating on how they make the programming process more efficient

---

* P. Morrison and E. Morrison, *Charles Babbage and His Calculating Engine* (New York: Dover, 1961).

- Take a necessarily brief look at the problems involved in translating high-level languages into a form that a computer can execute

THE BINARY MACHINE

> Machine language: The only language a computer's hardware can use.

A computer such as the Macintosh can run programs written in Hyper-Talk, Pascal, Logo, APL, LISP, Prolog, COBOL, and many others of the scores of programming languages available today. It appears that the computer is multilingual, but that's a fiction. In fact, every computer ever built "understands" one and only one language—the *machine language* it is wired to use. The machine language of the Macintosh is different from that of a Cray supercomputer, and neither is the same as the machine language of a VAX computer made by the Digital Equipment Corporation. How is it, then, that in spite of this Tower of Babel of different machine languages, all three computers can execute the same FORTRAN program? The answer is based upon our ability to write a program that allows the computer to translate a program written in a language such as FORTRAN into the computer's own machine language.

METAPHOR: THE ROSETTA STONE

At first glance, a program—particularly one in a language other than HyperTalk—might seem like so much hieroglyphics. Consider the two texts shown in Figure 5.1, one written in Egyptian hieroglyphics and the other written in the APL programming language. The APL sample comes from Terrence W. Pratt, *Programming Languages* (Englewood Cliffs, N.J.: Prentice-Hall, 1984). The hieroglyphic sample concerns a tax reduction in the time of Ptolemy V; the APL produces a list of prime numbers. If both seem confusing to you, you're in good company. You would have at last a chance of deciphering the hieroglyphic passage, given some help, but a computer would be completely lost. With the APL passage, both you and the computer are on equal grounds—both of you would have to rely on outside help to make any sense of the program.

FIGURE 5.1   Egyptian Hieroglyphics and APL

```
)CLEAR
∇RES ← PRIMES N; T
RES ← 2, T ← 3
→0 × ι N < ρ RES
T ← T + 2
→3 × ι v/0 = RES | T
RES ← RES, T
→2
∇
```

To understand the nature of the help that you and the computer need, we go back in time two hundred years. The eighteenth century was a time of increased interest in the artifacts of ancient Egypt. French explorations of Egypt unearthed countless artifacts of the time of the pharaohs, leading to adaptations of Egyptian style in architecture and interior design and to heightened scholarly activities in the period. Unfortunately, hieroglyphics, the language of scribes of ancient Egypt, resisted any attempts of translation until the discovery in 1799 of the Rosetta Stone. This basalt slab contained a royal proclamation, written in hieroglyphics, demotic (a cursive version of hieroglyphics), and Greek, and provided the first steps toward a translation of the formerly impenetrable pictorial language (see Figure 5.2).

This notion of translation is central to this module. A modern programming language is designed with two audiences in mind—the programmers who use the language to write programs for a computer, and the computer itself, which must execute the instructions in the language. Neither audience can use the programming language without some help; both must be taught to translate the language into what for each is a usable form. In this module, you will see what a programming language is, and what sort of outside help a computer requires to execute a program written in a programming language.

Æ STACKS: HOWARD STONE MEETS APPLE MACPIPPIN

We saw in Module 4 how collections of scripts can be integrated to form programs. Having identified the components of a program (the objects and scripts that comprise it), integration is accomplished by allowing components to communicate with one another. For components to communicate, there must be some standard notation for communicating—there must be a language.

The HyperTalk language is HyperCard's standard for communication. In writing a HyperTalk program we define scripts according to the language's syntax rules. That is, each script and each statement within a script must be written in a prescribed format. Despite HyperTalk's similarity to English and its relative flexibility, if we write a script that somehow violates the syntax rules of the language (for example, if we misspell a command word, forget to terminate an if command with end if, or forget to include the word on in the first line of a message handler), HyperCard cannot and does not respond to the script.

HyperTalk also has predefined semantics. Each of its special words, including its command words, has an established meaning that dictates how HyperCard interprets that word. Using information about the syntax and semantics of each command, along with its mechanism for interpretation (the object hierarchy), HyperCard can "understand" the HyperTalk language.

FIGURE 5.2   **The Rosetta Stone.** (Copyright © Archiv/Photo Researchers, Inc.)

The particular binary language that the Mac understands has a syntax and semantics that reflect its internal hardware. The Macintosh understands HyperTalk, or any high-level language, to the extent that it can translate the commands of the language into its machine language. In the lab exercises of this module we examine two stacks that illustrate some simple algorithms for translating text into its binary equivalent, and high-level programs into machine language.

LAB OBJECTIVES

In the disk part of this module, you will

- Use and examine the scripts of a stack that demonstrates the fundamentals of text translation
- Learn about some advanced features of HyperCard, including file processing and other features that are useful in translating text.
- Experiment with a stack that translates and executes PIPPIN programs

5.2   WHAT THE COMPUTER DOES

Here's a sample of a machine language program, written for a hypothetical computer:

```
0001000000001100
1001000000001101
0000000000001100
0111
```

Even if we told you that this program was designed to add the contents of memory locations 12 and 13, place the sum in memory location 12, overwriting whatever was originally stored in location 12, and then halt, you would probably still find these instructions about as understandable as the hieroglyphic text in Figure 5.1. In this section we will pick apart the machine language for an imaginary computer, and discover how to write programs in this language.

BINARY REPRESENTATION

> Modern computers must express all information in terms of 0 and 1.

Part of the difficulty of understanding the program just shown stems from the fact that these instructions are represented using just zeros and ones. We mentioned earlier that the nature of the machine language of a computer is a direct result of the way the computer was designed. You will see in the next module that a design feature common to all modern computers is that they represent all their information in *binary notation*—that is, as strings of zeros and ones. You will see that the decision to represent information in binary form is not made for capricious reasons or to confuse the layperson. Rather, it is a reflection of the fact that *at the fundamental hardware level, a modern computer can only distinguish between two values,* which we label 0 and 1 solely for our convenience.

If the computer can only work in terms of two values, 0 and 1, how are we to represent the information we want to store and manipulate? We are

BCD: A fixed-length code for digits.

comfortable with the notion of the computer as a number cruncher, so we will begin by considering representation of numbers using this limited alphabet $\{0,1\}$. An easy form of representation would be to use *binary-coded decimal* notation (BCD, for short), in which we invent a code for the digits 0, 1, 2, 3, 4, 5, 6, 7, 8, 9, and use this code to represent integers. For example, we might decide to use the following code:

DIGIT	CODE	DIGIT	CODE
0	0000	5	0101
1	0001	6	0110
2	0010	7	0111
3	0011	8	1000
4	0100	9	1001

With this choice of representation, the number 247 would be written as three groups of four digits: 0010 (for the 2), 0100 (for the 4), 0111 (for the 7), or 001001000111. Of course, we could have chosen any other collection of zeros and ones to represent the numbers, as long as our choice permitted a unique representation for integers.*

BCD representation has the advantage of being easy to read, but two disadvantages limit its use. First, it is not the most efficient in terms of space (in our sample code, for instance, a number that requires n decimal digits requires $4n$ binary digits to be represented in BCD form). Second, arithmetic on BCD numbers is complicated. For these reasons, the overwhelming majority of computers use a different form of representation of numbers, one that is somewhat more complicated to learn than BCD but quite a bit more efficient.

From our earliest years in grade school, we have been taught to represent information in *base-10 positional notation*. Positional notation means that the value represented by a digit in a number depends on where in the number that digit happens to be, and base-10 means that the value of any position is a multiple of a power of 10. The expression 247, for instance, is interpreted as the sum $(2 \times 100) + (4 \times 10) + (7 \times 1)$. Notice, too, that the multipliers 100, 10, and 1 are just powers of 10, arranged in increasing size from right to left, beginning with the 0-th power. Although most people don't give it any thought, the nice thing about positional notation is that it permits unique representation of integers: Every possible integer can be represented by this scheme, and every arrangement of strings of digits corresponds to one and only one integer.

---

* We could not have used, for instance, $1 \rightarrow 1$, $2 \rightarrow 11$, $3 \rightarrow 111$, and so on, since then the code 111 could be interpreted as any of the numbers 111, 12, 21, or 3.

There is nothing special about using 10 as our base—we use ten digits only because that's the way things have been done for several thousand years (perhaps having something to do with the fact that most of us have ten fingers). Since the computer could be regarded as having only two fingers, it is appropriate to use *base-2 positional notation*, also known as *binary notation*, instead. Let's see how that would work. The first few powers of 2 are 1, 2, 4 (= 2×2, or 2^2), 8 (= $2 \times 2 \times 2$, or 2^3), 16, 32, 64, 128, 256, 512, 1024, 2048, 4096, and 8192, where we form the sequence by beginning with 1 and multiplying each term by 2 to find the next one. Using only the "digits" 0 and 1 as multipliers of these powers of 2, we find, perhaps by trial and error, that the decimal number 247 would be represented in this scheme as

$$247 = (1 \times 128) + (1 \times 64) + (1 \times 32) + (1 \times 16) + (0 \times 8) + (1 \times 4) + (1 \times 2) + (1 \times 1)$$

or 11110111, as a binary number. Notice that this representation requires only 8 *bits* (*bi*nary dig*its*), whereas the BCD encoding takes 12.

To convert from binary representation to decimal is easy: Below the binary digits we write the powers of 2 in increasing order from right to left, then for each position, multiply the digit by its corresponding power of 2, and finally add the terms together.

> Binary numbers are just like decimal, except they use implied powers of 2 and the "digits" 0 and 1.

> To convert from binary to decimal, add powers of 2.

Example 1   To convert the binary number 10111 to decimal, we write

the binary string: 1 0 1 1 1
over the powers of 2:   16 8 4 2 1 = 16+4+2+1=23

Conversion in the opposite direction, from decimal to binary, is a trifle more complicated, but not much more once we realize that the last digit in the binary representation of n is just the remainder we get when we divide n by 2, and the next digit is obtained by repeating the division on the quotient of the first division. In other words, we can convert a decimal number to binary by repeatedly dividing by 2 and keeping track of the quotients and remainders.

> To convert from decimal to binary, repeatedly divide by 2 and write out the remainders.

Example 2   To convert the decimal number 23 to binary, we do the following divisions, recording the quotients and the remainders:

1. 23 divided by 2 has a quotient of 11 and a remainder of 1. We remember the remainder and use the quotient in the next step.
2. 11 divided by 2 has a quotient of 5 and a remainder of 1, which we also save.
3. 5 divided by 2 has a quotient of 2 and a remainder of 1.
4. 2 divided by 2 has a quotient of 1 and a remainder of 0.

5. 1 divided by 2 has a quotient of 0 and a remainder of 1. We have a zero quotient, so we stop the process.

6. The sequence of remainders we obtained, when read *from right to left*, is the binary representation of 23, namely 10111.

In more compact notation, our example might take the following form:

$$
\begin{array}{r r}
 & 0 \quad 1 \\
2\,\overline{)1} & 0 \\
2\,\overline{)2} & 1 \\
2\,\overline{)5} & 1 \\
2\,\overline{)11} & 1 \\
2\,\overline{)23} &
\end{array}
$$

Then the binary equivalent of 23 is found by reading the column of remainders from top to bottom—10111. We stop the process when we have a zero quotient, since any subsequent divisions by 2 will simply append zeros to the front of our binary answer, and it is clear that 00010111 and 10111 represent the same number.

Now that we can represent any nonnegative integer* as a binary number, we can expand this scheme to represent other information in the computer—we simply find a suitable coding for the information to be stored in integers and represent the integers as binary numbers. For example, to represent strings of characters, we first decide on a suitable integer code for each character. This coding varies from machine to machine, but many computers represent characters by what is known as ASCII code, where ASCII (pronounced "ask-ee") stands for American Standard Code for Information Interchange. Table 5.1 lists some characters and their ASCII codes.

> ASCII: Integer codes for characters.

To read the table, note that the code for a character is the sum of the digits in its row and column labels. For instance, the character *A* is in the row labeled 60 and the column labeled 5, so the ASCII code for *A* is 65. ASCII codes less than 32 are reserved for nonprinting characters, such as return and tab. The Macintosh uses an extended version of ASCII, in which codes between 128 and 216 are used for special characters such as •, ¶, and .

Using this representation of characters, we might decide to represent a string of characters by a number representing the length of the character string, followed by the codes for the characters. For example, the string CAB could be represented by the code for 3 (the number of characters in

---

* In the exercises, we explore some of the ways we might represent negative integers and real numbers such as 3.1415926535.

TABLE 5.1   ASCII Codes

Last Digit

First digits	0	1	2	3	4	5	6	7	8	9
30			space	!	"	#	$	%	&	'
40	(	)	*	+	,	-	.	/	0	1
50	2	3	4	5	6	7	8	9	:	;
60	<	=	>	?	@	A	B	C	D	E
70	F	G	H	I	J	K	L	M	N	O
80	P	Q	R	S	T	U	V	W	X	Y
90	Z	[	\	]	^	_	`		a	b	c
100	d	e	f	g	h	i	j	k	l	m
110	n	o	p	q	r	s	t	u	v	w
120	x	y	z	{			}	~			

CAB), followed by the codes for 67, 65, 66 (for the three letters). In the computer, then, this information would take the form 00000011 01000011 01000001 01000010; we've included spaces between groups of eight bits only to make it easier to read.

Æ LAB

LAB EXERCISE 1

The lab exercises for this module refer to two sample stacks on your disk. Both are tools for translation. The first, entitled "The Howard Stone"—we will refer to it simply as "Howard"—shows how easily text can be translated into binary form (see Figure 5.3). We will use Howard as a vehicle for discussing the programming techniques that underlie translator programs. The second is a PIPPIN assembler—that is, a program that translates programs written in PIPPIN into a binary form cor-

FIGURE 5.3   The Howard Stone Stack

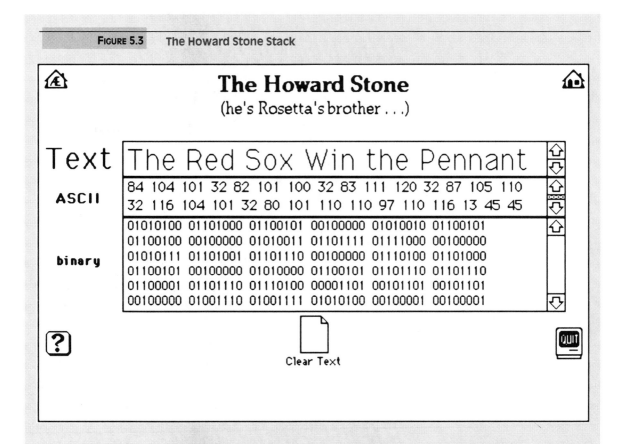

responding, in theory, to some computer's machine language. Our stack, named "Apple MacPippin," not only translates PIPPIN programs, but also simulates their execution, so you can use Apple MacPippin to watch your PIPPIN programs run.

As always, it will help considerably if you experiment with the sample stacks before proceeding with these exercises. We will concentrate for now on The Howard Stone.

1.1   Open The Howard Stone stack.

1.2   Use Howard to translate a variety of character strings. Try, for example:
       What a Cipher!
       UPPER AND LOWER CASE
       upper and lower case

1.3   Review Howard's scripts to the extent that you can

       a. Identify what event causes translation to occur
       b. Find the script that accomplishes the translation

closeField: **A message sent when we leave a field.**

Remember the object hierarchy from Module 4.

Looking at the scripts of card field "Text Field" as the lone background of the stack, you should see what event triggers translation—it is the closing of the field "Text Field." A closeField message is sent to a field each time that field goes from being "open" to being "closed." That is, when we click in or type in a field, that field is open. The field remains open until we close it. Closing is accomplished by pressing the Enter key, pressing the Tab key (which opens another field), or clicking the mouse outside the field's boundaries. In the case of Howard, any such event will send a translate message up the object hierarchy.

The translate message is received by and responded to by the background script, which is why a send command was not necessary in the script of "Text Field"—the desired recipient of the translate message is in the direct path of the message according to the object hierarchy. In fact, the translate message handler was not included directly in the "Text Field" script, but was put instead in the background, so that we could reference it from the Message box. Commands from the Message box enter the object hierarchy at the card level. Here is the entire script of the background, which includes the translate and makeBinary command handlers.

```
on translate
    put char 1 of card field "Text Field" into tempChar
    put charToNum(tempChar) into tempASCII
    put tempASCII & "" into card field "ASCII Field"
    put makeBinary(tempASCII) & "" into card field "Binary Field"
    repeat with i = 2 to the number of chars in card field "Text Field"
        put char i of card field "Text Field" into tempChar
        put charToNum(tempChar) into tempASCII
        put tempASCII & "" after card field "ASCII Field"
        put makeBinary(tempASCII) & "" after card field "Binary Field"
    end repeat
end translate

function makeBinary decimalValue
    --calculate the binary representation of decimalValue
    put decimalValue div 2 into quotient
    put decimalValue mod 2 into result
    repeat while quotient > 0
        put quotient mod 2 before result
        put quotient div 2 into quotient
    end repeat
    --"pad" the result to make it 8 bits long
    repeat with i = length of result + 1 to 8
        put 0 before result
    end repeat
    return result
end makeBinary
```

One of the first things you notice about Howard is that, like the Rosetta Stone, it accomplishes its translation in two stages. First, it translates each character into its ASCII code. So central is the need for representing textual information (characters) in numeric form that HyperTalk (and many other languages) provide commands that accomplish direct translations to and from ASCII. Looking at Howard's background script reveals that the first step in translating each character of the text entered is accomplished by using one of HyperTalk's translation commands, charToNum.

> Functions act differently from message handlers. See Module 4.

Notice that charToNum is referenced as a function handler, as described in Module 4. It doesn't appear as the first word of a command line. Rather, it occurs in the middle of a line (in this case, where a reference to some value is expected). Also, it is followed by a parenthesized expression indicating the parameters it is to operate on.

Functions, you will remember, are so called because they resemble mathematical functions in two essential ways. First, they are used to calculate and "return" distinct, single values for any input value provided. This is why function references occur in the middle of other HyperTalk commands. When the second put command in the background script is executed, the expression charToNum(tempChar) is evaluated and replaced by the value that the function calculates—that is, the ASCII code for tempChar.

> charToNum: A predefined function that returns the ASCII code for the character passed to it. numToChar: The inverse of charToNum.

The second way that HyperTalk functions are like mathematical ones is that they accept inputs or "parameters." The parenthesized expression following a reference to a function provides the parameters to be used in evaluating the function. The charToNum function accepts a single parameter, the character to be translated into ASCII. In general, functions may accept (require) any number of parameters.

To be precise, charToNum is an example of a "built-in" HyperTalk function like those we saw in Module 4 that process numeric information. Many others, including one named numToChar (which accepts an ASCII code as input and returns the corresponding character), are also provided and are described in detail in the Appendix.

Go back to Howard and do the following exercises.

1.4 Use Howard to translate the string "a b c X Y Z".

1.5 Use the charToNum function directly from the Message box to verify that each character was translated into its ASCII code correctly. (That is, type put charToNum ("a") in the Message box and press the Enter key; when put is used with no destination specified, it puts its value in the Message box!)

1.6 Use the numToChar function from the Message box to convince yourself that the translation works in both directions.

As easy to use as it is, the charToNum function accomplishes only half of the desired translation. For a given character, charToNum returns its ASCII code in decimal (base-10) notation. We must write—and we have—the

Defining our own message handlers.

HyperTalk code that accomplishes the second stage of the translation, from ASCII (decimal) notation to binary code. We have chosen to do so by taking advantage of HyperTalk's facility for defining our own functions.

The fourth line of the translate message handler makes reference to another function, makeBinary, which is not one of HyperTalk's built-in functions. Rather, we have defined makeBinary as part of the background script. As is the case with message handlers we define, this function can be used directly only by scripts that have access to it via the normal object hierarchy. Also remember, functions are useful only when a single, specific value is to be calculated. makeBinary is identified as a function (by the special word function) and is indicated to have a single parameter, named decimalValue. The word decimalValue is used as a placeholder by the function, and is automatically set to the value of whatever parameter is supplied with the function reference (in this case, the ASCII code stored in the variable tempASCII).

The commands in the function makeBinary implement the standard algorithm for translating decimal values into binary, described in Section 5.2. Obviously, the length of the binary result depends on the ASCII code provided as a parameter. For the sake of uniformity, the binary forms of ASCII codes are all prescribed to be eight bits long (in other words, ASCII is an eight-bit code). So, the rest of the function "pads" the result with however many zeros are needed to make the result eight bits long. The value to be "returned" to the translate message handler—that is, the one that will effectively replace the reference to makeBinary in translate— is specified in the final statement of makeBinary. Every function must contain at least one such return command.

It is interesting to note that the ability to define functions such as makeBinary is really just a notational convenience provided by HyperTalk. In fact, any calculation that can be accomplished with a user-defined function can also be accomplished using conventional message handlers and either global variables or parameters. Functions merely save us the trouble of using separate commands for declaring and setting parameters and for passing messages to other handlers. Also, functions help to make explicit where and what calculations are being performed within scripts.

1.7 Use the Message box to test the makeBinary function by giving it some simple decimal numbers to convert, and verify by hand that the conversions are correct. (Do this—it will help you later! Remember that makeBinary is a function, and so you must type, for example, put makeBinary(27) to invoke it from the Message box.)

1.8 Write a function called makeDecimal that accepts a binary value as a parameter and calculates its decimal equivalent; put it in the background script and test it from the Message box. Refer to Section 5.2 for a description of the required algorithm.

FIGURE 5.4	Coding an Instruction

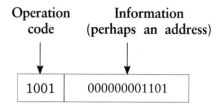

ENCODING INSTRUCTIONS

> Instructions are represented in binary, too.

Since modern computers represent information in binary, it is not hard now to see what form their instructions must take. Just as we decided to represent characters by a more-or-less arbitrary binary code, we can also represent instructions by deciding on a binary code for each instruction. In a hypothetical computer, we might decide that each instruction will be represented by a four-bit code, optionally followed by 12 more bits that provide details about what the operations will do, as shown in Figure 5.4.

To explain one possible use for the 12 extra bits of information, consider that our hypothetical computer will include some *memory*—that is, storage locations for binary information. You can think of a location in memory as a cell into which you can place a character or number. Each of these memory cells is referenced by an *address* (location number), and these addresses will range from 0 to 4095 in our computer. Since each number from 0 to 4095 can be expressed in 12 or fewer binary digits, we could use that part of the instruction code to refer to any location in memory—to store or retrieve the contents of that cell, for example.

We will also endow our computer with an *accumulator,* a special location used for storing intermediate results of computations. An accumulator is just the computer version of something we do all the time. If, for instance, we need to add 3 + 4 + 5, we might add 3 and 4, save the sum temporarily (in our mental accumulator), and then add 5 to the sum we saved. Our computer, then, takes the form illustrated in Figure 5.5. For this computer, the operations and their codes might include the following:

CODE	INFORMATION	ACTION
0000	X	Store accumulator value in memory location X.
0001	X	Load contents of memory location X into accumulator.
0010	X	Set accumulator to the value X.
0111	X	Halt execution.
1001	X	Add contents of memory location X to accumulator.

FIGURE 5.5   A Hypothetical Computer

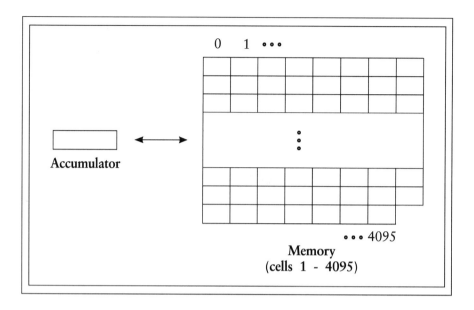

We can now read the program that appeared at the beginning of this section. We'll insert spaces to make it easier to read (although the computer has no need for them), and number the instructions for our reference:

```
[1]  0001  0000  0000  1100
[2]  1001  0000  0000  1101
[3]  0000  0000  0000  1100
[4]  0111
```

Instruction 1 begins with 0001, the code for "load accumulator from memory," and continues with the binary number 1100, equivalent to 12 in decimal. This instruction, then, tells the computer to make a copy of whatever is in memory cell 12 and place that value into the accumulator. Instruction 2 begins with 1001, the code for "add to accumulator," and continues with the binary representation for 13, so the computer will add a copy of whatever is in cell 13 to the accumulator. Instruction 3, with code 0000 and auxiliary information 1100, is a command to copy the value in the accumulator into memory cell 12. Instruction 4 tells the computer to halt. A trace of the action of this machine language program is given in Figure 5.6, in which we assume that memory location 12 originally contains the representation for the number 6 and location 13 originally contains the representation for 9.

There's probably little need for us to point out what would become very obvious if you tried to write a program of even moderate length in this language—programming in machine language is *hard*. As you'll see in the next module, the machine has no difficulty executing programs in machine language. After all, it was built from components designed to run programs in that language, and, in fact, machine language programs are all that it can execute. Machine languages were the only computer languages available to early programmers. Now that you have had some programming experience, you might be able to imagine how difficult it was for those hardy souls to write programs at all, much less debug the programs in the all too likely event that they didn't run perfectly the first time. Even when a machine language program was finally running more or less reliably, imagine the challenge of revising it at a later date. Suppose you were given someone else's program, a mountain of code in zeros and ones, and the boss said, "Smith's been transferred to our Seattle of-

FIGURE 5.6   Tracing the Action of a Program

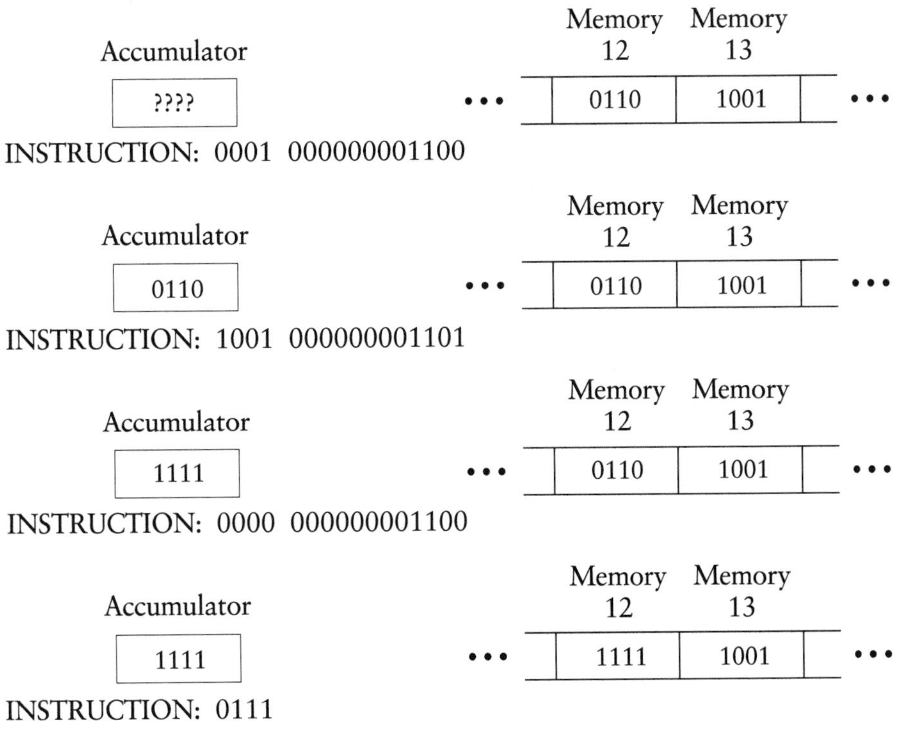

Accumulator		Memory 12	Memory 13	
????	• • •	0110	1001	• • •

INSTRUCTION: 0001 000000001100

Accumulator		Memory 12	Memory 13	
0110	• • •	0110	1001	• • •

INSTRUCTION: 1001 000000001101

Accumulator		Memory 12	Memory 13	
1111	• • •	0110	1001	• • •

INSTRUCTION: 0000 000000001100

Accumulator		Memory 12	Memory 13	
1111	• • •	1111	1001	• • •

INSTRUCTION: 0111

FIGURE 5.7   **Programming in Assembly Language**

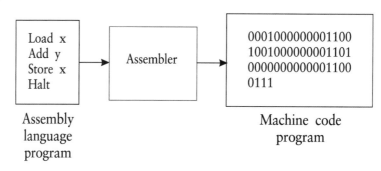

Load x
Add y
Store x
Halt

Assembler

0001000000001100
1001000000001101
0000000000001100
0111

Assembly
language
program

Machine code
program

---

fice; I want you to take over his accounts receivable program and fix it so that the quarterly report lists accounts by states, and alphabetically within states."

It didn't take early programmers long to see the shortcomings of machine language. Five or ten minutes is a good guess. It also didn't take them very long to arrive at a way to make their lives easier. It is likely that every programmer of those days kept a pad of paper at hand with something like this written on it:

(x = cell 12, y = cell 13)
        Load x
        Add y
        Store x
        Halt

> **Assembly language consists of word codes (easy for people) for machine language codes (necessary for computers).**

From there, it's a short step to the realization that one could write a program (in machine language, of course) that would translate these mnemonics to machine language, so that whenever the new program saw the characters "Add," it would produce output "1001." Thus was born the first program translator, the *assembler*. An assembler is a program that takes as its input a source code written in an *assembly language,* like the language of mnemonic names just shown, and produces the corresponding machine language program, or object code, by translating each line of assembly language into the corresponding machine language (see Figure 5.7).

> **A continuing theme in the history of computers is the move away from the tyranny of the machine.**

Source code is what goes into a program translator; *object code* is what comes out.

The invention of the assembler was the first step away from the tyranny of the machine and toward the realization that programs are written for people as well as for the machine. People must write, maintain, and modify programs, and programmers' time is expensive. Anything that makes programming more efficient not only makes the programmer's life easier, but also saves his or her employer money. Assemblers are still around today, despite the fact that higher-level languages such as HyperTalk are easier to use. Still, if you need direct, precise control of the computer's functions—for example, if your program must fit into a prescribed amount of memory, or if there is a piece of your program that absolutely must run as efficiently as possible—there is no better method than assembly language.

*SIDE TRIP: THE PIPPIN ASSEMBLER

So far, our excursion through the terrain of computer science has been more or less linear, like many commercial tours one arranges through a travel agent. In a manner of speaking, after each section you were herded onto the bus for the next section, and then the one after that, and the one after that, and so on. In the spirit of a deluxe tour, however, we have included a few optional side trips. These side trips are available at no extra cost, but each does take two or three days and, like a hiking tour of the Alps, may require a bit more effort than the rest of the adventure. Those of you who—for lack of time, effort, or interest—wish to pass up this side trip may feel free to do so; we'll rejoin the rest of the party at the beginning of Section 5.3. For those of you who elect to take this side trip, we'll provide a detailed look at a sample assembly language.

For reasons we'll make clear in the next module, we call our assembler PIPPIN. PIPPIN has 16 instructions, listed in the following User's Guide. For convenience, we assume that each PIPPIN program consists of a collection of statements, consecutively numbered from 1. In the User's Guide, we adopt the following conventions: (1) All variables refer to 12-bit binary numbers. (2) Unless the program instructs differently, execution begins with statement 1, and thereafter statement $n + 1$ is performed immediately after statement n. (3) Square brackets around a variable refer to the contents of the memory cell at the location indicated by that variable (so if X represents 13, then [X] refers not to 13 but rather to whatever is stored in memory cell 13). We also use the letter A to refer to the accumulator. An arrow refers to the operation of copying and moving information from one location (that to the left of the arrow) to another (to the right of the arrow). For example, the notation, $A \rightarrow X$ transfers a copy of A's data to location X. PIPPIN's 16 instructions can be divided into three groups: data flow, control, and arithmetic-logic.

---

* This section, like all side trips, is strictly optional.

The PIPPIN User's Guide

Data Flow
STO X   A → X, store accumulator in location X.
LOD X   [X] → A, load contents of X into accumulator.
SET X   X → A, place number X in accumulator.

Control
JMP X   Go to instruction number X.
JMZ X   If A = 0, then go to instruction number X, otherwise go to next
          instruction.
NOP   No operation, do nothing but go to next instruction.
HLT   Halt execution, don't go to any other instruction.

Arithmetic-Logic
ADI X   A + X → A (add immediate), add number X to accumulator.
ADD X   A + [X] → A (add direct), add contents of location X to
          accumulator.
SBI X   A − X → A (subtract immediate), subtract X from
          accumulator.
SBD X   A − [X] → A (subtract direct), subtract contents of
          location X from accumulator.
AND X   A **and** [X] → A, if contents of A and location X are both ≠ 0, set
          A to 1, otherwise set A to 0.
NOT   **not** A → A, if A = 0, set A to 1, otherwise set A to 0.
CPZ X   (Compare zero), if [X] = 0, then set A to 1, else set A to 0.
CPL X   (Compare less), if [X] < 0, then set A to 1, else set A to 0.

In the following examples, a semicolon signals a *comment*—anything from (and including) the semicolon to the end of the line is ignored by PIPPIN, and in fact will not be part of the PIPPIN input when you are writing PIPPIN programs in the lab exercises of this module.

Example 1   This program uses two numbers, stored in cells 11 and 12, which we refer to in the comments as X and Y. The program instructions themselves are stored in memory locations 1 through 10. If [X] < 2 * [Y], then cell 13, called ANS, is set to 0, otherwise ANS is set to 1.

```
        ;double the contents of Y (which is cell 12 here)
[1]     LOD 12      ;load [Y] into ACC
[2]     ADD 12      ;ACC now contains twice Y's value
[3]     STO 12      ;store new value back in Y
        ;store [X] - twice original [Y] value in cell Y
          (X is in cell 11)
[4]     LOD 11      ;load [X] into ACC
[5]     SBD 12      ;now ACC has what we'd call X - 2Y
```

```
[6]        STO 12      ;which we store in cell Y
        ;set answer to 0 if X < 2Y, otherwise set
          answer to 1
[7]        CPL 12      ;if X - 2Y < 0, put 1 into ACC,
                           else put 0
[8]        NOT         ;invert value in ACC (swap 0 ↔ 1)
[9]        STO 13      ;store the result in ANS (cell 12)
[10]       HLT         ;quit
[11]                   ;storage for X
[12]                   ;storage for Y
[13]                   ;storage for ANS
```

You might find it easier to understand the PIPPIN version if you keep the analogous HyperTalk version in mind:

[1]   Get y
    —recall from the Module 4 lab: "it" is a HyperTalk global variable
    —and "get" places the value in y into the variable "it"
    —here, we are using "it" to mimic the accumulator
[2]   add y to it
[3]   put it into y
[4]   get x
[5]   subtract y from it
[6]   put it into y
[7]   if y < 0 then
       put 1 into it
    else
       put 0 into it
[8]   put 1 − it into it
[9]   put it into ans

Notice that while we could simulate the PIPPIN program with HyperTalk (which is exactly what we will do with the PIPPIN assembler in the lab), the HyperTalk simulation is much wordier than it needs to be. We could have achieved exactly the same result with a single HyperTalk control structure:

if x < 2 * y then
    put 0 into ans
else
    put 1 into ans

> Don't lose heart—assembly language takes some getting used to.

In Section 5.3, we'll see how this more sophisticated program fragment would be translated into machine language.

Example 2   The following program computes the sum $1 + 2 + \cdots + limit$, for some positive integer *limit*. This program contains an example of a loop in which the index, stored in cell INDEX, successively takes on the values 1, 2, . . . , which are added into a running sum, stored in cell SUM. The loop terminates when the value in INDEX is equal to the value stored in LIMIT.

```
        ;initialize index (cell 17) to 1
[1]         SET 1               ;set ACC to 1
[2]         STO 17              ;and load that into
                                   cell INDEX
        ;initialize running sum (cell 18) to 0
[3]         SET 0
[4]         STO 18
        ;start of loop, if index > limit (cell 19), jump
                                   out of loop
[5]         LOD 17              ;load index into ACC
[6]         SBD 19              ;ACC now has index - limit
[7]         SBI 1               ;and now has index - limit
                                   -1
[8]         JMZ 16              ;if that's zero (so index =
                                   limit + 1), exit
        ;add index to running sum
[9]         LOD 18              ;load running sum into ACC
[10]        ADD 17              ;ACC has index + running
                                   sum
[11]        STO 18              ;which we store back in
                                   running sum
        ;increase index by 1
[12]        SET 1
[13]        ADD 17              ;ACC now has index + 1
[14]        STO 17              ;which we place back into
                                   index
[15]        JMP 5               ;jump to start of loop,
                                   line 5
[16]        HLT                 ;out of the loop from JMZ
                                   step, done
[17]                            ;INDEX
[18]                            ;SUM
[19]                             ;LIMIT
```

There's more to this example than might appear at first. Although much of the simplicity of this approach is obscured by the fact that it's written in

PIPPIN, the underlying idea is very tidy: We loop with INDEX varying from 1 to LIMIT, and in each iteration of the loop we add the current value of INDEX to the running SUM. In HyperTalk terms, we are doing this:

```
put 0 into sum
repeat with index = 1 to limit
   add index to sum
```

While this algorithm is simple enough, we can do better. Notice that the time it takes to compute the sum depends upon how large LIMIT is: If LIMIT is 10, we must run through the loop 10 times, and if LIMIT is 1000, we make 1000 iterations of the loop, which might take a considerable amount of time. A good programmer, though, has studied enough mathematics and theory of algorithms to realize that this sum is special. It happens that for any positive integer $n > 1$,

> It's better to work smart than work hard.

$$1 + 2 + 3 + \cdots + n = n(n + 1)/2 \quad \text{(See footnote)}^*$$

With this in mind, all we would have to do is compute limit * (limit + 1)/2, which takes a single statement (in HyperTalk, at least), no matter how large limit is. Of course, we can't do that in PIPPIN, since it doesn't have a multiplication operator, but it does show that as a general rule we cannot always count on the most obvious solution being the best.

It is worth noting in passing that there are two common features of assemblers that we left out of PIPPIN:

1. *Symbolic references* to variables—that is, the option to give names to location in memory, through the use of the EQ assembler directive. The statements TOTAL EQ 12, ADD TOTAL would together be equivalent to ADD 12. EQ statements are not translated into machine code; rather they provide information for use by the assembler.

2. *Statement Labels,* so that if statement 3 was HLT, we could label it as DONE:HLT and have another statement JMP DONE, which would, when encountered, transfer control directly to the statement with label DONE, which in this case would be equivalent to JMP 3.

These enhancements make assembly language programming simpler by increasing the readability of the programs. Consider, for instance, the program in Example 2. With symbolic references and statement labels, the program would take the following form:

```
INDEX  EQ  17

SUM  EQ  18
```

---

* You could prove this if you looked at, say $1 + 2 + \cdots + 9 + 10$. Add the numbers in pairs in a different order: $1 + 10 = 11$, $2 + 9 = 11$, $3 + 8 = 11$, and so on. There are five pairs, each of which is equal to 11, so the sum is $5 \times 11 = 55$. Now replace 10 everywhere by n and you have a proof.

```
                LIMIT EQ  19
                SET  1
                STO  INDEX
                SET  0
                STO  SUM
        LOOP:   LOD  INDEX
                SBD  LIMIT
                SBI  1
                JMZ  END
                LOD  SUM
                ADD  INDEX
                STO  SUM
                SET  1
                ADD  INDEX
                STO  INDEX
                JMP  LOOP
        END:    HLT
```

We think you would agree that this form is considerably easier to read, even without comments. Symbolic references and statement labels are actually just two aspects of the same thing, if you recall that a program is stored in memory just as its data are. Another benefit of symbolic variable references and statement labels is that we are not forced to place a program in a specified location in memory. A more sophisticated assembler would make these references available to the *loader* program, which could then place the assembler program and its data in an available location in memory. This is particularly important when your job must compete with others for space in a computer's memory.

REVIEW QUESTIONS

1. Count from 1 to 20 in binary.
2. Convert 704 to binary, and check your answer by converting it to decimal.
3. What string of characters does 1001111 1001011 0100001 represent?
4. What is an assembler? Why use one?
*5. Write PIPPIN programs to perform the following tasks:
    a. Triple the value presently in the accumulator.
    b. Move the contents of cell 12 to cell 13.

---

* Starred exercises are for those who took the side trip.

AE LAB

LAB EXERCISE 2

If you are interested in how the translation techniques embodied in Howard might manifest themselves in an honest-to-goodness program translator, look at the Apple MacPippin stack (Figure 5.8). Apple MacPippin allows you to enter manually or to read in from files PIPPIN programs, to translate them into a hypothetical machine language form, and to watch the effects of their execution. Open Apple MacPippin and do the following exercises.

2.1   Use the Open... command from the Pips menu to read in a file called Ex1 (which resides in a folder named PIPs on your Æ disk). This is the PIP-PIN program listed as Example 1 earlier in this section. It is intended to set location 13, currently labelled "ANS," to 0 if the value at location X is less than twice the value at location Y.

FIGURE 5.8   The Apple MacPippin Stack

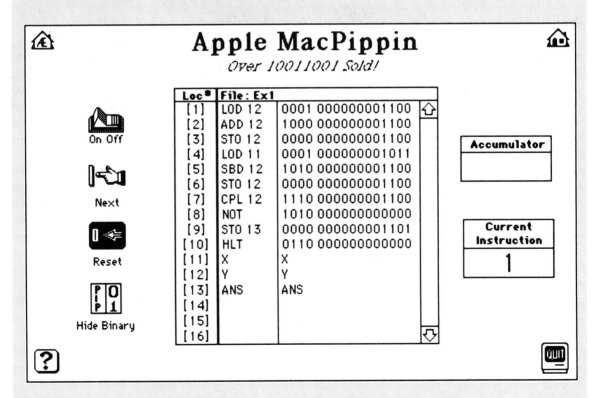

2.2 Click the Show Binary button to see the machine language form of Ex1.

2.3 Replace the X in line [11] of the PIPPIN window and the Y in line [12] by 3 and 201, respectively. These are the values we want to use for X and Y.

2.4 Run the program one instruction at a time using the Next button. Watch the values that appear in the "Accumulator" and "Current Instruction" boxes, and verify that the program performs as described.

5.3   WHAT PEOPLE DO

Among their other activities, people solve problems. For our purposes, that means that people write computer programs to help them solve problems. Writing programs in machine language is tedious, error prone, and time consuming, so much so that hardly anyone writes programs in machine language anymore. Writing programs in assembly language is less tedious and error prone, but is still time consuming. Assembly language programs seem to be (because they are) more verbose than they need to be: It is far more natural for us to think in terms of statements such as

```
put a + b into c
```

or, in Pascal,

```
c := a + b
```

rather than the assembler equivalent

```
LOD  A
ADD  B
STO  C
```

Clearly, a higher-level language—that is, a more expressive, natural one—would be closer to the terms we typically use for solving problems.

BEYOND THE ASSEMBLER

It's better to work smart than work hard—especially for programmers.

Verbosity is one reason why assembly language is time consuming. Some studies indicate that the total number of lines of debugged code a professional programmer can produce in a day is more or less independent of the language in which the programs are written. That means that if we could program in a language that used only one-fifth as many statements as assembly language (or, equivalently, machine language) to do the same task, it would be reasonable to expect that we could finish our programming task five times faster in the less verbose language.

We have already mentioned another reason why we would like to avoid having to write all our programs in assembly language—it's hard for most of us to think in assembler terms. A few decades ago, some linguists had the idea (largely discredited today) that one's native language dictates to a certain degree the way one thinks. A similar property does hold for computer languages, however. If we could design a programming language (without worrying for the moment about how to get a computer to "understand" programs in this language), it would certainly make good sense to design our language so that it makes writing, reading, and maintaining programs easier. In short, our goal should be to make the programming process as productive and efficient as possible.

One way of facilitating the programming process would be to sacrifice control over some aspects of the programming process, leaving them to the discretion of the computer, in return for the freedom to solve problems in higher-level terms. In particular, we could design our language so that much of the detail work was handled by the computer. After all, it is almost always easier to perform a large task if you are confident that the detail work is being handled for you—this is why you rarely see corporation presidents working on the production line or out in the field handling sales. Corporation presidents should concern themselves with corporate strategy and leave it to their subordinates to make sure that the doors are bolted on correctly and the bills get paid on time. This is an excellent strategy for programming, especially since detail work, done tirelessly and without flaw, is what the computer does best. What we want, then, is an "intelligent" programming language, one that handles the details of where to store information, when to move it, and so on, allowing us to concentrate on the Big Picture.

It's all very nice to make a wish list of features that a programming language should have, but such designing is purely an academic exercise unless we can figure out how to get a computer to execute programs in a language that it is not wired to recognize. The answer, of course, is simple—we need to construct our own Rosetta Stone. We want a program to do what an assembler does, only better, and in a more sophisticated fashion.

For every modern computer language, there is a program that takes a source code file in the high-level language and produces as its output object code in machine language, which the computer can then run. These translators come in two flavors, depending on whether they translate and run the source code one line at a time, or translate the entire source code at once and then turn it over to the machine to run. The first type of translator, which translates a line of source code into one or more lines of object code and then instructs the computer to perform those instructions until another line has to be translated, is called an *interpreter*. Interpreters have the advantages that they are fairly easy to write, and when the source code program produces an error, the interpreter can easily point to the line of source code that caused the error. The major disadvantage of interpret-

> Again, we're moving away from being dictated to by the machine.

> An interpreter says "Beat the eggs, beat the eggs, beat the eggs, . . ." as many times as it takes. A compiler says "Beat the eggs until they form soft peaks."

ers is that they are slow. A source code line inside a loop that is repeated 1000 times will be translated each of the 1000 times it's encountered, which could make a significant dent in execution time. BASIC, LISP, and HyperTalk are commonly implemented by interpreters.

If speed is of the essence, a better but more complicated solution is to use a *compiler,* which translates the source code once and for all, producing a complete machine language program. However, when the machine language program fails, it is much more difficult (though not impossible) to show the programmer where in the source code the error resides. But this disadvantage is offset by the increase in speed. In fact, since compilation and execution are separated, the time of translation has no direct effect on execution speed. After a correct program has been completely translated, you never have to translate it again. Pascal, C, and FORTRAN are languages that are generally compiled.

In theory, then, our job is simple. We can design a language of our own, by

1. Specifying precisely the form that statements in the language will take, and what each statement will do

2. Writing an interpreter or compiler that takes programs in our language and produces object code programs in the machine's language.

> So, to make the Mac run FORTRAN programs, all we need to do is buy a program that translates FORTRAN to the Mac's machine language.

That means that once we've written the translator, the user of our language does not need to be concerned with the details of the machine. A particular FORTRAN program should run identically on an Apple Macintosh or a Digital Equipment VAX or a Cray XM-P or any other computer, as long as there is a FORTRAN-to-machine-language translator program for that machine.* As far as the programmer is concerned, the FORTRAN program is written for a *virtual machine,* wired to run FORTRAN, which has nothing to do with the real machine being used. In other words, the fact that the FORTRAN program is being translated to run on a specific machine is of no concern to the programmer—he or she can pretend to be working on a machine that understands FORTRAN. We'll return to this idea in later modules.

DESIGNING A LANGUAGE

Machine language is dictated by the circuits inside the computer, as we'll see in Module 6. We as language designers don't have any control over that, in general. However, we can make our programming language take

---

* This is not completely true, since machines of different designs might, for instance, have different ways of representing numbers. A program that runs reliably on one computer might fail on another, because the latter might not be able to handle numbers as large as the former could. There is also widespread disagreement on what constitutes *standard* features in a given language, so statements recognized by one compiler might be unknown to another. You don't have to worry now about that, though, since there is only one version of HyperTalk, and it runs only on Macintoshes.

any form we want, subject only to the restriction that we can build a translator for it (which is why English isn't a programming language—we don't yet know how to write a program to translate all of English into any machine language). Most programming languages are designed to make the programmer's job easier, but exactly what this means has almost as many interpretations as there are languages. To take just a few examples, FORTRAN was designed for scientific and engineering programs; COBOL is tailored for business users; Pascal, BASIC, and Logo are teaching languages; Ada is a single standard for Department of Defense contractors; and HyperTalk provides a simple, flexible data management environment with a powerful graphic interface.

Scores of programming languages are available today, all with relative strengths and shortcomings. A programmer can do things in Pascal that require complicated workarounds in FORTRAN; a simple HyperCard stack would require a large and complicated Pascal program to duplicate; and a HyperCard stack would take an annoyingly long time to do some of the things that a FORTRAN program can do in seconds. In spite of the plethora of languages, a simple taxonomy serves to classify most languages into four major groups: imperative, functional, declarative, and object-oriented.

> The basic notion of imperative languages is "Do these operations."

In *imperative* languages the fundamental unit of abstraction is a procedure. That is, a program is composed of a group of procedures under the control of one "main" procedure. Each procedure is a group of statements describing in recipelike fashion the steps for accomplishing some portion of the program's processing. Consistent with this perspective, imperative languages tend to provide features that support the detailed description of algorithms—for example, if-then-else statements and while- and repeat-loops. FORTRAN, Pascal, and Ada are examples of imperative languages. Here is part of a program in Pascal that adds the odd numbers in a list of numbers:

```pascal
type TermIndex = 1 .. 100;
     TermArray = array [TermIndex] of integer;
var myTerms : TermArray;

procedure SumOdds(n : TermIndex;
                  terms : TermArray;
                  var sum : integer);
  var i : TermIndex;
begin
  sum := 0;
  for i := 1 to n do
    if Odd(terms[i]) then
        sum := sum + terms[i]
end;
```

From another perspective, a program can be viewed as an object that, given input parameters, computes and returns a particular value—like a mathematical function. *Functional* languages, such as LISP, afford programmers with language support for defining functions. Functions can be defined in terms of other functions (including themselves), which ultimately can be described as simple computations. There is no explicit notion in functional languages of a "main" program. Rather, there is one function to be evaluated for specific inputs that, in turn, can reference any number of other functions in the process of performing the calculations. Following is the LISP program to sum odd numbers. (This, and the Pascal version, are adapted from Lawrence G. Tesler, "Programming Languages," *Scientific American,* vol. 251, no. 3, September 1984, pp. 70–74.)

> The basic notion of functional languages is "Transform this information to this."

```
(DEFUN SUMODDS
  (LAMBDA  (TERMS)
   (COND
     ((NULL  TERMS)  0)
     ((ODD  (CAR  TERMS))  ((PLUS  (CAR  TERMS)
                                   (SUMODDS  (CDR  TERMS))))
     (T  SUMODDS  (CDR  TERMS))))))
```

For many applications (including much of what is commonly referred to as "data processing" or standard business applications, as well as knowledge-intensive tasks such as medical diagnosis systems and airline reservation systems), program complexity is not a function of complex calculations or algorithms, but one of the volume and complexity of the information being processed by the program. COBOL and Prolog are examples of *declarative* languages, in which the emphasis is on describing the information being processed by a program, as opposed to the processing algorithms themselves. Such languages offer only modest support for describing algorithms, but allow programmers to be very expressive about the type and format of the input and output data. The program to sum the odd numbers in Prolog would take the following form:

> The basic notion of declarative languages is "Describe what must be true about these data."

```
sumodds([],  0).
sumodds([H|T],N)  :-  sumodds(H,N1),  sumodds(T,N2),
                      sum(N1,N2,N),  !.
sumodds(X,N)  :-  mod(x 2 1),  eq(X,  N),  !.
sumodds(X,  0).
```

Object-oriented languages such as HyperTalk, C++, Object Pascal, and Smalltalk can be seen as hybrids that combine many of the features of the other three language classes. When the processing to be accomplished by a program is organized in terms of "objects" of the programming domain—

> The basic notion of object-oriented languages is "Pass this message to that object."

buttons, fields, files, and cards on a screen, for example—we first describe the organization of these objects and their interrelationships in detail, as we would in a declarative language. We can then associate imperative algorithms (such as scripts) with each of the program objects. Finally, we allow scripts and their corresponding objects to communicate by passing "messages" along communication lines that reflect their organization (the object hierarchy) or by explicitly invoking one another as functional objects. As with functional languages, there is no formal notion of a main program in object-oriented languages. Which part of a program (or which script in a stack) is executed first depends on the input the program is responding to, and then on which part of the program is designated to respond to that input. Finally, here is the program to sum the odd numbers (called a *method*) in Smalltalk:

```
sumOdds
  |total|
  total ← 0.
  self do: [ :each | each \\ 2 = 0 ifTrue: [total ←
      each + total]].
  ↑ total
```

Designing a computer language, in any of these categories, requires that we make decisions about several major features. First, we must decide exactly what information the language is capable of manipulating. PIPPIN is a very simple language in this respect—the only type of data available to it is integers, and only a small subset of the integers, at that. When designing a programming language, though, one typically keeps the needs of the user uppermost in mind, and so includes in the language the ability to handle the kind of data the user will commonly require. Such data almost always include integers and real numbers, such as −65.092615, and frequently include boolean data, which can be either *true* or *false,* and characters, such as A, $, ?, b, and so on.

> **Structured types are made of collections of simple types.**

Along with these simple types of data, we might wish to include *structured types,* consisting of logically grouped collections of simple data types. Some languages include *strings* of characters—such as 'MOON', 'this is a string', and 'FOOBAR456'—each consisting of a collection of characters arranged in order. A generalization of strings is the *array,* which, like a string, is a collection of data of a single type, each element of which can be accessed by specifying its position in the group. Figure 5.9 shows two examples of arrays.

Another common structured data type is the *record,* consisting of a named collection of data, not necessarily all of the same type. A record named "employee," for instance, might have *fields* called "name," consisting of a string; "age," which is an integer; and "payrate," a real number. For an example of a record, see Figure 5.10.

FIGURE 5.9   **Two Arrays**

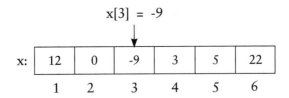

(a) A one-dimensional array of integers

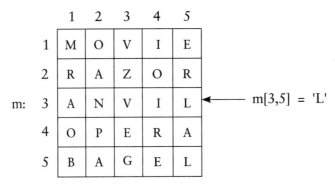

(b) A two-dimensional array of characters

HyperTalk doesn't explicitly support either arrays or records, although we can use collections of card fields to simulate both structured types. We've barely begun to list the types of data supported by all programming languages, but you have seen enough that you should be able to invent a new data type, perhaps one you'd like to see included in HyperCard.

FIGURE 5.10   **A Record with Three Fields**

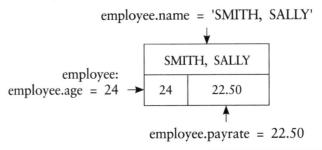

Data are not much use unless we can manipulate the data, so the next decision we need to make is what operations our language will permit on its data types. Most languages have some sort of assignment statement, to set one variable equal in value to another (put it into card field 1, for instance). To include assignment in any language, we must specify the form such statements will take (Pascal uses :=, HyperTalk uses put...into, other languages use = or ←, to name just a few). Not only do we have to specify the *syntax* of the assignment statement—that is, what form it must be written in—but we also have to specify its *semantics,* which is to say, precisely how it will work. Do we want to allow values of different types to be assigned to each other and let the compiler sort out what it means to assign the string "abc" to the variable *total,* which previously held an integer? This adds flexibility, but at the cost of making programs more difficult to understand and debug. At this stage we also have to decide on the set of arithmetic operations we will include, as well as how they will work. For instance, if our language supports integers and reals as distinct types, what type will we decide that the sum of an integer and a real number should be?

As if life weren't complicated enough, we also have to decide what *control structures* we will include in our language. If our language is imperative, with a program consisting of a sequence of statements to be executed in order, we'll need a way to alter the order of execution within the program, using constructs such as **if** statements and **repeat** loops. If our language is object-oriented, we need to be able to pass messages from one object to another, and to handle these messages, as HyperTalk does with statements such as on mouseUp. Unrestricted transfer of control, such as the BASIC GOTO statement or the PIPPIN JMP statement, enable the programmer to move freely from one statement to another, but at the price of producing code that can sometimes be exceedingly difficult to read and understand.

At a higher level of control, we might want to include unit-level transfers of control to subroutines, which are in effect mini-programs (like command and function handlers) that can be called upon by a main program. This makes a program easier to understand, since it hides the details of the action of a subunit from the reader, thereby making the action of the program easier to understand. The program

```
GetALetter(theLetter)
ConvertToASCII(theLetter,ASCIIValue)
ConvertToBinary(ASCIIValue,binaryValue)
put binaryValue into field 2
```

is relatively easy to understand, but might not be so easy if the 30 or more statements that made up the details of the subroutines GetALetter, Convert-ToASCII, and ConvertToBinary were listed directly in the main program in place of the calls to the subroutines. The price we have to pay for including subroutines, though, is greater complexity of our language, both syntactic and semantic.

As you can see, designing a programming language is anything but trivial. We haven't even mentioned the options available to handle input and output, or how our language will react to errors such as division by zero or an accidental call to a nonexistent subroutine. Language design is now, and likely will remain, more of an art than a science. As we have seen, "good" languages—languages that are flexible, powerful, general, easy to read and use, and simple to modify—can take many forms, depending upon one's emphasis. This is one of the reasons why there are so many different programming languages today. Eventually, we might be able to program a computer in a language close to English, using an intelligent compiler or interpreter that converts our fuzzy, possibly ambiguous specifications to a logically correct, precise machine language program. Although that day may seem to be in the distant future, look at the difference between HyperTalk and any machine language. We've come a long way already, and computer science is still in its infancy. It is unlikely, however, that programming languages will eventually all be like English or any other natural language—programmers will always be willing to pay the price of learning a precise and unambiguous language if they can thereby avoid having to answer a multitude of "Exactly what do you mean by this?" questions.

> Language design is an art, supported by a science.

LAB EXERCISE 3

Any program of consequence (including, for the sake of this discussion, The Howard Stone), is written with the intention of using it more than once. Most programs are created, edited, debugged (that is, made to work correctly), and ultimately saved on some external storage device (on a floppy disk, for example). Later, when one wants to run an existing program, the program is read back into the computer's memory from the storage device (this is essentially what happens when you open a stack). HyperTalk programs are created in text form, since we type out scripts using the full keyboard (not just the characters 0 and 1), and they are stored in binary form. Clearly, then, the processes of saving and retrieving programs involve translation.

Just as important, the same processes of saving and retrieving are involved when a program accesses files on an external storage device. Again, this notion of accessing external files is so central to computer applications that most programming languages provide commands to facilitate such access. HyperTalk is no exception. Four related HyperTalk commands can be used to save information in or retrieve information from files.

Let's imagine (this shouldn't be hard to do!) that we want to store in an external file the binary data produced as the result of using Howard to translate a text string. We would have to change Howard as follows. First, somewhere within Howard's scripts (and before we intend to access it), we have to alert HyperCard that Howard intends to reference an external file. This is accomplished by the open file command. For example, if the file Binary Data does not yet exist, the command open file "Binary Data" creates that file (on whatever disk contains the HyperCard program). The file Binary Data is thus hooked to our HyperCard stack and is ready to receive information.

> **Files provide permanent storage for data.**

> **open file: Creates a file with a given name, if one doesn't already exist, and allows a script to read from and write to it.**

Information—which can be the contents of a field, the value of a variable, or even the value returned by some function, can then be sent to the file by means of a write file command. The write file command has the general format write *thing to be written* to file *file name*. The command write makeBinary(tempASCII) to file "Binary Data" would copy one of our binary values into a file named Binary Data. Successive write commands append information directly to the end of the file (that is, all writing goes "after" what is already there). Returns and blank spaces are not included in a file unless put there explicitly by the program that creates the file.

> **write: Writes the given information at the end of a file.**

Once a stack is finished writing data to a file, the program should "close" the file—in other words, unhook it from the current stack and save it on the disk. This is accomplished, appropriately enough, by the close file command. In our example, the command close file "Binary Data" would separate from our stack and save the file containing the results of Howard's translation.

> **close file: Closes and saves a file.**

3.1 Fix Howard's background script so that it works as just described—that is, so that the binary representation of a text string is saved in a separate disk file. (*Note:* Don't worry about having a different file for each piece of text entered. Just translate one string and save its binary representation in some file.)

The primary reason for storing data in an external file is so that the data can be accessed and used without having to be recreated. Having created a file named Binary Data, we could have a script read a value from that file by using either version of HyperTalk's read from file command. One form of the command, read from file *file name* until *character*, reads from the specified file up to and including the next occurrence of the specified character. For example, if we wanted to read values from our Binary Data file until the first blank was encountered, we could issue the command read from file "Binary Data" until " ".

> **read: Reads from the current location in a file and advances to the next location.**

Similarly, we could read until the end of a line was encountered using the command read from file "Binary Data" until return. If we know precisely how many characters we want to read at one time, as we would if we were to read from our Binary Data file, we could use the other form of the read command. The command read from file "Binary Data" for 8 would read exactly eight characters (one ASCII code's worth) from the Binary Data file. Both versions of read store the values read in the global variable it. The variable it need not be declared as global (that's what it means to be a system variable), but can be referenced from within any message handler. The value of it is set by certain HyperTalk commands, such as read and answer, and remains unchanged until another command is executed that affects it.

Thus, to read in a value stored in the file Binary Data and to display it, say, in card field "Binary Field" as it was before it was written out, we could use the combination of statements:

```
read from file "binary data" for 8
put it & "" into card field "Binary Field"
```

Remember that we need to use open file and close file statements before any reading and after all reading has been completed, just as we did when we wanted our scripts to write to files. Since a file to be read must, by definition, already exist, the open file command does not create a new file if a file of the name specified is already on the disk. Instead, it readies the file so that it can be read from.

3.2   Add a new button that, when clicked, will read the data from the file Binary Data and display it in the card field "Binary Field."

By now, you have probably figured out what we are moving toward. We would like to extend Howard so that after it translates some text and stores the text's binary representation in a file, it can read the binary form back in and recreate the text. If you can create a working button as described in the previous exercise, you are two-thirds of the way there! Having successfully read the binary values into the card field "Binary Field" from the external file, all that we need to do is translate the binary codes back into their ASCII (decimal) equivalents. Then, we can use HyperTalk's numToChar function to translate the ASCII values into text. The trick is, thus, the binary-to-decimal conversion, and it really isn't that tricky—this is precisely what your makeDecimal function should have accomplished earlier.

3.3   Extend Howard so that it completes the translation just described. That is, clicking on the button you created in the past exercise should not only read in binary data from an external file, but should also translate it, first, into its ASCII equivalent and, finally, back into its original text form.

Translation of text into binary can thus be accomplished in stages and according to many different algorithms and representation schemes. Similarly, we have seen a number of different ways for HyperCard to interpret HyperTalk commands. Each method results in the same command being executed, but the methods differ in the amount of interpretation required. For example, HyperTalk commands can be executed as a result of being part of a message handler that is invoked according to its position in the object hierarchy. HyperTalk commands can also be executed by issuing them directly from the Message box.

Having nearly completed this lab, we can even imagine that HyperTalk scripts could be read in from an external file, saved in some field, and executed like a normal script. (Again, what do you think happens when you open a stack?) HyperCard affords us one final method for interpreting a HyperTalk command. The do command allows us to refer to a variable's value or a field's contents and have it executed as a HyperTalk command. If, for example, card field "opener" contained the text doMenu "Open Stack...", then the command do card field "opener" would result in the activation of the Open Stack...dialog box.

3.4 Extend your version of Howard so that when you enter a legitimate HyperTalk command (for example, hide menuBar) as the text to be translated, that command is executed after it is read back into and retranslated by Howard.

IMPLEMENTING A LANGUAGE

Once we have designed a language, how do we accomplish its translation? By now, you should know the answer—we write a program to do the translation for us. The assembler had a simple task: It translated assembly language into machine language on a one-statement-for-one-statement basis. With just a little more experience, you could write a PIPPIN assembler; we did, after all, and you can look at the scripts when you get to the disk part of this module. Translation is appreciably more complicated when you design a more sophisticated language, however. As you might expect, the more a language does for you, the harder it is to write its translator.

Generally, the action of any translating program can be divided into three phases:

> To translate (any) language we must recognize the words, use the words to recognize the ideas, and express the ideas in the target language.

1. *Scanning,* in which the source code—really nothing but a long string of characters—is broken down into *tokens,* the smallest chunks of characters that are meaningful in our language—for instance, words, names, numbers, and special symbols such as +. Scanning is the machine equivalent of what we do when we read a sentence and take note of the words it contains.

2. *Parsing,* in which the string of tokens is transformed into a *syntactic structure,* which represents the logical "sense" of the program. In human terms, this step is similar to recognizing the subject, verb, and object of a sentence.

3. *Code generation,* in which the syntactic structure that was constructed during the parsing phase is used to produce the output code,

just as we might paraphrase a sentence so that a six-year-old could understand it.

*SIDE TRIP: DETAILS

We've come to another optional part of our tour. This time your tour guides will take you kayaking through the rapids—we promise that the trip will be short but strenuous. If you want to sit this one out, we'll meet you at the end of this subsection. But if you want to know a little about the details of program translation, come along with us.

The scanning process is usually straightforward, if the language was carefully designed. HyperTalk variables, for instance, can be any collection of contiguous characters, subject to the restrictions that (1) they do not duplicate the words reserved for HyperTalk, such as put and on, (2) they begin with a letter and thereafter contain only letters, digits, or the underscore character, and (3) they are the largest consecutive collection of characters that meet the first two conditions. These rules for variables are not arbitrary, but rather exist to make scanning easy. To see this, consider the statement put a + b into mySum. This statement contains six tokens: 'put', 'a', '+', 'b', 'into', 'mySum'. Remember, a token is the smallest *meaningful* unit of information, which is why 'pu' or 't a +' or 'myS' wouldn't be considered tokens for this statement. To recognize that 'put' is a token, the scanner uses the rules that a HyperTalk variable or reserved word begins with a letter and ends at a blank, and that no other kind of token begins with a letter. The scanner identifies these tokens using a process that looks something like this:

```
repeat until the end of the line has been reached
  skip over blanks in the source string
  if a letter is seen then
    save it and all following characters, up to a blank or end of line
  else
    if a digit or minus sign or plus sign is seen then
      save it and all following characters, up to a blank or end of line
    else
      if a special symbol (like =) is seen then
        save that symbol
      else
        something wrong happened—send an error message
      end if
    end if
  end if
  send what has been saved to token storage
end repeat
```

---

* Remember, all side trips are optional.

FIGURE 5.11   A Parse Tree for x * (2 + y)

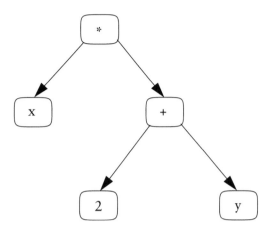

Of course, the scanner, or *lexical analyzer,* for HyperTalk is considerably more complicated than our previous example, but in principle it is just the same.

The lexical analyzer reads characters and returns tokens.

After receiving the tokens, the next part of the scanner replaces them by some convenient internal code, so that it no longer has to deal with strings of characters. In our previous example, the tokens in put a + b into mySum might be stored as the sequence of codes 157, 228, 34, 229, 136, 230.

Once the scanner is finished with its work, the parser takes over, trying to "make sense" of the string of tokens. This is the most difficult part of the translator to design. What usually happens in a compiler or interpreter is that the list of tokens is converted to a *parse tree* in memory via a complicated algorithm. To give you an idea of how a data structure could store meaning, consider the parse tree in Figure 5.11, which stores the "sense" of the algebraic expression $x*(2 + y)$.

This parse tree represents the sense of the algebraic expression in that we could reconstruct the expression (or evaluate it) from the parse tree. To understand a parse tree, we adopt the convention that each box with an operator in it operates on the results of evaluating the left and right subexpressions below it. We can't evaluate the expression until we first add 2 and y (that is, we evaluate from the bottom up), but having done that, we could then multiply x by the result to complete the expression.

Think of parse trees as sentence diagrams.

In a similar way, we could represent the sense of put a + b into mySum by the parse tree of Figure 5.12. In English, the parse tree says, "Add *a* and *b* first (since they're at the lowest level) and then put the result into *mySum*." How the parser converts tokens into parse trees is not for us to discover at

FIGURE 5.12   A Parse Tree for put a + b into mySum

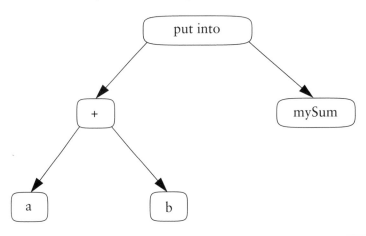

this stage; suffice it to say that this is a very complicated process that, like scanning, can be facilitated by careful design of the language.

Finally, to complete the translation process, these parse trees are used to generate code. Code generation is accomplished by tracking through the syntax tree in a systematic manner, using the information stored in the boxes to help us. Assume that we are generating PIPPIN code from the syntax tree of Figure 5.12. The code generator would act roughly as follows:

> We do parsing easily, but have trouble translating to another language. For computers it's just the opposite.

1. Using the table of symbols produced during the scanning phase, recognize that *a, b,* and *mySum* are variables, so assign a location in memory for each variable.

2. The top box is "put left part into right." Such boxes always result in the generation of PIPPIN code of the following form: STO RIGHT_-SIDE, where it is assumed that the left part has been evaluated and the result has been placed in the accumulator, and that RIGHT_-SIDE is the location in memory of the variable on the right. We look up the token for *c* and find it has been assigned memory cell, let's say, 6, so we'll eventually generate

   STO 6

   We will defer placing the STO instruction into our machine language listing until we have completed evaluating the left side of the parse tree.

3. The left side is an addition operation. For such boxes we generate ADD RIGHT_SIDE where we assume that the result of evaluating

the left part is in the accumulator. At this level in the tree, RIGHT_-
SIDE corresponds to *b,* which we have assigned memory cell 5. We
will list the instruction

```
ADD 5
```

as soon as we have evaluated the leftmost branch of our parse tree.

4. The left side at this level is the token for *a.* The variable *a* has been
    assigned cell 4, so we generate LOD 4, to place *a* in the accumulator.

5. We back our way out of these pending calculations, listing the in-
    structions produced along the way (comments included only for ben-
    efit of the reader):

```
LOD 4    ;place a into ACC
ADD 5    ;ACC now has a + b
STO 6    ;which we store in c
```

6. One statement has been translated from a high-level language into
    PIPPIN assembly language. All that remains is for the PIPPIN code
    to be translated to machine language, which we have seen is a rela-
    tively straightforward process. Then, at last, a computer could exe-
    cute our instruction.

GENERATIONS

We've covered a lot of ground in this module. It may seem confusing now,
but that's because this is the barest introduction to a very large and complicated subject, and, like it or not, some things are difficult by their very
nature. Just bear in mind that the fundamental ideas are simple, however
complex the details may be.

> We characterize gen-
> erations of lan-
> guages by how far
> they are from what
> the machine does and
> how close they are to
> what people do (our
> major theme, again).

We have traced the subject of program translation in roughly historical
order. In the passage from *first-generation languages* for the machine,
through *second-generation languages* with the development of the assembler, and *third-generation languages* such as Pascal, FORTRAN, and C,
we have seen an increasing independence of the programmer from the machine. A FORTRAN or C programmer doesn't even need to know what
kind of machine his or her program is running on, as long as there's a
compiler available for the language/machine combination. We have also
seen an increasing independence from the machine in the sense that more
and more of the details are handled invisibly to the programmer. A *fourth-
generation language* such as HyperTalk includes many software *agents*
that further extend the power of the language. For example, there are dozens of different ways to sort a list in increasing order—the standard text
on sorting and searching is 723 pages long! However, you can tell Hyper-
Card to sort a stack of cards without knowing even one sorting
algorithm—the sorting agent takes over and does the task for you.

We expect that future generations of languages will carry this process even further as software agents are designed to be increasingly clever. It's not unreasonable to expect a "smart" sorting agent, for example, that first looks at the data to be sorted and then chooses the appropriate algorithm for the data—perhaps a simple memory-hogging routine to sort short lists of data, and a complex but more memory-efficient one for long lists of data.

REVIEW QUESTIONS

1. What are the advantages and disadvantages of high-level languages over assembly languages?
2. What is the difference between an interpreter and a compiler?
3. Define the following language types: procedural, functional, declarative, object-oriented.
4. What do we mean by *syntax* and *semantics*? Explain, using English as an example.
*5. Draw the parse trees for the following expressions:

   a. $(3 * x) + (2 * (y - 4))$
   b. $1 + 2 * (3 + 4)$

Æ LAB　　LAB EXERCISE 4

4.1 Review the description of the program in Example 2 in Section 5.2 of the text. The disk version of this program is called Ex2.
4.2 Read Ex2 in your Apple MacPippin stack. Set the value of location LIMIT to 5, run the program, and verify that it performs as advertised.
4.3 Try using Apple MacPippin to write any of the programs described in the exercises at the end of this module.

5.4　EXERCISES

1. Convert the following binary numbers to decimal:

   a. 11111
   b. 101101
   c. 1100011

---

* Starred exercises are for those who took the side trip.

2. Convert the following decimal numbers to binary:

    a. 47
    b. 358
    c. 1023

3. Find a rule that describes which numbers have binary representations consisting solely of 1s.

4. If b is a binary number, what number is represented by $b0$—that is, what number do you get when you place a zero at the end of a binary number? What happens if you place two zeros at the end? Generalize your answer.

5. One way to represent fractions in binary (which, by the way, is not the way they are represented in most computers) is to mimic the way we represent decimal fractions: Each binary digit represents a power of 1/2, so, for instance, the binary fraction 0.1011 would represent

    $$1 \times (1/2) + 0 \times (1/4) + 1 \times (1/8) + 1 \times (1/16) = 11/16$$

    To convert a decimal fraction to this binary form, we could perform the following steps:

    (1) Take the original fraction, f, and repeat steps 2–4 until you have as many digits as you want.
    (2) Double f.
    (3) Write down the integer part (which will be 1 or 0).
    (4) Replace f with its fractional part.

    a. 11/16 has decimal representation 0.6875. Show that this algorithm, applied to 0.6875, yields the binary fraction 0.101100000. . . .
    b. Show that this algorithm represents 3/10 as the infinite repeating binary fraction 0.0100110011001. . . .

6. Write your name in ASCII, as we did in the text with the string "CAB."

*7. Write PIPPIN programs to perform the following tasks:

    a. Swap the contents of cells 12 and 13.
    b. If [X] < [Y] for two cells X and Y, then place 1 in the accumulator, otherwise place 0 in the accumulator.

*8. Write a PIPPIN program that will replace the contents of cell X with half its original value, ignoring any remainders, so the values 8 and 9 would both be replaced by 4.

9. Suppose a vending machine has a small computer embedded in it. The computer is programmable, so that the service person only needs to reprogram

---

* Starred exercises are for those who took the side trip.

the computer to modify its actions. Design a programming language for the vending machine's computer, paying attention to the data types and statements you will include. Assume that the vending machine has space for items of different kinds and prices, and that it can make change and detect counterfeit coins. In your language, write the program that would set the price of item 3 to 65 cents.

10. Some LISP compilers are written in LISP rather than in machine language. How is this possible? (*Hint:* The process may require more than one step. Think about attacking the problem in stages.)

11. HyperTalk terminates some if statements with end if. Is this for ease of scanning or parsing? What would happen if we eliminated end if from Hyper-Talk?

*12. Draw the parse trees for the following algebraic expressions:

a. $(x + (4 + y)) * (x + y)$
b. $1 + (2 * (1 + (2 * (1 + x))))$
c. $x * y + z$ (There are two different ways to parse this expression. Which is correct under the usual rules of algebra?)

*13. Describe the steps the code-generating process might take in translating the following statements:

a. add 1 to x
b. if x = 2 then
      put 0 into x

14. Look over the Pascal, LISP, Prolog, and Smalltalk versions of the program SumOdds. Which one seems easiest to understand? What syntactic features of the less comprehensible ones make them hard to read?

5.5   ADDITIONAL READINGS

BYTE Magazine. Issue on object-oriented programming. 11, no. 8 (Aug. 1986).

Dierker, P. F., and Voxman, W. L. *Discrete Mathematics.* San Diego: Harcourt Brace Jovanovich, 1986.

Lipschutz, S. *Essential Computer Mathematics.* Schaum's Outline Series. New York: McGraw-Hill, 1982.

Pratt, T. W. *Programming Languages: Design and Implementation.* 2d ed. Englewood Cliffs, N.J.: Prentice-Hall, 1984.

---

* Starred exercises are for those who took the side trip.

Sethi, R. *Programming Languages*. Addison-Wesley Series in Computer Science. Reading, Mass.: Addison-Wesley, 1989.

Tennent, R. D. *Principles of Programming Languages*. Englewood Cliffs, N.J.: Prentice-Hall, 1981.

Tesler, L. G. "Programming Languages." *Scientific American* 251, no. 3 (Sept. 1984): 70–78.

Wexelblat, R. L., ed. *History of Programming Languages*. ACM Monograph Series. New York: Academic Press, 1981.

Wulf, W. A.; Shaw, M.; Hilfinger, P. N.; and Flon, L. *Fundamental Structures of Computer Science*. Reading, Mass.: Addison-Wesley, 1981.

HARDWARE

6.1 INTRODUCTION

In the text part of this module, we will see how the computer, at the lowest level, is a physical embodiment of the rules of logic. Starting with simple switches, we will build increasingly complex hardware—using switches to construct simple circuits, then using these to construct a hierarchy of more complicated circuits, and finally connecting these circuits to build a computer. By the end of this module, you will have constructed, on paper at least, a simple but fully functioning computer with nearly all of the important features of real machines.

TEXT OBJECTIVES

In this module, we will

- Show how the circuit components of a computer are constructed, using a photographic process
- Discuss the hierarchy of complexity of a computer, combining switches to make gates, combining gates to make circuits, and constructing the architectural organization of the computer by combining circuits
- Come to understand that the ability of a computer to execute any program is based on wiring in all possible operations and using the program to switch on the proper operation when needed
- Learn how information may be stored in memory
- Explore the design of a small but complete microprocessor

THE LOGIC MACHINE

So far, we have been looking at computer science from the top down. Starting with high-level abstractions, we have seen how each level of our subject can be explained in terms of simpler levels. Applications were explained in terms of system design, systems were seen to be built from programs, and programs were translated into lower-level collections of machine language instructions. In this module, we find ourselves at the lowest level of interest to computer scientists—the hardware itself. To be sure, we don't have to stop there: Having explained how the hardware can be made to execute the statements of a program, a physicist might be interested in how the hardware itself operates. For our purposes, though, it will be enough to assume that the hardware works, without concerning ourselves with the quantum-mechanical details.

A computer is, or course, a demonstrably physical object, constructed of silicon, copper, gallium, arsenic, gold, phenolic resins, and the like. How can such an object run a program, which, after all, is really nothing but a collection of ideas? This is a simple version of a very old question: For centuries, philosophers have pondered the related problem of how brains can have thoughts. In the context of machines, it is fairly easy to imagine building a piece of equipment that can perform simple calculations—after all, the abacus can perform addition, and it is nothing but a collection of wires with beads strung on them. A computer, though, doesn't just add—it multiplies, compares, moves information, and performs a host of other basic tasks, all under the direction of a list of instructions called a program.

Imagine a collection of units—one to add, one to multiply, one to compare numbers, and so on—that can be used to build a computer. To visualize this, think of each unit as a smallish box with sockets on its front panel, and suppose that we have a storeroom full of these boxes along with a large collection of wires with plugs to fit into the sockets on the boxes, to connect the units together. Given a computational task to perform, all we need to do is get the right boxes from the storeroom, plug them together in the right way, and set them running.

The problem with such a computer, though, is that it needs to be rebuilt for every different task. In fact, this was just the way ENIAC (and the Difference Engine, for that matter) was designed. One didn't program ENIAC; one plugged it together. John von Neumann is largely responsible for the notion of a *stored-program* computer (though, to be fair, Babbage had a similar idea). A machine in which the instructions were stored in memory, just as any other data, represents a considerable conceptual leap over our original model. The feasibility of the idea that a machine can be built with the potential to perform *any* sequence of operations is certainly not obvious at first glance. Without this capability, however, computers would be little more than novelty items. After all, it is extremely unlikely that you would want to read through a hundred pages of instructions on how to rewire your machine to switch from word processing to working on a spreadsheet.

> Each program statement is a string of zeros and ones that control the flow of information in the computer by setting switches.

In what follows, we will investigate just how such a general computation device can be constructed. We will see that the components are connected in such a way that *the program itself controls the rewiring*, by signaling the hardware to switch on and off the components in the proper sequence.

METAPHOR: THE SWITCH

The metaphor for this module is the light switch, a box with a small lever and two wires attached. Flip the lever down and no current can flow through the wires; flip it up and current can pass. As we mentioned earlier, we won't worry about how things work inside the switch, because for our purposes, it is sufficient to assume that it does what we want. All we need to do to accomplish most of the mechanized computations we've described is remove the lever from the switch and replace it with an extra wire that can be used to control the switch. You will see that with enough of these switches, connected in the right way, we can perform any operation we want.

Æ STACKS: LOGG-O BUILDING BLOCKS

The Module 5 lab demonstrated both the feasibility and the necessity of using a binary language as a means for communicating with a computer. Why, though, do computers understand only such simple languages? Because there is a direct, but subtle, correlation between the binary number system and the hardware that constitutes most modern computers. Just as binary numbers are represented solely in terms of two symbols (0 and 1), a computer's memory can be thought of as a series of switches, each of which is either on or off at any given point in time. That is, both binary numbers and a computer's hardware are essentially two-valued systems and, as such, can be used to represent and implement boolean logic.

If we can build hardware units that implement the simple logical operations of conjunction, disjunction, and negation, these units can then be combined to produce circuits that, in turn, implement more complex operations such as addition, multiplication, and comparison of binary numbers. Computer scientists who study hardware are concerned with using existing circuits to design new ones that implement useful operations in efficient ways. As such circuits become refined and accepted, they become the building blocks of future computers and, ultimately, influence both the high-level languages programmers use for communicating with computers and the applications that are available to computer users.

In this lab part of the module, we provide you with a stack, called Logg-O, for designing and experimenting with simple logical circuits. While it is a far cry from the tools used for building modern, very-large-scale integrated circuits, it can—and will—be used to demonstrate the utility of logic for simulating useful instructions.

LAB OBJECTIVES

In the disk part of this module, you will

- Use the Logg-O stack to create and experiment with a variety of logical circuits
- Review the scripts of the Logg-O stack to see how it works
- Extend the stack by completing the script of one of the logical operations

---

6.2   THE GATE LEVEL

In modern computers, the devices we will discuss in this section are about the size of large bacteria, far too small to be seen by the naked eye. How are these components constructed in the first place, if they're that small? The answer rests in three technologies, two of which began during Babbage's lifetime and the other about a century later.

1. The idea of *representing information by electrical signals* led to the development of the telegraph in the mid-nineteenth century. In a fashion strikingly similar to that of modern computers, information was represented as a sequence of pulses of current in a wire, so that the letter *A* was represented as a short pulse followed by a longer one, for instance.

A number of devices were developed over the following years to control this current flow, but switching devices such as relays and vacuum tubes all suffered from the disadvantages of large size, high power consumption, and slow speed. The transistor, invented in the late 1940s, overcame all three of these disadvantages.

2. In essence, a *transistor* consists of three connected pieces of silicon with small amounts of impurities added, such as phosphorus or boron, along with a wire attached to each piece. The pieces are called the *collector,* the *emitter,* and the *base.* We can ignore here the details of how a transistor works—the important idea is that normally no current can flow between the collector and the emitter, but when an electrical signal is applied to the base a current can pass between the other two elements. In other words, a transistor is just an on-off switch with no moving parts.

The first transistor circuits were made by connecting the components with soldered wires. The size and complexity of such circuits are not limited by the size of the transistors—which, unlike relays or vacuum tubes, can be made very small indeed—but rather by the practical difficulties of soldering very small wires together in close quarters. One way around this problem is to use the last of our three contributing technologies, photography.

3. *Photography* was first successfully demonstrated at the very end of the eighteenth century, and by Babbage's time the technology was well enough developed to permit battlefield photography during the Crimean War in 1854. In essence, photography is based on the principle that some chemicals change their properties upon exposure to light. Silver nitrate, for example, when exposed to light and treated with the right chemicals, changes to metallic silver. This silver comprises the black portions of a photographic negative. It is also an excellent conductor of electricity, which brings us to our last development in circuits.

It is possible to "print" the wires of a circuit directly on a nonconducting base, using a four-step process. First, a sandwich is made by placing a layer of copper on the base board and covering the copper with a chemical that reacts to light, called a *photoresist*. A photographic negative of the circuit is then made and the base-copper-photochemical sandwich is exposed to light through the negative *mask*. Where the light hits the photochemical, the chemical hardens. The next step is to wash away the unhardened photochemical, leaving only the areas exposed to light. A second chemical bath follows, etching away the uncovered copper, and finally the hardened photoresist is removed in a third bath, leaving the wires photographically printed on the base board. Figure 6.1 illustrates this process.

With the photographically built printed circuit in hand, all that remains is to fit the components' wires into holes in the board and solder the whole assembly together. For a complicated circuit photographic construction saved considerable manufacturing time, with the added advantage that one mask can serve as the template for building as many boards as needed.

Building a transistor photographically is just like the process in Figure 6.1 with more steps.

In the 1950s, it became clear to many electrical engineers that the idea of constructing circuits photographically need not be limited to just the wires—the transistors and other components could themselves be produced by depositing the right chemicals in repeated applications of this process, thereby building an entire electronic device on a wafer of silicon. Such a device is known as an *integrated circuit*. The idea of using what is in essence the technology of the printing press to produce electronic equipment had several important consequences. The designed masks could be photographically reduced, permitting the manufacture of circuits that were far smaller than could be produced by any previous method. Additionally, the reduced masks could be duplicated, allowing dozens of identical circuits to be made at the same time on a single silicon wafer. This is particularly important because it is difficult to make large wafers of silicon, so there is a considerable saving of cost in having one wafer serve as

FIGURE 6.1   Constructing a Circuit Photographically

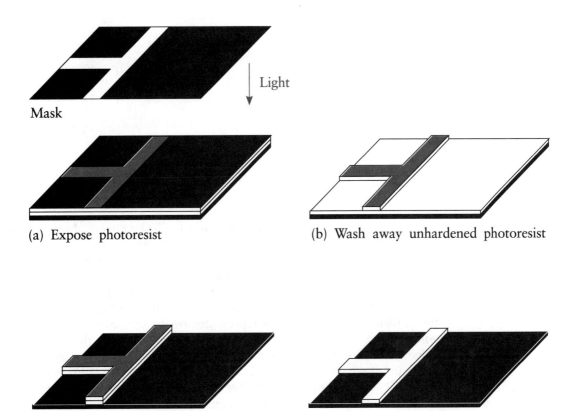

Mask

Light

(a) Expose photoresist

(b) Wash away unhardened photoresist

(c) Etch away uncovered copper

(d) Wash away photoresist

the base for many circuits. Indeed, the decreasing size of integrated circuits—about 50 percent per year over the past three decades—is driven more by economic reasons than by a desire for small size alone.

BUILDING BLOCKS

Now that we have an idea of how the microchip in a computer is built, we can turn our attention to the design of the circuits themselves, starting with our simple switch. We can think of a switch, such as a transistor, as a box with three wires connected to it, called *in, out,* and *control*. The *control* wire controls whether current can flow from the *in* wire to the *out*

FIGURE 6.2   A Normally Open Switch

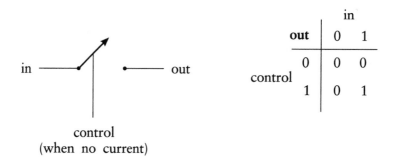

wire; it replaces the lever on our light switch. (To be honest, things are actually quite a bit more complicated at this level, but the details belong in a course on electrical engineering, not here.) Our switches will come in two basic varieties—"normally open" and "normally closed."

In a normally open switch (see Figure 6.2), current can pass from *in* to *out* only when there is a signal at the *control* wire. If we adopt the convention that a high voltage in a wire is represented by the symbol 1 and little or no voltage by 0, this switch can be viewed as a logic operator that says, "The value of *out* is 1 only when both *in* and *control* are 1, otherwise the value of *out* is 0." If we interpret 1 and 0 as numbers, then, we have made a device that can be interpreted as a multiplier in the universe of numbers {0,1}.

In a normally closed switch (see Figure 6.3), current can flow from *in* to *out* unless there is a signal in the *control* wire. Again, we could write 1 instead of "high voltage" and 0 instead of "low or no voltage," and look at

FIGURE 6.3   A Normally Closed Switch

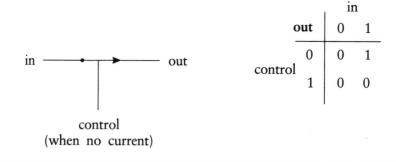

this switch as operating on the values of *in* and *control* to produce a value for *out*. In this case, the operation produces 1 only in the case that *control* is 0 (the switch is closed, allowing current to flow) and *in* is 1 (there is a current that can flow from *in*).

Instead of thinking of information represented by electrical current, you might find it helpful to think of information as automobiles. Then a normally closed switch would be represented as a highway junction. When there is no car on the *control* road, traffic along the main road from *in* to *out* can flow normally, but when a car comes along the *control* road and blocks the intersection, no traffic can flow from *in* to *out*.

LOGIC

The essential behavior of the normally open switch has nothing to do with electrical currents. In fact, to insist on clinging to descriptions that use the model of electricity actually obscures the basic nature of the switch, which is the same whether it controls a current of electricity, regulates the flow of water in pipes, or determines the rotation of shafts and gears. What is important is that, first, the information can be in one of two *states* (high/low voltage, water flow/no flow, or rotation/no rotation), which we can represent by 1 and 0, and, second, we can regard the switch as an operator that produces an output state depending only upon the input states.

Much of the power of mathematics stems from the fact that once we have isolated the essential behavior of a system, we often find that there are other systems which, under the proper interpretation, have the same essential behavior. This means that we don't have to reinvent the wheel to prove results about the new system—the new system will obey all the rules we discovered about the system we were investigating in the first place.

> Logic can be looked at as a collection of rules for manipulating zeros and ones.

For example, suppose we decide to interpret 0 as *false* and 1 as *true*. Then the action of the normally open switch is the same, under this interpretation, as that of the **and** operator in logic. The statement "*P* and *Q*" is true if and only of both *P* and *Q* are both true—for example, "Sally is here and Joe is happy" is true if and only if both statements "Sally is here" and "Joe is happy" are true. The value of *out* in the normally open switch, then, is equivalent to "*in* **and** *control*." Fortunately for us, a great amount of work has been done in the past three millennia to discover (or invent, depending on your philosophic point of view) the properties of logic, thereby relieving us of the chore of having to do the work again for our circuit model.

One fact that has been known for a long time, for instance, is that *any* logical operator can be made using only a combination of the operators **and, or,** and **not.** The **and** operator you have already seen—it is true precisely in the case that its two component parts are true. **Or,** in contrast, is true when either or both of its components are true, and false only when both are false. **Not,** of course, simply reverses the truth value of its associated statement, so "Joe is not happy" is true precisely when "Joe is happy" is false. We can express the actions of these three operators in tabular form, representing *true* by 1 and *false* by 0, and writing the **and** operator as if it were multiplication, **or** as if it were addition, and **not** with a prime after the expression to be negated.

Rules for Logical Operators (1 = *true*, 0 = *false*)

and				or				not	
P	*Q*	*PQ*		*P*	*Q*	*P + Q*		*P*	*P'*
1	1	1		1	1	1		1	0
1	0	0		1	0	1		0	1
0	1	0		0	1	1			
0	0	0		0	0	0			

An example should convince you that these three operators suffice to build an expression equivalent to any given logical expression. Suppose we want to produce an expression of the following form:

P	*Q*	RESULT
1	1	1
1	0	0
0	1	0
0	0	1

Of course, we could interpret *Result* as saying "*P* and *Q* are equal," but we want to show that there is an equivalent way to express this using only **and, or,** and **not.** We know how to obtain a 1 when *P* and *Q* are both 1— **and** will do nicely. Furthermore, the statement $P'Q'$ will take the value 1 only when its components, P' and Q', are 1—that is, when both *P* and *Q* are 0. We can now use **or** to put these statements together to produce a statement that has exactly the same values as *Result*:

P	*Q*	*PQ*	*P'*	*Q'*	*P'Q'*	*PQ + P'Q'*
1	1	1	0	0	0	1
1	0	0	0	1	0	0
0	1	0	1	0	0	0
0	0	0	1	1	1	1

> By combining **and, or,** and **not** gates, we can build expressions to represent *any* binary function.

In slightly more expansive notation we can say that *Result* is equivalent to (*P* **and** *Q*) **or** ((**not** *P*) **and** (**not** *Q*)). By similarly defining a collection of

> We can dispense with the **or** operator, by expressing **or** as a combination of an **and** and three **not**s.

and and **or** statements, with or without **not**s, we can obtain any result whatsoever.

Notice, by the way, that the column $P'Q'$ of the previous table is exactly the negation of the **or** operator $P + Q$. This means that we could dispense with **or** completely, since it can be duplicated by a suitable combination of **and** and three **not**s, since $P + Q = (P'Q')'$.

The general rule is clear: To construct an operator equivalent to any given one,

1. Look at each line in the table for which the result is 1.
2. For each of those:
   a. Find the P and Q values.
   b. Build an **and** statement with the variable itself, if its value is 1, and with the negation of the variable, if its table value is 0.
3. Use **or**s to connect the statements constructed in step 2.

For example, the following statement S is equivalent to $PQ + PQ' + P'Q'$.

P	Q	S	
1	1	1	*(This line is from PQ)*
1	0	1	*(This line is from PQ')*
0	1	0	
0	0	1	*(This line is from P'Q')*

> With n variables, there will be 2^n possible input combinations (and that many rows in the logic table).

Although we've only stated the results for two-variable statements, the same technique will work for an arbitrary number of variables—there will just be more variables in each **and** statement.

So, to build any logical expression, three kinds of operators suffice (or even just two, since we also showed that we can duplicate the action of **or** with an **and** and three **not** operators). Why is this important? Let's return to our circuit model. The principles we just demonstrated, translated into circuit terminology, state that any circuit made of switches can be made by properly connecting three types of components, which we will call *gates:* an **and** gate, an **or** gate, and a **not** gate. Figure 6.4 illustrates the drawing conventions for these three types of gates. In each case, the input lines, representing the values on which the gates operate, are on the left, while the output line leaves from the right of the gate.

FIGURE 6.4   Three Types of Gates

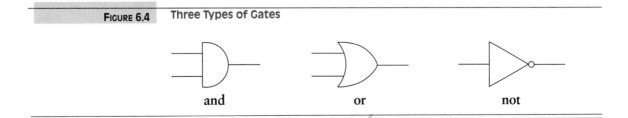

and   or   not

LAB EXERCISE 1

Before sending you off to experiment with Logg-O, a brief description is in order. The stack is intended to provide you with an automated "breadboard," a board on which you can lay out, hook up, and test combinations of gates. The stack provides you with unlimited supplies of four different gate types—AND, OR, NOT, and NAND (a negated AND)—that you can click on and position on the board. Having clicked, for example, on the AND gate, you are asked to click on the board to position the gate where you want it. (Where a gate is positioned on the board affects only the appearance of the circuit; it has no effect on performance.)

You are then asked to connect the gate to the board's "pins," which are its connections to inputs or outputs. An AND gate (just like a logical **and** operation) takes two values as input and produces as output a third value (the logical **and** of its inputs). The input and output values come from the pins that border the breadboard (see Figure 6.5).

| FIGURE 6.5 | The Logg-O Stack |

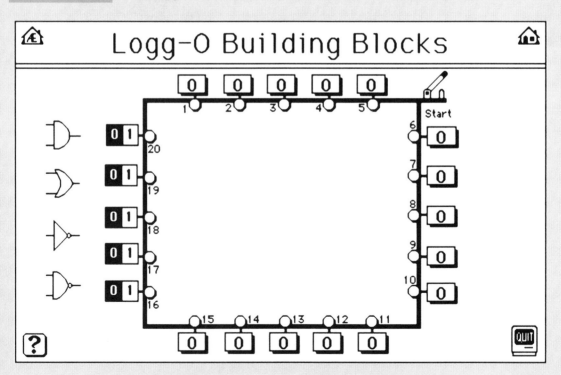

Logg-O's pins are represented as small circles around the perimeter of the board. The value (0 or 1) of each pin is displayed in the rectangle adjacent to the circle. The pins along the left edge of the board are special in that their values can be set by clicking on the appropriate value. These pins should be used for input. Any of the other pins may be used for saving the output of a gate. A given pin may serve as the output of only one gate, but can be an input to many gates.

You will be prompted in like manner to connect whichever type of gate you choose (avoid the NAND gate for now!). Note that the NOT gate accepts only a single input and, so, you will be asked only to make connections for one input and one output.

The completed circuit is "turned on" by clicking the Start lever in the upper right corner of the board. The circuit remains on until the lever is clicked again, turning the circuit off.

Logg-O also provides you with two menus that contain commands that are useful for saving and editing your work. The Circuits menu contains familiar Macintosh-like commands for creating new circuits, opening an existing circuit file, and saving the current circuit in a disk file. The Remove command in the Gates menu lets you remove a single gate and its connections from the board (just click on the gate to be removed). The Clear command removes all gates and connections from the board, allowing you to start over again with, literally, a clean slate.

Now you are ready to open the stack Logg-O. Design and test circuits that demonstrate:

1.1   1 AND 0 is 0.
1.2   1 AND 1 is 1.
1.3   0 OR 1 is 1.
1.4   0 OR 0 is 0.
1.5   NOT 0 is 1.
1.6   NOT 1 is 0.

GATES

We already have shown that **and** and **not** are sufficient to produce any logical operator; all we need to complete the translation of this result to circuits is to show that we can build the gates from switches. We do this in Figure 6.6. In the **not** gate, notice that if we fix the input of a normally closed switch so that it is always 1, then if the control is 0, the 1 passes to the output line, and if the control is 1, the switch flips open, breaking the circuit and sending 0 to the output line. Similarly, we can implement an **and** gate, using a normally open switch where one value is connected to the switch's input line and the

FIGURE 6.6   Building **not** and **and** Gates with Switches

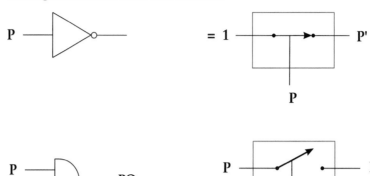

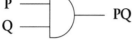

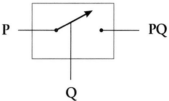

To build a circuit from an expression, work from the inside out, just as if you were evaluating the expression.

other is connected to the switch's control. In this case, the only time the output is 1 is when both the input (*P* in the figure) and the control(*Q*) are 1.

Confident that we can translate from gates to switches when the time comes to build a physical machine, we can now elevate our discussion and consider more complex collections of gates, called *circuits*.

In Figure 6.7 we illustrate a *one-bit comparator*, a circuit that sets the value of *R* to 1 if and only if *P* and *Q* have the same values. This is just the hardware equivalent of *PQ* + *P'Q'*, which we just saw is equivalent to the statement "*P* and *Q* are equal." To interpret this diagram, follow the

FIGURE 6.7   A One-Bit Comparator

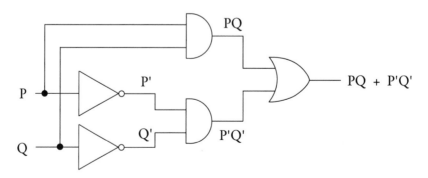

wires from P and Q: They go to the upper **and** gate (producing output PQ), and through the two **not** gates and the lower **and** gate (producing output $P'Q'$). The two outputs serve as input to the **or** gate, which produces the desired result.

We mentioned before that the important property of the simple switch is its binary nature. Up to now we have been using a logic model to help us design circuits, thinking of a signal as 1 or true, and no signal as 0 or false. But another model depends on just two possible values—namely, binary arithmetic. We're used to thinking of $1 + 1$ being equal to 2, but that's just because we customarily use decimal arithmetic. In binary notation, the equivalent expression would be $1 + 1 = 10$, since 10 is the binary representation of 2. Binary arithmetic would certainly make a grade-school student's life easier, since all one needs to know about binary arithmetic are two simple tables.

All You Need to Know about Binary Arithmetic

+	0	1		$\times$	0	1
0	0	1		0	0	0
1	1	10		1	0	1

> Arithmetic, then, is just a special case of logic.

If we think of our circuits using the binary arithmetic model, then we can design an adder that takes two digits a and b as input and returns the sum and the carry as outputs. The sum part is simple enough—the sum is 1 when $a = 1$ and $b = 0$ or when $a = 0$ and $b = 1$, and we can use our procedure to construct logic statements to construct the equivalent statement $ab' + a'b$. The carry part is even simpler—the carry is 1 exactly when a and b are both 1, which means we can use ab to represent the carry (notice that if we keep to our interpretation 1 = true, 0 = false, there is no difference between multiplication and the operator **and**). The only difference between this circuit and those we have seen previously, aside from the fact that we are now choosing to interpret the results in terms of binary arithmetic, is that this adding circuit has two outputs. Such a circuit is called a *half adder* (HA), where the adjective *half* indicates that such a circuit has a carry *out,* but no provision for a carry *in* to the sum (see Figure 6.8).

We can modify our adding circuit slightly to allow the possibility of hooking many of these circuits together to add strings of binary digits. In that case, when adding a and b we might have to take into account a carry coming in from another part—that is, another input. To do this, we recognize that we are performing two addition operations on *three* binary digits, so we use two half adders—one to add a and b, and another to add the carry in to the resulting sum. There will be a carry out precisely when either (or both) of the half sums has a carry, which produces the *full adder* (FA) shown in Figure 6.9.

Even at this level, when we combine gates to produce circuits that can perform arithmetic operations, the fundamental physical units are still not visi-

FIGURE 6.8   A One-Bit Half Adder (HA)

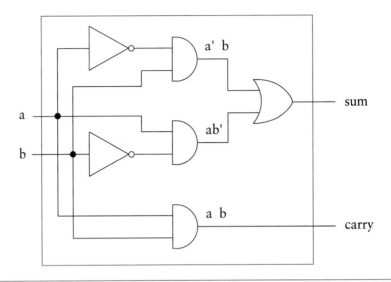

ble to the naked eye. Suppose that we expanded the Macintosh so that one of its full adders was the size of Figure 6.9. To get an idea of the scale involved, at this magnification the Macintosh in which this circuit resides would appear to be taller than any building in the world, the chip itself would just cover a football field, and a human hair would be nearly a foot thick.

REVIEW QUESTIONS

1. What were the three technologies that combined to make modern computers possible?

2. The logical operator **implies** is a formalization of what we mean when we say "if . . . then." In particular, P **implies** Q is false only in the case

FIGURE 6.9   A One-Bit Full Adder (FA)

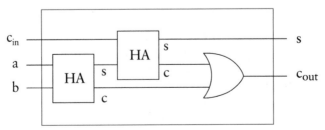

when P is true and Q is false—for example, "If it is sunny, then Sally is on the golf course" is a false statement only in the case that it is sunny and Sally isn't on the golf course. Find a way to express **implies** using some combination of **ands**, **ors**, and **nots**.

3. Create a circuit that implements the statement:

$$a \text{ and } (\text{not}(a \text{ or not } b)).$$

4. Show that it would be a waste of time to build the circuit in question 3, by finding the value of a **and** ($\text{not}(a$ **or not** $b)$) for all four possible values of a and b.

LAB EXERCISE 2

Circuits are typically composed of collections of primitive gates connected together to produce more complex logical behavior. Their complexity derives from the fact that the output of any gate may serve as an input to any gate (including itself!). This, coupled with the fact that any logical operation can be described as a combination of AND, OR, and NOT gates explains the logical power of circuits. For example, the circuit in Figure 6.10 implements a NAND gate, which is the logical negation of an **and** operation.

Note that the circuit accepts two inputs, as does a AND gate. (For the sake of discussion, we will refer to pins as being numbered 1 to 20, clockwise, beginning with the leftmost input pin at the top of the board.) We have chosen to use pins 19 and 20 for input. The result of ANDing the inputs is stored at pin 3. The value at pin 3 then serves as input to the NOT gate, the result of which—and that of the entire circuit—is stored at pin 8 (any of the unused pins would have sufficed).

You might describe the circuit in Figure 6.11 as a "four-way OR circuit." If any of its four inputs are 1, then the final result (stored at pin 8) is 1. Note that we need three simple OR gates to accomplish this, each of which still accepts only two inputs and produces a single output. What we have done is take the output of each successive OR (from pins 2 and 4) and used it as input to the next OR.

Using the logical operations available in Logg-O, design and test the following circuits. Once you are convinced each is implemented correctly, use Logg-O's Circuits menu to save each circuit in an appropriately named file.

2.1 A NOR circuit, which accepts two inputs (call them A and B) and produces 1 whenever (A OR B) is 0, and 0 whenever (A OR B) is 1

FIGURE 6.10 **Building a NAND Gate**

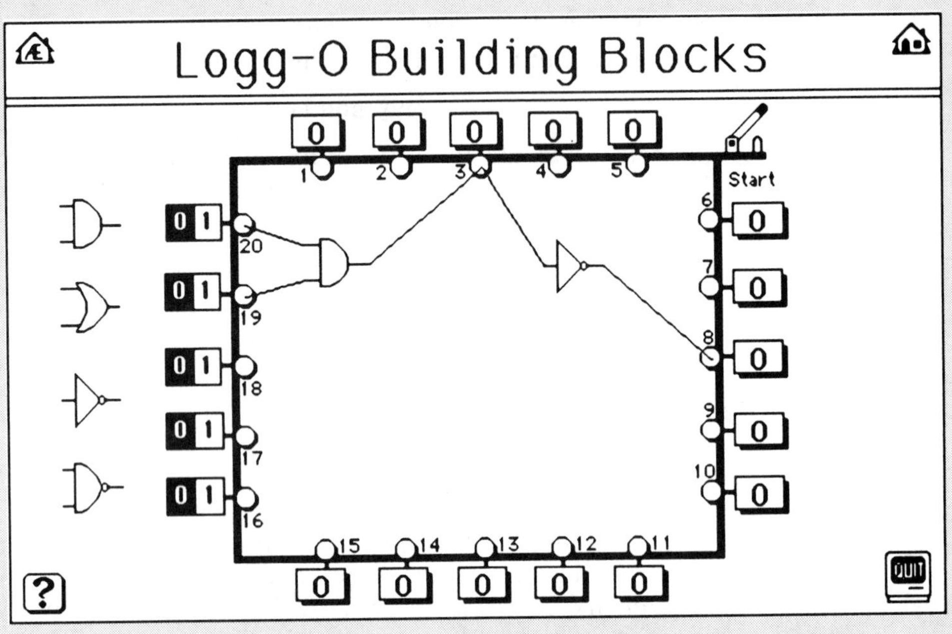

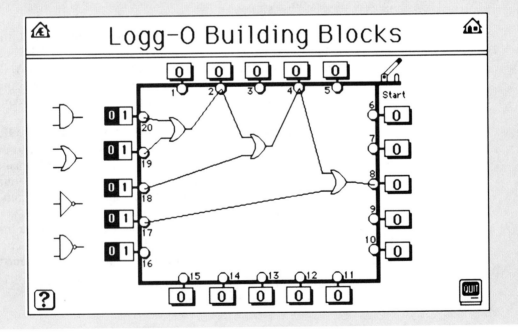

FIGURE 6.11   **A Four-Way OR Circuit**

2.2 A three-way AND circuit, which accepts three inputs and produces an output of 1 only when all three are 1; otherwise, it produces 0

2.3 An XOR ("exclusive OR") circuit, which accepts two inputs and produces output of 1 when the inputs are different, and 0 when the inputs are the same. *Hint:* A XOR B is logically equivalent to (A OR B) AND (NOT(A) OR NOT(B)).

6.3   THE ARITHMETIC LEVEL

The prospect of designing circuits that can operate on multiple binary inputs is an interesting one, especially if we want our computer to be able to handle numbers larger than 1. We do, indeed, and so we must decide how to represent larger numbers. Given the bi-state nature of our hardware, binary notation seems to be a natural choice. Again, we are in debt to von Neumann for this idea, although Atanasoff, in his earlier machines, also used binary representation. We don't have to use binary representation—some early machines used decimal representation, representing 1 by one volt, 2 by two volts, and so on. The problem with this representation, though, is that electrical signals in real circuits almost never can be fixed to exact values, and it is much easier and more reliable only to worry about high voltage versus low voltage, rather than trying to sort out ten possible voltages.

> An important theme in this chapter is that the efficiency of a computer comes from its doing many things at once—in parallel, that is.

If we are to represent the number 37 by its binary equivalent 100101, though, we still have to work out the details of this representation. One way would be to mimic the telegraph, and have the digits arranged in time, so 37 would be represented as a sequence of six pulses: high, low, low, high, low, high. This *serial* representation has the obvious disadvantage that it takes time, and as is often the case, time is of critical importance to us. It behooves us to trade an increase in complexity for a decrease in time and use a *parallel* representation for our numbers. In a parallel representation, we decide ahead of time how many digits our computer will use for numbers and assign a wire for each binary digit, as indicated in Figure 6.12. In this example, a number a is represented by six parallel wires, a_0 (representing the least significant or rightmost digit) to a_5 (representing the most significant or leftmost digit).

Since we are going to represent information in parallel, we will operate on this information as a unit, rather than a bit at a time, thereby complicating our circuits. For example, suppose we wish to design an adder in a machine that represents information with four parallel lines. The input to the adder would be four lines, a_3 to a_0, for one number and four lines, b_3 to b_0, for the other, and the output would be another four lines, s_3 to s_0, for the sum. We can build such a *four-bit adder* with four one-bit adders by linking the carry out of digit i to the carry in of digit $i + 1$, as shown in Figure 6.13.

FIGURE 6.12   Parallel Representation of 37

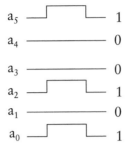

a_5 ⎯⎯⎯ 1
a_4 ⎯⎯⎯⎯⎯ 0
a_3 ⎯⎯⎯⎯⎯ 0
a_2 ⎯⎯⎯ 1
a_1 ⎯⎯⎯⎯⎯ 0
a_0 ⎯⎯⎯ 1

In the four-bit adder, the carry in line of the low-order adder (at the top of the figure) is always set to 0, reflecting that the least significant part of the sum has no incoming carry. The carry out line of the high-order adder signals an *overflow*, indicating that the sum is larger than can be expressed in four binary digits. This line might be used to turn on a light or other signal indicating that something went awry with an arithmetic calculation, for instance.

FIGURE 6.13   Building a Four-Bit Adder from Four One-Bit Full Adders

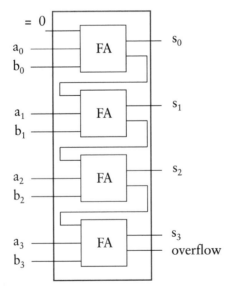

Using these simple principles, we can do more than just add. Binary multiplication looks just like decimal multiplication. For example, to multiply 12 (= 1100) by 7 (= 0111) we perform the following steps:

```
     0111    binary 7
    x1100    binary 12
     0000
     0000
    0111
   0111
  1010100    add four partial products = 84
```

Implementing multiplication by circuits is a trifle more complicated than implementing addition, but the essential idea is to be able to *shift* a number to the left by one position. For example, the four-bit number 0111, representing 7, would be shifted to the number 1110, representing 14, accomplishing a multiplication by 2. General binary multiplication can be accomplished by a collection of adds and shifts.

Notice that for multiplication, the result will generally require a larger output than the size of the numbers in our machine. With four-bit arithmetic, in which the numbers are limited to those expressible in four binary digits, multiplication might require two groups of four-bit numbers to express the result. We could deal with this in a real computer either by allowing two-group outputs, or by keeping to one group of four and signaling an overflow when the result would take more than the allowable number of bits.

LAB EXERCISE 3

If logical operations, no matter how sophisticated, were all we could simulate with boolean circuits, we might not have logic-based computers today. In fact, the expressive power of logical circuits extends far beyond conventional logic. As we have seen, a variety of arithmetic and manipulative operations can be defined in terms of these simple gates.

3.1 Use Logg-O to build a one-bit half adder using AND, OR, and NOT gates, as described in Figure 6.8. Test it using all possible combinations of inputs.

3.2 Save your circuit in a file named "My half adder".

3.3 Add to your half adder circuit the gates and connections necessary to implement a one-bit full adder, as depicted in Figure 6.9.

3.4 After testing your full adder, save it as "My full adder".

CONTROL

By now, it should seem reasonable that we can design circuits to perform all the operations we associate with modern computers, but we still haven't explained how to make these operations "programmable"—that is to say, we have avoided the question of how to make the computer a *universal* machine, capable of following the instructions of any program. There is a wonderfully clever trick that we use to solve this problem: A computer is designed so that every time it has to perform an operation, it performs *all* operations and lets the program set switches to determine which result will be used. In other words, when two numbers have to be added, the computer simultaneously adds them, subtracts them, multiplies them, compares them, **and**s them, **or**s them, and so on, and lets the program tell the computer which of the babble of results it wants.

We can do this with a *multiplexor,* which is a fancy word for a multi-way switch. In Figure 6.14 we illustrate a two-way multiplexor (MUX). (Note that in the figure we have adopted a shorthand convention for the **not** gate, representing it by a small circle.) In this example, we have a switch in which the *select* line determines whether to set the output line *out* to pass the value of the *a* line or the *b* line. When the *select* line is 1, the upper **and** gate allows current to pass, effectively setting the output *out* to the same as the input *a*, while blocking the current through the lower **and** gate. If *select* is 0, the upper **and** gate blocks the flow from *a* while allowing flow from *b*, setting *out* to the value of *b*.

(margin note) Parallelism, again.

FIGURE 6.14   A Two-Way Multiplexor (MUX)

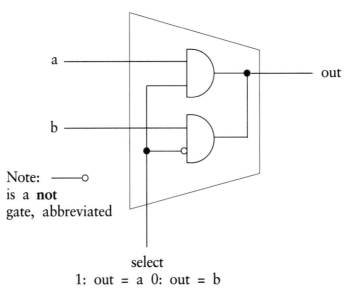

FIGURE 6.15   **A Two-Function Arithmetic Unit**

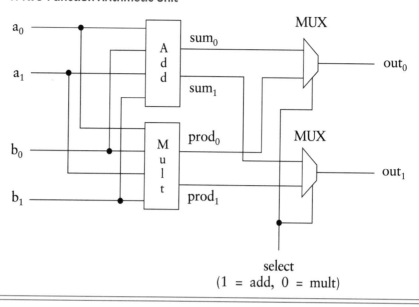

Now we can use our multiplexors to build a multifunction operator unit. Suppose, for example, we have a computer with an adder and a multiplier. We can combine these two operators into a single circuit, a simple *arithmetic unit* that acts as follows: The unit takes the two inputs a and b and a *selection* input; if the selection input is 1, the output will be $a + b$; if the selection is 0, the output will be the product ab. We accomplish this by feeding the inputs to both the adder and the multiplier and using several two-way multiplexors, one for each output line, to control whether the output is $a + b$ or ab (see Figure 6.15). To make the diagram simple, we assume that we have a two-bit circuit, one that performs arithmetic on two-digit binary numbers $a_1 a_0$ and $b_1 b_0$ (see Figure 6.16). The principle would be the same with numbers of more digits—we'd just need more wires and more MUXs.

It would not be much harder to make a more complicated *arithmetic unit*, or an *arithmetic-logic unit* (ALU), by including more operations, such as subtraction, division, comparison, and the logic operations. The action would be the same as in our two-function example—all possible operations would be performed on the inputs, but a more complicated multiplexor would be required to select the desired output from the many possibilities. In the exercises at the end of this module, we provide a circuit that we ask you to verify is a four-way multiplexor.

> With four output lines, we need two *select* lines to give all four address combinations. An eight-way decoder, then, would require three *select* lines.

The ALU simultaneously performs *all possible operations* on its inputs. The result that is chosen by the select lines is the one that becomes the output.

FIGURE 6.16   The Circuit Diagram Abbreviation of the Arithmetic Unit in Figure 6.15

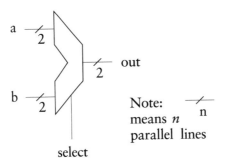

Finally, notice that we can work the multiplexor idea in reverse and construct a *decoder* that takes a single input and a selection and, depending on the value represented by *select*, sends the input to one of many output lines, as illustrated by the four-line decoder in Figure 6.17. In this example, we show a circuit in which input line x_i is selected only when the *select* lines represent the binary number i.

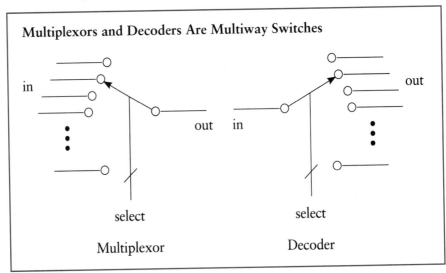

STORAGE

So far, none of the circuits we've built "remember" any of the information they have processed—when the current flow through them stops, they re-set themselves to a quiescent state. To complete construction of our "paper

FIGURE 6.17   A Four-Way Decoder

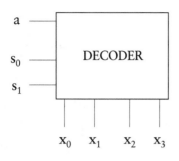

| | | select values | | a value |
		s_1	s_0	sent to
		0	0	x_0
		0	1	x_1
		1	0	x_2
		1	1	x_3

> We can build any circuit from just **nand** gates. Not only does this simplify design, but as a side benefit **nand** gates are usually smaller than **and** and **or** gates.

computer" we must find a way to save the information it is to manipulate. We will make just such a circuit, but first we will introduce a new gate, the **nand** gate. A **nand** gate is built by attaching a **not** gate to the output of an **and** gate (hence its name "n[ot]and"), so that P **nand** Q is false only when both P and Q are true.

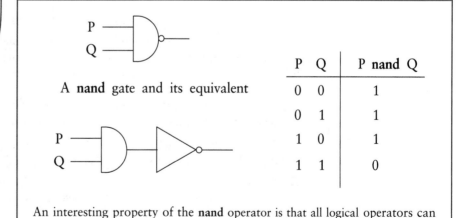

A **nand** gate and its equivalent

P	Q	P nand Q
0	0	1
0	1	1
1	0	1
1	1	0

An interesting property of the **nand** operator is that all logical operators can be constructed by a suitable combination of **nands** alone.

A *latch* is a circuit that can store a single 1 or 0 bit of information. It can be built from three **nand** gates and a **not** gate. A latch has two input lines that serve to set and reset its stored value, along with a single output line that yields the value of the "remembered" bit.

In the table of Figure 6.18, we analyze the behavior of this latch for the four possible combinations of the input lines d and g. In the figure, x, y,

FIGURE 6.18   A Latch

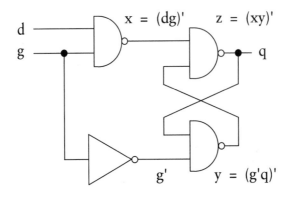

d	g	$x = (dg)'$	$y = (g'q)'$	$z = (xy)'$
0	0	$(00)'=0'=1$	$(1q)'=q'$	$(1q')'=q$
1	0	$(10)'=0'=1$	$(1q)'=q'$	$(1q')'=q$
0	1	$(01)'=0'=1$	$(0q)'=0'=1$	$(11)'=1'=0$
1	1	$(11)'=1'=0$	$(0q)'=0'=1$	$(01)'=0'=1$

and z represent the values of the output lines of the three **nand** gates. When reading the table, remember that the prime represents negation, changing 0 to 1 and vice versa, and that **and** is written as we would write single-digit multiplication, by the rules $00 = 0 \times 0 = 0$, $01 = 0 \times 1 = 0$, $10 = 1 \times 0 = 0$, and $11 = 1 \times 1 = 1$. A helpful consequence of the behavior of **and** is that $1p = p$, and $0p = 0$, no matter what value p is. There are two main types of behavior, depending on the value of g:

> The **g** line enables the latch, allowing it to be set to the value of the **d** line.

1. When $g = 0$, the value of q, the circuit's lone output, is unchanged, since the new value for z is the same as the old value of q.

2. When $g = 1$, the value of z is forced to be whatever d is, regardless of the original value of q. So in this case, the value of q is eventually forced to be the same as that of d.

Aha! We have a circuit that remembers! To store a value in this circuit, we send that value in as d, set g to 1, and thus force q to have the same value as d. Thereafter, as long as g stays quiescent at 0, the value of q will stay as it was set, until we change it by sending new data in via d, along with a value of 1 for g. Figure 6.19 illustrates what happens when we force q to be 0, by setting $d = 0$ and $g = 1$. In the figure, lines with 1 are colored.

Using the latch principles, we can build a one-bit memory unit as follows. We want to be able to store and retrieve data from memory, so we will have a *data line* that will pass information to and from memory; a *read/write line* that when set to 0 will cause data to be read from memory and appear on the data line, and when set to 1 will cause the latch to be set to the value on the data line; and a *select line* that will activate the memory, allowing reading or writing, when it is set to 1. Figure 6.20 illustrates this one-bit memory cell.

Notice in Figure 6.20 that we are using the two **and** gates labelled 2 and 3 as normally open switches. When *select* is 0, the two gates will not pass any information, effectively shutting off the memory. When *select* is 1, it is as if the two lower **and** gates were just horizontal wires, allowing information to pass. When *select* is 1 and *read/write* is 0, no signal passes to g, so the value of q is passed through the **and** gate labelled 1, then through the lower right gate and out the *data* line, thereby copying the memory to

> We're using **and** gates as traffic controllers. We'll do more of this shortly.

FIGURE 6.19   Setting a Latch

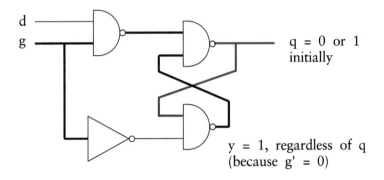

(a) Before z has had a chance to stabilize

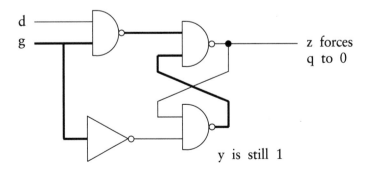

(b) After z has remained 0 long enough

FIGURE 6.20   A One-Bit Memory Cell

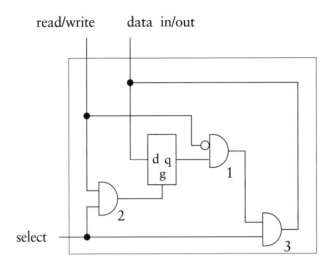

data. Finally, when *select* and *read/write* are 1, *g* is activated, *q* is forced to equal *data,* and the signal from *q* is blocked at the upper **and** gate, thus writing to memory.

Our memory cell acts like this:

1. When *select* = 0, nothing happens (the cell is inactive).

2. When *select* = 1 and *read/write* = 0, a copy of the memory is sent along the *data* line (reading from the cell).

3. When *select* = 1 and *read/write* = 1, the memory cell is set to whatever the value of *data* is (writing to the cell).

> Just as we stacked one-bit arithmetic circuits to build a four-way adder, we stack one-bit memory cells in two dimensions to build bigger memories.

We can build larger memory circuits from smaller ones, forming a *four-bit memory* capable of reading or writing a four-bit number (Figure 6.21). Then we can use four of these four-bit memory cells and a four-way decoder to form a *4 × 4-bit memory,* capable of storing four different words of four bits each (Figure 6.22).

You should be able to verify that our 4 × 4-bit memory would require 100 **and** gates and 82 **not** gates, if built from our standard components. We've skimped on the details, but the broad picture should be enough to show you how you would build a memory for a typical modern computer, in which data are represented in 32-bit groups (usually divided into four groups of eight-bit *bytes*), and memory contains a million bytes, more or less.

FIGURE 6.21   A Four-Bit Memory, Containing a Four-Digit Binary Number

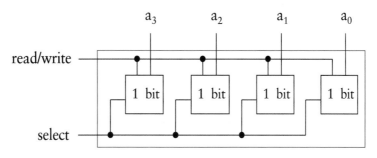

FIGURE 6.22   A 4 x 4-Bit Memory, Containing Four Four-Bit Numbers

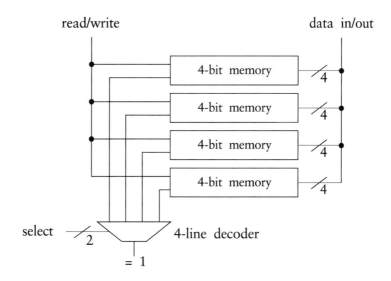

The important thing to realize is that our memory *does everything at once,* just as the arithmetic-logic unit does. When a request comes to read from memory location 1288, for example, the request is sent to all memory cells simultaneously, but the address decoder only activates cell 1288. All the other cells of memory remain unselected, unable to respond to the request.

REVIEW QUESTIONS

1. What are the advantages of parallel representation of information in a computer? What are the disadvantages?
2. Multiply binary numbers 1011×1101, and check your answer by converting to decimal.
3. What is the important principle behind the working of a computer?
4. How can we use **and** gates as switches?
5. What are multiplexors and decoders, and why are they important?
6. What do the d, g, and q lines in a latch do?

LAB EXERCISE 4

Your Æ Stacks disk contains a folder named "Circuits," which includes a file named "Latch." This file is a Logg-O description of a latch as depicted in Figure 6.18. Open Logg-O now, and do the following exercises.

4.1 Use the Open... command from the Circuits menu to load the latch into Logg-O.

4.2 Test it out to verify that it performs as described in the text.

4.3 Use Figure 6.20 to guide you in adding the gates and connections necessary to convert the latch into a one-bit memory cell.

4.4 Once you have convinced yourself that your new circuit performs as it should, save it on disk in file "Memory".

6.4 ARCHITECTURE

We are now ready to move up one more conceptual level. You can forget about gates now, just as you could forget about switches when we moved to the gate level. At this new level of organization, the pieces of a real computer are just barely visible to the naked eye. We have, in our imagination at least, a large collection of building blocks—an arithmetic-logic unit to perform the basic calculations under the direction of selection lines that tell which of the operations will be allowed to pass its output to the rest of the components, and a memory, which allows us to store not only the data, but the program instructions themselves. In this section we will use these building blocks to construct a computer.

This level is called the architecture level for good reason. Just as the architect of a building can concentrate on the design of a building, leaving for others the questions of how a window is constructed from glass, steel, and wood, so too can the computer architect concentrate on the larger ideas of how to fit the components together, leaving to the engineers the problem of designing the integrated circuits that will eventually realize the large ideas in physical form. At this language level, we have access to the structure of the real machine, not just the virtual machine visible to a high-level programmer.

The architecture of a computer is sometimes defined as "that which is visible to an assembly language programmer." Although HyperTalk and Pascal programmers can act most of the time as if the machine is actually wired to perform HyperTalk scripts or Pascal statements, at the architecture level there is no compiler sitting between us and the machine—all that's there is the assembler, generating machine code on a statement-for-statement basis from the assembly language source code. When we design a computer, the decisions we make are reflected directly in the form that the machine language takes.

THE MICROSCOPIC DANCE

A single processor executes the instructions of a program sequentially,[*] employing what is known as the *fetch-execute cycle*. At each iteration of this cycle, the next program instruction is fetched from memory, and that statement is used to determine the action of the machine. The fetch-execute cycle is implemented in an orderly fashion by endowing the computer with a sense of time.

A charming definition of time, attributed to an anonymous child, is "Time is what keeps everything from happening at once." To keep our computer from trying to do everything at once, we include a clock at the heart of the circuitry, marking off the steps of the fetch-execute cycle like an electronic metronome. At one tick, the machine fetches an instruction from its memory. At the next tick it begins to execute the instruction. At subsequent ticks the machine finishes executing the instruction, fetches the next instruction, and starts the cycle over again. This cycle continues until such time as the program signals the computer to halt, or the computer halts by itself due to a program error that makes further execution impossible. Thus, we can envision the action of the computer as an elaborate

---

[*] In recent years, *parallel* processors have been developed that are capable of executing a number of instructions simultaneously. Such parallel machines typically are constructed from a collection of sequential processors and thus represent yet another conceptual level, one higher than we are discussing here.

dance with thousands of performers, choreographed by the program, and conducted by the clock, at a rate of millions of steps per second.*

DESIGN DECISIONS

We are at last ready to build our computer. It's a standing joke among computer engineers that the first decision to accompany the birth of a new machine is what to name it and how to design the T-shirts for the project team. Since this course would not be possible without the products of Apple Computer, Inc. (and since our computer company is hypothetical, thereby relieving us of worry about the legal problems of trademark infringement), and since our computer will be very small, we'll name our computer Pip. Smaller than a minicomputer, smaller than a microcomputer, Pip is the world's first *nano*computer. We leak our release date to the trade press, along with some extravagant claims about Pip's performance, have a company party in celebration of our new venture, and set to work designing Pip the next day.

> Pip: A small seed, as of an apple.

The first real decision we need to make is the size of the fundamental unit of data. This is generally one of the easier decisions, since it is dictated by the iron hand of economics. In our hypothetical computer the economic measure is one of complexity, rather than money, but the principles are the same. A two- or three-bit unit of data is really too small to be of any practical use, but anything like a contemporary 32-bit computer is obviously far too complex for us to build, even in our imaginations. So, let's settle on the eight-bit *byte* as the fundamental unit of information.

With eight bits, we can express 256 different binary numbers, so our computer will be limited in the size of the numbers on which it can operate. Pip will have 256 bytes of memory, with addresses from 0 to 255 (00000000 to 11111111 in binary), so we will need eight bits to address memory. For reasons that will be made clear later, though, we will use 12-bit addresses, even though we don't need all of them to address our memory. To satisfy the bean counters in the accounting department, we remark that our 256×8 memory (including a 256-way decoder) will cost us 12,750 **and** gates and 10,455 **not** gates and will use up an area on the chip roughly twice the size of the period at the end of this sentence.

The next decision we must make is to determine the *instruction format*—that is, how will the machine language instructions be stored in memory? We could, for instance, use a *two-address format,* in which an ADD instruction, for instance, would take the form ADD X Y and would be interpreted as "add the contents of memory location Y to the contents of memory location X and store the result in location X." The problem

---

* With the right equipment, it is actually possible to hear or see this dance, since the circuits of a computer emit faint but detectable radio signals.

with that format, though, is that two addresses would eat up too much memory. Instead, we'll use a *single-address format* and rely on a hardware *accumulator* (a special storage unit) to assist us in our calculations. Our accumulator is capable of holding eight bits of information, so our ADD instruction will look like ADD X and will be interpreted to mean "add the contents of byte X to the value stored in the accumulator, and store the result in the accumulator."

Since the instructions for Pip will be stored in memory, we must decide how these instructions will be stored. We can only address memory by bytes, so it will make the design easier if we store instructions in one or two bytes, depending on whether the instruction requires extra information. To make life simple, we'll code the operation (that is, what the instruction does) in four bits, and leave the other four bits in the byte unused. (That will give us four extra bits to play with if we decide to introduce Pip II later.) If the instruction requires extra information (such as an address of data on which to operate, as ADD requires), we'll store that *operand* in the byte that follows the operation code. Figure 6.23 shows Pip's instruction format.

With four bits for the address, we have four bits left over for the instruction code itself. This means that Pip will be limited to no more than 16 different instructions. As we just noted, if you want to include more instructions in a later model of Pip, we have the four unused bits that we can use. Or, if we decide to stay with 16 instructions, we could employ the unused bits to expand the addressing capabilities of Pip, so we could expand memory from 256 to 4096 bytes.

So, we are interested in defining a single-address language with 16 instructions. Now we can let you in on the secret—PIPPIN stands for "PIP Program INstruction language." To save you the trouble of looking up the PIPPIN User's Guide in Module 5, we'll reproduce it here, along with the

> The 4096 x 8 bit memory of Pip II would be about a fifth of an inch on a side and would require almost exactly 400,000 gates.

FIGURE 6.23   Pip Instruction Formats

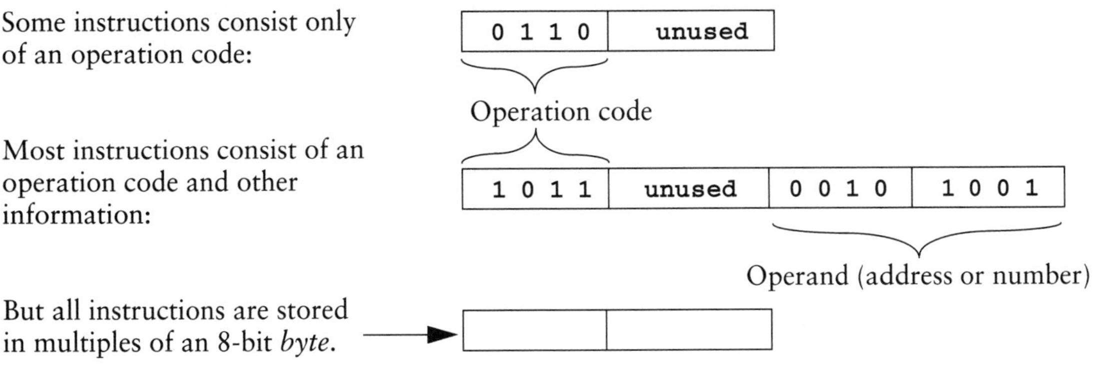

Some instructions consist only of an operation code:

0 1 1 0 | unused

Operation code

Most instructions consist of an operation code and other information:

1 0 1 1 | unused | 0 0 1 0 | 1 0 0 1

Operand (address or number)

But all instructions are stored in multiples of an 8-bit *byte*.

four-bit instruction code for each of the operations. Remember, A stands for the accumulator; X stands for an address or a number, and if X is an address, [X] stands for the contents of the byte at memory location X; and PC stands for the program counter (the address in memory of the instruction that is currently being executed).

Data Flow
0000	STO X	A → X
0001	LOD X	[X] → A
0010	SET X	X → A

Control
0100	JMP X	X → PC
0101	JMZ X	if A = 0, then X → PC
0110	NOP	no operation
0111	HLT	halt execution

Arithmetic-Logic
1000	ADI X	A + X → A
1001	ADD X	A + [X] → A
1010	SBI X	A − X → A
1011	SBD X	A − [X] → A
1100	AND X	A **and** [X] → A
1101	NOT	**not** A → A
1110	CPZ X	if [X] = 0, then 1 → A, else 0 → A
1111	CPL X	if [X] < 0, then 1 → A, else 0 → A

We've put the cart somewhat before the horse here for pedagogical reasons. Normally, the format of a language would be dictated by the architecture of the computer, and not the other way around. But we already have defined PIPPIN and don't want to invent another language after we have designed our machine.

We now have all we need to design Pip. We have seen the fundamental ideas behind the design of a modern computer:

1. Information is represented in binary form, using as many parallel sets of wires as we need to move this information.

2. Program instructions are stored in memory, just as any other information.

3. When the current program instruction is executed, all possible operations are executed simultaneously, and the current instruction is used to select among the choices for the result.

We have a machine language of instructions, we have discussed how the arithmetic and logic operations are implemented by circuits, and we know how we can use memory to store information and recall that information for later use. The rest of the design process is little more than working out the details.

*SIDE TRIP: PIP DETAILS

We end this section with the last side trip of this module. Although we have seen the important ideas behind the workings of a computer, we are not quite ready to actually construct a computer of our own—there is still some detail work to be done. In keeping with our student-as-tourist view of this text, this is where we get off the bus and spend some time getting to know the locals and their society firsthand.

Pip, as illustrated in Figure 6.24, consists of six main parts:

1. The *program counter* (PC), which stores the eight-bit address in the memory of the current instruction

2. The *instruction register* (IR), which stores the current instruction, divided into two eight-bit pieces: the *instruction code* in IR_H (the high-order, leftmost bits) and the *operand* in IR_L (the low-order, rightmost bits)

FIGURE 6.24   Pip Revealed

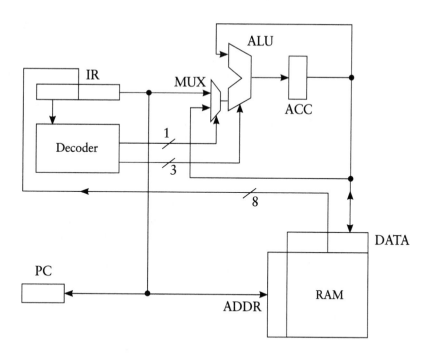

---

* All side trips are optional.

3. The *decoder,* which takes the instruction code as input and produces several control signals as output

4. The *arithmetic-logic unit* (ALU), which takes, generally, two data inputs and a selection and, based on the selection from the decoder, performs one of eight operations on its data inputs

5. The *accumulator* (ACC), used to store the results of calculations from the ALU

6. The *random access memory* (RAM), which takes an address and a read/write signal from the decoder and reads or writes information to the specified address.

For simplicity's sake we have not drawn several lines, particularly those from the decoder and the clock. The discussion that follows, wherein we run Pip and trace its operation, will enable you to fill in the missing pieces.

The fetch part of the fetch-execute cycle is quite simple: (1) Pip sends the contents of the PC to the ADDR part of RAM, thereby activating the memory location containing the instruction it wants. (2) Then Pip sends the contents of that location from DATA to IR. (3) It increments PC by 1 or 2 (depending on how long the instruction was), so that PC will refer to the next instruction in the program.

Given an instruction code and an operand, Pip must execute the operation described by the code. The four-bit instruction code is sent to a 16-way decoder, and exactly one of the 16 output wires is selected. When you look at Pip in Figure 6.24, you'll notice that we have drawn only four output lines: one to the multiplexor and three to the ALU. Each of the output wires, including the 12 not drawn in the diagram, controls some action by Pip—we will give an example from each of the three main instruction categories.

DATA FLOW Wires 0, 1, and 2 from the decoder implement one of the three data flow instructions. Suppose the instruction code is 0000, the STO X instruction. To store a copy of the accumulator into address X, Pip must (1) turn on the switches to send IR_L to ADDR, while it (2) turns on the switches to send ACC to DATA. This is what we meant when we said that the schematic of Pip's internal workings in Figure 6.24 is incomplete—the black dots connecting the groups of wires are actually collections of **and** gates controlling the flow of information, depending on the values of the control wires from the decoder. The 12 invisible lines from the decoder act as traffic controllers. In this example, the leftmost two dots would be expanded as in Figure 6.25 (and of course, we would have two similar controls for the path from ACC to DATA).

CONTROL Wires 4 through 7 from the decoder govern the sequence of steps in the program. Suppose that the instruction to be executed is 0100, the JMP X instruction, indicating that the next statement to be fetched

FIGURE 6.25   Controlling Data Flow

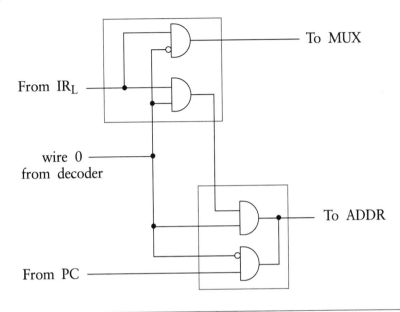

will be found in memory location X. In this case, Pip must use wire 4 to control the flow of data in such a way that the contents of IR_L are passed to PC, since IR_L contains the address of the next statement to be executed. In other words, we need to further complicate the switches as shown in Figure 6.26.

ARITHMETIC-LOGIC Finally, wires 8 through 15 control the execution of arithmetic operations. If operation 1001, ADD X, is selected, Pip must perform four tasks: (1) send the address X from IR_L to ADDR, (2) send the selected memory value from DATA to the multiplexor MUX, (3) control MUX so that the value of DATA (rather than IR_L) gets sent to ALU, and (4) control ALU so that addition is performed.

We're done; we have a computer (on paper, anyhow). Counting the memory, Pip requires approximately 25,000 **and** and **not** gates, almost all of which comprise the memory. If we sent our design off to the integrated circuit shop for fabrication, we would find that—as with most microprocessors—the majority of the chip area is taken up by connecting wires, and not by the components themselves. Even with all the wires, though, the finished computer is so small that a careless sneeze could lose it forever. Pip is well named—the complete computer would be about the size of an apple seed.

FIGURE 6.26   More Detail of the Data Flow (We promise there won't be any more pictures like this.)

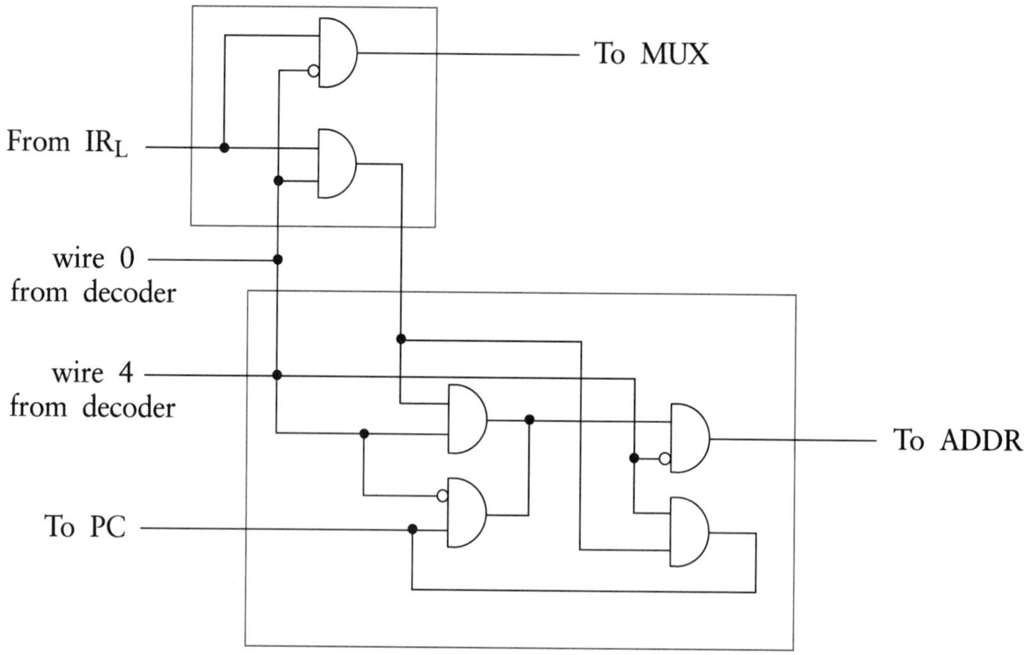

THE STATE OF THE ART

Just how far is Pip from a contemporary computer? Well, in purely numeric terms the answer depends upon the context of the question. In terms of sophistication of its architecture, Pip is about 30 years behind the times; in terms of complexity, it's about a hundred times simpler than the chip in the Macintosh.

This is not a course in microelectronic technology. In an attempt to understand that ideas behind the development and practice of microprocessor design, we have taken steps that would likely distress anyone in advanced courses in engineering school. We did this deliberately and owe no apologies therefrom. As a result, though, much is missing in Pip. Here, we list some of the features present in modern computers and absent in Pip.

SOPHISTICATED ADDRESSING Because of its simple architecture, many things would be difficult to do with Pip. Even such a simple problem as setting memory addresses X to X + 10 all equal to 1 requires a complicated workaround in PIPPIN. The fault lies partly in a lack of *addressing modes,* ways of specifying where information resides. True direct mode operations, for example, allow one to specify a memory location by its *off-set* from the current PC, rather than its absolute location in memory. This allows a program to be movable in memory, a handy feature for sophisticated operating systems, which often relocate items in an attempt to allocate memory more efficiently.

ADVANCED INSTRUCTION SET Another shortcoming of Pip is its limited instruction set. While one can do most things in PIPPIN that a program should be able to do, it often takes many statements to perform what are conceptually very simple processes. In the past two decades, the number of tasks that are wired directly into hardware has increased to the point that the MC68030 in a modern Macintosh has about 80 varieties of operation in its instruction set, with many of these available in different modes, for a total of around 600 different assembly language commands. In fact, this burgeoning instruction set has led to a reaction among some computer scientists who are now investigating *reduced instruction set computers* (RISC, for short), which use a small but powerful set of instructions in an effort not only to increase ease of use, but also to increase the speed of the computers themselves. In a related vein, a computer designer may decide to keep a complicated instruction set and still have a fairly simple processor by employing *microprogramming,* in which the instructions are translated at the hardware level into instructions for the simple processor, in effect adopting a hard-wired interpreter at a very low level.

SPEED ENHANCEMENT To further increase the efficiency of our processor, we could have introduced *pipelining,* in which we fetch the next instruction at the same time we are executing the current one. We could also add circuitry for *caching,* in which a memory access results in loading not only the desired memory value, but several of its adjacent values into a separate, very fast, small memory called the *cache.* The advantage to caching comes from the *principle of locality,* which stems from the observation that if one memory location is needed, it is likely that its neighbors will be used shortly. There are many such interesting topics in computer architecture—as we said, we've only scratched the surface.

Ultimately, though, the shortcomings of Pip stem from its size. As long as we have the ideas at hand, little more than problems of scale separate Pip from the chip in the Macintosh, with its hundreds of thousands of gates and approximately half a mile of connecting wires.

REVIEW QUESTIONS

1. What do we mean by "the architecture of a computer"?
2. Describe the fetch-execute cycle.
3. Why did we decide to address memory in Pip by bytes, rather than by bits?

4. What decisions were involved in the choice of Pip's instruction format?

5. Describe two ways in which Pip is more primitive than modern computers.

*6. What are the six major parts of Pip, and what are their functions?

LAB EXERCISE 5

It is worth considering how the Logg-O stack works before continuing with the remaining exercises. Its complexity may surprise you. Briefly, each of the four basic logical gates is a button covered by a transparent field. The script of the button implements the corresponding logical operation. The script of the field is responsible for making a copy of the corresponding gate, for positioning it on the grid, and for establishing its input and output pins. The latter two operations require the help of the user.

Look, for example, at the script of the **or** gate:

```
on mouseUp
    global waitingForAPin
    if waitingForAPin is true then exit mouseUp
    put the number of the target into tempGate
    put word 2 of line tempGate of field "GATES" into A
    put word 3 of line tempGate of field "GATES" into B
    put word 4 of line tempGate of field "GATES" into R
    if (field A is empty) or (field B is empty) then exit mouseUp
    if (field A contains 0) and (field B contains 0) then
        put 0 into field R
    else
        put 1 into field R
    end if
end mouseUp
```

The if statements accomplish the logical **or** operation. To understand the four preceding put statements, we must remember that every time the transparent **or** field is clicked, another **or** gate with this exact same script is created and pasted onto the circuit board. Somehow, each **or** gate in the circuit must know where to get its inputs and where to send its outputs. This is where the field "GATES" comes into play. As each logical gate is created, a new line is entered into the field "Gates" that records, among other things, the pins to which the gate is connected. The following lines show what the field "GATES" looks like (it is normally hidden) after creating the three-way **or** circuit:

---

* Starred exercises are for those who took the side trip.

OR pin20 pin19 pin2 173, 149 157, 137 157, 155 189, 146
OR pin2 pin18 pin4 242, 175 226, 163 226, 181 258, 172
OR pin4 pin17 pin8 321, 217 305, 205 305, 223 337, 214

When an **or** gate is executed (that is, when we click on it), the **or** button's script must decide which **or** was clicked (there may be many **or** buttons). The first statement in the script uses HyperTalk's special word target to determine which **or** button was clicked. The next three put statements retrieve the pins to be used as input and output from the "GATES" field line that contains the pin information for the chosen button. These values (there are three in the case of the **or** gate—two inputs and one output) are stored in local variables A, B, and R. The logical **or** is then carried out using the values of the pin fields, as dictated by A, B, and R.

Nand was included in Logg-O because it is a particularly powerful logical operation. Indeed, each of our other primitives (and, thus, any logical operation at all) can be described solely in terms of **nand** gates. For example, the same effect as a **not** gate can be achieved by the circuit shown in Figure 6.27 (where both inputs come from pin 19 and the output is sent to pin 7).

FIGURE 6.27   Building a **not** Gate from a **nand**

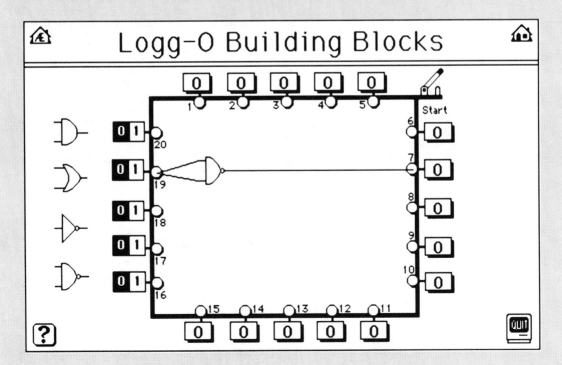

FIGURE 6.28   Building an **or** Gate from Three **nand**s

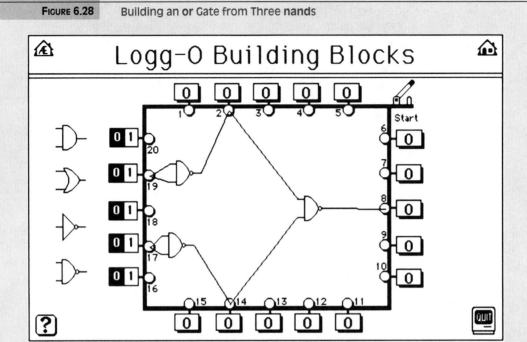

The circuit in Figure 6.28 simulates an **or** gate using only **nand**s (inputs are at pins 17 and 19, output at pin 8). The circuit in Figure 6.29 does the same for an **and** gate (inputs at pins 19 and 20, output at pin 8).

5.1 Build and test a **not** circuit using only **nand** gates.

5.2 Add a **not** gate directly to your circuit from exercise 5.1. Connect it so that it uses the same input pins as does your **nand**-based circuit, but sends its output to an unused pin.

5.3 Verify that your **nand**-based **not** circuit produces the same output for all inputs as does the direct **not** gate.

5.4 Build, test, and verify the performance of a **nand**-based **or** circuit, like you did in exercises 5.1–5.3.

 Æ LAB   **EXTENDED LAB EXERCISES**

1. Build and test a one-bit half adder using only **nand** gates.

2. Modify Logg-O so that circuits are more fully editable. For example, try extending the stack's editing facilities so that gates can be repositioned on the board without having to be recreated.

FIGURE 6.29   Building an **and** Gate from Two **nands**

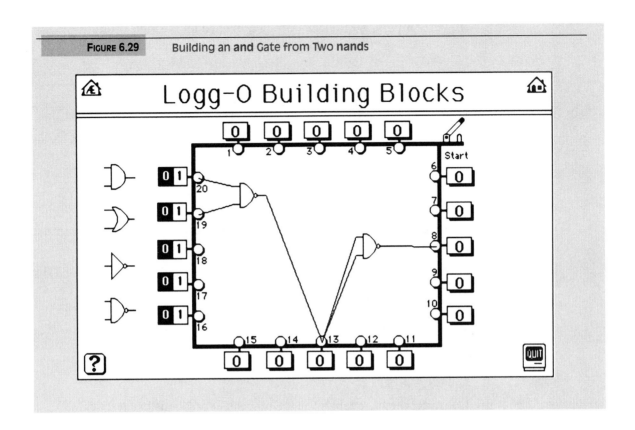

6.5   EXERCISES

1. Using only **nand** gates construct circuits that are equivalent to

    a. not (*x* **and** *y*)
    b. *x* **or** (**not** *y*)

2. Using **and, or,** and **not** gates, construct circuits with the following proper-
    ties:

    a. Two inputs, *a* and *b*, one output *z*, with *z* defined by the logic table:

a	b	z
1	1	0
1	0	1
0	1	1
0	0	1

b. Three inputs, *a*, *b*, *c*, one output *z*, defined by the logic table:

a	b	c	z
1	1	1	1
1	0	0	0
1	0	1	1
1	0	0	0
0	1	1	0
0	1	0	1
0	0	1	0
0	0	0	1

3. Construct circuits with output *z* equivalent to the following boolean expressions:

   a. $a(a' + b) + ab'$
   b. $(a + a')b$
   c. $abc + a'bc + ab'c + abc'$

4. Using logic tables, show that the following identities hold:

   a. $a1 = a$
   b. $a(a + b) = a$
   c. $(ab)' = a' + b'$

5. Construct the logic tables for the boolean expressions in exercise 3.

6. Fill in the logic table that describes the action of the following circuits, and give the equivalent boolean expressions for the output.

   a.

   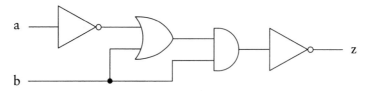

   b. (Recall that the small circles represent **not** gates.)

   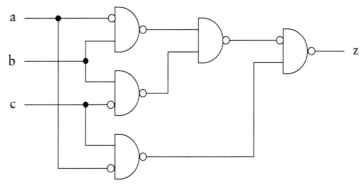

7. Find a simpler circuit equivalent to that of

    a. Exercise 3b
    b. Exercise 6a

8. Construct the following circuits:

    a. A three-input **and** gate, which has output 1 if and only if all three inputs are 1
    b. A three-input **or** gate, which has output 1 if and only if at least one of the three inputs are 1

    3-input **and**   3-input **or**

9. Construct a *majority circuit,* which has three inputs and one output; the output is 1 if and only if at least two of the inputs are 1. To make your design simpler, you may use multi-input **and** and **or** gates.

10. Verify that the following circuit is a four-way multiplexor, and describe how it works.

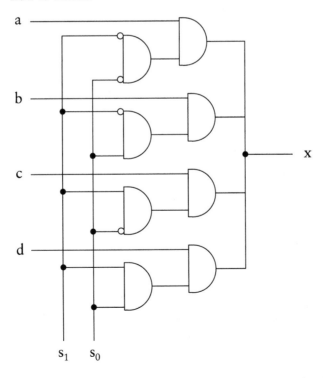

11. Using four four-way multiplexors, construct a *cyclic shifter,* which has four input lines a_3, a_2, a_1, a_0, two select lines s_1, s_0, and four output lines z_3, z_2, z_1, z_0, defined as follows:

s_1	s_0	z_3	z_2	z_1	z_0
1	1	a_0	a_3	a_2	a_1
1	0	a_1	a_0	a_3	a_2
0	1	a_2	a_1	a_0	a_3
0	0	a_3	a_2	a_1	a_0

In other words, if $s_1 s_0$ is the binary representation of the number n, the output will consist of the input shifted n bits to the left (or, if you prefer, $4 - n$ bits to the right).

12. Verify that the following circuit represents a four-way decoder, as described in Figure 6.17.

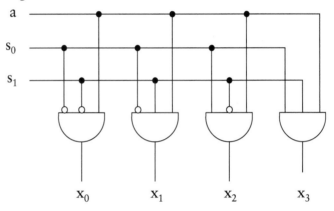

13. a. Show that the 4×4 bit memory of Figure 6.22 requires 100 **and** gates and 82 **not** gates.
    b. Using the conversion of exercise 1, how many **nand** gates would be required to construct the memory?
    c. How many **and** and **not** gates would be required to construct an 8×14-bit memory (with eight cells of four bits each)? There are many possible answers to this question, so be sure to describe the memory circuit precisely.

*14. Show the steps Pip would make when executing the following statements:

    a. LOD X
    b. ADI X

15. Recall that in a computer with a *pipelined architecture,* the fetch and execute steps are overlapped, so that the next instruction is fetched at the same time the present one is being executed.

    a. Show how this change could make a computer run faster.

---

* Starred exercises are for those who took the side trip.

b. It is not enough to simply get the next instruction while the current one is being executed. What statement must be handled specially, and why?

c. Redesign Pip with a pipelined architecture.

6.6 ADDITIONAL READINGS

Forester, T., ed. *The Microelectronics Revolution.* Cambridge, Mass.: MIT Press, 1980.

Gray, N. A. B. *Introduction to Computer Systems.* Sydney: Prentice-Hall of Australia, 1987.

Johnsonbaugh, R. *Essential Discrete Mathematics.* New York: Macmillan, 1987.

Kolman, B., and Busby, R. C. *Introductory Discrete Structures with Applications.* Englewood Cliffs, N.J.: Prentice-Hall, 1987.

Mano, M. M. *Computer Engineering: Hardware Design.* Englewood Cliffs, N.J.: Prentice-Hall, 1988.

Newell, S. *Introduction to Microcomputing.* New York: Harper & Row, 1982.
Scientific American. Microelectronics theme issue. 237, no. 3 (Sept. 1977).

THEORY OF COMPUTATION

INTRODUCTION

Herbert Simon has argued that the solar system can be viewed as an information processor, flawlessly computing the position of the planets by placing them exactly where they should go at each instant. The solar system, under this interpretation, differs from what we would call a computer in that it is, like the Difference Engine, a single-purpose information processor. Indeed, little of what we think of as natural science embodies the salient features of either computers or computation. Computer science is different from other sciences in that it devotes its attention to the study of an artifact of human design. In this regard, computer science is closer to the study and practice of literature than it is, say, to physics.

There is a time-honored tradition that theoretical discussions intended for a lay audience are often presented as dialogs, and we will hold to that tradition here. We do this not merely out of a sense of historical homage, but because we believe in the importance of the way of thinking espoused by the late Ted Sturgeon: "Ask the next question." We hope that you will not be content to hear that "this is the way it is" without asking, "Why is this the way it is?" and "What are the implications, then?" We designed this module—and those that follow—with that way of thinking in mind.

TEXT OBJECTIVES

In this module, we will

- Essentially ignore the physical computer, and concentrate on the view of a program as defining an abstract machine
- Consider two ways of looking at these abstract machines: as black boxes that match input strings to outputs, and as clear boxes consisting of programs in a very simple language
- Investigate the Turing Machine, a simple but powerful model of "clear box" computation

- Provide arguments that make it reasonable to believe that any programs are equivalent to Turing Machine programs
- Show that some problems cannot be solved by Turing Machines, and hence, probably cannot be solved by any programs for any computers.

THE ABSTRACT MACHINE

A poem and a computer program are different, surely, but there are similarities as well. First, a poem and a program result from the author's intentional use of symbols. In the case of a poem, the intent is to communicate ideas and feelings to the reader, and in the case of a program, the intent is to cause the computer to perform certain actions. When Carl Sandberg wrote, "The fog comes/On little cat feet," he obviously didn't intend to imply that a fog bank had identifiable feet. More likely, his intent was to point out to the reader that incoming fog moves in a quiet and stealthy way similar to the way a cat walks. He may also have intended to invoke the connection between a soft, light gray cat and the soft gray nature of fog.

In the same way, a programmer who writes

    put height * width into area

may intend that height and width represent the values of the height and width of a rectangle, and that the resulting area be stored in the container labelled area. The computer doesn't "know" the programmer's intended interpretation of these variables, any more than the printed page "knows" the intended interpretation of the movement of a fog bank as catlike. If, for instance, the programmer wrote

    put height + width into area

the HyperTalk interpreter would faithfully translate the line into a series of instructions to be performed, in spite of the fact that the instructions would be incorrect under the programmer's assumptions of what the script was to do.

Poems and programs are not merely collections of symbols; they are produced within a framework of rules for symbol usage. The rules for constructing programs are more restrictive than those for poems, if for no other reason than people can interpret symbols better than computers. But the fact remains that rules, whether formal or informal, can be ignored only at the risk of not communicating effectively. The line "The fog creeps in two eggs over easy, coffee, no cream" is little better for its intended purpose than

    put height multiply width upon area

Keep this in mind when we get to the Halting Problem later.

Finally, we will see that an important aspect of computer science is that programs, like poems, can be *self-referential*. Just as a poem can have itself as its subject, or can talk of the nature of poetry, a program can accept other programs as input, produce other programs as output, or be written to modify itself. We saw just this behavior in Module 6, when we observed that a compiler or interpreter is nothing more than a program that takes a source code program as input and produces an object code program as its output. Indeed, a compiler could take a copy of itself as input and produce a compiled (object) version of itself as output.

In this module, we adopt the approach that *a computer scientist studies The Computer in much the same way that a student of literature studies The Poem,* and we will consider some of the tools and ways of thinking that are involved in this study. Our approach so far has been top-down, from applications to hardware, via design, programming, and program translation. Now that we've seen what programs are and how a computer can be designed to do what a program instructs it to do, we will try to go beyond computers to the nature of computation itself. We will ask what a computer is, in essence; we will ask what *computation* means; and we will see what computers can and cannot do—not just today's computers, but anything that we can imagine as a "computer." In short, the text part of this module is devoted to the Big Questions about computer science.

METAPHOR: THE TURING MACHINE

The metaphor for this module is the Turing Machine, a simple imaginary device invented by Alan Turing *before* there were any such things as computers. The Turing Machine consists of a tape of unlimited length, along with a device that can read symbols on the tape, write new symbols on the tape, and move to adjacent locations on the tape. We will see that this simple machine is powerful enough to embody all that we would consider as "computation," and will serve as the vehicle for our discussion of what computation is all about.

Æ STACKS: ITM

This claim—that the Turing Machine not only is equal in power to any computer available today, but is also powerful enough to perform anything that we would consider as "computation"—is strong indeed, and you have every right to be skeptical. In the lab part of this module, we will provide you with a Turing Machine of your own, and encourage you to write some programs for this machine to see just how powerful it is.

LAB OBJECTIVES

In the lab part of this module, you will

- Use a Turing Machine simulator to experiment with some simple Turing Machines
- Develop an appreciation for the simplicity and the power of these machines, and for the nature of symbolic computation

- Be exposed to some additional features of HyperTalk, including its facilities for controlling the screen and for monitoring the mouse

7.2   TWO WAYS OF THINKING ABOUT PROGRAMS

You said that a computer scientist studies The Computer, in much the same way that a student of literature studies The Poem. What is this capitalized "Computer" you're talking about?

First of all, it certainly doesn't have anything to do with a particular technology; we've seen that already. The Analytical Engine was purely mechanical. Though it was never finished (thereby putting it in contention for the first instance of "vaporware"—promised but not delivered—in the history of computer science), the principles of its design were theoretically sound. Modern computers are electronic, but developments today in areas other than electronics might lead to future computers that use an entirely different technology. Just as words can be penciled on paper, graven in stone, printed on a press, or displayed on a video screen, the technology of the device that allows words to take physical form is less important than the notion of writing itself.

> For example, there's a growing body of research on *photonic* circuits, where information is carried by light rather than electricity.

Using your writing analogy, then, it seems that for our purposes, the technology of the computer is there to support the more basic notion of The Program. (I've capitalized to conform to your convention of Big Ideas.)

Right. The program is the important part. After all, the notion of an abstract machine shouldn't require too much of a conceptual leap, since every time you write a program, you act as if you're writing a program for an abstract machine. When you write a HyperTalk script, you don't need to concern yourself with the fact that your program runs on a Macintosh with an MC68030 central processor, four megabytes of RAM, an 80M hard disk, and a 1.4M floppy, connected to a LaserWriter. As far as you're concerned, your script can be written for an imaginary HyperTalk computer that executes your instructions directly. Figure 7.1 contrasts the image of the imaginary, virtual computer with the real one. We can take a more general example and say, for instance, that a correctly written Pascal program should produce the same results on *any* computer equipped with a functional Pascal compiler. When we talk about processing information, it is clearly the program—rather than the computer on which the program runs—that is of interest to us.

I'll accept the idea that The Program is the important notion, but that just substitutes one question for another. What is a program?

There are two answers. We'll first take a "black box" approach. A program processes data. In essence, a program is a rule (perhaps a very complicated rule) that describes how input data are transformed to output data. For our

FIGURE 7.1   Programming a Virtual Machine

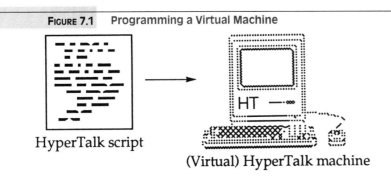

HyperTalk script

(Virtual) HyperTalk machine

(a) Image

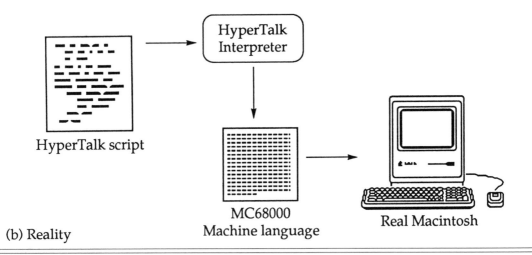

HyperTalk script

HyperTalk Interpreter

MC68000
Machine language

Real Macintosh

(b) Reality

"Meaning" is a slippery and messy concept, so we'll simply ignore it here.

purposes, we'll define *data* as equivalent to a "binary string." This relieves us of having to deal with the question of meaning. The binary string 01000011010000010100010 is data with no particular meaning. We could interpret it as the string "CAB" if we think of it as the ASCII codes (in binary) for the three letters; or we could interpret it as the binary representation of the integer 4,407,618; or we could even interpret it as part of a picture, where the 1s represent dark squares, and the 0s white:

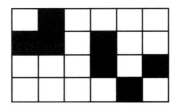

The meaning of the data, if any, lies in the encoding scheme we adopt to interpret the string—but that's our problem, not the program's.

One of the reasons we adopt this approach is that we want to consider *all* programs, not just those that are correctly written to perform some well-defined task that humans understand. Our first definition is general enough to allow such a broad interpretation:

Black Box Definition

A *program* is a matching from the set of all possible finite binary (input) strings to some members of the set of all possible finite binary (output) strings.

> In technical terms, a program may be regarded as a partial function on the set of all finite strings of zeros and ones.

In this view, we don't care at all what happens "inside" a program. All that's of interest to us is that for each binary input, a program does one of two things: (1) It eventually halts on the input string, producing no more output, in which case we say that the program matches that input with whatever output (if any) it produces, or (2) the program produces output forever, in which case we say that there is no string that the program matches to that input.

Alternatively, a given program might not "run correctly" with all possible inputs. Our black box definition takes care of that, too. If a program is written so that it runs correctly only on inputs of three binary digits, say, and we give it 01 as input, the program might "hang up," waiting forever for the third input. In that case, its output would just be the empty string, consisting of no zeros or ones at all. In other words, our definition not only includes all possible programs, it also includes all possible actions of these programs, both "correct" and "incorrect." (Figure 7.2 illustrates this matching process.)

THE TURING MACHINE

> *That's not a very satisfying answer. First of all, to me, a definition is a statement that says that something is equal to something else. Your definition is akin to saying "a person is a mammal." Do you mean that every matching of inputs to outputs is a program? Second, your definition is way too abstract—a program does indeed associate an output string with every input string, but I'm much more interested in how that association is performed.*

You're right on both counts. We are not claiming that every possible input-output matching is a program. In fact, we'll show shortly that that's not the case at all—there are matchings that cannot be realized by programs. Now it's our turn to ask a question: If you're not happy with the definition of a program as a function from binary strings to binary strings, what definition of *program* would make you happy?

> *I suppose it would have to do with functionality—we need to settle on what a program can do internally.*

FIGURE 7.2   **Describing a Program as a Matching of Input Strings to Output Strings**

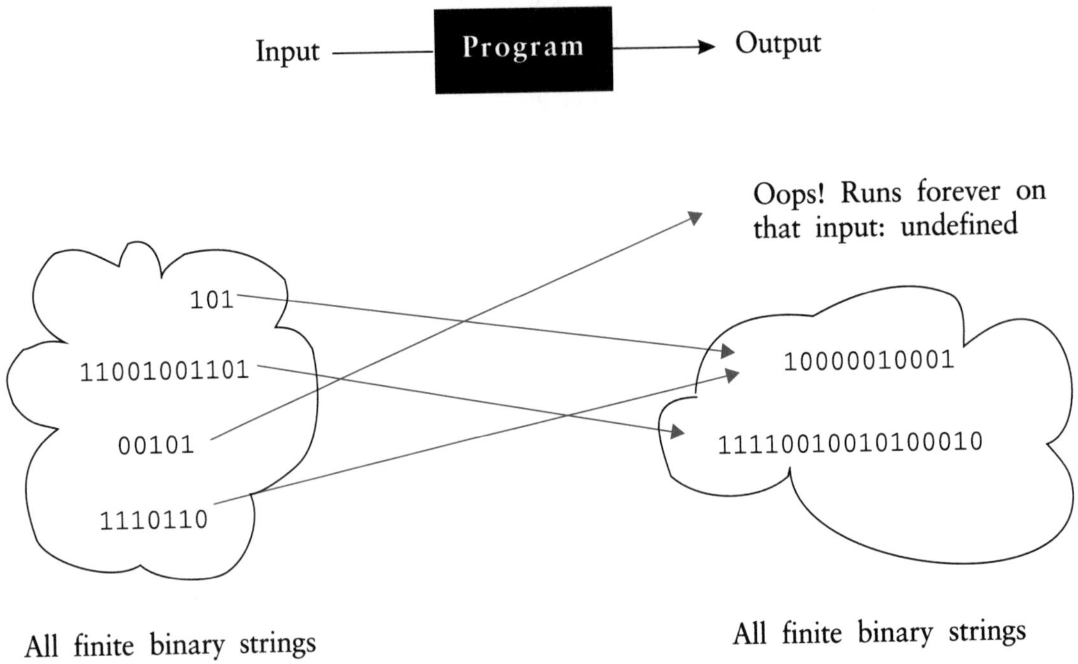

OK. But to make it easy for us to talk about programs without having to talk about specific languages or specific machines, how would you re-phrase your question?

> *What is the simplest machine that is sufficiently powerful to perform everything we mean when we talk about computation?*

Congratulations! You've hit upon the heart of the matter. We want a simple model of computation. We could equally well look at the abstract notion of "computation" from the point of view of what we do with the computers we're familiar with. Modern computers, though, with their registers, busses, random access memories, and the like are just too complicated to be of any theoretical use to us. The answer we seek lies in a 1936 paper by Alan Turing.* In this paper, Turing showed that what we gener-

---

* The 1930s was a significant decade for theoretical computer science. Not only did Turing publish his paper on computation, but the mathematician Kurt Gödel, using a "diagonalization" argument similar to one we will see later, demonstrated that there are theorems in arithmetic that can be stated but cannot be proved to be true or false.

ally mean by "computation" could be satisfied by a simple, abstract machine, such as the one diagrammed in Figure 7.3, that consisted of:

1. A tape of discrete cells and unlimited length, along with
2. A device with a finite number of *states* that could

   a. Read one symbol from the tape, and, based on that symbol and the current state,
   b. Write another symbol over the current symbol,
   c. Change the current state, and
   d. Move left or right on the tape.

> We could dispense with the blank symbol by suitably encoding a blank as, for instance, "11011".

The tape is used for recording input and output, one symbol (0,1, or blank) per cell. Initially, the string to serve as input to our computation is recorded in the leftmost cells of the tape, and the read/write head is positioned at the leftmost tape cell.

The control device embodies the machine's program. It uses a collection of rules, its notion of "state," and the contents of the tape to determine how to process the input symbols. Each rule is a statement of the form: "In state *n*, if the head is reading symbol *x*, write symbol *y*, move left or right one cell on the tape, and change the state to *m*." One of the states is singled out as the "initial state," the state that the machine regards itself as being in when the computation begins. Such a machine is referred to as Turing Machine (or TM, for short).

> *Sounds like a pretty simple machine. . . . You'll have to convince me that it can accomplish everything I call computation.*

OK, let's try. Here are the rules for a particular TM with five states and initial state 1 (we'll always use state 1 as the initial state):

PRESENT STATE	PRESENT SYMBOL	WRITE	MOVE	NEW STATE
1	0	0	Right	2
2	0	0	Right	3
2	1	1	Right	2
3	0	blank	Left	5
3	1	0	Left	4
4	0	1	Right	2

We could simplify this table by writing each row within parentheses, so the TM program would have statements (1, 0, 0, R, 2), (2, 0, 0, R, 3), (2, 1, 1, R, 2), (3, 0, b, L, 5), (3, 1, 0, L, 4), and (4, 0, 1, R, 2).

Although it is not obvious at first, this TM accomplishes integer addition, if we interpret the input in a particular way. We will decide that the input will represent the numbers to be added in *unary* notation—in other words, that *n* will be represented as *n* consecutive ones. Suppose we agree that the integers *n* and *m* are represented on the tape, from left

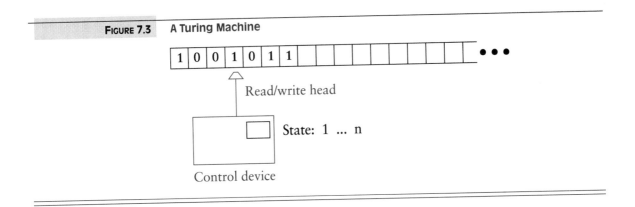

FIGURE 7.3   A Turing Machine

to right, as 0, followed by n 1s, followed by 0, then m 1s, followed by 0, so that the pair of integers (1, 2) would be represented on the tape as 010110. Then, given such an input, this TM will leave the tape with 0, followed by $n + m$ 1s, followed by 0. Using our example input 010110, and writing the present state below the symbol being read, the TM's action would be:

> In these descriptions, the current state is written immediately below the current cell on the tape.

```
0  1 0 1 1 0
1                    Start: Go right.


0  1  0 1 1 0
   2                 Scan past 1s.


0 1  0  1 1 0
     2               End of first string, go to next.


0 1 0  1  1 0
       3             Change 1 to 0, go back.


0 1  0  0 1 0
     4               Copy the 1, return to second string.


0 1 1  0  1 0
       2             End of first string, go to next.


0 1 1 0  1  0
         3           Change 1 to 0, go back.


0 1 1  0  0 0
       4             Copy the 1, return to second string.
```

```
0  1  1  1  0  0
               2                    End of first string, go to next.

0  1  1  1  0  0
                  3                 Oops! No second string. Erase last 0.

0  1  1  1  0
            5                       Halt—no further moves possible.
```

We could make the description of this sample TM easier to understand if we include comments, describing the intended interpretation of every statement.

```
(1, 0, 0, R, 2)      --move right, past the first 0
(2, 0, 0, R, 3)      --we've come to the end of a string of 1s
(2, 1, 1, R, 2)      --move right past all the 1s
(3, 0, b, L, 5)      --we've moved past the last 1—done
(3, 1, 0, L, 4)      --just hit the second string of 1s, shift the 0
(4, 0, 1, R, 2)      --finish shifting the 0, and go back to state 2
```

Notice that a TM "program" need not include rules for every state/symbol combination. If a TM encounters a state/symbol combination for which no rule is defined, we imagine the machine simply halts without making any further moves, as it did in the example when it reached state 5, reading a zero.

The "backing-and-filling" movement of our sample machine is characteristic of TM programs. We didn't say that TM computations were efficient, but we do claim that they are effective—they work, however slowly. The lab part of this module will explore some of the other computational capacities of the TM model. For now we'll assert without proof that a TM cannot only add; when programmed with suitable rules it can subtract, multiply, divide, compute logarithms and powers, and compare two data elements for equality or size. A TM can move information from one place on the tape to another, set aside locations to act as memory, and, in general, perform any operation that a contemporary computer can perform.

Only "contemporary computers"?

No. Turing Machines are actually more powerful than any piece of hardware that could be built. Since the tape of a TM is of potentially unlimited length (one of the beauties of abstraction!), we can store more information in a TM than we can with any real computer that we can possibly build. That's not important to us here, though, since you recall that we quite purposely stepped beyond hardware at the very beginning of this discussion. Remember, we are concerned with programs, not hardware. We are interested in achieving the functionality of the imaginary machines for which we write our programs—the virtual HyperTalk machine (or Pascal machine, or FORTRAN or LISP or Ada machine). The definitions of programming languages almost never mention the kind of machine on which they will run, so for our purposes, we can think of these virtual machines as being as unlimited as the Turing Machine is. Pick your favorite language, and we can prove that any program in that language can be simulated by a TM, in the sense that the TM will produce the same input-output matching that your program does. Thus, we have the basis for another definition:

Clear Box Definition

When we talk about programs, it is sufficient to talk about Turing Machines, in the sense that everything you can do with a program you can do with a suitable TM.

This makes life much easier for the theorist—TMs function as the *lingua franca* of programming. If we want to show that a property is true for all programs, it is sufficient to show that that property is true for Turing Machines. In some sense, the Turing Machine is a minimal device that still contains the full functionality of what we call computers.

That's still not very satisfying. You are trying to get a handle on the nature of computation by looking at contemporary computers and languages. Although I can't describe what they would be like, I can imagine that the intelligent artichokes of Planet X might have developed machines that operate on conceptual principles that are completely different from those of our computers. What happens to your abstract framework then?

Nothing at all, at least if you believe our third definition:

Optimistic Clear Box Definition

Any reasonable definition of computability is equivalent to "computability by Turing Machines."

The intelligent artichokes of Planet X may have machines that operate on principles we never dreamed of, but, by this definition (more commonly referred to as the Church-Turing thesis, after its creators), if we could call what their machines can do "computing," then we could simulate the action of their machines by Turing Machines.

I get the feeling I'm being flim-flammed by a smooth-talking logician turned confidence man. It's time to put up or shut up. Why should I believe the Church-Turing thesis? Can you prove it?

No. That's why it's called a thesis, rather than a theorem. To prove it, we'd have to agree once and for all what constitutes a "reasonable" notion of computability. Certainly, we would agree that whatever computability means, it must at least include the ability to do arithmetic calculations. Beyond that, deciding what to include becomes a rather murky question. During the early part of this century, logicians such as Church, Post, and Turing worked long and hard to provide a theoretical framework for what the nature of computation was. They came up with several definitions, each of which seemed quite general and powerful, and each of which took very different forms from the others. In all cases, it was eventually shown that anything "computable" by their definitions was computable by Turing Machines.

The Church-Turing thesis stemmed from a growing conviction that the equivalence of these definitions to Turing computability was not a fluke, but rather a fact. The Church-Turing thesis was, in essence, a confident challenge: "If you come up with a definition of what computability means, and if we are content that your definition includes all the things that we customarily call computations, then we'll be willing to bet that your definition includes only those things computable by Turing Machines."

LAB EXERCISE 1

The lab part of this module, like previous labs, revolves around a sample stack that is useful for conveying features of the HyperTalk language as well as some interesting insights into a particular aspect of computer science. The stack, named "ITM," is a Turing Machine simulator that allows you to define or read in descriptions of Turing Machines (TMs) and to watch them go through their paces. Unlike previous labs, this one is divided into two sections, one devoted to using the ITM stack and one to programming this stack. We will concentrate first on using ITM with some sample TMs that we have already defined.

The first thing you will notice about the ITM stack (see Figure 7.4) is that it represents all of the components of a TM. The "tape" stretches horizontally across the top of the screen, with an arrow beneath it indicating the current position of the scanning head. The large, scrollable field contains the rules, one per line, of the TM being simulated. Fields are also provided for displaying the start state, the current state, and the number of the rule used to make the last move. This graphic description of a TM is surrounded by buttons and a special "TMs" menu that allow us to define, manipulate, and execute the machine described.

Selecting "New" from the TMs menu clears all of the fields so that information describing a new TM can be entered. You can define your own

FIGURE 7.4   The ITM Stack

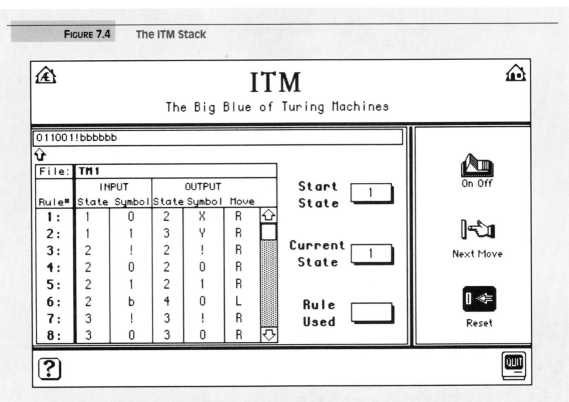

TM by clicking and typing directly in any of these fields. You can set the tape to contain the desired symbols, you can define rules (using the columns in the "Rules" field as guides for separating the entries in a given rule) to process the tape, and you can initialize the start and current states so that processing can proceed. You can even save a TM description (its rules, its initial tape, and its start state) by selecting the Save or Save as... commands from the TMs menu, in typical Macintosh fashion.

More commonly in this module, you will have ITM open an existing description of a sample TM from a file and experiment with it. Opening a machine description is accomplished by selecting the Open... command from the TMs menu. Doing so presents you with a standard Macintosh dialog box for choosing a file to open. A folder on your Æ Stacks disk, named "TMs", contains descriptions of machines that we will ask you to experiment with. Clicking on the desired file and opening it allows the stack to fill in values for the tape, the rules, the start and current states, and to execute the machine that they describe.

Execution can be accomplished "manually"—one move at a time— by clicking on the Next Move button. HyperCard searches the list of rules for one with input fields that match the current state and symbol being scanned. If a matching rule is found, the move is executed: The tape, the position of the scanning head, and the current state are all updated as prescribed by the rule.

A TM can also be executed to completion automatically by clicking the On/Off button at any point. The stack will process the current tape, using the rules provided, until either the TM reaches a state and symbol combination for which no rule exists or you click the On/Off button again. The Reset button is used to put the current TM back into its original condition. That is, its tape and current state are set to their initial values, as described in the file description of the TM.

Open the ITM stack now, and complete the following exercises.

1.1 Use the Open... command from the TMs menu to read in the TM described in file TM1.

1.2 Record on a separate sheet of paper the initial contents of TM1's tape.

1.3 Run TM1 to completion one rule at a time using the Next Move button. You will know TM1 is finished when the current state, the rule used, and the tape marker stop changing.

1.4 Record the final condition of the tape.

1.5 Use the Reset button to put TM1 back into its original condition.

1.6 Now, rerun TM1 to completion by clicking the On/Off button.

You may have enjoyed watching TM1 work under the control of ITM, but unless you knew something about TM1 beforehand, the connection between its initial and final tapes remains a mystery. In fact, in order to make sense out of any TM, one needs to know a great deal about the assumptions under which it was developed. At the very least, the notion of a start state seems to be important. While in the abstract a given TM can apply its rules equally well, beginning from any of its states, it must start in one particular state if we are to have any hope of obtaining the intended "results."

Similarly, one has complete freedom in ITM to define the tape processed by a TM. It would be pointless, however, to define the tape to contain symbols that are unrecognized in the TM's rules. Why, though, are initial tape values stored with each machine description? It is not enough to use symbols from the machine's "alphabet," the tape must also be in a particular format. While there is nothing explicit in the machine's rules about format, the required format is implied by the rules. A TM will process (perhaps vacuously) any tape, but only those composed from its alphabet and in its implied format can be processed in a useful or meaningful way.

What, though, is the meaning or utility of a TM? The utility of many TMs is evident from the results of their processing. As long as one has started the machine in its start state and has provided a valid input tape, the task accomplished by the machine is clear. TM1 is such a machine. The start state of TM1 is 1, and its alphabet is the set of symbols 0, 1, and b.* The required input format for the tape of machine TM1 is any collection of zeros and ones, followed by a single !, followed by a sequence of bs of equal (or greater) length to the leading zeros and ones. The result? TM1 makes a copy of the zero-and-one portion of its tape at another location on the tape. While this may seem a trivial use for a TM, think of the value of this operation to modern computers!

1.7 Now, open the Turing Machine described in file TM2. (There is no need to "save" TM1, since a copy of it already exists on your Æ Stacks disk.)

1.8 Write down the initial contents of TM2's tape on a piece of paper.

1.9 Run TM2 to completion by clicking the On/Off button.

1.10 Record the final contents of the tape.

The performance of TM2 was undoubtedly more baffling to you. Indeed, to appreciate the meaning of TM2, we need to know more than its start state, its alphabet, and the format of its tape. We need to know how to interpret the tape. Suppose, for example, we tell you that the initial tape configuration of TM2 is intended to represent the integer 3. That is, TM2 uses strings of ones to represent positive integers. On input 111b it produces 1111; on input 1111b it produces 11111; ... see the pattern? TM2 adds 1 to a positive integer.

SERIAL NUMBERS FOR PROGRAMS

OK. I'm willing to accept for the time being that computability by what I call "programs" is the same as computability by Turing Machines, but where does that leave us? What do we gain by equating programs and Turing Machines?

In a word, simplicity. For example, one thing it allows us to do is make a list of all possible TMs, and hence, by the Church-Turing thesis, all possible programs. This by itself is no mean feat. Since TMs are uniquely described by their rules, we can associate with each TM a unique "serial number," if you will, constructed from a description of its rules.

Each rule is a statement of the same general format, involving five variables: "If the machine is in state i, reading tape symbol j, then write symbol k, move in direction l, and change the state to m." We code each rule

> This is one way to encode TMs—it is certainly not the only way. You may want to experiment with a different encoding technique.

---

* Note that TMs are traditionally described as having a blank character as part of their alphabets. Since "" is sometimes difficult to discern on the screen, we have adopted the habit of using lowercase b in place of a blank. Therein lies one of the beauties of symbolic computation. The symbols themselves mean nothing to the machine and, as long as we are consistent in their usage within a TM, there is no difference in the machine's performance.

by representing the current state in unary, using zeros, so state *n* will be represented by *n* zeros. Also, we encode the tape symbol 0 by 0, symbol 1 by 00, and *blank* by 000. Direction *left* we code by 0, and direction *right* we represent by the integer 00. We represent the rule (*i, j, k, l, m*) by the binary string

$$\underbrace{0\ldots0}_{\substack{i \\ \text{times}}}\ 1\ \underbrace{0\ldots0}_{\substack{j \\ \text{times}}}\ 1\ \underbrace{0\ldots0}_{\substack{k \\ \text{times}}}\ 1\ \underbrace{0\ldots0}_{\substack{l \\ \text{times}}}\ 1\ \underbrace{0\ldots0}_{\substack{m \\ \text{times}}}$$

so that the rule "In state 3, reading 1, write blank, move left and change state to 2" would correspond to the 5-tuple (3, 1, b, L, 2) and thence to the binary string 000100100010100.

Now we can code an entire TM by listing its move codes, separated by pairs of ones, and enclosed on both ends by three ones:

111 first move code 11 second move code 11 ... 11 last move code 111

For example, the simple TM that puts a zero after its input (remember, we always begin a TM with its input written on the left end of the tape) has the following program

PRESENT STATE	PRESENT SYMBOL	WRITE	MOVE	NEW STATE
1	0	0	Right	1
1	1	1	Right	1
1	blank	0	Right	2

and has the move 5-tuples (1, 0, 0, R, 1), (1, 1, 1, R, 1), and (1, b, 0, R, 2), and so would be assigned the serial number

111 0101010010 11 010010010010 11 0100010100100 111

We've put spaces in the binary string to make it easier to read; they wouldn't actually be part of the serial number. If binary strings give you the willies, we could convert each TM serial number to decimal, so the simple TM just shown would have the rather massive serial number 32,241,552,672,039.

> If you're diligent, you might check this.

This notion of assigning a binary string to a Turing Machine is not too unusual; in fact, you've seen something very much like it already. Remember, we can compile a program in Pascal, say, to produce an output in machine language for some computer. But you've already seen that we can regard a machine language program as nothing but a collection of zeros and ones. All we have to do is take care of the details of how to separate statements, and we have a single (very long) string of zeros and ones that encodes our Pascal source code program. In encoding Turing Machines, all we're doing is simplifying our model, by using a simple language and doing the compiling ourselves, as it were (see Figure 7.5).

FIGURE 7.5   Encoding Turing Machines as Binary Strings

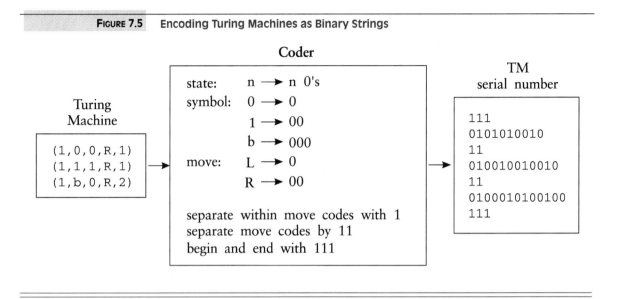

Notice that we can reconstruct any TM from its serial number. We convert the number to a binary string, if it's not already, then observe that the move codes are separated by double ones, and within the move codes, the values of i,j,k,l, and m are separated by single ones. We then count zeros to obtain the individual components of the move codes, and we're done. Notice also that there are many numbers that couldn't possibly be serial numbers for TMs, just as there are many nine-digit numbers that are not legal social security numbers. For instance, any binary number that doesn't begin and end with 111 could not be a legal serial number. Indeed, the smallest legal TM serial number is 63, which in binary is 111111. This is the serial number for the TM with *no* moves—on any input, it simply sits there and does nothing. Looked at as a matching between input and output strings, this is the identity function, where the output is just the input.

Well, that's moderately interesting, I'll admit. There's a certain tidiness in being able to encode all possible Turing Machines, but I must confess that the association of a serial number with every TM seems to be more of a curiosity than anything else. Does this TM encoding have any use?

Two uses, in fact. First, the ability to encode Turing Machines as binary strings allows us to build a TM that accepts these coded descriptions as input. Although it would take us too long to prove here, it is possible to build a *Universal Turing Machine* (UTM), which, when given the description of a TM along with an input for that machine, simulates the action of the coded machine, reading, writing, and moving along the tape just as if it were the original machine. In a sense, the TMs we have seen so far are like the old ENIAC machine, which had to be rewired for each new task. A UTM is more like a modern computer in that it interprets a description of a TM program and then performs the tasks that the program described.

The second use that arises from this encoding is really the heart of this module. If we extend the notion of encoding the objects we're working with, we can combine the definitions of programs as (1) functions on binary strings and (2) Turing Machines, to prove what you may have felt all along—that there are some things that programs simply can't do.

We begin by encoding all finite binary strings as integers, in much the same way that we encoded TMs by integers. Make a list of all possible binary strings, initially in order of length and then by numeric order within collections of strings of equal length, as follows:

STRING	CODE
empty string	1
0	2
1	3
00	4
01	5
10	6
11	7
000	8
001	9
010	10

In this coding, every binary string corresponds to a unique positive integer, and any positive integer encodes a unique string. In fact, the rule for this code is simple to state: A binary string of length n that is equal in binary to the number b has code $2^n + b$. For example, the string 001001 has length 6 and is the binary representation of the number 9, so its code would be $2^6 + 9 = 73$ (as illustrated in Figure 7.6), which you could easily verify by continuing the table. Similarly, the string 0100001101000001010000010, which we earlier interpreted three ways, would have code 21,184,834. With this encoding in mind, we could say:

Black Box Definition (Integer Version)

A program is a matching from all positive integers to (possibly a subset of) the positive integers.

Figure 7.7 illustrates this definition.

For example, we've already seen a program that appends a zero to the right end of the input string. Thus, given 001001 as input, the program

---

FIGURE 7.6 **Encoding Binary Strings as Integers**

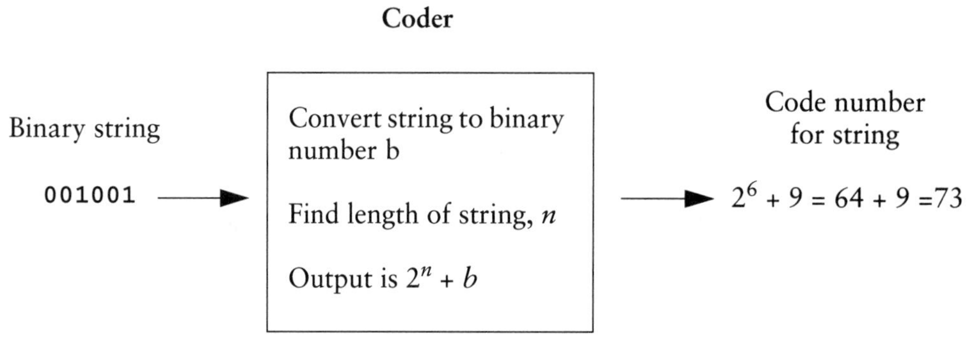

Coder

Binary string

001001 →

Convert string to binary number b

Find length of string, n

Output is $2^n + b$

Code number for string

→ $2^6 + 9 = 64 + 9 = 73$

FIGURE 7.7   **Figure 7.2 Rewritten with Integer Codes for Binary Strings**

Input ——— **Program** ——→ Output

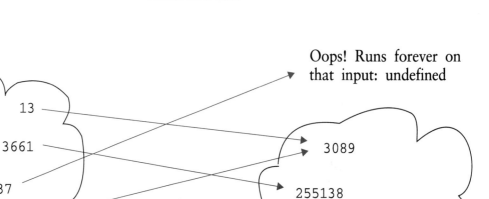

Oops! Runs forever on that input: undefined

13

3661

37

246

3089

255138

All finite binary strings, coded as integers

All finite binary strings, coded as integers

---

produces output equal to 0010010. Looked at as a matching P from the positive integers to themselves, this program has a very simple interpretation: If the input code is n, the code for the output will be $2n$, so the program would correspond to the matching that we would write as $P(n) = 2n$. For instance, if the input is 001001, with code $n = 73$, the output will be 0010010, with code $146 = 2 * 73 = 2n$.

REVIEW QUESTIONS

1. What do we mean by "virtual machine"? Give a similar situation outside computer science, where what you think you are seeing or doing is not actually what you are seeing or doing.

2. In the black box definition of a program, why do we say that some input strings may not match any output strings? Can an input string match two or more output strings? Is every output string matched to some input string, in general? Explain.

3. Which definition includes more objects: the black box or the clear box? Which is the correct definition of *program*?

Æ LAB

LAB EXERCISE 2

Following are descriptions of four other TMs, cleverly disguised on your disks as files TM3, TM4, TM5, and TM6. Your task is to experiment with each in the interest of guessing its purpose. For each TM, write English descriptions of what information its initial tape contains and what processing is accomplished by its rules. For TMs 5 and 6 you should also try to figure out what the symbols T, F, N, and P stand for.

		START STATE	ALPHABET	TAPE FORMAT
2.1	TM3	0	1,!,b	two strings of ones, separated by a !
2.2	TM4	0	1,0,b	two strings of ones, separated by a ! and followed by a b
2.3	TM5	3	1,b,T,F	a string of ones followed by a b
2.4	TM6	1	0,1,b,N,P	any string of zeros and ones followed by a b

7.3   IMPOSSIBLE PROGRAMS

We're back to the black box definition of programs; all you've done is replace binary strings with their integer codes. Aside from the fact that integer codes take less room to write than the original strings, what does this buy us? Aren't we trying to relate programs to computation? Our definitions keep flipping back and forth.

Be patient. Now comes something rather remarkable. Imagine that we have a list of all possible TMs, arranged in increasing order of their serial numbers. We'll write this list $M_1, M_2, M_3, \ldots$. In particular, M_1 is the TM with code 63 (111111 in binary), which has no moves; M_2, with code 111010101010111 (30,039 in decimal) is the TM that has one "statement" (1, 0, 0, L, 1), since that's the next-largest TM code.

M_2 is simple enough to describe—if the input tape begins with a 0, this TM writes a 0 and then "falls off" the left end of the tape, thereby halting. Since there is no move description to cover any other input tape, the TM halts immediately on all other inputs. In other words, no matter what the input is, M_2 will (quickly) halt and leave its tape unchanged. As a black box, M_2 is just the identity function that matches each input string to itself. Many TMs in our list are equally uninteresting: out of the first twelve, only M_4 and M_5 modify their tapes at all.

If you accept the Church-Turing thesis, then *everything* you consider to be a program is somewhere in this list (along with many "nonprograms" that produce infinite output, like (1, 0, 0, R, 1), (1, 1, 0, R, 1), (1, b, 0, R, 1), which writes a never-ending string of zeros on its tape). Now we'll construct an input-output matching function P from our list of TMs. P will match every finite string of zeros and ones to either '0' or the blank string by the following rules. For each positive integer n:

1. Find the binary string s_n whose code is n.
2. Feed s_n as input to machine M_n and look at the output.

   a. If M_n produces no output (that is, if the tape is blank when the TM stops), define $P(s_n)$ to be the symbol '0'.
   b. If M_n produces any output, including infinite output, define $P(s_n)$ to be the empty string.

In Figure 7.8 we demonstrate the process we use to create the matching P.

The important thing to realize is that we are constructing the input-output matching P that is by definition *different* from that of every other machine. M_1 cannot produce the matching given by P, since M_1 acts differently from P on input s_1. M_2 cannot produce the matching given by P, since M_2 acts differently from P in input s_2. In fact, *no* TM in the list produces the input-output matching described by P, because we designed P for just that purpose. Since the TM serial number for every program is

FIGURE 7.8   Generating an Input-Output Matching

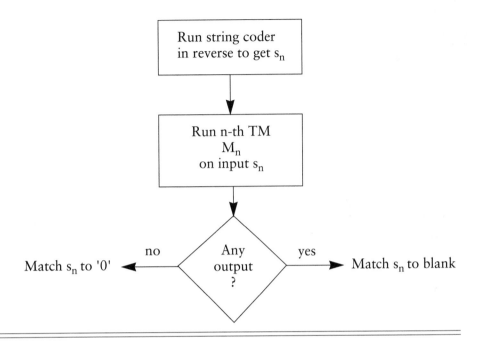

somewhere in the list, we must conclude that no possible program can produce the input-output matching described by *P*. In simple terms:

> There is at least one function from input string to corresponding output string that cannot be computed by any program at all. In other words, *every clear box program (TM) is a black box program (matching), but there are black box programs that are not clear box programs.*

The situation is even bleaker than that, though. Our argument was based on the fact (which surprises almost everyone the first time they see it) that infinity comes in different sizes. Although there are infinitely many possible programs, and infinitely many different ways of matching inputs to outputs, the infinity of possible matchings is vastly larger than the infinity of possible programs. Stated another way,

> A negligibly small proportion of all possible input-output matchings can be realized by Turing Machines.

Computers cannot only not do everything; when we think of computers and their programs as matching outputs to inputs, they can hardly do anything at all. Or, if you will, there just aren't enough programs to produce all possible input-output matchings.

> *That's very impressive, but isn't this example somewhat contrived? There's no possible way you could describe what the function P is without describing every TM in your list, running each on its associated input string and looking at the results. Anyhow, the fact that there are many things that we cannot compute is of no real importance to us so long as we can compute the things we want to compute.*

In mathematical terms, there is a *countable infinity* of all TMs (clear boxes), but an *uncountable* infinity of input-output matchings (black boxes).

Right and wrong. You are correct that there is no easy way too describe what P does. We could start the process by recalling that the lowest-numbered TM, M_1, with serial number 63, is the identity machine. M_1 gives empty output on empty input, and so P would pair the empty input to the output '0'. With some more work, we could find the next-lowest-numbered TM and run it on '0' (the string with code 2), and so on, but it appears that while we know that P exists, it would take us infinitely long to tell what it is.

The matching *P* is pretty boring. $P(s_1) =$ '0', but after that $P(s_n)$ is the empty (blank) string until some $n > 2317$.

That is exactly as it should be. Suppose we discovered some "shortcut" way to determine what P is, such as "P produces output '0' precisely when the input has code that is divisible by 3." In that case, we could make up a program to apply the shortcut rule to input strings, thereby producing a program that acts like P. But that would contradict our findings that there is no program that acts like P. In other words, the fact that we have proved there is no program that acts like P guarantees that there is no effective shortcut to describing P. P would take infinitely long to describe precisely because we designed it that way.

Where you go wrong, though, is in thinking that the only instances of problems that we cannot solve by computers are peculiar ones like the example we just used. In fact, there is a very simple example of a problem we would very much like to solve, but cannot. This problem even sounds like it could be solved by a computer program, unlike the problems of prejudice or world hunger, which seem too ill posed and "fuzzy" to be amenable to computer solution. We could have given you that problem at the start, but we needed to introduce the notion of encoding first.

THE HALTING PROBLEM

Consider this problem: A perennial error that programmers face is described as an "infinite loop." Here's a simple HyperTalk example:

```
on mouseUp
    put 3 into card field 1
    repeat until card field 1 = 0
        beep
        put 3 into card field 1
```

```
      end repeat
      end mouseUp
```

Perhaps the programmer intended to include an additional statement in the interior of the loop. We'll never know, but it's clear that this script will run (noisily) forever. It would be very nice to have a program that takes as its input (1) the listing of this or any other program, along with (2) a sample input for that program, and answers either "Your program will never halt on this input" or "Your program will eventually halt on this input." Believe us, a program that could do that would make its creator wealthy beyond any dreams of avarice—there's not a professional programmer alive who couldn't benefit from such an application. Why hasn't someone written it, then?

Because it's impossible? You'll have to do a lot more convincing before I'll believe you can prove that. I'd be perfectly willing to accept the fact that such a program doesn't exist because it's tricky to write, but because it absolutely can't be written? That's another matter entirely.

It's true, though. We can prove it to you, and we will, for two reasons. First, because we want to give an example of a reasonable-sounding problem for which there is *provably* no program to solve it, and second, for purely aesthetic reasons. The proof, while a bit tricky, is so pretty that it would be a shame not to share it with you.

We'll adopt a common proof technique, known as *proof by contradiction.* In such a proof, you want to show that something, call it Q, cannot happen. You begin by supposing that Q can happen, and then argue to a conclusion that is patently false, like $2 + 2 = 5$. If the steps of your argument are valid, but you still reach a false conclusion, then the only thing that could have led you to that false conclusion is your original assumption, that Q could have ever been true. Since your original assumption must have been false, the only possible state of affairs is that Q could never happen in the first place.

> In detective stories, this technique takes the form, "If we assume the butler did it, we must then conclude that he had to be in two places at the same time. Therefore, the butler is innocent."

So, let's assume that we could somehow make a halt-testing program, H. The specifications of this program are as follows:

1. H takes as its input

   a. a suitably encoded description of a program P (in binary, say);
   b. a binary string s denoting an input.

2. For any pair (P, s) as described in item 1, H eventually halts and answers

   a. "yes," if P will eventually halt on input s, or
   b. "no," if P would run forever on input s.

There are two important properties of H that deserve notice:

- *Property 1:* We require that H itself will always halt. That means we couldn't design H as a compiler that just runs P on s. Such a scheme

---

FIGURE 7.9   **The Halt-Testing Program H**

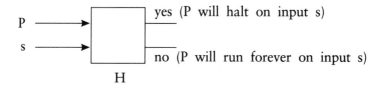

P ⟶

s ⟶

H

yes (P will halt on input s)

no (P will run forever on input s)

---

would always give a correct answer if P halted on s, but we'd have to wait forever to get an answer if P ran forever on s—we could never know, in other words, if P halted or not on s.

- *Property 2.* We want H to work correctly—that is, we want H to give the right answer for *every* program-input pair, even if the input were something peculiar that P would never expect to get in the normal course of affairs. After all, operators make mistakes entering data, and we'd like to be able to test P on all kinds of input, good and bad.

Summing up, we assume that H is designed so that it will halt and provide an answer, no matter what the strings P and s are. Figure 7.9 is a graphic description of H.

Now we're ready to begin. Assuming that we have such a program H, we'll use H to construct another program, H'. H' will use H as a subroutine, as follows:

1. H' will take a single binary string x as input.
2. H' will first make a copy of x and will send x twice to H': once as P, and once for s. That is, x will serve as both the program and input for H.
3. Depending on the answer returned from H, H' will do one of two things:

   a. If the answer returned from H is "yes" (indicating that program x will indeed halt on input x), then H' will deliberately go into an infinite loop and run forever.
   b. If the answer from H' is "no" (program x will run forever on input x), then H' will stop immediately.

Figure 7.10 shows H'.

Now, H' is a pretty peculiar object, but it certainly is a program, as long as H is a program, too. What does it do? If x is the encoding of a program, the subroutine H determines whether program x will halt, *when given its own descriptions as input*. There's nothing at all wrong with giving a program is own description to work on—we could use a word processor to edit a copy of its own code for publication purposes, for example.

| FIGURE 7.10 | Program *H'* |

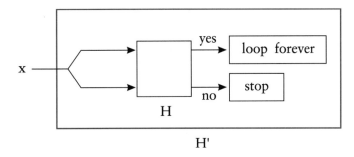

So, if *x* is an encoding of a program, *H'* is designed to halt if program *x* will run forever on its own description, and to run forever if program *x* will eventually halt on its own description. That bears repeating:

> *H'*, when given an encoding of a program, *x*, will halt if and only if program *x* will not halt when given its own encoding.

Now, what happens when we give *H'* its own description? Think about it, replacing *x* in the boxed sentence with *H'*. Take your time, we'll wait.

*   *   *

Got it? The conclusion is that we have built a program *H'* that will halt when given its own description if and only if it will *not* halt when given its own description! In other words, we have a program that, for at least one input, will halt only if it never halts, and will run forever only if it eventually halts. Well, that can't possibly be correct—that's as bad as saying "I'll pass this course if and only if I fail."

We've reached the contradiction we promised at the beginning. Since *H'* acts so bizarrely, it can't possibly be a program, but the only thing that could stand in the way of its being a program is our assumption that we could have built its subroutine *H* in the first place. We have to conclude that there is no possible program that will do what *H* does. In other words, *H* is one of the possible black box matchings, but we can never write a clear box TM program to do what we want *H* to do.

Don't feel bad if you're confused over what just went on. This argument is probably as subtle as any you've seen recently, and almost everyone has trouble with it the first time out. If you're still confused, take the time to look over the argument again—it's well worth the effort. The important thing to realize is that there are reasonable-sounding problems that can never be solved by programs.

The original problem that *H* was designed to solve is known as the *Halting Problem*. In technical terms, what we have just done is to prove that there is no effective procedure (that is, program) that will solve the Halting Problem.

I'm almost afraid to ask—is the Halting Problem the only interesting one for which there is no effective procedure?

Nope. In fact, there are many related problems that are *undecidable*—that is, for which we cannot write a program that answers all possible instances. We'll finish with a few samples, just to give you the flavor.

1. Given a program P and a string x, will P ever write x as part of its output?
2. Given programs P and Q, are P and Q equivalent in the sense that for every input s, P and Q started on s will have the same output?
3. Given P and s as usual, and a state n of P, will P started on s ever be in state n?
4. Given a program P, will P halt on all possible inputs?
5. Given a program P, will P halt when started on a blank tape?
6. Given a suitably encoded description of what P should do, will P actually act as described?

> That is to say, self-referentiality is almost always problematic for programs.

Basically, it is very difficult to come up with decision procedures for any interesting questions about programs. In fact, there is an honest-to-gosh theorem, due to H. G. Rice, that states, in our terms, "Any nontrivial property of programs is undecidable." In this theorem *nontrivial* has a complicated technical definition, but you can almost capture the truth of the theorem if you use the customary definition of the term. You can write programs to do many things, but you can't do everything with computers—in particular, it is very hard to find programs that can answer questions about programs.

> More generally, we can't write a program that can determine whether an arbitrary mathematical statement is true or false. Unfortunately for students, we'll never mechanize all of mathematics.

Undecidable problems are not restricted to problems about programs, either. There are many undecidable problems in other areas, such as mathematics and game playing. Consider the following:

1. Given a collection of *Diophantine equations*, polynomial equations to be solved in integers, such as

$$xy - 3x^2z + 62xyz = 14, \; 13xy^2 + y = xz = 9$$

find a solution (or even tell whether there is a solution).

2. Given a collection of square tiles with colored sides, can these tiles be used to cover the plane, subject to the restriction that tiles with a common edge must have matching colors along those edges? You are not allowed to rotate the tiles. (Refer to Figure 7.11.)

The last two problems point out an important idea about undecidable problems, or about using programs to solve problems in general. When we say that a problem can (or cannot) be solved by a program, we mean that there is (or is not) a program that gives the correct solution for *any* in-

FIGURE 7.11   Tiling the Plane: An Undecidable Problem

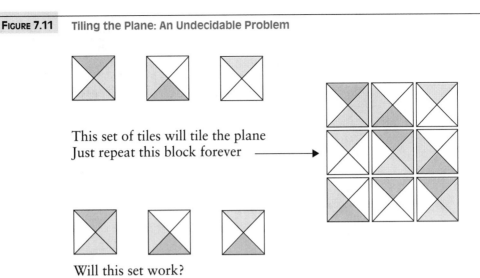

This set of tiles will tile the plane
Just repeat this block forever ─────────▶

Will this set work?

stance of the problem. The tiling problem does not ask you to write a program for a specific set of tiles, but rather requires that you find a program that will allow you to send it as input any possible set of tiles, and will give the correct answer. In essence, you probably could answer the problem for any particular (reasonably small) set of tiles, but your solutions would be *ad hoc*—tailored to the specific set you were given, rather than general and applicable to all sets of tiles.

REVIEW QUESTIONS

1. Give two reasons why encodings of Turing Machines are useful.
2. Why is the argument in which we show that the matching *P* cannot correspond to any TM called a "diagonalization" argument?
3. What is the Halting Problem? Why is it important?

LAB EXERCISE 3

What we have done in the previous lab exercises is to help you interpret a few simple Turing Machines. As you have seen, a great deal of interpretation is required for such machines to be seen as meaningful or useful in any way. The amount of interpretation reflects the conceptual simplicity of TMs and of symbolic computation in general. If nothing else, this brief excursion into the world of computer science theory should help you to appreciate the expressive power of a language such as HyperTalk, wherein the bulk of the burden of interpretation rests with the Macintosh, not with the programmer.

Speaking of HyperTalk, let's turn to the scripts of the ITM stack to see some features of the language that we have not used before. As you can imagine, most of ITM's processing is described in the script of the Next Move button:

```
on mouseUp
    global ruleNumber, inState, inSymbol
    put 0 into ruleNumber
    put field "Current State" into inState
    put field "Current Cell" into cell
    put char cell of field "Tape" into inSymbol
    findMove
        if ruleNumber < 0 then
            put ruleNumber into field "Current Rule"
            update Tape
            moveLR
            setState
        end if
end mouseUp
```

Looking at the mouseUp handler provides us with an overview of the processing. In fact, we chose to define separate handlers for finding a rule, for updating the tape, for setting the new state, and for moving the scan head, precisely so that the mouseUp handler would convey its processing clearly at first glance. Reading it tells us that the current state and current symbol from the tape are used to look up the rule to apply. If a rule is found (indicated by global variable ruleNumber being set to some nonzero line number in the field "Rules") that applies to the current situation, then the tape is updated, the scan head is moved left or right, and the new state is set.

The findMove handler simply searches through the "Rules" field for a rule that matches the current state (inState) and tape symbol (inSymbol):

```
on findMove
--returns a rule # if one exists, else no change
    global ruleNumber, inState, inSymbol
    put 1 into lineNumber
    --keep looking until a match is found or no rules left
    repeat until (ruleNumber > 0) or (lineNumber > 50)
        put word 1 of line lineNumber of field "Rules" into thisState
```

```
      put word 2 of line lineNumber of field "Rules" into thisSymbol
      if (thisState = inState) and (thisSymbol = inSymbol) then
        put lineNumber into ruleNumber
      else
        add 1 to lineNumber
      end if
    end repeat
  end findMove
```

Notice the use of "word" to pick out parts of each line of the field "Rules" for comparison (a "word" of a line in a field is a collection of characters surrounded by blanks). Global variable ruleNumber, which is set to zero in the mouseUp handler prior to invoking findMove, is set to the matching line number for the "Rules" field, if one is found.

3.1 The number 50 in the repeat loop of findMove derives from the fact that the field "Rules" is initially set up to have 50 lines (room for 50 rules). In fact, each machine we have investigated so far has had far fewer than 50 rules, in which case the remaining lines in the field "Rules" are empty. Fix this script so that it searches only those lines of the field "Rules" that actually contain rules.

The updating of the tape is accomplished, appropriately enough, in the updateTape handler:

```
on updateTape
  global ruleNumber
  put word 4 of line ruleNumber of field "Rules" into newSymbol
  put field "Current Cell" into newSpot
  put newSymbol into char newSpot of field "Tape"
end updateTape
```

The new symbol to be written onto the tape is copied out of the selected rule, and then placed directly "into" the location on the tape where the scanning head is currently located (as indicated by an invisible field named "Current Cell").

The arrow beneath the "Tape" field is actually a button with no mouseUp handler of its own. We simply wanted to create a graphic arrow the location of which we could control. This arrow could have been created with HyperCard's drawing tools, and its location could have been manipulated using the selection tool and HyperTalk's drag... to command from within moveLR, but using a button is much simpler.

```
on moveLR
  global ruleNumber
  put location of background button "Tape Marker" into arrowLoc
```

```
        put word 5 of line ruleNumber of field "Rules" into direction
        if direction contains "L" then
            if field "Current Cell" > 1 then
                subtract 1 from field "Current Cell"
                subtract 6 from item 1 of arrowLoc
            else
                Answer "Attempt to move off left end of tape" with "Stop"
                put 0 into ruleNumber
            end if
        else
            if direction contains "R" then
                add 1 to field "Current Cell"
                if field "Current Cell" < 50 then add 6 to item 1 of arrowLoc
            end if
        end if
        set location of background button "Tape Marker" to arrowLoc
    end moveLR
```

It's simple to move a button because buttons and fields have "location" properties that can be obtained and set directly in HyperTalk. Notice how the moveLR message handler alters the location of the arrow named "Tape Marker." The location of the button is retrieved and saved in the first put statement (as variable arrowLoc).

An object's location is represented as an ordered pair of screen coordinates—for example, a location of 100,200 means that the object's center is 100 dots horizontally and 200 dots vertically from the upper left corner of the screen (location 0,0). Recall that individual components of a location can be referenced in HyperTalk using the term "item." Asking, for instance, for "item 1" of a location returns its horizontal component. Thus, the statements that add 6 to and subtract 6 from "item 1 of arrowLoc" are merely adjusting the horizontal component of the arrow button's location by 6 (which is the width of one character in the "Tape" field). Notice also how the location of the arrow button is reset directly in the scripts of button Reset and the NewTM handler of the ITM stack.

Let's look at the script of the button On/Off for a demonstration of how screen coordinates can be used from within a script in another interesting way.

```
on mouseUp
    global ruleNumber
    if field "Current State" is empty then
        Answer "Enter a value for Current State" with "OK"
    else
        set the icon of background button id 11 to "On"
        send mouseUp to background button "Next Move"
        put item 1 of the rect of background button id 11 into h1
```

```
                    put item 2 of the rect of background button id 11 into v1
                    put item 3 of the rect of background button id 11 into h2
                    put item 4 of the rect of background button id 11 into v2
                    repeat until (ruleNumber = 0)
                       if the mouseClick then
                          if withinRect(item 1 of the mouseLoc, item 2 of the ¬
                             mouseLoc, h1, v1, h2, v2) then
                             set the icon of background button id 11 to "Off"
                             exit mouseUp
                          else
                             send mouseUp to background button "Next Move"
                          end if
                       else
                          send mouseUp to background button "Next Move"
                       end if
                    end repeat
                    set the icon of background button id 11 to "Off"
                 end if
              end mouseUp

              function inBetween x, low, hi
                 return ((x)>=low) and (x(<=hi))
              end inBetween

              function withinRect h,v,h1,v1,h2,v2
                 return (inBetween(h,h1,h2) and inBetween(v,v1,v2))
              end withinRect
```

> mouseClick: **A HyperTalk function that returns** true **if the mouse button has been clicked and** false **if it has not.** mouseLoc: **A HyperTalk function that returns the point on the screen where the pointer is currently located. The return value is of the form** *horizontal, vertical*.

On/Off sets the current TM to run automatically. It accomplishes this by repeatedly invoking (via a send command) the Next Move script until either no applicable rule is found (indicated by a ruleNumber of 0), or until the user clicks the On/Off button again. The reclicking of the button, not mentioned explicitly in the script at all, is monitored by the nested if statements within the repeat loop, which use two interesting HyperTalk functions.

The if statement begins by invoking HyperTalk's built-in mouseClick function, which returns true or false to indicate whether or not the mouse has been clicked since the last check. If it has—that is, if mouse-Click returns true—we invoke another built-in function, mouseLoc, to get the location of the mouse when it was clicked.* We then check the

---

* There is a third mouse-related built-in function called clickLoc, which in essence combines the functions of mouseclick and mouseloc—that is, it returns the location of the most recent mouse click. Unfortunately, when referenced from within a script, it does not get updated. That is, clickLoc will return the same location every time it is referenced from within a script—the location of the last click before the script began. The mouseClick and mouseLoc functions are updated each time they are invoked and, thus, are better suited to the kind of repeated monitoring being done in the script of the button On/Off.

horizontal (item 1) and vertical (item 2) positions of the clicked location to see if they fall in a certain range on the screen. The numbers used to specify the range are, not coincidentally, precisely those that describe the bounding rectangle of background button id 11, that is the On/Off button.

Finally, look at ITM's stack script to see how the handlers NewTM, OpenTM, and SaveTM manipulate the files that describe TMs. Files are stored in three pieces. Line 1 stores the start state for the TM, line 2 contains the initial tape to be used, and lines 3 through the end of the file record the list of TM rules, one per line. The only tricky thing in any of these file-related scripts has to do with how they handle carriage returns. Notice that in order to have file entries occur on different lines, it is necessary to send return characters concatenated to the end of each line sent to the file.

When these lines are read back into the ITM stack with a read ... until return statement, the return characters become part of the fields they are read into. For example, if a file contains a first line of 1 <return> (indicating a start state of 1), when that file is read, the TM's start state field would be set to 1 <return>. If we then made modifications to the corresponding TM's rules and saved it again (in modified form), its start state would be recorded in the new file as 1 <return> <return>—oops! At any rate, the statements in the OpenTM script that subtract 1 from the length of each line read in from a file get around this problem.

EXTENDED LAB EXERCISES

1. While there is nothing wrong with a TM being incomplete—that is, not having a rule to cover every input state–input symbol combination—it is incorrect for a TM to have an ambiguous rule set. It should not provide two rules that address the same input conditions. Nothing in the stack ITM precludes this. No checks are made prior to saving a file to ensure that its rules are unambiguous. Implement such a checker.

2. Write and test your own TMs to accomplish
   a. Clearing a tape (that is, setting it to all blanks)
   b. *Proper integer subtraction*, also called *monus*, in which $m - n = 0$, if $n > m$
   c. Integer multiplication

3. As currently defined, the stack ITM always assumes a tape is to be scanned beginning at its left edge. The Reset, OpenTM, and NewTM

handlers all initialize the scan head to point to (and read from) the first character on the tape. Given the freedom we have in designing TMs, we can imagine that a machine could be defined to start operating from somewhere in the middle of its tape. Fix ITM so that it allows one to specify, prior to saving a TM description on a file, which position on the tape is to be used as the initial one for the scan head.

7.4 EXERCISES

1. The string 1110010010100101001011001001010001 represents a rectangular picture, as specified in the text. What familiar object is pictured?

2. Write the move description for a TM that blanks its tape and halts after replacing every zero or one with a blank. Remember that initially all the non-blank characters are in consecutive cells at the left end of the tape.

3. In computing the serial numbers of Turing Machines, why did we begin and end with 111? Could we have left the ones off and still had the correspondence between integers and TMs that we desired?

4. Suppose that the tape of a TM initially contained 0 at the far left, followed by the binary representation of the integer n. Assume that the start state was state 1. What would be the action of the following TM?

PRESENT STATE	PRESENT SYMBOL	WRITE	MOVE	NEW STATE
1	1	1	Right	1
1	0	0	Right	1
1	blank	blank	Left	2
2	0	1	Right	3
2	1	0	Left	2

5. What is the encoding for the TM of exercise 10? Only masochists need express their answer as a decimal number.

6. Design a TM that appends 0 to the *left* of its input. (*Hint:* The addition TM in the text contains a helpful idea.)

7. Describe the action of the TM with the following serial number, again assuming that state 1 was the start state.

1110101001001011010010100101101000100101 00111

8. M_4, the first TM that changes its input tape (some of the time) has code 1110100101010111. What does M_4 do, and under what conditions will it modify its input?

9. In the text, you saw the rule for finding the code of a binary string. How would you reverse this process, finding the string that has code n? What string has code 467?

10. When we found the matching P that didn't correspond to any program, we ignored the fact that most TMs appeared several times in the list M_1, M_2, M_3, . . . , since identical TMs that had their move descriptions listed in different orders would be assigned different codes, in spite of the fact that they act in exactly the same ways on all inputs. Does this affect the construction of the function P in any way? Explain.

11. What is $P('0')$? To do this exercise, you'll have to find M_2.

12. **a.** Describe M_1–M_{10}. This is not an exercise for the faint-hearted. (*Hint:* 63; 30,039; 58,711; 59,735; 59,991; 60,055; 60,071; 116,055; 117,079; 117,335.)
    b. Describe the mapping P on the first ten binary strings, s_1–s_{10}.

13. Some problems have the property that it is much easier to verify a solution than it is to produce a solution. Consider the *equal sum problem:* Given a set of numbers, separate them into two sets that have the same sum, if possible.

    a. For the set {1, 5, 8, 10, 12, 15, 16, 17, 21, 34, 47, 51, 52, 53, 65, 77, 100}, verify that one solution is the pair of sets {1, 5, 10, 12, 15, 16, 17, 51, 65, 100} and {8, 21, 34, 47, 52, 53, 77}.
    b. Find a different solution. (*Hint:* All the numbers sum to 584, so you need to find a collection with sum 292.)
    c. If you are very ambitious, describe a process that will solve the equal sum problem for any input set. It's a bit easier to find a process that tells whether there is a solution or not, without actually producing the solution.

14. Extending exercise 13, there are even some undecidable problems for which it is easy to verify a solution, in spite of the fact that there is no program that will find a solution in all instances. The *Post Correspondence Problem* is one of these. In this problem, you are given a collection of dominos with patterns of white and colored dots on the top and bottom:

You must find an arrangement of these dominos in a row (repeating dominos as necessary, but without inverting any of the dominos) that yields the same sequence of dots in the top and bottom rows, as in the following solution:

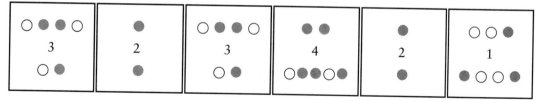

Solution sequence: 3, 2, 3, 4, 2, 1

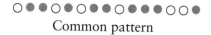

Common pattern

a. Verify this solution.

b. Find a solution to the following Post Correspondence Problems, or show why there is no possible solution. Was this harder than part a?

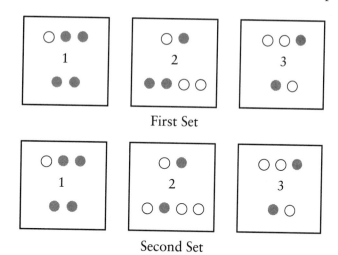

c. Describe a process you could use to tell whether or not there is a solution to *some* special instances of the Post Correspondence Problem, even though your process wouldn't work on all instances.

15. (This is a very tricky problem.) There are infinitely many integer solutions in positive integers x, y, z to the equation $x^2 + y^2 = z^2$. For example, $x = 3$, $y = 4$, $z = 5$ and $x = 5$, $y = 12$, $z = 13$ are two solutions to this equation. For

higher exponents n, however, there don't seem to be any solutions to $x^n + y^n = z^n$ except for the trivial ones in which one or more of the terms is zero. About 1637, the brilliant French mathematician Pierre de Fermat wrote in the margin of one of his books that the equation $x^n + y^n = z^n$ has no solutions in positive numbers when $n > 2$, and added the note, "I have discovered a truly remarkable proof which this margin is too small to contain." The statement

$$x^n + y^n = z^n \text{ has no solutions in positive numbers when } n > 2$$

is known as *Fermat's Last Theorem* and has been neither proved nor disproved to this day.* Could that be due to the fact that it is undecidable? In other words, if we consider the quoted statement as a problem, is it an undecidable problem?

16. Discuss the following assertion:

> I am not a computer, and here's the reason why. A computer, or at least anything we would want to call a computer, cannot be programmed to solve an undecidable problem, such as the Halting Problem or the Post Correspondence Problem of Exercise 14. Given enough time, though, I'm sure I could solve any individual instance of one of these undecidable problems—after all, decidability or undecidability just asks *can* you solve these, not how long will it take. The way in which I am better than a computer is that I can tailor my solution to the particular instance, rather than having to use the same procedure on all instances. I have enough confidence in my problem-solving abilities to assert that with enough time I could solve any instance of, say, the Halting Problem. Therefore, I represent a "meta-program," which is beyond the range of any computer, and so I cannot be a computer, nor could I be simulated by one.

7.5   ADDITIONAL READINGS

Bird, R. *Programs and Machines: An Introduction to the Theory of Computation.* New York: John Wiley & Sons, 1976.

Brookshear, J. G. *Theory of Computation: Formal Languages, Automata, and Complexity.* Redwood City, Calif.: Benjamin/Cummings, 1989.

Garey, M. R., and Johnson, D. S. *Computers and Intractability: A Guide to NP-Completeness.* San Francisco: W.H. Freeman, 1979.

---

* In June, 1993, Andrew Wilkes, a British mathematician working at Princeton, announced the proof of a result that would imply that Fermat was right, but at the time of this writing, there hadn't been time for other mathematicians to verify Wilkes's apparent proof. In any case, the likely affirmative answer to the question has no bearing on the answer to this exercise.

Harel, D. *Algorithmics: The Spirit of Computing.* Reading, Mass.: Addison-Wesley, 1987.

Hofstadter, D. R. *Gödel, Escher, Bach: An Eternal Golden Braid.* New York: Basic Books, 1979.

Hopcroft, J. E., and Ullman, J. D. *Introduction to Automata Theory, Languages, and Computation.* Reading, Mass.: Addison-Wesley, 1983.

Minsky, M. *Computation: Finite and Infinite Machines.* Englewood Cliffs, N.J.: Prentice-Hall, 1967.

Stockmeyer, L. J., and Chandra, A. K. "Intrinsically Difficult Problems." *Scientific American* 240, no. 5 (May 1979): 140–159.

Turing, A. M. "On Computable Numbers with an Application to the Entscheidungsproblem." *Proc. London Math. Soc.* vol. 2 (1936): 230–265.

ARTIFICIAL INTELLIGENCE

8.1   INTRODUCTION

In 1956 John McCarthy coined the phrase "artificial intelligence" to apply to the use of computers for studying and modeling certain problem-solving tasks that were, prior to the invention of the computer, thought to be uniquely human. Whereas the theoretical limitations of computation were reasonably well understood at that time, little was known about the practical limits of the computer as a problem-solving medium. Computers were expensive, second-generation behemoths available to only a handful of governmental agencies, research universities, and large corporations, and accessible only to the few specialists who could communicate with these machines in what were the first primitive programming languages. Yet, these computers were powerful enough to inspire their programmers to try to develop programs that played checkers and chess, translated natural languages, proved theorems, and learned from their experiences.

Even more interesting is the fact that some of these early programs were successful. Indeed, many of the tasks that had been historically equated with superior human "intelligence" (such as chess playing and theorem proving) were among the first to be simulated successfully by a computer. Others that at a casual glance seemed readily amenable to automation (natural language translation, commonsense reasoning) have to this day proven elusive. All of the successes and failures have contributed to our understanding both of the practical powers of digital computers and of how we as humans perform a variety of intellectual tasks.

After nearly 40 years, artificial intelligence (AI) is a central and exciting part of the computer science landscape. Still, the phrase means different things to different people, and each definition illuminates a slightly different perspective of the field. In this module we will explore some of these perspectives and their historical bases, as well as the primary areas of AI research. We will measure our progress to date against the standard provided by a fictional (at least, for now) computer named HAL.

TEXT OBJECTIVES

In this module, we will

- Discuss the notion of embodying intelligence in a machine, and consider Alan Turing's operational test for machine intelligence
- Explore the nature of human intelligence
- Discuss the physical differences between brains and computers
- Look at some of the major directions in artificial intelligence research
- Investigate some of the reactions to AI products and possible future directions in AI

COGNITIVE COMPUTERS?

We first met Alan Turing in Module 1, where we described his activities during World War II using the Colossus computer to crack the secrets of the German Enigma machine. In Module 7 we saw Turing's connection with another device, a *Gedankenmaschine,* or "thought engine"—the abstract computer that bears his name. In discussing artificial intelligence, we return to Alan Turing again, for the third and final time in this text. Turing's 1950 paper, entitled "Computing Machinery and Intelligence," is generally regarded as the first to propose that the computer be brought to bear on the problem of simulating human behavior. It was certainly the first to juxtapose the words *computing* and *intelligence* and, in so doing, propose the computer as a metaphor for human intelligence—a metaphor that permeates our culture today. Although the paper was (and remains) highly controversial in content, it is highly readable and downright entertaining throughout. In it, Turing sets out to consider the question "Can machines think?" by proposing a test for intelligence. He ends his treatise with the thought-provoking—and apparently serious—prediction: ". . . I believe that at the end of the century the use of words and general educated opinion will have altered so much that one will be able to speak of machines thinking without expecting to be contradicted." To be sure, things have changed in the last 40 years to the extent that we now talk about AI to the generally educated. But, thinking machines? By the end of the century? Aside from a time discrepancy of one year, Arthur C. Clarke, author of *2001: a Space Odyssey* and creator of the fictional HAL 9000 computer, apparently concurs.

This is a good time to pester your instructor to show the film. Even better, what about an Intelligent Machines Film Festival?

METAPHOR: HAL

The HAL 9000 computer—or as "he" is referred to in the film, HAL—is "the latest result in machine intelligence." Specifically, HAL* is the computer that controls virtually the entire operation of a space vehicle on its

---

* Short for "Heuristically programmed ALgorithmic computer."

way from Earth to Jupiter. The 9000 series computers, we are told, can reproduce "most of the activities of the human brain, and with incalculably greater speed and reliability," and have a perfect operational record. In HAL's own words, "We are, by any practical definitions of the words, foolproof and incapable of error."

Beyond monitoring and directing the functions of the ship itself, HAL's responsibilities include maintaining life support services for the crew of five scientists on board. Three of the crew members are in "hibernation" (asleep and frozen), to be awakened when the ship arrives at Jupiter. HAL regulates the temperature and oxygen flow in the hibernation chambers and monitors the vital signs of the sleeping scientists. It is in HAL's interactions with the two active crew members that we see clear evidence of what can only be described as intelligent behavior.

HAL speaks and gives the appearance of understanding English as well as any human. He sees and responds to everything that is going on in his visual field, which includes the entire ship. He appears to have a wealth of knowledge about a variety of topics, and the knowledge seems to be interrelated in sophisticated ways. He can develop plans to solve problems in both general and highly specialized domains. His behavior gives evidence of an ability to acquire and assimilate new information—to learn. Perhaps most interesting are HAL's seemingly personal attributes. He expresses his feelings, opinions, and fears just as humans do. It is little consolation when we are assured by one of the crew members that HAL has been programmed to do so in the interest of making it easier for the crew to interact with him. This programming obviously worked because the crew members admit to regarding HAL as "just another person."

Few who have read Clarke's novel or seen the film version would deny that HAL has skills and attributes that would allow him to conform to any definition of AI. As such, HAL serves as a point of departure for discussing many of the issues currently being investigated by AI researchers.

Æ STACKS: HYPE-KU AND HYPERCHARS

By definition, AI programs are intended to give the appearance of human behavior. Some exhibit human-like problem-solving skills in prescriptive, logical, or rule-based domains, whereas others endeavor to capture human attributes such as intuition, judgment, and creativity. Most AI programs, though, achieve their behavior using techniques that, intuitively at least, bear little resemblance to those used by humans. These programs, like the Turing Machines in Module 7, merely manipulate information. We, the users of the programs, interpret the information so as to be meaningful to us and, thereby, endow the program with intelligence. In this lab module we provide you with two stacks that embody all of these traits.

The stack named "Hype-KU" (it produces haiku poetry) is rule-based to the extent that its data can be manipulated to produce dramatic differences in program behavior. The behavior it produces can be considered creative, even artistic. As we shall see, Hype-KU achieves its behavior by thoroughly artificial, counterintuitive means. It uses fixed grammatical forms and a carefully chosen vocabulary to produce otherwise random strings of characters as output that, when interpreted by humans, evoke beautiful images and conjure profound thoughts.

Similarly, the second lab stack, named HyerChars, uses two decidedly mechanical techniques for learning and recognizing simple characters as they are drawn on the screen. HyperChars also illustrates how such a seemingly simple task, easy even for school-age children, can confound—or, at least, confuse—a modern computer.

LAB OBJECTIVES

In the disk part of this module, you will

- Experiment with a stack that demonstrates both artificial skills (a facility with natural language) and artificial attributes (a seeming artistic flair)

- Expand the stack's vocabulary and grammar, and analyze its behavior

- Experiment with a stack that illustrates a primitive ability to learn

---

8.2   INTELLIGENT AUTOMATA

> Pamela McCorduck refers to the goals of Artificial Intelligence as "forging the gods," in both senses of "forging."

The word *automata,* used today to describe anything that acts on its own, derives from the Greek *automatos,* meaning "self-moving." In fact, humanity's fascination with developing machines that somehow mimic human action (what J. David Bolter refers to as "The Technology of Making Man") goes back at least to the ancient Greeks. In many societies since, one finds evidence of automata that reflects both the available technologies of the day and the prevalent view of the workings of human beings. Examples include ancient clay sculptures of human figures, the great clocks of the Middle Ages that were adorned with human and animal figures, and the humanlike toys (some of which wrote messages, drew pictures, and played instruments) that amused the courts of baroque Europe. A celebrated automaton was The Turk, a machine that played chess. The Turk toured America and Europe in the early nineteenth century, astounding all those who saw it, except perhaps Edgar Allan Poe. In his essay, "Malzel's Chessplayer," Poe demonstrated the likelihood that The Turk was actually controlled by a human operator, sitting cramped in the base of the machine. Of course, knowing what we do today, Poe's conclusions seem perfectly reasonable, but they caused a minor storm of controversy at the time. Unfortunately for us, The Turk has vanished and is presumed to have been destroyed.

Until the twentieth century, such automata were constrained in the sense that they imitated only the appearances and visible actions of humans. With the advent of circuits and motors, attention turned to developing machines that embodied the other sense of *automatos*—the thinking machines. In the first quarter of the century a few bold scientists openly (if guardedly) postulated that sophisticated electromechanical automata might be capable of simulating more subtle, intellectual forms of human behavior. Over the next few decades the definitions of *machine* evolved to include a few "robots," one of which even played chess. Still, these devices were, as before, regarded as merely mechanical curiosities. By the 1950s, though, technological revolutions, most notably the development of computers, heralded a new age of automation.

The man who introduced us to this age was Alan Turing, who only a few years earlier had published his seminal works in the theory of computation. In 1950, he asked, "Can machines think?" In the interest of avoiding the philosophical pitfalls of this question (such as, What does it mean to think? How would we recognize machine thought?), Turing proposed a test as a more workable substitute. He called this test the "imitation game"; it is better known today as the "Turing test." Simply stated, the Turing test involves two humans and a computer. One of the humans plays the role of interrogator and is isolated in a separate room from the computer and the other person. The interrogator communicates with the computer and the other human by means of some form of teletype device that serves to conceal the identities of those involved. The computer can be said to have exhibited intelligence if the interrogator fails to distinguish the responses of the computer from those of the human.

> More precisely, Turing's test involved the computer pretending to be a human and the human player trying to fool the interrogator into thinking he or she (the player) was a computer.

In one stroke, Turing sidestepped the difficult philosophical questions of the nature of Mind by proposing that if a computer *acts* intelligently, then it *is* intelligent. In his paper, Turing envisioned the following dialog:

> *Q:* Please write me a sonnet on the subject of the Forth Bridge.
> *A:* Count me out on this one. I never could write poetry.
> *Q:* Add 34957 to 70764.
> *A:* (Pause about 30 seconds and then give as answer) 105621.
> *Q:* Do you play chess?
> *A:* Yes.
> *Q:* I have K at my K1, and no other pieces. You have only K at K6 and R at R1. It is your move. What do you play?
> *A:* (After a pause of 15 seconds) R-R8 mate.

> It's not surprising that the inventor of the abstract Turing Machine would have been able to look beyond then-existing technology.

Turing's paper is remarkable for many reasons, not the least of which is the state of computer technology in 1950. Few, if anyone besides Turing, were in a position to appreciate the potential richness of the computational metaphor for intelligence in a day when the first modern computers had just been built. It was Turing, after all, who helped to define the power and the limitations of symbolic computation, as we saw in Module 7. Note, too, that the Turing test is intentionally designed to remove physical characteristics from consideration in determining whether the machine has exhibited intelligence: Turing consciously directed us to consider intellectual automata, as opposed to those based on appearance or overt action.

Turing's foresight was not limited to proposing this new metaphor. Most of the paper is in fact dedicated to anticipating and responding to a full range of objections (grounded in everything from theology and mathematics to extrasensory perception!) to the validity of both the original question (Can machines think?) and the proposed test. One suspects that he would be disappointed if there was a consensus today as to what constitutes AI. He needn't have worried.

There is no such consensus today. The field admits a number of definitions, each amounting to a different interpretation of the metaphor. Many adhere to Marvin Minsky's definition that AI is "the science of making machines do things that would require intelligence if done by man." Those who accept Minsky's definition follow most literally Turing's ideas that the details of how the machine achieves its behavior are unimportant, even irrelevant. All that matters, according to this definition, is that the machine perform like a human would in a prescribed task. Such performance-oriented research tends to focus on algorithms and programming techniques, and serves to pursue the metaphor by seeing to what degree the computer can be considered "human."

Other researchers are concerned with the extent to which humans can be considered "computers." They might define AI as does Patrick Hayes: "the study of intelligence as computation." Indeed, the analogy between human and machine problem solving is paramount for many researchers. They seek (perhaps a bit more directly) to understand how humans solve problems and perform sensory tasks, and attempt to model their understanding as computer programs. Their interest is in using the computer to simulate and evaluate theories of intelligence.

A third definition, credited to Tessler, is somewhat less formal but equally perceptive. He defined AI, only somewhat facetiously, as "whatever hasn't been done yet." This description emphasizes the elusive natures of both intelligence and computation. Because we tend to regard ourselves as something more than mechanical symbol processors, we often dismiss any behavior that can be simulated by a computer as "unintelligent." As soon as a program is written that demonstrates some humanlike skill or attribute, that skill or attribute is dismissed as merely mechanical. Indeed, our notion of a computer continues to expand, as does our understanding of human development and behavior. If history is an accurate predictor, there is every reason to believe AI will continue to present a moving target toward which our scientific energies will be directed.

REVIEW QUESTIONS

1. Describe three of Alan Turing's contributions to the history of computer science.

2. Think of an aspect of intelligence that in your opinion would *not* be captured by the Turing test.

3. In the sample Turing test dialog given in the text, Turing deliberately built in a subtle point about A's behavior. Find and discuss that point. What do you suppose was Turing's intent?

4. Discuss the differences among the definitions of artificial intelligence given by Minsky, Hayes, and Tessler.

Æ LAB

LAB EXERCISE 1

Since the Æ stacks that support this lab module attempt to simulate two particularly "human" tasks (creating poetry and recognizing written characters), we begin these exercises by asking you to do some things on your own—without the aid of your computer. Essentially, we are asking you now to collect some data that will allow us to apply the Turing test to our "artificially intelligent" stacks in subsequent exercises.

1.1 Record on a sheet of paper three haiku verses that you find interesting. You can select poems from any source that is available to you (there are volumes full of verses composed by masters of the haiku form), or you can try your own hand at writing a verse. A verse may be "interesting" in the sense that it is particularly meaningful to you, it is particularly evocative, or just because you like it.

1.2 For each of the characters, *C, S,* and *N,* record on a sheet of paper five different versions of the character. As above, you can transcribe a typeface you see printed in some text, newspaper, or magazine, or you can create your own "fonts."

8.3   PEOPLE AND MACHINES

Before we discuss further what artificial intelligence is, we will discuss what it is *not*. One thing AI workers are not doing at present is making HAL. At least for the time being, that goal is not yet in sight. Philosophers have devoted centuries to the problem of human intelligence, psychologists have spent decades, and we still have only the most rudimentary knowledge of what constitutes intelligence or even intelligent behavior.

THINKING EFFORTLESSLY

Some things about intelligence are clear, however. Whatever intelligence is, it is not simply cognition. In fact, the hardest things to simulate with machinery seem to be precisely those things that we do with little or no conscious thought. We understand natural languages effortlessly, for the most part, but we will see that natural language processing is one of the most difficult tasks to perform on a machine. In spite of the fact that the sentences we generate and receive are certainly of human origin, we must treat them as foreign objects when we seek rules to determine what is a comprehensible sentence and what is not. In other words, being able to use language is a far cry from understanding how we use it.

In a similar way, we can make sense of the visual images around us without any apparent effort on our part. Almost from birth, infants respond to faces, and a child can readily tell the difference between an adult face and that of a teenager, a task that is still beyond the powers of today's computers and their programs. There is a growing body of evidence, in fact, to support the commonsense notion that much of our facility with vision and language comes from the fact that we are "wired" to be adept at these tasks. Of course, in one sense our superiority over computers in these areas should not be surprising at all, given that our design is the result of eons of evolution, while computers and programs have been around only for four decades or so. Although progress is being made in these areas, AI researchers are handicapped by having to play the computer game in the human home court. We should not be discouraged that programs cannot duplicate human behavior in these areas yet—humans, after all, have a million-year head start.

THINKING DEEPLY

If we move up from the deepest levels of human intelligence, we are little better off in an attempt to mimic human attributes. One important feature of human intelligence is our facility with analogy and metaphor. We often base our behavior of understanding in new situations on the similarity of the situation to something known. A child on his or her first trip to a restaurant recognizes that it is like a dining room and will have at least an idea of what to expect, however different the details may be. Similarly, we can read part of Shakespeare's sonnet 73,

> That time of year thou may'st in me behold
> When yellow leaves, or none, or few, do hang
> Upon those boughs which shake against the cold,
> Bare ruin'd choirs, where late the sweet birds sang

and know, even without further context, that the narrator is elderly, comparing his stage of life with the late winter stage of the year. We understand that "bare ruin'd choirs" refer to the leafless branches of the trees in winter, recalling the branchlike vaulting ribs of a ruined cathedral, bereft of roof or windows. We use analogy to make the unfamiliar familiar, just as we, your authors, did when we designed each module of this text around a single metaphor. Yet we have no idea about the workings of the process that allows us to understand that a life is "like" a year in Shakespeare's sonnet, or that a restaurant is "like" a dining room; we just know it works. Again, some progress is being made in designing programs to act according to analogy—you will soon see some programs that are written to demonstrate a rudimentary ability in analogy. But again, the task is a difficult one, if only because a human being, even a child, "knows" vastly more than any computer yet built.

THINKING HARD

When the brain's "wetware" we were born with is not enough to help us, and when analogy fails, then we have to think hard. If we are presented with an optical illusion that represents something we know cannot be as it appears, we have to reason about what we are seeing, thinking, "How could that object be constructed so that it looks like stairs ascending forever?" If we are faced with a situation that has no analogue, we must reason "Tom's not here when I expected to meet him. Maybe it's because he overslept or misunderstood me when I said to 'meet me at the entrance.' The nearest phone is closer than the entrance on the other side, so I guess I should try calling him first, before I walk around the block." Of course, in both of these examples, we are relying on a large stock of acquired knowledge: knowledge about how physical objects are constructed, about Tom's sleeping habits and the vagaries of verbal communication, about telephones, about being late for appointments, and about nearby locations being closer in travel time than more distant ones.

If we ignore for the moment our obvious advantage over programs in the number of things we know, we have an area in artificial intelligence where clear progress is being made. Among other attributes, computers are quintessential logic machines. A computer can perform logical inferences at a speed that far surpasses our own and, properly programmed in an area where the relevant knowledge can be included as part of the data, can outstrip our meager abilities by a large factor. Ironically, this supposedly "highest" level of human intelligence is the one at which the computer is most adept. The rules of logic are simple and can be programmed easily—we are playing in the computer's home court when we reason logically. It is relatively easy, at least compared to visual or language processing, to write a program that exhibits goal-directed behavior and explores the moves it must make to reach the desired end and to choose among options to select the most efficient path to the goal. In the next section, we will introduce you to some of the techniques used to write programs capable of a limited form of reasoning.

THINKING ABOUT COMPUTERS

Certainly, one of the major difficulties faced in artificial intelligence research is lack of knowledge about its subject matter, the human intellect. Although we have been talking about simulating human intelligence, there is another equally valid point of view held by many AI researchers. Instead of looking at the goal of AI as producing intelligent machines, many researchers regard their work as being directed more toward understanding intelligence. In this view, the computer is seen as a simple testbed that can be used to provide insights into the ways in which human intelligence might actually work. Roughly speaking, this way of looking at artificial intelligence can be called "experimental cognition." We cannot modify the internal workings of a person to test a theory of intelligence, but there are no legal or moral restrictions to modifying a program or redesigning a machine and then testing it to see if it exhibits a greater or lesser degree of what we consider to be intelligent behavior. For instance, to test a theory that sentences are generated by applying a collection of generation and transformation rules, we could program a set of rules, use them to generate sentences, and apply our intuitive familiarity with natural languages to rate how well our set of rules generates sentences. As a matter of fact, that is exactly what you will do in the lab portion of this module.

Regardless of our view of the work of artificial intelligence, before we leave this section we can at least make some comparisons between the physical objects involved—brains and computers. We will look at three aspects of our subjects: storage, complexity, and speed.

> How did we come up with this estimate? Try to come up with one of your own.

In terms of raw storage of data, brains have a significant advantage over machines. Although estimates of the storage capacity of the human brain are open to varying interpretations, it is safe to say that the capacity of the brain is somewhere around the equivalent of 50 trillion bits (5×10^{13}, in scientific notation). In contrast, the largest computers available today can store about 1 trillion bits, giving us a fiftyfold advantage over computers in that aspect, at least at present.

In terms of complexity, brains have an even larger edge over computers. Each neuron in the human brain is connected to about 5000 others, on the average. In practical terms, this means that the brain is capable of massively parallel computations. The ability of a processor, either organic or inorganic, to break a task into many subtasks that are performed simultaneously can lead to considerable gains in computation speed, in much the same way that a house can be constructed more rapidly if one crew is

Very small and simple processors, we'll admit.

working on the plumbing while another is doing the wiring and another is completing the roof. The most advanced parallel computers today may have a few thousand processors, each connected to perhaps a hundred others, while the brain's architecture consists of the equivalent of millions of processors, each connected to thousands of others. The brain has a clear advantage over a computer in connection complexity, which could be one reason why we do so well on highly complicated tasks requiring parallel computations, such as language and visual processing. Any attempt to quantify this advantage would be more guesswork than anything else, but it would not be unreasonable to assign us a ten- to thousandfold advantage over computers.

One way of looking at the connection complexity of the brain in comparison to that of an electronic computer is to say that the brain needs to be massively parallel to perform as well as it does, because the transfer of information in the brain is so slow in comparison with that in a computer. Information is transferred from one neuron to another by chemical means, involving the release and capture of chemicals called neurotransmitters, while information in a computer is transferred via electrons in the circuit wires. Signals travel through our nerve cells at the rate of perhaps 1000 feet per second, while the speed of electrons through a wire is almost the speed of light, nearly a million times faster. In addition, the *cycle time,* the time it takes one circuit element (neuron or gate) to change from one state to another, is similarly faster in a computer, giving the computer a ten thousand- to millionfold advantage over the brain.

Considering all three factors together, and not placing too much credence in the numbers we used, we can conclude that brains still have an edge over computers, at least for those kinds of AI tasks for which brains are specialized. We cannot even approach the speed of computers for simple, repetitive, serial (rather than parallel) performance, but brains still have an edge over computers in computations that are complex, high level, and parallel. We should not ignore, however, the enormous differences in the rate of evolution of the two systems we have been considering. Natural evolution is so slow as to be almost unobservable on a human time scale—in essence, human "hardware" has not changed at all in the past 100,000 years. In contrast, in the span of just 50 years computers have evolved from machines such as ENIAC to modern supercomputers, with a corresponding improvement in power of something like a million. Although brains are better equipped for what they do than are computers, the gap between brainpower and computer power is rapidly diminishing. It is reasonable to expect that AI research will not suffer in the future due to lack of raw processing power. The important question will be how much progress we can make in defining and solving the questions about how to implement human skills on these powerful machines.

REVIEW QUESTIONS

1. Give examples of tasks that involve our innate abilities, our ability to use analogy, and our use of reasoning, and give a task that uses a mixture of at least two of these abilities.

2. Consider the following problem:

   Three missionaries and three cannibals have to cross a river. They have a boat that can carry at most two people and that can be used by any combination of missionaries and cannibals. Because of the habits of the cannibals, it is unsafe to have a group on either bank in which the missionaries are outnumbered by the cannibals. How can the missionaries and cannibals get across the river safely?

   Solve this problem, and describe some of the knowledge of the real world that is implicit in your solution (such as the fact that people cannot walk across water).

3. What is the rough correspondence between the things we do easily and the things computers can easily be programmed to do?

4. Will future progress in AI be limited more by hardware or by software limitations?

8.4 ARTIFICIAL SKILLS

In describing HAL's discernible skills it is interesting to note at the outset that, popular images to the contrary, HAL is not portrayed as a clanking android. Indeed, aside from his omnipresent eye, we never really see HAL until the end of the film, when one of the human crew members (the only one left alive) has to do some major surgery on HAL's "brain." To be sure, HAL exhibits robotlike control over numerous ship devices. However, just as he controls the temperature of the hibernation chambers without explicitly turning a dial on a thermostat, HAL moves chairs, opens and closes doors, manipulates equipment, and navigates the ship without any obvious appendages that we would recognize as hands, arms, or legs. HAL simply controls parts of the ship by means of the ship itself—in a sense, the ship is HAL's body.

This notion of an invisible robot is consistent with the predictions of many of today's scientists, who foresee computer-controlled offices, factories, and even cities. In such environments, the controlling computers will not be the ones (if there are any) sitting on people's desks. Rather, they will be hidden away, essentially inaccessible to humans, free to interact with those agents in their environment that they are designed to control. These other agents may themselves be special-purpose computers or may be human workers. In any case, this image of the smart machine is perfectly consistent with Turing's emphasis on simulating human intellectual, as opposed to physical, prowess.

LANGUAGE PROCESSING

The fact that in his paper Turing describes his hypothetical computer by using sample dialogs between the interrogator and the computer is testimony to the perceived centrality of language to all intellectual activity. Language is regarded by many as a skill that distinguishes humans from other species and, as such, is considered a potentially fruitful source of insight into our intellectual behavior. Similarly, there is great practical motivation for developing computers that understand language. Needless to say, researchers have been writing programs to process and respond to natural language input, in both typed and spoken form, since the early days of computing.

Programs of the late 1950s focused on translating one natural language into another and were seen as a potential solution to the "worldwide translation problem." These programs were endowed with large bilingual dictionaries and did little more than translate on a word-by-word basis, rearranging word order to reflect different languages. As this approach proved inadequate even for what was considered to be the straightforward task of translation, scientists came to understand that there is more to language than meets the eye (or the ear). For example, there is more to meaning than the sum of the meanings of individual words. An old story about an English-to-Russian computer translator tells of how the program translated "The spirit is willing, but the flesh is weak" into the Russian equivalent of "The vodka is acceptable, but the meat has spoiled." So research in this area shifted toward language understanding—programs that used a working knowledge of not only the elements (words) of a language, but also of its grammatical structure. Not coincidentally, this shift of attention coincided with breakthroughs in programming language development (facilitating the development of more complex, high-level programs) and linguistic theory in the early 1960s.

> This might be pure folklore, but like good folklore it has a truth that's independent of whether or not it really happened.

This cycle of (1) write a program that reflects a theory or approach to language understanding, (2) test the program, identify, and explain its shortcomings, (3) revise the theory to reflect both the performance of the program and recent developments in language research, and (4) start again (which is common to most subfields of AI), has repeated itself many times since then. In rough chronological succession, language understanding programs have grown to incorporate:

1. Sophisticated parsing techniques that help both in determining the grammatical correctness of statements and in identifying which words in a statement are serving which roles (subject, predicate, object). To use a famous example by Noam Chomsky, we know that "Colorless green ideas sleep furiously" is a grammatical sentence,

even though it is nonsensical, while "Furiously sleep ideas green colorless" is both nonsensical and ungrammatical.

2. More complex techniques for semantic analysis to address—for example, the problem of determining the sense of a particular word using surrounding words. A program that was capable of such analysis would match *lies* with *reclines*, rather than *deceives,* in the sentence "Ron lies asleep in his bed."

3. A model of dialog "context" so that a program can make use of information about the topic of conversation in interpreting a particular utterance. For example, in a conversation about tonight's seafood dinner, the sentence "The clams are ready to eat" would be given the interpretation "The clams are ready to [be] eat[en by us]," rather than "The clams are ready to eat [because it's their dinnertime and they're hungry]."

4. Informal rules of conversation that describe, for instance, our expectation that when we ask someone if they know the time, we expect more than a yes or no answer.

5. An extensive and shared knowledge about the real world that transcends language *per se.* For instance, suppose we read, "Sally was fed up. She got up angrily from her table at the restaurant and left just enough to cover the check. The waitress sneered at her as she walked out." Few of us would have difficulty in answering the question "Why did the waitress sneer?" but we are only beginning to understand how to incorporate our background knowledge into a program.

All of these types of information have been demonstrated as useful in getting programs to approximate human performance in language understanding. Each problem is also much larger than we might at first expect. That is, we as humans have seemingly endless lists of rules that govern our understanding of language, not to mention our experiential knowledge of the real world. Consider, for instance, the two interpretations of *flies* in "Time flies like an arrow; fruit flies like a banana." How do we know one is a verb and one is a noun? To date, programs have been limited by their ability to capture all of the knowledge involved. Still, there are programs today that are capable of carrying on humanlike conversations about a restricted range of topics. They tend to emphasize the integration and coordination of these different types of information.

An early language-processing program was ELIZA, developed by Joseph Weizenbaum during the mid-1960s. ELIZA, like its namesake in George Bernard Shaw's *Pygmalion,* could learn to speak increasingly well, a fact that has gone largely unnoticed behind the misplaced fascination with the program's other abilities. ELIZA's "conversations" were governed by scripts, described by Weizenbaum as "a set of rules largely like those that might be given to an actor who is to use them to improvise around a certain theme. Thus, ELIZA could be given a script to enable it to maintain a conversation about cooking eggs or about managing a bank checking account, and so on." In its best-known incarnation, ELIZA was given a script that permitted it to play the role of a neutral psychotherapist, producing the following dialog, taken from Weizenbaum's *Computer Power and Human Reason* (pp. 3–4). In this dialog, the computer's responses are written in capitals.

> Men are all alike.
> IN WHAT WAY
> They're always bugging us about something or other.
> CAN YOU THINK OF A SPECIFIC EXAMPLE
> Well, my boyfriend made me come here.
> YOUR BOYFRIEND MADE YOU COME HERE
> He says I'm depressed much of the time.
> I AM SORRY TO HEAR YOU ARE DEPRESSED
> It's true. I am unhappy.
> DO YOU THINK COMING HERE WILL HELP YOU NOT TO BE UNHAPPY
> I need some help, that much seems certain.
> WHAT WOULD IT MEAN TO YOU IF YOU GOT SOME HELP
> Perhaps I could learn to get along with my mother.
> TELL ME MORE ABOUT YOUR FAMILY
> My mother takes care of me.
> WHO ELSE IN YOUR FAMILY TAKES CARE OF YOU
> My father.
> YOUR FATHER
> You are like my father in some ways.
> WHAT RESEMBLANCE DO YOU SEE
> You are not very aggressive but I think you don't want me to notice that.
> WHAT MAKES YOU THINK I AM NOT VERY AGGRESSIVE
> You don't argue with me.
> WHY DO YOU THINK I DON'T ARGUE WITH YOU
> You are afraid of me.
> DOES IT PLEASE YOU TO BELIEVE I AM AFRAID OF YOU
> My father is afraid of everybody.
> WHAT ELSE COMES TO MIND WHEN YOU THINK OF YOUR FATHER
> Bullies.
> DOES THAT HAVE ANYTHING TO DO WITH THE FACT THAT YOUR BOYFRIEND MADE YOU COME HERE

> The last response sounds much more insightful than it really is. What sorts of rules could have caused ELIZA to say what it did here?

Weizenbaum makes it very clear that there is no "understanding" going on here. Many of the responses, as you can see, are of certain forms: "YOU <some text>. WHY DO YOU THINK I <the same text>." "HOW DO YOU FEEL ABOUT <one of the keywords in an earlier response>." ELIZA also used neutral responses such as "CAN YOU THINK OF A SPECIFIC EXAMPLE." By now, you should be able to imagine how you could write a program like ELIZA.

Because of its open-ended nature and the nature of its subject matter, artificial intelligence seems to inspire unfortunate flights of fantasy, even among people who should know better. One of the things that disturbed Weizenbaum greatly was the ready tendency of people to anthropomorphize the ELIZA program, to become emotionally attached to it and to assign to it spurious emotions such as compassion and empathy. We shall have more to say about this misguided but all-too-common response in the next module.

"Understanding" in programs such as ELIZA is demonstrated by accepting natural language text from the keyboard as input and either producing comprehensible text on the screen or carrying out some motor command as output. An entirely separate branch of AI is devoted to the problems of getting computers to "hear" natural language. Because these problems deal with physical phenomena (sound waves) and require special equipment to record and produce the data upon which they operate, this subfield takes on an engineering, as opposed to psychological, flavor. Despite this difference, the field has evolved along the same lines of language understanding.

The difficulties of speech recognition are precisely those aspects of language that we take for granted in processing typed text. Typed text is uniform. That is, every time you type a particular word, it appears the same on the screen. Every time we say a particular word, it sounds ever so slightly different, depending on, for example, the acoustics of the room we are in, the words that come before and after the particular word, and whether we just woke up or not. Also, typed text is disconnected, that is, words are separated by blanks and other forms of punctuation. Real speech is connected. Not only does this make word identification more difficult, but it makes it difficult to even detect word boundaries in an utterance.

Not surprisingly, early speech recognition systems were isolated word detectors. They processed a single word by matching the digitized version of its waveform (represented in the computer as a series of numbers) against a collection of "templates," waveforms representing words the program "knew." The computer would choose the word corresponding to the template that was the best match for the input. Until recently, such systems suffered from extreme sensitivity to noise (background sounds that interfered with the specific signal to be processed) and a lack of generality. That is, they might work well for one person, but not for another. More sophisticated recording and digitizing techniques, and decreases in the cost of the associated technologies, have spurred the development of commercially viable—although, still expensive—isolated word systems with general vocabularies in the hundreds of words and accuracy rates of about 90 percent.

Connected speech recognition systems are not yet commercially viable. Difficulties encountered in developing systems that both detect word boundaries and identify individual words in different contexts have led us to believe, in this case, that there is indeed more here than meets the ear. Researchers speculate that a hearer of language has expectations about

Discrete speech recognition systems are commercially available today. Connected to the operating system of a computer, they can be of great help to users whose limited mobility makes typing difficult or impossible.

speech as it is being processed. That is, we know, based on our syntactic and semantic knowledge of a particular language, what types of words can follow each other in speech, and these expectations help us to break apart and decode a continuous signal (a process exemplified by the annoying habit some people have of completing your sentences for you). As a result, emphasis in connected speech research has shifted from recognition to "understanding," and is in many ways coming together with research in language understanding.

HAL's humanlike facility with language is perhaps his most obvious and stunning skill. He converses about a remarkable variety of topics (engineering, art, chess, the mission to Jupiter, the personalities of the crew members) with equal fluidity and has an exceptional vocabulary (". . . forgive me for being so inquisitive, but . . .", "I never gave these stories much credence . . ."). He understands a full range of grammatical—and ungrammatical, natural-sounding—structures as they occur in normal human discourse and carries on conversations according to normal protocols ("Well, HAL, I'll be damned if I can find anything wrong with it." "Yes, it's puzzling."). HAL clearly has a sense of context. That is, he carries on dialog with an awareness of both the topic of conversation and the conversation to date ("Certainly no one could have been unaware of the many strange stories floating around before we left, rumors about something being dug up on the moon."). This allows him to use and understand pronouns, and to make references to related topics and previous discussions ("Would you put it on in here and take me in a bit?"). He recognizes voice inflections, pauses, and other subtleties that contribute to communication ("You don't mind talking about it, do you, Dave?") and uses them in his own speech ("Well . . . it's rather difficult to define." "Wait a minute! . . . Wait a minute!).

Why are there no HAL-like programs for processing natural language? The obstacles to language understanding appear to be equally practical and theoretical. While AI researchers today recognize the role and the necessity of real-world knowledge to our understanding language, we as yet have no effective means for transferring a human's collective experience to a computer. The problems of identifying and describing such information at all, much less efficiently, must be overcome before computers will understand language with skills approaching those of HAL.

Æ LAB

LAB EXERCISE 2

Earlier in this module we discussed the importance of metaphor and analogy to human intelligence. Language, for example, is meaningful to us to the extent that it relates to familiar forms, concepts, and experiences.

FIGURE 8.1   The Hype-KU Stack

FIGURE 8.1   The Hype-KU Stack

Literature "moves" us when it strikes a particular, personal chord or when it casts old ideas in a new light. The haiku poem, which originated in Japan centuries ago, is intended to do just that—to move us by capturing a deep, personal feeling and presenting it in haiku form.

Classically, a haiku verse consists of three lines of five, seven, and five syllables, respectively. Modern haiku poets (particularly those not writing in Japanese) rarely restrict themselves to the classic pattern, since the Japanese concept of "syllable" is not equivalent to that in many other languages, including English. Still this relatively rigid form, coupled with a tendency to use natural images as the bases for metaphor, makes haiku amenable to computer simulation.

There is not much you need to know in order to use the Hype-KU stack, as pictured in Figure 8.1. Every time you click on the Write a Poem button, a new haiku verse will (after a few seconds of "thought") appear on the screen. While the poems produced do not conform to the 5-7-5 syllable pattern, they are undeniably thought-provoking in the traditional haiku style.

2.1 Open the Hype-KU stack. Have it produce as many poems as you like.

2.2 As you did in Lab Exercise 1 with the human-generated verses, record three verses that strike you as particularly interesting. In this case, your notion of interesting may expand to include verses that are particularly silly, meaningless, or otherwise not humanlike.

KNOWLEDGE PROCESSING

Knowledge representation is an implicit concern of all computer programs, although *knowledge* is a term that is usually reserved for AI programs (for more conventional programs we typically refer to *information* or *data*). For AI programs, representation schemes merit additional attention for two reasons. First, the adequacy of the chosen method for representing knowledge often dictates more than the storage or processing efficiency of the program. The method may determine what kinds of behavior can be achieved by a program and ultimately whether or not the program is judged a success. Second, given that the domain of AI is human intellectual tasks, programs that experiment with knowledge representation schemes are a means for evaluating and refining theories of human memory.

Research in knowledge representation was the foundation for most early AI work. In fact, much of what we know today about the strengths and limitations of different knowledge representation schemes grew out of early AI studies that nominally were devoted to other AI application areas. For example, early game-playing and problem-solving programs used what is referred to as a "state-space description" of their domains. That is, a particular game, such as chess, was described as beginning with the game pieces arranged in a certain way on the board, in a particular "state." The game proceeds through a series of such states, where the possible states that one can move to from a given state (the set of legal moves) are well defined. A "game tree" describing alternative moves from a given state can be developed based on this scheme that allows a program to make intelligent choices about its moves. This same scheme is applicable to any problem or game in which the "states" and "moves" are well defined and discrete (see Figure 8.2).

In much the same way, early research in theorem proving demonstrated both the utility and the limitations of predicate logic as a knowledge representation scheme. Logic-based schemes describe their domains in a "declarative" manner—that is, as collections of facts and inference rules for deriving new facts. Logic is the basis of the knowledge representation scheme embodied today in the programming language Prolog. A slightly more expressive scheme for representing rules of inference, the production system, evolved out of early work in problem-solving systems. In a production system, knowledge is represented as a series of condition-action pairs

> We used symmetry to reduce the number of game states in Figure 8.2, but the game tree still gets pretty big. About how many nodes (game states) would be in the full tree?

> Recall the declarative languages we mentioned in Module 5.

FIGURE 8.2   Part of the Game Tree for Tic-Tac-Toe

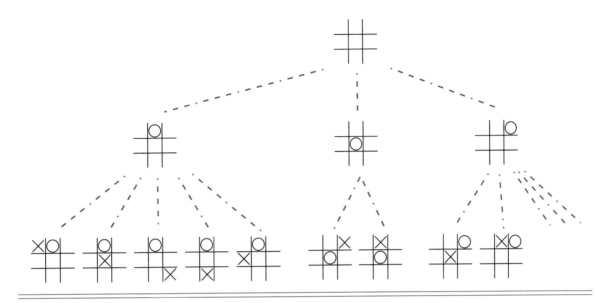

in the form of if-then rules, which describe what actions a program can take when a certain condition becomes true. For example, a production system for diagnosing car problems might contain rules like the following:

- *If* the engine won't turn over and the lights won't turn on, *then* check the battery.
- *If* checking the battery and the connectors are corroded, *then* first clean the connectors and then try to start the car.
- *If* the engine won't turn over and the lights work, *then* check the starter solenoid.
- *If* the engine turns over and the car won't start, *then* check the fuel gauge.

Programs that demonstrated facility with natural language gave rise to the notion that knowledge could be represented as a "semantic net," a graphlike structure where the elements of the graph represent objects in the domain being modeled and the links between the elements represent relations between the objects. Figure 8.3 shows an example of a semantic net. This notion of pieces of knowledge being related in arbitrarily complex ways evolved into the "procedural" representation scheme, wherein all knowledge is stored in the form of programs that may refer to (or call) other programs. Minsky's work in computer vision led to the theory of

FIGURE 8.3   A Simple Semantic Net

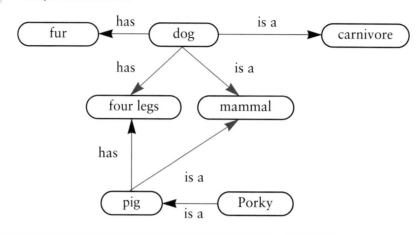

"frames" as a model for knowledge representation. A frame is a collection of knowledge about a particular thing. Frames can contain both declarative and procedural information, and can be related to other frames in numerous useful ways (for example, a frame for a particular restaurant can be a "kind" of generic restaurant frame). Frames, along with "scripts" (which are framelike structures for describing events, such as going to a restaurant, as opposed to things), represent the current state of the art in knowledge representation schemes.

Numerous philosophical and psychological issues have cropped up in the process of defining this range of schemes for representing knowledge. Aside from the obvious question of What is knowledge?, researchers have been forced to address questions such as: What kinds of knowledge do we have, and what kinds are needed to accomplish different tasks? How do different types of knowledge interact? How much knowledge is needed to solve a particular problem? Are certain knowledge representation schemes more "economical"—that is, less redundant—than others? What are the primitive units of a knowledge representation scheme? That is, in what terms are more complex knowledge structures described? Are there universal semantic primitives in terms of which a variety of knowledge types can be expressed? How is knowledge about knowledge (for example, telling us when to use some rule or information) represented? Our collective experience in developing AI programs has afforded us insights into each of these questions that introspection alone could not have.

While variations and combinations of the knowledge representation techniques appear, at least in principle, to be adequate for expressing our—and HAL's—knowledge, numerous practical problems remain. The first, the problem of articulating all of the components of our knowledge (in particular, our meta-knowledge, or knowledge about knowledge), we have already mentioned. Beyond this, there are the problems of endowing the machine with the undoubtedly vast amounts of information (do we include it as part of the machine's program, or provide the computer with a program that can learn on its own?) and making it efficient. How knowledge is represented in a computer goes hand in hand with how knowledge is retrieved and used in the process of reasoning. Whatever representation scheme is used, it must be compatible with efficient algorithms for choosing among and using the knowledge represented.

In fact, a great deal of energy has been expended, particularly in the early days of AI, on identifying and improving the efficiency of algorithms for using knowledge. Algorithms for searching complex knowledge structures have received the most attention because, like concerns about knowledge representation, they are generally applicable to many programs, AI and otherwise.

Many AI programs give the appearance of intelligent behavior using a technique known as "generate and test." That is, they generate a list of all possible moves or solutions to a problem and then search through the list, testing alternatives until maximal or optimal conditions are met. Game-playing programs and mechanical theorem provers are common examples of this type of behavior. For a game-playing program, the list of alternatives would contain all legal moves that could be made from a given position. In programs that "look ahead" to anticipate subsequent moves, the list would also contain all legal moves that could be made for some number of moves in the future. Such lists grow quickly and proportionally with the number of alternative moves (for instance, it is estimated that there are about 10^{120} possible board positions in chess) and the extent to which a program looks ahead. The success of such programs depends in large part on the ability to search through the list of alternatives efficiently.

Early optimism about the generate-and-test techniques, along with other general techniques based on tightly coupled knowledge representation schemes and searching algorithms (most notably, "means-ends analysis"), spawned a series of programs that were said to model general problem-solving skills. In fact, a program based on means-ends analysis, called "General Problem Solver" (GPS), was an explicit attempt to formalize what was thought to be a thoroughly general human problem-solving technique. General Problem Solver was applied to a variety of tasks, including robot control, and means-ends analysis today is incorporated into many programs that must develop and carry out their own plans.

Practically speaking, these general techniques have proven adequate for some AI applications and inadequate for others. As our experience with them has grown, it has become clear that different applications require slightly different techniques. That is, while techniques such as generate and test are to a certain degree generic, variations of them prove more suc-

> Means-ends analysis: Identify a solution state and use a collection of general rules to move to a state that is closer to the solution than you are now. Repeat as needed.

> GPS, invented by Newell, Shaw, and Simon way back in the late 1950s, could not, or course, be truly "general" in the sense that it could solve all suitably worded problems. We saw in Module 7 that such a goal is impossible.

cessful in simulating specific behaviors. As our understanding of particular domains has increased, and as programs are pushed to higher levels of sophistication, the need for domain-specific information (much of it metaknowledge) has become evident. Many of today's "expert systems," programs that perform humanlike diagnostic and analysis functions in a specific field or task, are based on general problem-solving techniques that have been customized to incorporate and take advantage of domain-specific information.

An interesting outgrowth of the trend toward highly specialized expert systems has been a better understanding of the types of knowledge that are brought to bear on particularly human problems and how such knowledge is used. Many tasks, for example, require of humans that we make judgments based on incomplete information, that we qualify our judgments as falling somewhere between true and false, and that we be able to explain how it was that we arrived at our judgments. These considerations, like the knowledge representation considerations that preceded them chronologically, are addressed implicitly in most programs today. Various expert systems, particularly those based on production systems and procedural representation schemes, have displayed an ability to explain their reasoning processes. The problems of getting computers to perform as well as humans do with incomplete information and of expressing degrees of certainty have been identified only within the last ten years or so, and remain topics of theoretical research.

> You can imagine that having a program explain its reasoning would be useful—even necessary—in critical applications like medical diagnosis.

The creators of HAL apparently overcame all of our current obstacles to implementing knowledge representation schemes and problem-solving skills. HAL clearly maintains a superhuman database of factual and algorithmic information. He instantly answers questions that require direct responses (when asked, as he is sure that there are no known incidents of a 9000 series computer failure, he responds, "None whatsoever"). He plays a great game of chess, anticipating his victory many moves in advance. He demonstrates detailed expertise about all of the hardware devices he controls and maintains (HAL knows—or thinks he does—when a remote sensor is about to fail and can even predict its time of failure). In expert system fashion, HAL is also capable of explaining his reasoning (he admits, for example, that the reason he is questioning one of the crew members is that he is in the process of completing his crew psychology report).

> It's easy to write a program that lies; it's much harder to write a program that lies well.

HAL also shows a powerful propensity for developing general plans in response to perceived situations. After detecting the fault in the sensor and finding nothing wrong with the device itself, HAL devises a plan to test his prediction (replace the unit and wait until it fails). Even more ambitious and intricate is his plan to take over complete control of the ship and the mission by doing away with the human crew members. He even lies to one of the humans to accomplish the intermediate goal of getting the human to leave the ship.

HAL's knowledge representation scheme must also account for uncertain information. Indeed, many of his actions are based on his *beliefs* about people and events. His plan to take control of the ship is based on his belief that the crew will attempt to disconnect him. There are more subtle indications of uncertain behavior throughout the mission. HAL wonders about the feelings of crew members, admits that he is suspicious about certain aspects of the mission, confesses to not being able to totally dismiss rumors about the mission from his mind, and expresses confidence that his "work will be back to normal."

Ironically, the most telling indication of the power of HAL's memory, and the degree to which it reproduces human performance, comes when HAL's memory is being disconnected. Even prior to disconnecting HAL, the crew members speak of having "to cut his higher brain functions without disturbing his purely automatic and regulatory systems." As he is being disconnected, however, HAL noticeably regresses, essentially to his "childhood" state. As individual memory units are removed, HAL feels his mind "going" ("There is no question about it—I can feel it") and ultimately begins reciting lessons he learned for his first demonstration. He loses "consciousness" while singing "On a Bicycle Built for Two."

Æ LAB

LAB EXERCISE 3

How does the Hype-KU stack produce such realistic poetry? Actually, it works in a manner similar to Weizenbaum's ELIZA program (and, for that matter, all key-word analysis programs). Both programs use stored grammatical templates, or "forms," and prescribed vocabularies to produce their output.

It is interesting to note that, despite its creative nature, the Hype-KU program is not (and need not be) nearly as sophisticated as ELIZA. The interactive nature of ELIZA required that it incorporate some of the user's vocabulary into its responses. The vocabulary of Hype-KU, however, is internal to the program and (although it can be modified by the user) is extremely sensitive. At present it consists of only 124 carefully chosen words from volumes of haiku. Also, depending on their complexity, ELIZA-like programs are required to perform some level of syntactic manipulation in order to use their grammatical templates to produce responses. The verses produced by Hype-KU come directly from the program's templates, by simply filling them in with stock vocabulary items.

Figure 8.4 shows the Hype-KU screen as it appears after clicking on the Show Forms and Show Vocabulary buttons. When asked to "Write a

| FIGURE 8.4 | Hype-KU, Showing Forms and Vocabulary |

Form #1:
Article Adjective Noun
Article Noun Verb Preposition Article Noun
Adjective Adjective Noun

Form #2:
Noun Preposition Article Noun
Article Adjective Noun Preposition Article Noun
Adjective Noun

Form #3:
Article Adjective Adjective Noun
Preposition Article Adjective Noun
Article Noun Verb

Form #4:
Article Adjective Noun Verb
Article Adjective Adjective Noun
Preposition Article Adjective Noun

Articles:
a
the
an
the

Adjectives:
autumn
hidden
bitter
misty

Nouns:
waterfall
river
breeze
moon
rain
wind
sea
morning
snow
lake

Prepositions:
on
in
of
under

Verbs:
shakes
drifts
has stopped
struggles
has fallen

Write a Poem

Hide Forms   Hide Vocabulary

Poem," the Hype-KU program first chooses one of the forms to use. It then uses that form to choose successive words of the prescribed grammatical classes from the vocabulary fields, and strings them together. When using Form 1, for example, Hype-KU randomly chooses an article, an adjective, and a noun, and concatenates them to produce line 1 of the verse. Line 2 is similarly composed from an article, a noun, a verb, a preposition, an article, and a noun. Line 3 is two adjectives followed by a noun.

You can see that the underlying details are really very simple. The verses produced, however, can be downright insightful and melodic. This is mostly a reflection of the vocabulary chosen and its relation to the grammatical forms. Both the vocabulary and the forms are Hyper-Card fields that, in fact, can be edited to produce different program behavior. Open Hype-KU again to perform the following exercises.

> It's also a function of our ability to read meaning into randomly chosen strings of words.

3.1   Save a copy of Hype-KU, and open the new copy.

3.2   Click on Show Forms and Show Vocabulary.

3.3 Examine the grammatical forms. Edit them to include what you think might be interesting forms.

3.4 Use the revised forms to produce some new verses. How do the results compare with those produced by the original stack?

3.5 Do the same for the vocabulary fields. Add words to different classes and see what poems result.

3.6 Record on a sheet of paper three interesting verses that are produced by your modified version of Hype-KU.

3.7 Now, pick one verse each from your lists of poems produced by humans, the original Hype-KU stack, and the modified Hype-KU. Pass the three poems chosen to a classmate, friend, or your instructor, and see if they can determine the "author" of each verse.

VISUAL PROCESSING

> Recent research indicates that we are born with many more neural connections than we need, and that experience strengthens the ones that produce useful information (like recognition of faces, for instance).

HAL's ability to process visual information is every bit as impressive as are his language and memory skills, if less obvious. While HAL sees and reacts to everything that goes on inside and around the ship (by means of cameralike "eyes" located throughout the spacecraft), we as observers have no clear evidence as to how or when HAL uses this facility. Nor do we have any indication of what influences HAL's visual acuity. The same can be said for human vision. Despite (or, perhaps, because of) the fact that we humans are normally vision experts at a very young age, we have very little intuition about either how vision develops or how we accomplish seeing. This lack of discernible data compounds the already difficult problems of devising and testing theories of vision, and is only one of many difficulties faced by researchers in computer vision. Again, as with language processing, the most difficult tasks to simulate mechanically are precisely those that are easiest for humans—those that are "wired" in our nervous systems as the result of several million years of evolution.

Other major difficulties in computer vision research stem from the complex nature of visual data. First, our ability to understand a visual image is dependent, in part, on the quality of the image. Poor lighting, for example, can make it difficult to "see." Second, as anyone who has looked at an optical illusion can attest, a great deal of information can be lost in representing a three-dimensional image (what we see) as a two-dimensional picture (what a computer "sees"). Even to humans, pictures are often ambiguous. It appears that we rely on a complex system of visual cues (about, for example, distances, and shadows, and implicit edges) to help us to disambiguate scenes.

Further, we have expectations about what we are looking at (for instance, this is a picture of my dog) that contribute to our understanding of a picture. Real-world knowledge, about, for example, the shapes of objects, also seems to play a role in our understanding. Finally, even without these other complications, visual data are voluminous. Even a small image, when represented as a two-dimensional array of light intensities, requires tremendous amounts of memory and processing.

It has taken years of vision research just to appreciate these problems. The first applications of computers to vision addressed only the problems of enhancing images (say, of a satellite photo) so that they could be better understood by human inspectors. Complex numerical algorithms were developed that helped to identify and eliminate extraneous "noise" from a computer's representation of an image, so as to produce a sharper picture. These algorithms were eventually extended to allow for edge detection between objects in a scene, for gross classification of objects in a scene (based, as were speech recognition systems, on a collection of stored templates), and subsequently for constructing line drawings of a scene. Today's vision programs, which are what might be called the first generation of image-understanding systems, combine these facilities with models of objects being viewed and heuristic rules that together help to identify objects in a scene.

If nothing else is clear from this description, it should be obvious that we are not yet capable of producing computers with a sense of vision approaching that of HAL. Even today's most sophisticated image-understanding systems are constrained to be brute-force approaches by both the complexity of the task and our lack of understanding of the problems involved. This is not to say that there haven't been any practical applications of computer vision research. On the contrary, advances in medical applications (imaging and analysis systems), remote sensing applications (resource analysis by satellite), and industrial applications (robot vision) have been, and continue to be, dramatic.

As a simple example of the difficulties inherent in visual processing, consider the problem of optical character recognition (OCR). OCR technology has been with us for a number of years—the rather peculiar typeface used for the numbers on the bottom of bank checks is specifically designed to be read by special hardware and translated by a computer. Again, however, we see the asymmetry between people and computers, in that the typefaces that are easy for a computer to interpret are difficult for people to read. In Module 9, we will explore the notion that we are entering a transition period between our traditional reliance primarily on printed media for information storage and the coming reliance on electronic storage of information. In this transitional period, we need a way of translating words on a page into character codes in a computer. There are many large texts that we would like to have stored electronically: company financial and personnel records, the Oxford English Dictionary, the complete works of Shakespeare, and so on. Of course, the traditional method of performing this translation is to hire a battery of typists to key

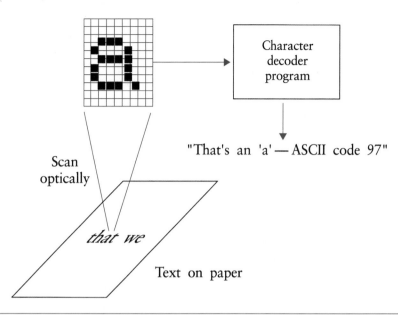

FIGURE 8.5   Optical Character Recognition

in all of the text into a suitable program, but this is clearly inefficient. A much more cost-effective solution would be a machine that might look like a copier with a computer attached. All we would have to do is place a page of text into the machine and it would translate the text into a suitable form for computer manipulation.

Such OCR machines do indeed exist today, but they are still somewhat limited in what they can do. Typically, the text is first scanned to produce a matrix of black and white dots, much as letters are represented on the screen of the Macintosh. The hard part of the process is designing a program that decodes the matrix and decides which letters are represented. Figure 8.5 diagrams the OCR process.

There are two approaches to character recognition. If we happen to know the typeface used in the original document, we can provide the decoder program with a matrix image for each character and test a character by matching the scanned image against the stored images for each character. This *matrix matching* is fairly simple to do but requires that we have at least some idea of what we're looking at. A more sophisticated approach is *pattern extraction*. In this technique, the program stores the "essence" of each character—for example, recognizing that a lowercase *i* is made by a short vertical line with a dot above it. Both techniques suffer from the lack of detail in the stored image—many optical scanners cannot distinguish features that are less than 1/300 of an inch in size, so a stray black mark near an *o* could result in the *o* being misinterpreted as a *p, q, b,* or *d,* for instance. The second approach, that of pattern extraction, is the most promising, but also the one most fraught with difficulties. What rules, for instance, govern the appearance of an *a?* Consider the four typefaces in Figure 8.6. In three of the samples, the *a* has an arc at the top, but that arc is missing in Zapf Chancery. If that weren't bad enough, look at the *g* in the four samples and try to decide what determines the essence of *g.*

Most OCR programs use a combination of matrix matching and pattern extraction, using matrix matching for monospaced typefaces such as Courier, in which all of the characters have the same width, and pattern extraction for proportional typefaces such as Palatino and Helvetica. In addition, most OCR programs can be "taught" to recognize a character, by displaying the questionable character and asking the operator what the interpretation should be. Despite the sophistication of today's OCR programs, though, the rate of correctly read characters is still in the range of 96–99 percent. That may seem rather impressive, but it would mean that in a manuscript the size of this text, about 10,000 characters would have to be corrected in the scanned product.

Perhaps the most dramatic demonstration of HAL's visual skills is the scene in the story when the crew members hatch a plot to disconnect him. After taking pains to ensure that HAL cannot hear them, the humans assume HAL cannot see them and they begin their discussion. Much to their ultimate chagrin, HAL not only sees them, but he succeeds in reading their

---

FIGURE 8.6   Four Typefaces in the Same Point Size

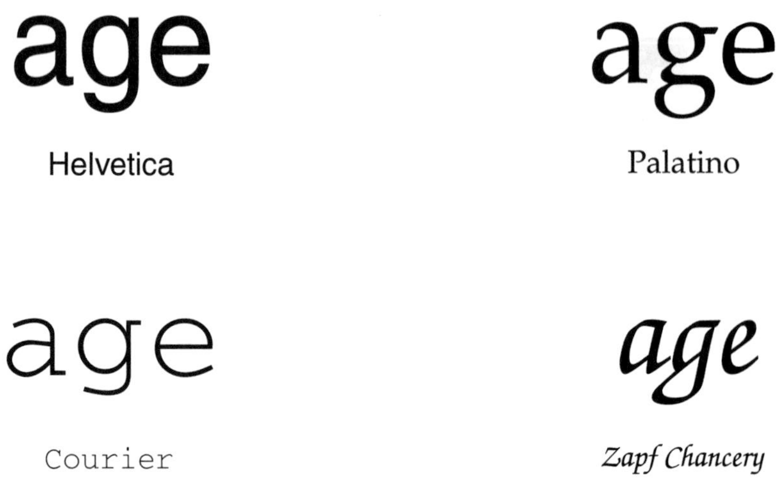

Helvetica

Palatino

Courier

Zapf Chancery

lips. HAL's field of vision was so complete that there was no escaping it. Even more impressive is the fact that the ability to read lips entails, at least intuitively, the integration of sophisticated visual and language skills far beyond anything available today.

Æ LAB

LAB EXERCISE 4

The second Æ stack that accompanies this lab module is a simple OCR program, entitled "HyperChars" (Figure 8.7). HyperChars provides you with a 12-by-12 grid of "dots" on which you can draw a character. Clicking on a dot turns it black, clicking again turns it back to white. Once you have drawn a character, you can tell the stack to "Learn It" or to "Guess" which character it might be.

Both learning and guessing are accomplished by two distinct methods. The first is a simple matrix matching method like that described in the

FIGURE 8.7   The HyperChars Stack

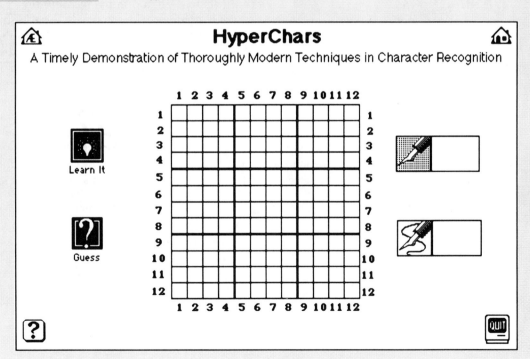

previous section. That is, to learn a character the stack simply encodes the patterns of black and white dots as a string of zeros and ones (0 representing a white/off dot; 1 representing a black/on dot). When asked to guess the character currently on the grid, the stack encodes the current grid according to the same scheme and compares the resulting pattern to those it has already learned. The guess produced (which appears in the "pen" field with the dotted background) is the learned template that most closely matches the dot pattern on the grid.

The second encoding technique is an implementation of one of the earliest successful pattern extraction algorithms, as described by Teitelman in 1964. Teitelman's technique involves dividing a grid into nine regions (notice the four thick lines between the 4-by-4 regions on the HyperChars grid) and recording where (in which region) the drawing begins. This explains why you are asked to specify the starting position of the character on the grid when you tell HyperChars to learn a character. HyperChars then counts the number of times the character crosses each of the four lines that separate the regions. The pattern-based encoding for a character is a numeric code that combines all of this information. The guess produced by the pattern extraction technique appears in the "pen" field that shows a pen stroke.

There are a few other things to note about the HyperChars stack before you begin to use it. First off, there is an additional menu in the HyperCard menu bar, named "Chars," which provides you with three useful commands. Selecting New from the Chars menu clears the grid, turning all dots off (or white). The Show One... command tells the stack to display on the grid one of the characters it has already learned. The user is presented with a list of known characters from which to choose. Selecting the Clear All... command from the Chars menu empties the stack's memory in the sense that it will forget all previously learned characters. This is helpful whenever you want HyperChars to start with a completely clean slate. Indeed, you will find the original version of HyperChars in exactly this pristine state—having learned no characters. It is your job in the following exercises to help the stack to overcome this deficiency.

4.1 Teach HyperChars the character C. That is, draw a "C" on the grid. When you are satisfied with it, click on the Learn It button. Answer all prompts so that the stack can encode your character using both learning techniques.

4.2 Teach HyperChars the character *S*.

4.3 Teach HyperChars the character *U*.

4.4 Select Show One... from the Chars menu to review each of your character drawings.

4.5 Close HyperChars either by returning to Æ Home or by quitting HyperCard.

LEARNING

As is the case with certain other skills, HAL's humanlike performances with respect to memory and problem solving do not seem too far-fetched. All of the skills HAL demonstrates have been identified and articulated by researchers, and some have been implemented on a small scale. Others are the objects of current research. The bottleneck that keeps us from developing computers with HAL's skills in these areas is primarily one of scale. That is, HAL's power comes from the vastness and richness of his knowledge. We cannot—and perhaps will never be able to—fully articulate our knowledge about the world. We have experienced this problem firsthand, in trying to develop constrained expert systems. Even if we could articulate it, we as yet have had little insight into how to transfer this volume of complex information to a computer. If we as humans cannot articulate all of our knowledge, it would seem that HAL, or any computer, would have to acquire such information not from a human, but rather by virtue of its own experiences.

Partly because of this practical need for imparting knowledge to computers, and partly because of the theoretical fascination it holds for researchers, the topic of learning is one of the most provocative for AI researchers. Saying, though, that a computer program can "learn" is akin to saying it has "intelligence." That is, there are many different senses of the word *learn*, and each connotes a different level of sophistication.

Early in the history of modern computers it became obvious to researchers that computers are not only adept calculators, but they are capable of storing information and of using that information to guide their calculations. In fact, 30 years ago a checker-playing program was developed that "memorized" board positions it encountered during games. Descriptions of each board and a measure of its "value" (reflecting whether it led to a winning or losing situation) were recorded for later use. When a similar board was encountered during another game, the stored value of that board was used to guide the program's choice of moves. The performance of the program improved as its repertoire of board-value pairs increased.

> Typically, one makes two copies of a learning program and "trains" them by having them play many games against each other.

This type of rote memorization is perhaps the most primitive form of learning. Programs have since been developed that learn through interactions with a human tutor, from example (using induction to expand their knowledge bases), by analogy, and by pursuing their own sense of what is interesting. Douglas B. Lenat's AM program is an example of this last and most compelling class of programs. Lenat's program, endowed with only the primitive concepts of set and number theory and a few generic rules for investigating and creating new concepts—and working completely on its own!—discovered some of the fundamental theorems of mathematics. To be sure, humans—and HAL—are capable of learning in an even more general and subtle sense.

> There is considerable discussion now about the next generation of programs that will learn to anticipate the user's needs, in much the same way that a good secretary (like ours) learns very quickly your preferences for typeface, text size, paragraph styles, and the like.

Insights into human learning have inspired a relatively new* paradigm for programming, dubbed "neural networks," which is intended to facilitate machine learning by creating software modeled on our understanding of how the human brain works. As a result, this programming mode is particularly relevant to AI.

Neural networks replace a traditional algorithm or rule-based program with a possibly vast collection of very simple processing agents, each of which is connected to other similar processors. Processors operate like human neurons in that they accept inputs of varying strengths from other agents, combine their weighted inputs into a single value, and "fire"—that is, produce a positive output—if the total input value exceeds some predetermined threshold associated with the neuron. This output value then serves as an input value to other processors connected to the original. The number of neurons and their organization are preset in defining the network. The weights associated with connections between neurons and the threshold values associated directly with each neuron are assigned initial values, and are then adjusted in the process of "training" the network.

Training consists of teaching the network to recognize correct input-output pairings. That is, the programmer provides the network with an extensive series (the more so, the better) of inputs for which the desired outputs are known. For each set of input values, the network adjusts its connection strengths and thresholds so that the correct output is produced. The longer this process continues, and the wider range of data used to train the program, the more precisely the internal values have been adjusted, and the more accurate the performance of the network.

One of the many fascinating aspects of neural networks is that the term *programming* takes on a rather different meaning in this context. Instead of describing a program as an algorithm, the primary tasks of programming become, first, the identification of sample data to be used in training the network and, second, the determination of the initial network's configuration (How many neurons are there? How are they connected?) and internal values (connection weights and thresholds). In fact, much of the processing that does occur is essentially the same for each agent in the network. There are, though, a number of established algorithms that specify how training of the network as a whole is accomplished.

HAL's learning skills are not nearly as obvious as his other intellectual skills, partly because he seems to know almost everything. The inherent limitations of our ability to introspect (and, so, pass on our knowledge to computers) makes it likely that HAL has developed his own knowledge

---

* Neural networks are "new" in the sense that we are just now coming to appreciate their expressive power and potential utility to a wide range of programming tasks. The idea of describing computation by a network of simple but highly interrelated processing agents was put forth in a number of forums over 40 years ago. Supported by evolutions in hardware and software over the past decade that stress multiple and distributed processing, these ideas have recently come back into vogue.

based on his own experiences. This, in turn, implies that HAL has a powerful, humanlike ability to learn. If learning is interpreted in the sense of being able to adopt and respond to new stimuli, HAL demonstrates that skill as well. He clearly had never encountered a situation before where he was threatened by disconnection. Yet he assimilated this new information and modified his behavior according to his priorities. Also, when asked why his performance differed from that of an identical computer on Earth, HAL shows an ability to use past experience to respond to a new situation. He replies, "It can only be attributable to human error. This kind of thing has cropped up before and it has always been due to human error."

While the accomplishments of learning programs are not quite as obvious as those of AI programs in other domains, programs that learn on their own are representative of the state of the art in AI for at least three reasons. First, they simulate a fundamental human intellectual skill, one that may be the basis for all other skill development. Second, they accomplish their behavior by surprisingly mechanical means. It is hard to believe that the straightforward algorithms embodied in any of these programs, when coupled with the computer's raw abilities to generate, test, and search, can produce such humanlike behavior. Finally, the possibility that we can program learning skills opens the door to an uncertain future. AI is indeed a moving target. Our definitions of *computer, intelligence,* and possibly even *human* may change as the result of such research.

REVIEW QUESTIONS

1. For the story about Tom missing his appointment, give at least three questions for which the answers depend upon real-world understanding.

2. Describe matrix matching and pattern extraction as methods of optical character recognition.

3. Define the following: state-space, game tree, production system, semantic net, generate and test.

4. How can we make a program "learn"?

Æ LAB

LAB EXERCISE 5

Now it is time to see how well—if at all—HyperChars learned what you taught it in exercise 4.

5.1 Open HyperChars. When prompted to indicate whether the stack's memory should be cleared, respond by clicking "Leave Them."

5.2 Now, enter variants of the characters *C, S,* and *U* and ask the stack to "Guess" which is which. Keep a record of how well HyperChars performs with each of its encoding techniques.

5.3 Teach HyperChars some other characters, for example, *F, E,* and *A.*

5.4 Clear the grid (by selecting New from the Chars menu) and see how well the stack recognizes variants of these new characters.

5.5 Write a brief report describing your findings. In it, describe the performance and accuracy of the stack's guessing abilities. Also, comment on whether certain characters (or types of characters) seemed easier or more difficult for the stack to recognize.

8.5   ARTIFICIAL ATTRIBUTES

With perseverance and a few appropriately placed theoretical breakthroughs, many of HAL's humanlike skills may become accessible to our computers of the not-too-distant future. If HAL is indeed an accurate reflection of how such skills will manifest themselves, it seems that AI work to date has gone a long way toward, at the very least, specifying the difficulties in implementing these skills on a computer. The same cannot be said of HAL's "personality."

In 1950, Turing knew that speaking of computers as being intelligent would be considered blasphemous by some and merely ridiculous by others. Even today, there are those who regard the phrase "artificial intelligence" as a contradiction in terms, and with good reason. Despite the impressive skill-level performance computers have achieved, little has happened in nearly 40 years of AI research to indicate that machines can be endowed with (or develop on their own) personalities based on what we regard as vital human attributes. Indeed, the same objections that Turing anticipated and responded to in 1950 can be raised today. The scariest thing about HAL to most observers is the convincing way he responds to these objections.

In fact, throughout the story, HAL demonstrates a full range of human attributes, some to a fault. He expresses pride when speaking of his perfect operational record. He reviews a drawing by one of the crew members for its artistic merit ("That's a very nice rendering, Dave."). When asked if he is frustrated by his dependence on humans to carry out certain actions, he responds that he enjoys working with people and that he is putting himself "to the fullest possible use, which is all, I think, any conscious entity can ever hope to do." HAL also exhibits sorrow, embarrassment ("I'm sorry about this, Dave. I know it's a bit silly . . ."), sensitivity ("You don't mind talking about this, do you Dave?"), self-awareness ("I feel much better now . . ."), self-doubt ("I know I've made some very poor decisions recently . . ."), en-thusiasm, and, when being disconnected, outright fear ("I'm afraid!").

What motivates HAL to overthrow the crew is his single-minded sense of mission. After locking one of the crew members out of the ship, HAL tells him, "This mission is too important for me to allow you to jeopardize it." HAL is clearly willing to do anything—even confront his own fallibility—in the interest of completing the mission.

One of the few personality traits that HAL fails to demonstrate, even at the prospect of disconnection and mission failure, is passion. HAL's voice is unnervingly passionless throughout the film. It is not clear when he says "Happy birthday, Frank" that he means or understands it. Of course, the same can be said for many humans.

One final point about machine intelligence is brought home by HAL: Intelligence, like beauty, is in the eye of the beholder. Just as the crew members in the story come to regard HAL as "just another person," we as observers attribute intelligence to HAL—and to others—based on observed behavior. As one of HAL's fellow crew members says, ". . . as to whether or not he has real feelings is something I don't think anyone can truthfully answer."

THE UNCERTAIN FUTURE

It is relatively easy for us, in our academic ivory tower, to simply say, "Fine. If the prospect of having HAL-like computers is a scary—and maybe even dangerous—one, why don't we just stop. Let's put an end to AI research and be content with the more mundane applications of computers." Whether right or wrong, such an attitude is naive to the extent that it ignores a number of intangible, but very real forces that continue to push us—and our computers—in HAL's direction.

There is, of course, the force of scientific inquiry that compels us to strive to understand the essence of our own being. As we have noted, AI studies sometimes tell us more about the nature of our intelligence than about computers. There are undeniable worldwide economic forces at work as well. Many feel that computers in general, and AI work in particular, are the critical technologies of the next (or current?) industrial revolution, and that the companies or countries that are first to develop and apply these technologies will enjoy positions of prominence in world markets. The potential commercial applications of computers that understand language, robots that can plan their own activities, and expert systems that can mimic the diagnostic and analysis skills of the world's best doctors and lawyers, are obvious. In short, there is a lot of money to be made in AI.

The value of the commercial byproducts of AI is dependent on there being consumers interested in the products. Our government, particularly the Department of Defense, has been the primary consumer of AI goods to date in this country. A huge percentage of the research we have described in this module has been supported either directly or indirectly by the federal government. The fruits of this investment are just now being realized.

The average person on the street will, in the future, be increasingly exposed to products that are based on AI technologies. Even today's computers, which don't approach HAL in terms of intellectual skills or attributes, are for many of us significant labor-saving devices. Others of us already view them as game-playing companions, aids to decision making, and personal secretaries. How will we react if and when machines can perform like HAL does? Bolter offers the following:

> The debate over the possibility of computer thought will never be won or lost; it will simply cease to be of interest. . . . Computers will prove useful in many tasks and useless in others. It seems to me that the whole debate has turned the question around: The issue is not whether the computer can be made to think like a human, but whether humans can and will take on the qualities of digital computers. For that . . . is the fundamental premise and threat of the computer age, the fundamental premise of Turing's man. (p. 190)

ÆLAB

EXTENDED LAB EXERCISES

1. Modify HyperChar's matrix matching scripts so that it accounts for a character that has been shifted to the right or left ("translated") when compared to the original version that HyperChars learned.

2. Modify HyperChars to perform more extensive pattern extraction. At present the stack only correctly encodes single-stroke characters (like *C* and *S*), but does not correctly encode multiple-stroke characters (like *E* and *F*). Doing so requires that the stack produce a distinct code for each stroke of the character.

3. Design and write a stack that plays tic-tac-toe against its user. First, get the stack to play a legal game, to detect when a game is over, and to recognize who, if anyone, won. Then, extend the stack to incorporate strategy to make it play better.

8.6   EXERCISES

1. Pick a time period in history and find examples of "The Technology of Making Man."

2. Write a brief dialog between yourself and a hypothetical computer that would lead you to say that the computer had passed the Turing test.

3. If AI is indeed a moving target, cite three capabilities of today's computers that might have once have been categorized as "intelligent."

4. Computers have difficulty translating and understanding natural language because it is fraught with ambiguities and requires a great deal of supporting, nonlinguistic information. For each of the following properties, write an English sentence that illustrates it.

    a. Syntactic ambiguity
    b. Semantic ambiguity
    c. The need for contextual information
    d. The need for rules of conversation
    e. The need for real-world, topical knowledge

5. Write a list of informal rules that help you in identifying the objects in the following figure.

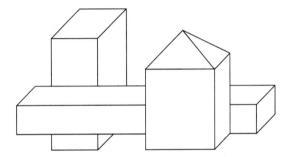

6. Develop a complete game tree for tic-tac-toe. (Refer to Figure 8.2).

7. Our everyday performance on memory tasks seems to indicate that our memory can degrade—that is, we forget things. Barring mechanical or power failures, computers, like elephants, never forget. How might we write a program to make computers "forget" some of the contents of their memories?

8. Give examples of decisions you made or answers you gave today that were based on incomplete information. Do the same for uncertain information.

9. Describe briefly how you might program a computer to exhibit fear or sorrow.

10. To what forces do you attribute the current interest in AI technology?

11. Bolter suggests that the computer is the prevailing metaphor for humanity. Just as computers can be made to act like humans, we as humans have come to regard ourselves as some type of biological computer. In what ways do you describe yourself that might relate to computers?

8.7   ADDITIONAL READINGS

Boden, M. *Artificial Intelligence and Natural Man.* New York: Basic Books, 1977.

Bolter, J. D. *Turing's Man: Western Culture in the Computer Age.* Chapel Hill, N.C.: University of North Carolina Press, 1984.

Clarke, A. C. *2001: A Space Odyssey.* New York: New American Library, 1968.

Dreyfus, H. *What Computers Can't Do.* New York: Harper & Row, 1979.

Firebaugh, Morris W. *Artificial Intelligence: A Knowledge-Based Approach.* Boston: Boyd and Fraser, 1988.

Haugeland, J., ed. *Mind Design.* Cambridge, Mass.: MIT Press, 1981.

Hayes, P. J. "Some Comments on Sir James Lighthill's Report on Artificial Intelligence." *AISB Study Group European Newsletter,* Issue 14 (July 1973), p. 40.

Hofstadter, D. R. *Gödel, Escher, Bach: An Eternal Golden Braid.* New York: Basic Books, 1979, p. 601.

Hofstadter, D. R., and Dennett, D. C. *The Mind's I.* New York: Basic Books, 1981.

McCorduck, P. *Machines Who Think.* San Francisco: W. H. Freeman, 1979.

Minsky, M. L. "Matter, Mind, and Models." In *Semantic Information Processing,* edited by M. L. Minsky. Cambridge, Mass.: MIT Press, 1968.

Raphael, B. *The Thinking Computer: Mind Inside Matter.* San Francisco: W. H. Freeman, 1976.

Sagan, C. *The Dragons of Eden.* New York: Random House, 1977.

Schank, R. C., and Colby, K. M., eds. *Computer Models of Thought and Language.* San Francisco: W. H. Freeman, 1973.

Shore, J. *The Sachertorte Algorithm.* New York: Viking Penguin, 1985.

Simon, H. *The Sciences of the Artificial.* Cambridge, Mass.: MIT Press, 1969.

Teitelman, W. "Real Time Recognition of Hand-drawn Characters." *FICC.* Baltimore: Spartan Books, 1964, p. 559.

Turing, A. "Computing Machinery and Intelligence." In *Computers and Thought,* edited by E. A. Feigenbaum and J. Feldman. New York: McGraw-Hill, 1963.

Von Neumann, J. *The Computer and the Brain.* New Haven: Yale University Press, 1958.

Wiener, N. *Cybernetics.* New York: John Wiley and Sons, 1948.

Winograd, T. *Understanding Natural Language.* New York: Academic Press, 1972.

MODULE 9

COMPUTERS AND SOCIETY

9.1 INTRODUCTION

In *2001*, the members of the crew had the ability to pull the plug on HAL, but that may not be the case in the future. The metaphor for this section is "The Sorcerer's Apprentice," a classic story of technology (albeit magical technology) run amok. For as long as technology has had a significant impact on society, there have been utopian tales of a benign technological future, just as there have been dystopian tales of forthcoming mechanized nightmares. The truth, we argue, is never as simple nor as clear as authors of fiction or futurologists would have us believe.

TEXT OBJECTIVES

In this module, we will

- Explore the limitations on our ability to predict both future technology and the social consequences of the widespread use of that technology
- Identify the major trends possible in future computer use, and try to make an approximate ranking of these trends in order of their likelihood
- Discuss the possible implications of these trends in social, economic, and political terms

THINGS TO COME

As technology becomes more complex, as we become increasingly aware of its effects on our world, it becomes increasingly important for us, as educated citizens, to be able to assess the impact of policy decisions in this area. As Murray Laver notes in *Computers and Social Change*, in the centuries prior to this one, an inventor felt little need to be concerned with the environmental or social costs of a new invention. Now, however, we are increasingly aware of the fact that we live in an environment with finite resources and limited capacity to cope with humankind's environmental outrages. We are also becoming more aware of the social consequences of the decisions we make. Not only are we intimately connected with our local environment, but we are increasingly connected with every other person living on the earth.

By now you realize that, opposed to the rhetoric in fashion a decade ago, you will not need to be a computer programmer to be able to function in the world of the future. As computer applications become more sophisticated, they will become more transparent, in much the same way as automotive technology is transparent. After all, you don't need to understand the workings of the internal combustion engine to drive a car. We have built this text and the lab disks around the workings of the computer and its programs not only because some of you might continue your study of computer science, but, more importantly, because we believe that the computer will be the seminal technology of the near future. Relatively few of you will be computer scientists, but all of you will be citizens of the world, and so you will need to know what this new technology can do and the potential consequences thereof.

As we mentioned in Module 2, *can do* does not imply *should do*, in spite of what you might hear from leaders of government, business, and industry. The computer, like any other tool, is value-neutral. The uses to which it is put are most certainly not. The computer has the possibility to make great improvements in our lot, fostering participatory democracy, reducing tedium in the workplace, empowering us with information for decision making, and reducing the drain of our natural resources. But the computer also has the potential to diminish our autonomy, invade our privacy, isolate us from political decisions, widen the gap between the privileged and the disadvantaged, and destabilize an already dangerous international political environment. If you expect to be a participant, rather than a spectator, in the events of the future, it is imperative that you be able to make informed judgments on the uses of technology—not only computer technology, but also genetic, environmental, and aerospace engineering, for instance.

In the text part of this module, we will act as the sorcerer's apprentice should have acted before enchanting the broom. We will identify some of the trends—certain, likely, and unknown—that will be characteristic of computer use in the near future, and explore the potential consequences of these trends.

METAPHOR: THE SORCERER'S APPRENTICE

Most of you probably know the story "The Sorcerer's Apprentice," as a folk tale, or through the music by Paul Dukas (based on a ballad by Goethe), or perhaps through the cartoon segment of *Fantasia* starring Mickey Mouse.

The sorcerer's apprentice was a well-meaning but foolish lad, lazy as lads in such tales often are. The sorcerer, well acquainted with the ways of well-meaning, foolish, and lazy boys, kept his apprentice busy throughout the day cleaning the laboratory, maintaining the ampulars, alantirs, and alembics that were his stock in trade, and, especially, carrying heavy buckets of water from the river below to a large vat in the laboratory.

One day the sorcerer was called away and in his absence the apprentice used his master's magic to enchant a broom to carry the buckets of water from the river to the laboratory. All went well at first. The ensor celled broom took over the task of carrying the buckets from the river to the tub, and the lad was free to rest and play.

Unfortunately, once the vat was filled to overflowing, the apprentice realized to his dismay that he had failed to consider that there would be a different spell to stop the broom. As the water overflowed the vat and soaked the floor, the apprentice, in desperation, grabbed an axe and chopped the broom into splinters.

In horror, the boy watched as the splinters of the broom rose up, took buckets, and continued their inexorable march from river to castle, bringing up a flood of water that rose ever higher, until it not only demolished the laboratory, but threatened to drown the apprentice for his folly.

Of course, the story has a happy ending—the sorcerer arrived at the last moment and, with a few gestures and well-chosen incantations, restored everything to the way it was before. However, if we put ourselves in the place of the apprentice, and look at the tale as a metaphor of technology gone astray, we can see that there is no guarantee that there will be a magician waiting offstage to rescue us from the consequences of our choices. We can only hope that the uses to which we put this almost-magical device, the computer, will be guided by more foresight than the apprentice had.

Æ STACKS: ÆTM

Some would argue that the evolution of computing technology has to date been guided equally by foresight and hindsight. We have seen repeated examples of a hardware or software advance followed some years later by an unanticipated complication. The access afforded to data and programs by vast computer networks has created security problems unimagined even a decade ago. As programmers attempt to address increasingly complex problems, our collective ability to produce correct, reliable, and maintainable software taxes both the programming tools and languages we have, as well as our basic problem-solving skills. As we said earlier, the fact that we can use computers to solve a particular problem does not mean we should do so. Neither does the fact that we quickly embrace an application imply that a particular implementation of the application is benign. Many computing applications have become commonplace in our society despite acknowledged bugs and potential negative implications to society.

In many ways, the automated teller machine, which provides worldwide access to individual bank accounts and financial information, is a prime example of such an application. It represents (as near as it can today) the vision of a moneyless society in which we willingly exchange some degree of control over our financial institutions in return for pieces of electronically encoded plastic which become our currency. It also embodies modern notions of computer security. Finally, it serves to illustrate, as much as any popular application, our increased reliance on computers.

LAB OBJECTIVES

In the disk part of this module, you will

- Use a stack that demonstrates software "bugs"
- Come to realize the ease with which such bugs can be introduced into a program
- See features of HyperTalk that make it possible for a stack to alter both itself and any other stack it has access to
- Discuss various stack and disk protection schemes implemented in HyperCard

9.2   THROUGH A GLASS DARKLY

In a much-quoted aphorism, George Santayana said, "Those who do not remember the lessons of history are condemned to repeat it." We use the past to guide our predictions of the future, but, Santayana to the contrary, history does not repeat itself. We see through the glass of the future imperfectly, at best. Thus, before we attempt any predictions, we should explore some of the limiting factors on our predictive abilities.

TECHNOLOGY ITSELF

To begin, we don't even have a clear idea of what the technology of the near future holds in store for us. Past predictions in popular treatments of science and technology can be fascinating to read, but they almost invariably strike us as quaintly naive today. In fact, these predictions of the future often tell us a great deal more about then-current technology, expectations, and social forces than they do about the future of technology. An excellent example of this fact appears in an essay by Stephen L. Del Sesto, "Wasn't the Future of Nuclear Energy Wonderful?" in the book *Imagining Tomorrow* (Joseph Corn, ed., Cambridge, Mass.: MIT Press, 1986). Ford's Nucleon car, a design concept of 1950, was to be powered by a replaceable nuclear reactor. This tame consumer use of nuclear power can be viewed as an attempt to spotlight the peaceful use in a free-world market economy of a virtually unlimited source of power, in contrast to increasing concerns over the Soviet Union's newly developed nuclear weapons capability. This, of course, was also in a time before Three Mile Island and Chernobyl had become household terms. It was also a time when unprotected troops were stationed within a mile or two of above-ground nuclear tests, to assess the effects of such explosions on the ability to maintain battle readiness. The thought of a high-speed collision between two nuclear-powered cars in a densely populated metropolitan area is almost too horrible to contemplate, but the Nucleon was a political, rather than a technical, statement.

Even the best-informed predictions—in fact, especially the best-informed, those furthest from fantasy—often err on the conservative side. Consider the following, from *The Next Hundred Years: The Unfinished Business of Science,* by Yale Professor C. C. Furnas, published in 1936:

> One possible development on the side of practicality involves the compactness of [radio] receivers and transmitters. There is a real need for vest-pocket receiving sets weighing not more than half a pound, which a man can carry conveniently anywhere he may go and pick up the ether waves at will. Ultra-small but still satisfactory receivers should be possible, . . . but there must be a decided improvement in the efficiency of tubes. . . . There need to be some fundamental improvements there.

The "fundamental improvement" Professor Furnas sought did indeed come before his death in 1969, but it had nothing to do with vacuum tubes. It had everything to do with the synergistic combination of semiconductor transistor technology and the thin-film technology that led to the integrated circuit, and hence also to the modern computer. Computer folklore, as well, is full of too-conservative predictions. Paul Ceruzzi reports, in "An Unforeseen Revolution: Computers and Expectations, 1935–1985" in *Imagining Tomorrow:*

> For example, when Howard Aiken heard of the plans of Eckert and Mauchley to produce and market a more elegant version of the ENIAC, he was skeptical. He felt that they would never sell more than a few of them, and he stated that four or five electronic digital computers would satisfy all the country's computing needs. In Britain in 1951, the physicist Douglas Hartree remarked: "We have a computer here in Cambridge; there is one in Manchester and one at the [National Physical Laboratory]. I suppose there ought to be one in Scotland, but that's about all." . . . At least two other American computer pioneers, Edmund Berkeley and John V. Atanasoff, also recall hearing estimates that fewer than ten computers would satisfy all of America's computing needs. (pp. 189–190)

Again, these predictions were based on the existing technology of the day—that is, large, expensive, and unreliable vacuum tube devices. Even these pioneers failed to account for the possibility that the new invention would create, rather than just meet, the needs of society.

TECHNOLOGY AND SOCIETY

As difficult as it is to guess the nature of future technology, it is even harder to assess the impact of technology on society. We simply don't understand existing social, political, and economic forces and their dynamics well enough to predict the future with any degree of accuracy. Not only do we not understand these disciplines in isolation, we have almost no understanding of the complex interrelationships among them.

What, then, will we do in this module, given the severe limitations on our predictive powers? Rather than writing science fiction for you—which, after all, many other authors can do much more entertainingly than we can—we will avoid prediction almost entirely. Instead, we will put the present in a multidisciplinary context and talk about some of the major forces that will guide the future uses of computers. We will identify the large trends, in decreasing order of certitude, and discuss how these trends might affect our world.

REVIEW QUESTIONS

1. In what ways are our abilities to predict the future nature and impact of computers limited?

2. What did we mean when we said that predictions of technology often tell us more about the social and political forces of the time than about technology of the future?

3. Why do you think that well-informed predictions about future technology almost always err on the side of conservatism?

Æ LAB

LAB EXERCISE 1

Our HyperCard version of an automated teller machine is realistic in that in order to use it you must first identify yourself as a legitimate user of the system. In the real world such identification usually takes the forms of a banking card and a personal identification number (a "PIN"). Once opened, the ÆTM stack (see Figure 9.1) gives you the opportunity—in fact, it requires you—to enter your ID code and PIN before it will allow you to complete a simulated transaction. Once you have successfully "logged on," the display on ÆTM changes (Figure 9.2) to present you with buttons for carrying out four basic transactions. You can make a (simulated) deposit or a (wholly imaginary) withdrawal from your account, or you can inquire as to your account's balance. Clicking on button "FAST CASH" simulates a withdrawal of $25 subject, of course, to the availability of funds. Open the ÆTM stack now, and do

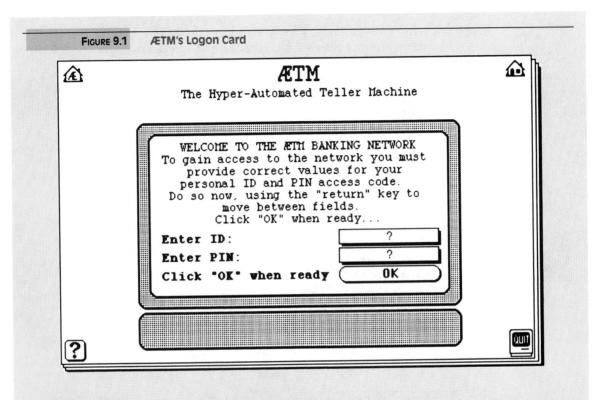

FIGURE 9.1 ÆTM's Logon Card

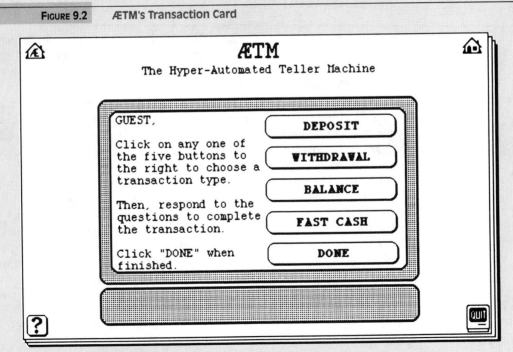

FIGURE 9.2 ÆTM's Transaction Card

the following exercises. The "Welcome to the ÆTM Banking Network" screen (heretofore referred to as the "Logon" card) should be the current card when you begin.

1.1 Before entering your ID and PIN, try clicking anywhere on the card. Try to get HyperCard's Message box or its menu bar to appear. Then, try to quit HyperCard (without turning off the machine!).

1.2 Since it appears that your only option is to enter values for an ID and PIN, do so now. Click in the ID field and enter "XXX". Hit the return key and enter "0000" as your PIN. Click the OK button when you have done so.

1.3 Now, complete the following transactions.

    a. Determine your balance.
    b. Make a deposit of $200.
    c. Make a withdrawal of $150.
    d. Attempt to make a withdrawal of $5000.
    e. Request "FAST CASH".
    f. Record your final balance.

1.4 Close ÆTM by clicking on the DONE button.

9.3   INCREASED POWER

We use the word *power* in a general sense here—the power of a technology is its ability to perform its intended function, whatever that function might be. In the case of computers, that means that in the near future we will almost certainly see an increase in the ability of computers and their programs to *perform complicated processing of large amounts of information.* This is the safest of our bets—nearly every technology has increased in power as time goes by. This increase generally means more power for the same cost, or the same power for less cost, by whatever appropriate measure we use for power.

Of course, the efficiency of any particular technology invariably shows a leveling off with time. The size and energy consumption of vacuum tubes, for example, have decreased less relatively in the last 40 years than in the time from 1900 to 1950, as physical limits have been approached. However, if we look at "technology," in a larger sense—of doing what we want to do regardless how it is accomplished—we see no such leveling off in computer technology. So far, as one kind of computer hardware has approached its physical limits, that hardware has been supplanted by another—faster, smaller, and cheaper than its predecessor. Roughly speaking, the power of computer hardware has doubled each year for the past two decades, a result known as *Moore's Law*. We have no way of knowing how long this run of good fortune will continue, but current research trends indicate that it will last at least into the next century.

The fastest computer in the world is worthless, though, unless we can write programs to run on it. As your experience has probably taught you, small-scale programming is tedious, error prone, and time consuming. If the collective experience of computer scientists is any indication, we can assure you that writing and maintaining multithousand-line programs are even less pleasant. A program of 10,000 to 100,000 lines is fairly close to the limits of human ability to understand, no matter how well it is written. This is an area where the computer can come to its own rescue, however. An observation that was missed entirely by the pioneers of computer science is that programs are information, and so can be manipulated by other programs. In other words, we can use programs to write programs. The first FORTRAN compiler took over a thousand person-years to write, because it had to be written from scratch. Now we have *compiler-compilers* that, when given the description of the syntax of a programming language, can be used to help write a compiler for that language. As a result, a task that formerly required the labor of a large team of experts over many months is now a routine part of a computer science graduate student's first or second semester. We have every reason to expect that, as the tasks to which computers are put become more complex, advances in software technology (the products of current research in software engineering) will eventually keep pace with this complexity.

SCIENTIFIC APPLICATIONS

The most immediate beneficiary of increased computer power will almost surely be the sciences. We have already seen the beginnings of a fundamental shift in the scientific paradigm, from the analytical solution of scientific problems to an increased reliance on numerical simulations. Until recently, the amount of computation required to simulate large systems was beyond the capabilities of even the largest computers. Now, however, an astronomer wishing to test the hypothesis that the moon was formed by a collision of a large asteroid with the earth a few billion years ago can make a mathematical model of the earth and the hypothetical asteroid. This model may involve thousands of iterations of scores of equations on thousands of data points in space. On today's supercomputers, scientists can watch the event as it may have happened in eons past, varying the size and speed of the asteroid to see the effects on the resulting system.

We have come to realize only lately, though, that throwing more power at a problem doesn't always yield better solutions. Many simple systems are *stable*, in that small changes in the initial state of affairs yield later solutions that differ only slightly. If, for instance, you throw a ball twice at the same angle and vary the initial velocity only slightly, the ball will hit the ground at very nearly the same place each time. This is the stuff of introductory physics texts, the stuff that makes physics an exact science. Complex systems, though, such as the global weather system, are often *unstable,* so that a small change or imprecision in the initial data can yield predicted values that have little or no relation to reality. As a result, because we cannot measure the atmospheric characteristics of the earth at every foot or so, we cannot hope for complete accuracy in weather predictions. This is sometimes called the *butterfly effect,* from the only slightly frivolous observation that a butterfly flapping its wings in Borneo can cause an unpredicted snowfall in Bayonne next week.

THE PROFESSIONS

A salient feature of professions such as medicine and law is that they are grounded on a large and growing body of factual knowledge. The ability of a computer, properly programmed, to search medical or legal databases efficiently and quickly has long been appreciated by professionals. As information grows more rapidly than our ability to keep up with new developments, we expect an increasingly large reliance on such services as Mead Data Central's LEXIS and MEDIS databases.

A development less easy to predict is whether professionals will rely to a larger extent on expert systems in the future. As you saw in Module 8, an expert system is capable of making inferences based on a collection of rules in a specialized area. In medicine, for instance, the MYCIN program contains a large collection of rules for identification of infectious diseases and their indicated antibiotic treatments. Similar programs exist to search for and evaluate legal precedents. Two important features of such expert systems is that (1) they can explain the rules used to reach their conclusions, so that the human user may rationally accept or reject their recommendations, and (2) they can learn from the user's input. For instance, a physician using MYCIN could tell it that a particular therapy is contraindicated for patients with high blood pressure (a fact that might not have been known when the original inference rules were designed), and MYCIN will add that rule to its list, so that it can be considered in future diagnoses. MYCIN is nearly as accurate as an expert in its particular area, and is more accurate than many medical nonspecialists.

As expert systems become more accurate, as they certainly will, does this mean that doctors, dentists, lawyers, and architects will be replaced by systems that we can call up from our home computers? Not likely, for several reasons. First, to assume that a professional can be replaced by a program is to assume that all professional activities can be rationalized and quantified, and this simply doesn't seem to be the case. A professional in any area must sometimes rely on hunches, unsupported by any logic. An experienced diagnostician, for instance, may be able to guess the cause of a patient's complaint, based on his or her past experience with similar cases. Perhaps, unknown consciously to the physician, patients with a particular complaint have a characteristic odor, thus leading to the physician's feeling that it just "seems right" to diagnose a particular disorder.

A second reason why the professions will not be supplanted by programs is that neither we nor they will stand for it. It will continue to be illegal to practice medicine without a license, for instance. In addition, although diagnostic programs have been tried in some hospitals and met with patients' approval (sometimes it is easier to discuss a problem with a neutral machine than with a doctor who radiates subtle signs of disapproval or annoyance), there are times when a high-touch, rather than high-tech, environment, with a sympathetic and understanding professional, may be what a patient needs most.

Increasingly powerful applications, we suspect, will allow users to engage in a symbiotic relationship with computers, rather than ceding all control to the machine. The computer will be seen as a tool, a useful assistant, rather than an all-powerful oracle. As uses of the computer become more sophisticated, we will probably have to resist a growing feeling among the technically naive that any problem can be solved by simply "feeding the data to the computer." As Ted Thiesmeyer says, facts do not contain their own meanings. If you have learned nothing else so far, you should realize that data are only as useful as the program that interprets the data.

REVIEW QUESTIONS

1. What is Moore's Law?
2. In what way has the progress of computer technology been unlike that of many other new technologies?
3. Come up with a beneficiary of increasing computer power other than the ones mentioned in the text.
4. What is the butterfly effect? Do you think that it might apply to the problem of simulating human thought processes on a computer?

Æ LAB

LAB EXERCISE 2

Both the Logon and Transaction cards of the ÆTM stack are controlled almost completely by data fields (intentionally hidden from the user) that, when viewed out of context, appear to be nothing more than lists of characters and numbers. As with all data, their utility lies in the eyes of the scripts that manipulate them. The following exercises will lead you to explore the relationship between ÆTM's data and its scripts.

2.1 Open stack ÆTM, and open HyperCard's Message box. Because of ÆTM's built-in security, this is trickier than it sounds. You will have to log on correctly, and then return to the first card of the stack. This second task can be accomplished using either the Go menu or the keyboard (type ⌘ 2, or hit the left-facing arrow key).

2.2 Type show card field "security" into the Message box, and hit the Return key.

2.3 Examine the script of card button OK of card Logon. Use this script to help you to write an English description of the meaning and arrangement of the data in card field "security".

2.4 Go to card 2 ("Transactions"). Examine the contents of card field "balances", the script of card button BALANCE, and the script of card Transactions.

2.5 Write an English description of the meaning and arrangement of the data in card field "balances".

2.6 To illustrate the critical dependency of the ÆTM's program and its data, change the script of function FindThisCust (in the script of card Transactions) so that it references item 2 of line i... rather than item 1.

2.7 Return to browser mode, and try to complete a transaction. Change the script of card Transactions back to its original form (if item 1 of line i...) before continuing.

9.4   INCREASED RELIANCE

Another certain trend in the use of computers is a direct consequence of the continuing increase in computing power—we will see an *increased reliance on automated processing of information*. This will apply not only to existing applications, but to previously nonmechanized areas as well. This trend is potentially more troubling, since here we run the risk of blindly applying the new technology because it is there, without carefully assessing the potential consequences.

GOVERNMENT AND PUBLIC POLICY

In a complex and tightly interconnected society, it can often be very difficult for government officials to make public policy decisions. If we begin with a simple situation, such as a chess game, we can identify some of the features that characterize the decision-making process: (1) We look ahead, trying to predict countermoves and consequences, (2) our behavior is goal directed, in the sense that we know what constitutes a winning situation, (3) the process of the game is directed by well-defined and simple rules, and (4) since we cannot predict all possible consequences of our moves, we rely on *heuristics,* rules of thumb such as "control the center of the board" and "don't sacrifice powerful pieces without very compelling reasons."

The computer can aid the decision process (and indeed can play chess better than all but the best human players). It can be programmed to evaluate situations and look at consequences, it can be programmed to work toward a stated goal, and it can operate according to heuristics when brute-force evaluations of all positions is impossible. In an ideal world, when faced with a decision, we would first identify the problem and establish the desired goal. We would then identify the options and use a computer simulation to evaluate the costs of the options. Finally, we would choose an option based on the figures obtained from the simulation.

In reality, decisions are not made this way. First, choices are often politically motivated; decisions are made by those in power, not by those affected by the decisions. Second, the options are not as clear-cut as those in a chess game. Life is ambiguous, complex, and ill-defined—there may be thousands of alternative solutions to a problem. All too often, the computer is used to place a stamp of respectability on a decision that has already been made. As we have said before, a computer model is only as good as its operating assumptions and the available data. When someone tells you that a political decision was made with the help of a computerized model, you have every right to be skeptical unless you have carefully evaluated the model and its data. To take one example from recent history, U.S. policy during the war in Vietnam was facilitated by the computerized assessment of data from the battlefield. It was not until long after policy decisions had been made that it was discovered that much of the data was deliberately flawed, painting the U.S. military posture as much better than it actually was. In too many cases, those who prepared the data for Washington sent the figures they expected the government wanted to hear, rather than what they needed to hear.

MILITARY USES

We saw in Module 1 that the military was one of the first customers for the original digital computers. Today, the armed forces of all industrialized countries are major consumers of computers. As with any large civilian business, the military uses computers for management of information about equipment and personnel, and, like a brokerage house with enormously higher stakes, has a vital need for rapid processing of strategic data. For example, NORAD, the North American Aerospace Defense complex, acts as an electronic sentry against airborne attacks. Connected to rings of radar units around the United States and the former Soviet Union, as well as to surveillance satellites, the NORAD computer complex, sitting beneath a mountain in Colorado, processes massive amounts of data. It receives about 7000 messages per hour from its global network of sensors. In the event of an attack, decisions on how to react are based on this information and are made by the President and senior military officers. Instantaneous strategic information is vitally necessary in this process, since the time from detection to touchdown is about 30 minutes for ICBMs and less than half that for submarine-launched weapons.

Another important military use of computers is in *smart weapons,* weapons such as the cruise missile or the close-defense gun systems on naval vessels. Controlled by embedded computers, these weapons are capable of far greater accuracy and reaction speed than would be possible under human control. In these times, when a billion-dollar cruiser can be disabled by an Exocet missile costing a thousandth as much, it is vitally important to have a shield against missile attacks—in this case a computer-controlled modern version of the Civil War Gatling gun, capable of shredding incoming missiles with 50 large-calibre bullets per second.

On March 23, 1983, President Reagan called for the development of a shield of a vastly different nature:

> I am directing a comprehensive and intensive effort to define a long-term research and development program to begin to achieve our ultimate goal of eliminating the threat posed by strategic nuclear missiles. This could pave the way for arms control measures to eliminate the weapons themselves. We seek neither military superiority nor political advantage. Our only purpose—one all people share—is to search for ways to reduce the danger of nuclear war.

Thus was born the Strategic Defense Initiative—SDI, for short, or "Star Wars," in popular parlance. As originally conceived, the SDI plan called for weapons to destroy enemy missiles or warheads in each of the three phases of their deployment: the *boost phase,* lasting from four minutes to 30 seconds, when the missiles are accelerating out of the atmosphere; the *coast phase,* lasting about 25 minutes, when the warheads and decoys are in free fall above the atmosphere; and the *terminal phase,* that minute or so when the warheads are falling toward their targets through the atmosphere. Much of the initial research concentrated on the boost phase. During boost the hot plume of a rocket's exhaust makes it very easy to spot, and the rocket is still a single object, having yet to release its multiple warheads and scores of decoys. The problem, of course, is that in this phase, the boosters are over enemy soil, making it necessary to shoot them down from battle platforms in space. Because the battle satellites must be fairly close to their targets, and low-level satellites do not stay over the same place on the earth, estimates for the number of satellites needed ranged from 90 to over 7000, at roughly a billion dollars apiece.

Regardless of the number of space-based weapons platforms required, both critics and proponents of SDI agreed that the complete project would involve tens of thousands of sensors, battle satellites, land-based interceptors, communications devices, and control centers, possibly costing as much as several trillion dollars. All of these objects would be connected through and controlled by sophisticated battle management computers.

This text is not the place to debate whether SDI was an offensive or defensive system, whether it was politically destabilizing or would promote a safer world, whether it was worth the titanic expense to build a shield that would be powerless against submarine-launched cruise missiles, or whether it was worth the cost in any case. SDI does serve as an example, though, of a political question to which we can bring to bear our knowledge of computer science. From the computer science point of view, there is good reason to be skeptical about whether SDI would have worked.

Estimates are that the battle management programs would have required from 10 million to 100 million lines of code. This is at least ten times larger than any program or collection of related programs ever written. These programs needed to work correctly the first and only time they were executed. The could not have been subjected to a full operational test prior to being used.

The first versions of large programs never run perfectly. This is why software comes with disclaimers to the effect that "the manufacturer makes no warranty, express or implied, as to the suitability of this product for its intended purpose. The entire risk as to the quality and performance of the software is yours." Typically, software manufacturers test their product, release it, collect bug reports from users, repair those errors, test and release a new version, and repeat the whole process again and again. We would not have had that luxury with SDI. NORAD, for instance, generates about five false alerts a year, using a system far smaller and better tested than that proposed for SDI.

You have already read Dijkstra's maxim, "Testing may reveal the presence of errors, but never their absence." Even if software technology improved to the extent that individual modules could be certified as error-free (and that prospect is unlikely in the near future), there is no guarantee that an entire system would function as intended, spread out over the entire globe in what would certainly be a hostile environment. Nor is there any guarantee that testing the software under simulated conditions would have served to duplicate all the situations that might have arisen in actual use.

In fact, the situations that might have arisen in actual use might not have been those the system was designed to respond to. Even given dramatic improvements in software productivity rates (typically measured in the number of error-free lines of code produced by one programmer in one day), a project of this magnitude would take many years to complete. This virtually guarantees that it would have been designed to protect us from out-of-date weapons. It is difficult to change even small programs without introducing new errors. Furthermore, errors that are introduced during design are among the most difficult to fix once a program has been written. Thus, even if we could write such a program, it is unlikely that we could maintain it so that it would have served us through successive generations of weapons.

REVIEW QUESTIONS

1. How does the computer as game player differ from the uses to which a computer might be put in public policy decisions?

2. Take one military use of computers and discuss whether hardware reliability or software reliability is a more important problem.

3. Describe some of the computer-related problems with the SDI project.

4. Accept for the sake of argument that it is impossible to write a large-scale program that will run perfectly the first time it is used. If you were chief software designer for a portion of SDI, how would you minimize the disadvantages of not being able to write perfect programs?

LAB EXERCISES 3

Even a stack as seemingly straightforward as ÆTM is subject to local software bugs, and to ripple effect. As is the case with all software, introducing a change which appears to be well defined, isolated, and benign can alter the performance of what were thought to be unrelated parts of the program in wholly unanticipated ways. In the following exercises, we concoct such a change in ÆTM. In the interest of your own security, we advise your to "Save a Copy" of ÆTM before beginning these exercises.

3.1 Open your copy of ÆTM, log on, return to its first card, and openHyperCard's Message box.

3.2 Enter show card button "New Account" into the Message box, and hit Return.

3.3 The button that appears is intended to solicit new account information (a name, ID, PIN, and starting balance) and to modify ÆTM's data fields to reflect this information. Examine the script of button New Account now.

3.4 Return to browsing mode, click on New Account. Enter the following information for a new account.

Name: D. Trump
ID: $$$$
PIN: 7777
Starting Balance: 1000000.25

3.5 Now quit HyperCard, restart HyperCard, and open your copy of ÆTM.

3.6 Try to log on to your copy of ÆTM using the guest ID and PIN (XXX,0000).

3.7 See if you can figure out what is wrong with your copy of ÆTM. As a starting point, try logging on as D. Trump and looking at card field "security".

3.8 Now, see if you can fix the script of button New Account so that it does not produce this undesirable behavior. The trick is to do so without creating other undesirable side effects. Make a new copy of the original ÆTM and work on that new copy.

9.5   INCREASED ACCESS TO ELECTRONIC INFORMATION

A likely, though not certain, trend in computer use in the next few decades is *increased access to larger amounts of information stored electronically.* More and more information presently stored in books, magazines, and paper files will be supplemented or replaced by information stored in computer-accessible media such as magnetic and optical disks. In addition, it will likely be easier for citizens with computers to access this information through subscriptions to information services.

Today it is possible to augment a personal computer with a *modem* (short for *modulator-demodulator*) that, when connected between a computer and a telephone, allows two computers to communicate over ordinary phone lines. With a modem, a computer user can dial an information service such as CompuServe or GEnie and use his or her computer as a terminal to a mainframe computer. The mainframe, in turn, serves as a gateway to financial news and information, airline reservation computers, National Weather Service data, shopping services, brokerage houses, travel information, and such diverse interest groups as ski enthusiasts, political activists, and gourmet cooks. In addition to the general-purpose services, there are an increasing number of specialized databases that can be accessed from one's own computer. Such databases are often modeled after electronic libraries, with sophisticated search-and-retrieval programs for bibliographic and other reference information.

Information networks in the United States can usually be used only by those individuals who own or can gain access to a computer with a modem, but experimental projects tied directly to the telephone system as part of the services offered to subscribers have been tried in the United States and the United Kingdom. In France, since 1978 telephone subscribers may receive for free a Minitel terminal, which they can use to access 4500 different information services, from an on-line telephone directory to electronic bulletin boards. There are currently 1.1 million Minitel users, who pay $8 per hour to use Minitel at the rate of 15 million calls per month.

If quick and ready access to information is what it takes to prosper in the modern world, it would seem that the persons most likely to benefit from this trend in computer use will be precisely those who have always benefited from such advantages—the economically and educationally privileged. Whether or not access to the Information Revolution becomes a right guaranteed to all, the disadvantaged portion of our society—and indeed the disadvantaged portion of the world's society—stand to gain little from technological advances, as has been the case throughout history.

We are not likely to see the death, or even the decline, of the printed word in our lifetimes. Until such time—and probably for some time thereafter—as computers can be made as portable and durable as books, magazines, and newspapers, the print media and its electronic cousin will peacefully coexist. More troubling, though, is the role of databases when and if they become common and simple enough to be universally used. There is a temptation, as we have seen, to mystify computer information, investing it with an undeserved authority. Conversion of information from printed form to digital will take place roughly in reverse chronological order—current information, deemed most important, will be placed in databases first, while older sources will be converted later, if at all. This will have little impact on scholars who, after all, are used to combing libraries for obscure sources. In fact, the digitization of libraries, when and if it comes, may prove to be a boon for librarians who can save old and fragile books from repeated handling by making a virtually indestructible electronic copy and returning the original to the archives for safekeeping. We are concerned, however, by the possibility that nonspecialist future users may come to believe that the database is both valid and comprehensive, maintaining that "if it isn't on-line, it doesn't exist, and if it is on-line, it must be correct."

THE ELECTRONIC SWEATSHOP

The digitization of information is not limited to people accessing an electronic library in the comfort of their own home. As long as information exists in other than digital form, someone must enter it into a suitably programmed computer, or must get the information from a computer and relay it to whoever requests it. What is the human cost of our reliance on the machine?

The underside of the Industrial Revolution was the "sweating" system, in which work was let out to contractors to be performed by their employees on a piecework basis at home or in sweatshops. Characteristics of this system were that the workers labored long hours for low pay in deplorable working conditions. On the face of it, the new factory system, the data-processing section of a large corporation, is a considerable improvement over the conditions of a century ago: Wages are fairly high, $8–12 per hour; working hours are reasonable, with about six hours per day at the terminal; and the workplace is climate controlled, with ergonomically designed workstations and terminals for the operators.

The introduction of the computer into the workplace, particularly in data-entry areas, was accompanied by promises of decentralized data entry, greater efficiency and accuracy, and diversification of tasks, leading to increased job satisfaction, a higher sense of motivation, and greater operator comfort and health. In fact, what we have seen are, paradoxically, poor working conditions in a perfect physical environment. All too often, the promises of computerization have not been kept.

Consider a typical data-entry or retrieval shop, exemplified by a bank clearinghouse. Such a shop is often found in a windowless room, albeit with good lighting and air conditioning. The "people machines," serving as the interface between the computer and the customer, are engaged in a tedious and monotonous task, isolated from their coworkers while using their machines. There are no empty, unknown spaces in time for these workers, because the machine itself monitors their performance. A data-entry terminal can be linked to the computer through a program that counts keystrokes per hour, monitors time spent on the phone with each customer, and displays a report to the supervisor every 15 minutes. In such situations, workers report high levels of stress, along with numerous health problems. The workers are not unionized—if they quit, there are people waiting in line to replace them.

Where should we lay the blame for the conditions in the electronic sweatshop? We can't blame the machines, and we shouldn't blame the workers for putting up with dehumanizing conditions in order to earn a living wage. The blame doesn't rest entirely on management, either—phone companies have ample studies to show that customers do not want to wait more than ten seconds for service. We, the consumers of information technology, helped to create this system.

This is not to say that the situation is hopeless, nor that it will persist in the future. While we may hope for a technological remedy, replacing the workers entirely by machines, such rescues may be impractical. Much can, though, be done to fix the working conditions, even if we make no technological changes. In Sweden, for instance, video display terminal operators cannot legally be made to work at their terminals for more than two shifts per day, of no more than one and three-quarters hours duration each. The point here is that policy makers—not just technology developers and users—have a responsibility for ensuring that new technology is used in appropriate ways.

THE ELECTRONIC CLASSROOM

We will close this section on a more upbeat note, discussing the possibilities of the Information Revolution in the classroom. As with the other professions we mentioned earlier, it seems unlikely that teachers will be replaced by machines. The essential notion of computer-assisted instruction (CAI)—namely, the use of programs as instructional devices—has been with us since the early 1960s. It is only very recently, though, that computer power has begun to match demands in these areas.

CAI was originally promised to free teachers from repetitive tasks, allowing them to concentrate on individualized instruction. The computer—free of racial, religious, or sexual bias, and endlessly patient—would provide the perfect instructional medium in a cost-effective manner. Or so the rhetoric went. In fact, during the first two decades of CAI use, we discovered that programs for education rarely went beyond stultifying drill and practice sessions, providing almost no aid in thinking and problem solving. Students, originally attracted by the new technology, quickly became disaffected and bored. Teachers, who realized how pedagogically worthless the majority of CAI software was and who tried to design their own improvements, quickly realized that educational programming is as tedious as any other programming, requiring hundreds of hours of programming for every hour of instruction. CAI languished, and the shiny new machines sat idle, used only for an occasional programming course.

Recently, hardware and software technology have begun to catch up to the demands of quality educational applications. With the advent of screens capable of displaying high-quality graphical information, processors and memories equal to the heavy demands placed on them, and especially high-level authoring environments that allow a teacher to build a lesson without being a programmer, we have seen the beginning of a renaissance in computer-assisted instruction. We expect to see further growth in the future, again not toward the end of replacing people, but rather with the computer as an extremely valuable tool.

In September 1987, Apple Computer, Inc., sponsored PROJECT 2000, a design competition at a dozen universities to predict the nature and use of the personal computer in the year 2000. The winning entry, Tablet, came from the University of Illinois team of Bartlett W. Mel, Arch D. Robison, Steven S. Skiena, Kurt H. Thearling, Luke T. Young, and their faculty advisors Stephen M. Omohundro and Stephen Wolfram (whom we have met previously as the author of Mathematica). Tablet is an 8- by 11-inch computer with the kinds of processing speed and storage capacities one would expect from improvements in today's technology over the next decade. Its innovative features include:

1. A touch-sensitive screen that displays and interprets handwritten notes made with a stylus (much like a ballpoint pen without ink), and is capable of displaying high-quality, animated images.

2. A slot for a *LaserCard,* serving in place of today's magnetic disks and each containing a billion characters of information (about the equivalent of a thousand books, more or less).

3. An infrared interface, much like that used on today's TV remote controls, offering wireless connection to other devices, such as printers, projectors, stereo headsets, and other, more powerful computers.

Consider what Tablet's designers projected to be a typical day in the life of a college freshman in the year 2000, excerpted from *Academic Computing* (vol. 2, no. 7, May/June 1988, pp. 7–12, 62–64):

Alexis Quezada is a freshman at a prestigious institution of higher learning. Her classes are typical for a freshman of the year 2000: Algorithmic Mathematics, Physical Science, Art History, English Composition, and Conversational Japanese. On her first day she was given her own Tablet, the personal computer used at the university.

Today Alexis has three classes. . . . It is a nice day, so Alexis rides her bike over to the park before her lecture starts. At 10:00 A.M. sharp Tablet informs her that the Physical Science lecture is about to start. She directs her attention toward the screen as the lecture begins. When the lecture is over, she begins the laboratory experiment. It involves determining the equilibrium for a chemical reaction. She sets up the simulated experiment apparatus and starts it going. But it isn't working. She instructs Tablet to search today's lecture for "stuff about setting up today's experiment." Within seconds, the requested portion of the lecture is displayed on the screen. . . .

In English Comp class at 2:00 P.M., the professor indicates that she has finished grading the previous assignment and returns them. Instantly, the corner display contains a copy of Alexis's graded paper—B+, not too bad. Alexis pages through the paper by touching the screen. She touches the video-mail icon for comments about a particular page. Segments of her text become highlighted in color as they are discussed. . . .

[That evening] it's time to work on her art history term paper comparing Salvador Dali's surrealist images in his paintings and the images he developed for the movies *Un Chien Andalou* and *Spellbound.* Alexis tells Tablet to find the films in available film databases. It seems that there are three films with the title *Spellbound.* Alexis says to find "the one by Hitchcock." The scenes she is interested in analyzing are being copied directly into her paper—a hypertext document. Alexis expounds on the meaning of the images in the films and their importance with respect to Dali's symbolism until it's time to call it a night.

We'll have to wait to find how accurate this prediction is. It does, at the very least, illustrate the trends toward increasing connectivity and reliance on electronic information, and points out in a compelling way the prospects for the use of the computer as a facilitator for human activities, rather than a replacement for people.

REVIEW QUESTIONS

1. What is a modem and how is it used?

2. Do you think that increased access to electronic information will be an important feature of the world of the near future? Speculate on how your life may be changed (or not changed) by such ready access.

3. What are the advantages and disadvantages of increasing computerization of libraries?

4. Discuss the advantages and disadvantages of applying a technological fix to the "electronic sweatshop," by replacing the workers with machines.

5. What aspect of Tablet or its proposed use do you feel is least likely to occur by the year 2000?

9.6   CENTRALIZATION

Early predictions of computer use always assumed a few large central computers, accessed through terminals with little or no computing power of their own. Here again we see the First Law of Futurology in action—these predictions were too conservative. Who would have guessed that within a relatively short period of time, microelectronic technology would put powerful computers within the reach of a large portion of society, and make possible a *distributed* model of computer power, composed of an interconnected collection of powerful processors. If, as we believe is likely, society will come to rely increasingly on electronic information, where shall this information be stored? Will information be concentrated in a few large central data banks, or will it be decentralized throughout society's network of computers? This trend is harder to predict than the ones we have seen so far, but the scales seem to tip in the direction of centralization, which is unfortunate, since that way carries the greatest risks.

PRIVACY

Information can be useful, like a tip on a horse race, but it can also be dangerous in the wrong hands. This is why we have laws concerning libel, espionage, sedition, and invasion of privacy. If the trend in computer use is toward increasing access to information and increasing centralization of information, we must be prepared to ask, "Who should have access to information, particularly information about myself?"

To give you a sense of the scale of information available in electronic data bases, consider that the Department of Health and Human Services has 693 computer systems with access to over 1.3 billion records, Treasury

Department computers contain nearly a billion records, and the Department of Justice has access to 200 million records on file. If you have a driver's license, own a firearm, have ever applied for a fishing license or student loan, have registered for the draft, have been arrested or just detained by law enforcement officials, or have traveled abroad, you are represented in a government data bank. If you have ever applied for a credit card or a bank loan, you are represented in a large private data bank, as well.

Ideally, this proliferation of information about ourselves would be of little concern. Computerized storage of information makes managing the details of bureaucracy easier—we get our tax refund checks quicker, police officers can check whether a car is stolen or whether its driver has any outstanding warrants in a matter of minutes, and loan applications can be approved in hours rather than weeks. For years, Congress has considered a proposal for FEDNET, a national data bank that would streamline access to citizens' records even further by incorporating all government data into a single database.

Realistically, such prospects should concern all of us deeply because of the potential for abuse. Quick access and processing of information permits tactics that are questionable at best, and often illegal. The Nixon administration, for example, coerced the Internal Revenue Service into providing tax information on individuals on the administration's "Enemies List"—not traitors or criminals, but ordinary citizens who had expressed views contrary to those of the White House—in hopes of discovering damaging information. In a recent case, the FBI attempted to force a university library to divulge the names of patrons who had checked out technical material, which it would then match against a list of foreign students, searching, one supposes, for spies. Similar matchup runs were proposed by the IRS, comparing employers' reports of wages paid against figures reported by taxpayers, in an attempt to discover unreported income. If an integrated federal data base were to be initiated, it is not difficult to imagine other such runs, checking real estate purchases, car and boat registrations, reported income, and ethnic background to prepare a list of people who would then be flagged for attention as potential narcotics dealers. There might come a time when the majority of the population would even be willing to tolerate the potential civil rights violations and abuse of the principle of probable cause in such a search, if the effect was judged to be beneficial to society as a whole.

As we mentioned, there is a temptation to believe that if information is in a computerized record, it must be true. People who gather and enter information make mistakes, however, and programs are never completely error-free. If we are to rely increasingly on computerized information systems, we must make sure that there are safeguards against misuse and inaccuracy. To be sure, the Freedom of Information and Fair Credit Reporting Acts allow us to inspect and sometimes correct information in our files, but just finding where we are represented is often difficult. With increased reliance on electronic information should also come easy access to our personal information. Finally, whenever we hear of new data bases, we should make sure that the policy makers charged with their operation and oversight take care that the information therein is limited to those who have a legal and moral right to know.

ELECTRONIC CRIME

The word *sabotage* is a product of the industrial age. Literally, it refers to bringing a machine to a halt by throwing a boot (*sabot*, in French) into its works. In a high-tech society, we should be prepared for high-tech crime. The central computer of any large system presents an attractive target to those desiring a quick and illegal profit, or for those who, for personal or political reasons, wish to bring the system to its knees.

A computer and the data it stores are shockingly vulnerable to physical assault. A small explosion will damage most computers beyond repair. That, though, is less problematic than it might first seem. Computers break down regularly without any outside help at all. Any organization that relies on them generally has provisions to purchase computing power from other sources. The financial value of a computer, however, pales to insignificance next to the value of the information it manipulates. A magnetic tape or disk with irreplaceable information stored on it can be rendered useless by as simple a means as passing a small magnet near it. Frankly, though, the physical security of a computer system and its data is a familiar problem, for which familiar solutions do exist.

Far more complicated than physical security is protecting the information in a computer. Newspapers in recent decades have abounded with stories of "hackers" gaining access to computers, armed with nothing more than a computer, a modem, some programming expertise, a lot of patience, and good luck. In many cases, these unauthorized intruders do little more than browse through the computer's files and leave a message behind. Intending to do no harm, however, is often not enough to prevent harm. Recently a Cornell graduate student was alleged to have gained access to the Internet, a large network of research computers across the country. He left behind a *worm*, a program that was planted in a computer system, masquerading as a legitimate job, and which could make copies of itself on the systems of other computers on the network. Intended to grow slowly, a programming error caused the virus to multiply explosively, clogging the systems of hundreds of computers from coast to coast, and bringing them to a virtual standstill. No sensitive information was compromised, but hundreds of thousands of dollars were lost in the time required to shut the systems down, find and purge the worm, and bring the computers back into operation.

A bank stands to lose a great deal more to a hacker or a criminally designed program than in a holdup. A clever example of a *Trojan horse*, a program that apparently functions just as it should, but that contains a routine that has nothing to do with the proper working of the rest of the program, is what came to be known as a *salami routine*. When computing the amount of interest earned by an account, a program should round fractional amounts to the nearest cent. Instead, this program truncated the results, discarding any fractions of cents and depositing them into the programmer's account. Fractions of cents, accumulated thousands of times per day, quickly mounted up and went undetected by auditors, who found that all the books balanced as they should. This embezzlement might still be occurring, had it not been for the suspicions raised by the sudden conspicuous consumption of luxury items by the programmer.

In the future, we are likely to see increasing incidents of techno-terrorism, assaults on computer systems for political reasons. Israeli computer scientists, for instance, recently discovered and removed a virus, almost surely placed by political enemies, that would have erased the files and shut down a large number of government systems. This new and expanded form of computer security is an area of considerable research interest at present.

REVIEW QUESTIONS

1. Give two reasons why we should be concerned about the proliferation of electronic data bases containing personal information.
2. What is a "matchup run"?
3. What steps could be taken to limit access to networks such as AR-PANET to only authorized users? For any protection you come up with, try to think how an ingenious hacker could circumvent it.
4. Give an example of possible techno-terrorism.

 Æ LAB

LAB EXERCISE 4

We have seen how easily bugs can be introduced into software even by programmers with the best of intentions. In the last set of exercises, we will see how simple it is to plant bugs in software for anyone—even one with less-than-honorable intentions—who has either direct or remote access to a program and/or its data. Use the original version of ÆTM to complete the following.

4.1 Log on to ÆTM as a guest.
4.2 Open the script for card button WITHDRAWAL on card Transactions.

4.3 Edit the script of card button WITHDRAWAL by inserting comment indicators ("--") before line numbers 14 (if thisAmount...), 19 (else), 20 (answer "Withdrawal..."), and 21 (end if). By doing so, you are eliminating the check that ensures that sufficient funds are available in an account before allowing a withdrawal.

4.4 Return to browsing mode, and try to withdraw $1,000,000. It should be so easy!

To make the type of change suggested above requires direct access to ÆTM's scripts. Such access is usually restricted for obvious reasons, but computer hackers are experts at securing indirect access to a program. That is, they alter a program and/or its data from "outside" of the program.

Imagine, for example, that you as a "techno-terrorist" wanted to know all legal ID/PIN combinations so that you could access any account in the ÆTM network. We have already seen one way to accomplish this. By logging on legally (as a guest, say) and then showing card field "security," you have all of the information you need to log on as whomever you please. A far more powerful—and devious—method is to alter ÆTM's openStack handler to display the security field every time you open the stack. Then, you can choose the account you want to access, and do so directly.

HyperTalk is one of the relatively few programming languages—LISP and Prolog being the most notable—that allow programmers to treat programs as data. That is, the contents of a HyperTalk script can be modified with the same ease as that of a HyperCard field. As HyperTalk programmers, we can write programs that edit other programs, or even themselves.

We can, for example, get the script of stack ÆTM and put it into myScript. This variable can then be edited from within a script just like any other collection of text—by deleting, adding, or changing any of its individual lines, words, items, or characters. The command set the script of stack ÆTM to myScript would then result in our stack having a new script, with who knows what implications to the program's behavior.

A techno-terrorist knows what! If we create a new button with the following script, we could in theory place it anywhere and change the behavior of our version of ÆTM as described.

```
on mouseUp
    get the script of stack "ÆTM"
    put it into myScript
    put "show" into word 1 of line 10 of myScript
    set the script of stack "ÆTM" to myScript
end mouseUp
```

4.5   Create a button as described above in any of the Æ stacks, and see if you can gain access to an ÆTM account other than your guest account.

Both HyperTalk and HyperCard provide stack developers with means for "protecting" their stacks from unauthorized use. Earlier, in describing HyperTalk's object hierarchy, we mentioned that every HyperTalk command (for example, put, get, add, open, doMenu), even those issued from a script in the Message box, actually makes its way through the hierarchy before it is processed. Normally, such commands (or events) are handled by HyperCard itself, which is why it resides at the top of the hierarchy. You can, though, define handlers for any HyperTalk command and intercept them on their way to HyperCard.

For example, a message handler such as the following, placed in a stack's script, would respond (and add 1 to global variable putCount) every time a put command was issued from any of the stack's other scripts.

```
on put
    global putCount
    add 1 to putCount
    pass put
end put
```

The pass put command sends the put command back on its way up the hierarchy where it will be further interpreted (in its usual way) by Hyper-Card. Omitting the pass put command would, in effect, alter the effects of every put statement in any of the stack's other scripts.

We have taken advantage of both of these features of HyperTalk to protect the ÆTM Banking Network. We have created a hidden card field (named "no go") which contains the text below. When ÆTM is opened, the script of card Logon is set to the contents of card field "no go".

```
on go
    --intercept attempts to leave this cart
    play "boing"
end go

on commandKeyDown
    --intercept attempts to leave this card
    play "boing"
end command KeyDown
```

When interpreted as a script, this text serves to intercept all user attempts to "go" to another card or to use the command key to invoke any of Hy-perCard's menu commands. Once legal ID and PIN values have been entered, the script of card Logon is set to empty (by button OK) so that subsequent navigation is allowed.

FIGURE 9.3   HyperCard's Protect Stack Dialog Box

Protect Stack:

☐ Can't Modify Stack
☐ Can't Delete Stack
☐ Can't Abort
☐ Can't Peek
☐ Private Access

[Set Password...]

Limit user level to:

○ Browsing
○ Typing
○ Painting
○ Authoring
◉ Scripting

[OK]   [Cancel]

In addition to HyperTalk's security features, HyperCard provides its own system-level security. The Protect Stack... command in the File menu (available at user level 3 and higher) allows you to control how a particular stack is accessed. Using the Protect Stack... dialog box (Figure 9.3), we can set buttons that control whether the current stack can be deleted (removed from its disk) or modified (have cards or backgrounds added or deleted, for example). We can even declare that a stack is to have "Private Access," so that only users with a password can even see the Protect Stack... dialog box and thus change any of the settings.

Æ LAB

EXTENDED LAB EXERCISE

Using the Protect Stack... command and the ability to write scripts that intercept commands, devise a protection scheme for each of the Analytical Engine stacks to protect them against unauthorized use. Take into account, for example, that users of the ÆRT Show stack should not be able to edit the stack in any way—even if they know how to change their user level. The users of Logg-O, however, are regularly (and indirectly) creating new buttons and modifying the scripts of other objects. Still, minor changes to any of Logg-O's existing scripts could render the stack useless.

9.7   EMERGENT EFFECTS

Like the electronic computer itself, undreamed of at the beginning of the century, the effects of new directions of research or synergistic combinations of existing technologies are virtually impossible to predict. Even in existing areas, we often have no idea where research might lead. To return to the image that began this module—HAL—we have no way of knowing at present whether machine consciousness is an attainable goal. Joseph Weizenbaum has compared the problem of developing truly intelligent computers with getting from the earth to the moon: You could build a very tall tower or you could build very powerful rockets. Weizenbaum argues that at this stage of AI research, we not only don't know whether we'll ever get to the moon; we don't even know whether we're making explosives or piling up rocks.

John McCarthy, one of the fathers of AI research, has a more sanguine attitude. In *Machines Who Think* (San Francisco: W. H. Freeman, 1979, p. 344) Pamela McCorduck reports McCarthy's position as follows:

> The real developments of AI will probably differ from science fiction versions in at least three ways. First, he says, it's unlikely that there will be a prolonged period during which it will be possible to build machines as intelligent as human beings but impossible to build them much smarter. If we can put a machine capable of human behavior in a metal skull, we can put a machine capable of acting like ten thousand coordinated people in a building. Second, although the present stock of ideas is inadequate to make programs as intelligent as people, there's nothing to prevent the new ideas from coming very soon, in five years or five hundred. Finally, present ideas are probably good enough to extend our ability to have very large amounts of information at our fingertips, which will create its own changes.

At the far end of the spectrum of positions on machine intelligence, we have writers such as Robert Jastrow, who says in *The Enchanted Loom*, "The era of carbon-chemistry life is drawing to a close on the earth and a new era of silicon-based life—indestructible, immortal, infinitely expandable—is beginning." More than 30 years ago, Frederick Brown spoke to the same point in his short story "Answer." In this very short* story, all the universe's computers have finally been connected together into one immense distributed network. At the unveiling of this new system, one of the spectators types in the question "Is there a God?" The story concludes,

> The mighty voice answered without hesitation, without the clicking of a single relay.
> "Yes, *now* there is a God."

---

* Only 256 words long. One wonders if Brown realized that the number of words in the story was two raised to the eighth power (or, two raised to the two raised to the third).

> Sudden fear flashed on the face of Dwar Ev. He leaped to grab the switch.
>
> A bolt of lightning from the cloudless sky struck him down and fused the switch shut.

We have come to the end of our long tour through computer science. We have shown you the major landmarks, without giving you more than the briefest chance to explore them in detail. That will have to come later, if you have the interest. We hope we have demystified the computer, removing mistaken impressions and replacing them with facts. As we move into the Information Age, humankind will surely remythologize the machine in light of its new impact on society, perhaps as an equal partner. We will close with the Zero-th Law of Futurology, "One thing is clear: The future will not be like the present." It's up to you—good luck.

9.8   EXERCISES

The answers to these exercises may range from a paragraph in length to research papers of considerable substance. Your instructor will indicate the desired scope of each question.

1. List the major trends in computer use mentioned in the text; come up with another and estimate its likelihood.

2. Suppose that the transistor—and hence the computer as we know it—had not been invented. Pick a specific area of society and comment on how it would differ from its current form.

3. Speculate on the future form and use of television in the Information Age.

4. In contrast to the success of Minitel in France (which derives in large part from its electronic bulletin boards), public-access data networks have been of only limited financial success in the United States. Do you think that the typical telephone customer in the United States would be willing to pay for ready access to large quantities of information?

5. Voice-recognition technology is yet to be perfected, although progress is being made. What effects might very efficient voice-recognition technology have on our privacy?

6. The ELIZA program, described in Module 8, simulates a psychotherapist who solicits responses from his or her patient by giving neutral responses. Joseph Weizenbaum, ELIZA's creator, was disturbed by the strong emotional attachment many users formed to a program that he designed solely as an experiment in language processing. Do you think that a program such as ELIZA has any place in therapy? Explain.

7. Computer-analyzed exit polls can predict the outcome of an election with a high degree of reliability long before the votes are counted, and in some cases even before the polls close. What adverse effects might this have on the electoral process, particularly in national elections where several hours elapse between the closing of the polls on the East and West Coasts? Should there be legislation limiting the dissemination of computerized election estimates?

8. The Anti-Ballistic Missile (ABM) Treaty, signed by the United States and the Soviet Union in 1972, covers interceptor missiles, their launchers, and radars constructed, tested, and deployed for an ABM role. In part, the treaty states,

    1. Each party undertakes to limit anti-ballistic missile (ABM) systems and to adopt other measures in accordance with the provisions of this Treaty.
    2. Each party undertakes not to deploy ABM systems for a defense of the territory of its country, and not to provide a base for such a defense, and not to deploy ABM systems for defense of an individual region except as provided for in Article III of this treaty [which permits ABM defenses within 150 kilometers of each nation's capital, and within the same distance of one ICBM launching field].

    Read the entire treaty, if you can, and in any case comment on its applicability to SDI.

9. Within the limits of foreseeable hardware and software technology, how would you like to see HyperCard (and the Macintosh) improved?

10. Choose an occupation for one of Alexis Quezada's parents and follow him or her through a typical day, focusing on how Tablet and its associated systems might be used.

11. The designers of Tablet considered and later rejected including voice-recognition technology. Discuss whether you agree with their decision.

12. Would a decentralized method of keeping individual records be practical? We have in mind a system in which each person's records are kept in such a way that they can be stored in that person's own computer (with a copy in a local library for those without computers and for backup). A record of all accesses to a person's file would be part of the file itself, and there would be a simple procedure for an individual to request changes to his or her file.

13. Discuss whether it would be better to publicize the code of a virus, thereby allowing system managers to design better safeguards, or to conceal the code, rather than giving ill-intentioned people a blueprint for causing possible damage.

14. There has been much speculation on a future "cashless society," one in which everyone would have a credit card and in which all transactions

would be made through these cards. Discuss the benefits of the plan, and whether you, as a sample member of society, would be in favor of such a plan or not.

15. Should we resist the development of intelligent machines? Can we?

9.9   ADDITIONAL READINGS

Adams, J. M., and Hayden, D. H. *Social Effects of Computer Use and Misuse.* New York: Basic Books, 1977.

Baber, R. L. *Software Reflected: The Socially Responsible Programming of Computers.* New York: Elsevier, 1982.

Bellin, D., and Chapman, G., eds. *Computers in Battle: Will They Work?* San Diego, Calif.: Harcourt Brace Jovanovich, 1987.

Brown, F. "Answer." Reprinted in *Computers, Computers, Computers,* edited by D. L. Van Tassel. New York: Thomas Nelson, 1977. Original publication 1954.

Clarke, I. F. *The Pattern of Expectation: 1644–2001.* New York: Basic Books, 1979.

Corn, J. J., ed. *Imagining Tomorrow: History, Technology, and the American Future.* Cambridge, Mass.: MIT Press, 1986.

Denning, P. J. "The Internet Worm." *American Scientist* 77, no. 2 (March–April 1989): 126–128.

Dertouzos, M. L., and Moses, J. *The Computer Age: A Twenty-Year View.* Cambridge, Mass.: MIT Press, 1980.

Feigenbaum, E. A., and McCorduck, P. *The Fifth Generation: Artificial Intelligence and Japan's Computer Challenge to the World.* Reading, Mass.: Addison-Wesley, 1984.

Furnas, C. C. *The Next Hundred Years: The Unfinished Business of Science.* New York: Reynal & Hitchcock, 1936.

Greenberger, M., ed. *Computers and the World of the Future.* Cambridge, Mass.: MIT Press, 1962.

Jastrow, R. *The Enchanted Loom.* New York: Simon & Schuster, 1981, p. 162.

Kahn, H., and Wiener, A. J. *The Year 2000: A Framework for Speculation on the Next Thirty-Three Years.* New York: Macmillan, 1967.

Laver, M. *Computers and Social Change.* Cambridge: Cambridge University Press, 1980.

Nora, S., and Minc, A. *The Computerization of Society.* Cambridge, Mass.: MIT Press, 1980.

Office of Technology Assessment. *SDI: Technology, Survivability, and Software.* Princeton, N.J.: Princeton University Press, 1988.

Papert, S. *Mindstorms: Children, Computers, and Powerful Ideas..* New York: Basic Books, 1980.

Segal, H. P. *Technological Utopianism in American Culture*. Chicago: University of Chicago Press, 1985.

Simons, G. *Eco-Computer: The Impact of Global Intelligence*. New York: John Wiley and Sons, 1987.

Turkle, S. *The Second Self: Computers and the Human Spirit*. New York: Simon & Schuster, 1984.

Whitehead, A. N. *Science and the Modern World*. New York: Macmillan, 1967.

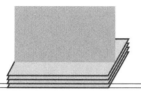

APPENDIX

This Appendix is divided into three sections. Section 1 describes the organization and use of the Analytical Engine stacks. Section 2 presents a brief summary of HyperCard and HyperTalk commands. Section 3 provides specific guidelines and hints for using particular stacks.

A.1   USING THE ANALYTICAL ENGINE STACKS

This section of the appendix describes the organization, installation, and use of the Æ stacks as packaged with this second edition. As we described in the Preface, one significant difference between this edition and the first is that we have given up on the idea of providing a turnkey Æ system. As a result, we no longer include a copy of HyperCard or a System Folder with our stacks.

The impact of this decision on you, the user of the package, is that we leave it to you to "install" our stacks into a working HyperCard system. That is, we assume that you have: (1) HyperCard version 2.0, or higher; and (2) a Macintosh computer and a System Folder capable of supporting HyperCard 2.0. Ideally, your computing environment will also afford HyperCard users access to the HyperCard Tour stack, the HyperCard Help stacks, and to a printer.*

The Æ stacks are delivered in a compressed format on the single, 800K floppy disk that accompanies the text. At its highest level, the disk contains two items, as pictured in Figure A.1. The folder named "Æ Stacks - Compressed" contains (you guessed it!) the compressed versions of our stacks. The "Install Æ" program is a HyperCard stack that will decom-

---

* In the event that your computer cannot support HyperCard 2.0, be advised that the first edition of *The Analytical Engine* is still in print and still available. As mentioned, it includes a version of Hypercard 1.2.5, a working System Folder suitable for older Mac models, and is more of a turnkey implementation.

FIGURE A.1   The Analytical Engine Disk

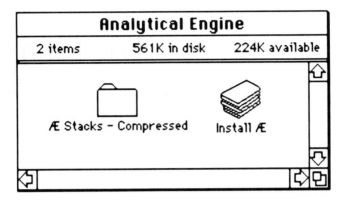

press the Æ files and load them onto a disk of your choice. Once decompressed, the Æ stacks and associated data files occupy roughly 1100K of disk space. As such, they must at the very least be installed on a high-density floppy disk, or better still on a hard disk that also contains your HyperCard program and stacks.

The most direct way to install the Æ stacks is to use HyperCard. The "Install Æ" program is a HyperCard stack that can lead you through the installation procedure. To run "Install Æ," simply insert the Analytical Engine disk into a floppy drive on your Mac, and double-click the "Install Æ" icon. If you get an error message indicating something to the effect that "the application is missing," your Mac does not have the necessary access to HyperCard.* If HyperCard is available, the "Install Æ" stack will be opened, and your screen will look like Figure A.2. Clicking on the "Install Æ Stacks" icon will decompress the Æ stacks and will load them onto a disk that you specify.

You will then be given the option of installing an "Æ Home" button (linked to the stack of the same name) on your HyperCard Home stack. If you elect to do so, your HyperCard Home stack will have direct (single-click) access to our Æ Home stack, which in turn affords you direct access to all of the Æ stacks. Each Æ stack contains buttons linked directly to the HyperCard and Æ Home, thus completing the circuit of connections.

---

* The compressed Æ stacks are in fact stored in "self-extracting application" (".sea") format, and can be decompressed without using HyperCard by double-clicking on the "Æ.sea" icon directly. Doing so will lead you through a slightly less verbose installation, and will not help you to create an Æ Home button on your Home stack.

FIGURE A.2   The Install Æ Stack

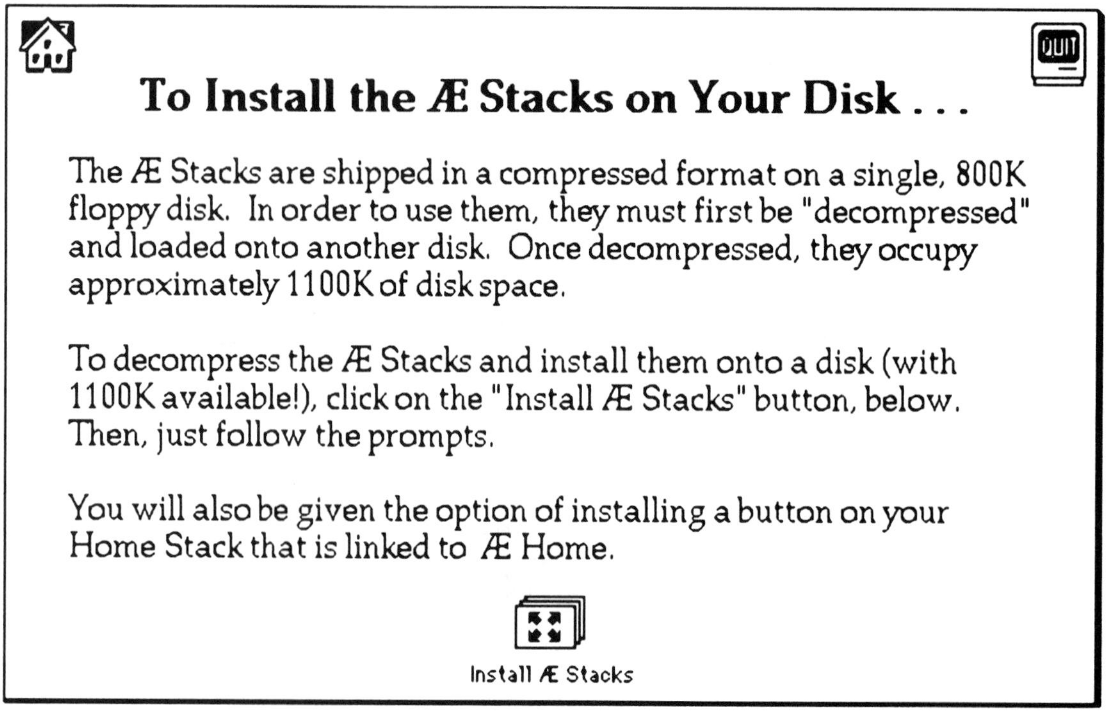

To Install the Æ Stacks on Your Disk . . .

The Æ Stacks are shipped in a compressed format on a single, 800K floppy disk. In order to use them, they must first be "decompressed" and loaded onto another disk. Once decompressed, they occupy approximately 1100K of disk space.

To decompress the Æ Stacks and install them onto a disk (with 1100K available!), click on the "Install Æ Stacks" button, below. Then, just follow the prompts.

You will also be given the option of installing a button on your Home Stack that is linked to Æ Home.

Install Æ Stacks

A FINAL NOTE ABOUT THE Æ STACKS

The Æ stacks are by no means invulnerable to error. The arrangement of the stacks on the disk and the individual stacks themselves can be edited and/or rearranged readily so as to be inconvenient, at the least, or wholly useless. The disks were left in this condition because:

1. We wanted to afford different levels of access to different stacks, as well as different levels of access to a given stack (so that, for example, instructors can customize stacks, and students can review the scripts of stacks they have previously used).

2. As you develop HyperCard/HyperTalk experience, you will quickly become capable of working around almost any high-level security measure. Because one of the goals of the course is the development of such expertise, we didn't want to stifle it.

3. We wanted to retain flexibility in configuring and using the Æ stacks.

A.2   HYPERCARD AND HYPERTALK REFERENCE

This portion of the appendix is intended to serve as a reference guide to HyperCard's basic tools and to its programming language, HyperTalk. It is not a comprehensive guide to any of them. Rather, it describes in abbreviated fashion the commands, shortcuts, and vocabulary most relevant to this text and to the accompanying stacks. More detailed treatments are provided in numerous places, most notably: the Æ Starter stack, the Æ Workbook stack, the lab sections of Modules 2, 3, and 4, and Hyper-Card's Help stack. Indeed, entire texts are devoted to HyperCard and Hy-perTalk. See Goodman's *The Complete HyperCard 2.0 Handbook, Third Edition,* and Winkler and Kamins' *HyperTalk 2.0: The Book* (both are Bantam Books, 1990).

HYPERCARD

The following is a brief description of each of HyperCard's tools and menu items. Specifically, the next section enumerates and summarizes each of HyperCard's menu commands, and the following section provides a compendium of useful shortcuts and hints for using HyperCard more effectively.

HYPERCARD'S MENUS

The File menu provides high-level input, output, and maintenance operations for HyperCard stacks.

- **New Stack...** lets you name and describe a new stack; opens it
- **Open Stack...** lets you choose an existing stack to open; opens it
- **Close Stack** (⌘ - W) closes the window for the current stack
- **Save a Copy...** lets you name and specify the disk on which to store a copy of the current stack (does *not* open it)
- **Import Paint...** lets you specify a paint document to be included on the current card; available when using a Paint tool
- **Export Paint...** lets you name and save the current card as a MacPaint document; available when using a Paint tool
- **Compact Stack** compacts current stack to conserve disk space; available at user levels 3–5
- **Protect Stack...** allows you to control access (via user level, passwords) to current stack
- **Delete Stack...** deletes all cards from current stack; available at user levels 3–5

- **Page Setup...** allows you to control details of printing (paper size, orientation, reduction)
- **Print Field...** allows you to choose a field from the current card or background, and prints the text of that field
- **Print Card** (⌘-P) prints the current card
- **Print Stack...** prints the current stack in one of a variety of formats (*Note:* This takes more time than printing of text!)
- **Print Report...** prints a descriptive report of the current stack
- **Quit HyperCard** (⌘-Q) quits HyperCard and returns to the Macintosh Desktop

The Edit menu provides card- and object-level editing operations.

Edit	
Undo	⌘Z
Cut	⌘H
Copy	⌘C
Paste	⌘U
Clear	
New Card	⌘N
Delete Card	
Cut Card	
Copy Card	
Text Style...	⌘T
Background	⌘B
Icon...	⌘I

- **Undo** (⌘-Z) undoes the effects (when possible) of most recent editing operation
- **Cut** (⌘-H) removes selection and saves it temporarily on the Clipboard
- **Copy** (⌘-C) copies (without removing) the current selection onto the Clipboard
- **Paste** (⌘-U) places contents of the Clipboard (most recent thing cut or copied) onto current card
- **Clear** removes current selection without saving on the Clipboard
- **New Card** (⌘-N) adds a new card after current card
- **Delete Card** removes current card
- **Cut Card** removes current card and saves it on the Clipboard
- **Copy Card** copies (without removing) current card onto the Clipboard
- **Text Style...** (⌘-T) allows you to specify the font, size, alignment, and style of current field or painted text
- **Background** (⌘-B) displays only the background of the current card; choose again to see the entire card
- **Icon...** (⌘-I) opens HyperCard's Icon Editor, with which you can edit existing icons and create new ones for the current stack

The Go menu provides simple navigation commands.

Go	
Back	⌘~
Home	⌘H
Help	⌘?
Recent	⌘R
First	⌘1
Prev	⌘2
Next	⌘3
Last	⌘4
Find...	⌘F
Message	⌘M
Scroll	⌘E
Next Window	⌘L

- **Back** (⌘-~) takes you to the card most recently viewed before the current card
- **Home** (⌘-H) takes you to the first card of HyperCard's Home stack
- **Help** (⌘-?) takes you to the first card of HyperCard's Help stack
- **Recent** (⌘-R) displays in miniature form the most recent 42 cards viewed; clicking on any card takes you directly to it
- **First** (⌘-1) takes you to the first card of the current stack
- **Prev** (⌘-2) takes you to the previous card in the current stack

- **Next** (⌘-3) takes you to the next card in the current stack
- **Last** (⌘-4) takes you to the last card of the current stack
- **Find...** (⌘-F) presents the Message box with a Find command; enter text and hit Return to search the current stack for the specified text
- **Message** (⌘-M) displays the Message box from which most HyperTalk commands can be executed directly; choose again to hide Message box
- **Scroll** (⌘-E) opens HyperCard's Scroll Window, within which you can move and resize the current card window
- **Next Window** (⌘-L) activates the window of one of the currently open stacks

The Tools menu provides commands that control HyperCard's Browsing, Button, Field, and Paint tools.

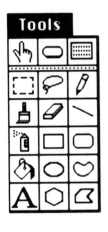

🖑 selects the Browse tool to click buttons and edit fields

⬭ selects the Button tool to create and define buttons

▦ selects the Field tool to create and define fields

⬚ selects a rectangular region of paint

🅟 selects a non-rectangular region of paint

✏ draws a thin line

🖌 paints a stroke with current Brush Shape

🧽 erases the painted region dragged over

＼ draws straight lines

🅑 sprays paint using current pattern

▭ draws hollow or filled rectangles

⬭ draws hollow or filled rounded rectangles

🖌 fills an enclosed area with current pattern

◯ draws hollow or filled ovals

♡ draws freehand shapes

A paints text at insertion point

⬡ draws regular polygons

◿ draws irregular polygons

The Objects menu allows you to define and set the properties of objects.

- **Button Info...** presents the dialog box used to specify the selected button's properties

```
┌─────────────────────────┐
│      Objects            │
├─────────────────────────┤
│ Button Info...          │
│ Field Info...           │
│ Card Info...            │
│ Bkgnd Info...           │
│ Stack Info...           │
│·························│
│ Bring Closer     ⌘+     │
│ Send Farther     ⌘-     │
│·························│
│ New Button              │
│ New Field               │
│ New Background          │
└─────────────────────────┘
```

- **Field Info...** presents the dialog box used to specify the selected field's properties
- **Card Info...** presents the dialog box used to specify the current card's properties
- **Bkgnd Info...** presents the dialog box used to specify the current background's properties
- **Stack Info...** presents the dialog box used to specify the current stack's properties
- **Bring Closer** (⌘+) moves the selected button or field one level closer to user's view
- **Send Farther** (⌘–) moves the selected button or field one level farther from user's view
- **New Button** creates a generic button
- **New Field** creates a generic field
- **New Background** creates a blank card with a blank background after current card

The Paint menu is only available when a Paint tool is in use. It provides operations to edit the current paint selection.

```
┌─────────────────────────┐
│      Paint              │
├─────────────────────────┤
│ Select          ⌘S      │
│ Select All      ⌘A      │
│·························│
│ Fill                    │
│ Invert                  │
│ Pickup                  │
│ Darken                  │
│ Lighten                 │
│ Trace Edges             │
│ Rotate Left             │
│ Rotate Right            │
│ Flip Vertical           │
│ Flip Horizontal         │
│·························│
│ Opaque                  │
│ Transparent             │
│·························│
│ Keep            ⌘K      │
│ Revert                  │
└─────────────────────────┘
```

- **Select** (⌘-S) selects the shape most recently drawn
- **Select All** (⌘-A) selects the entire card or background picture
- **Fill** fills the selected area with the current pattern
- **Invert** changes black to white and white to black in selected area
- **Pickup** acts like a stamp pad to pick up images of desired patterns in specified shapes
- **Darken** makes the selected picture area darker
- **Lighten** makes the selected picture area lighter
- **Trace Edges** outlines the black in the selected area
- **Rotate Left** rotates the selected area counterclockwise 90 degrees
- **Rotate Right** rotates the selected area clockwise 90 degrees
- **Flip Vertical** flips the selected area vertically
- **Flip Horizontal** flips the selected area horizontally
- **Opaque** makes the selected area opaque
- **Transparent** makes the selected area transparent
- **Keep** (⌘-K) remembers the current card or background picture so that after subsequent editing it can be "reverted" to
- **Revert** reverts to most recently "kept" picture

The Options menu appears when a Paint tool is in use. It provides operations to control the details of painting.

Options

Grid
FatBits
Power Keys

Line Size...
Brush Shape...
Edit Pattern...
Polygon Sides...

Draw Filled
Draw Centered
Draw Multiple

Rotate
Slant
Distort
Perspective

- **Grid** overlays a grid pattern to guide painting
- **FatBits** acts like a zoom lens to magnify selected area and allow fine detail work
- **Power Keys** lets you perform Paint commands from the keyboard
- **Line Size...** lets you choose the width at which subsequent lines will be drawn
- **Brush Shape...** lets you choose a brush shape for subsequent painting
- **Edit Pattern...** lets you edit the current pattern
- **Polygon Sides...** lets you select the number of sides for subsequent polygons
- **Draw Filled:** subsequent enclosed shapes will be filled with current pattern
- **Draw Centered:** subsequent enclosed shapes will be drawn centered as opposed to from their upper left corners
- **Draw Multiple** allows you to draw repeated copies of a shape at specified offsets
- **Rotate** allows you to rotate a selected rectangular graphic region by dragging its "handles"
- **Slant** allows you to slant a selected rectangular graphic region by dragging its "handles"
- **Distort** allows you to distort a selected rectangular graphic region by dragging its "handles"
- **Perspective** allows you to impose perspective on a selected rectangular graphic region by dragging its "handles"

The Patterns menu appears when a Paint Tool is selected. It is used to specify the current pattern for all paint operations.

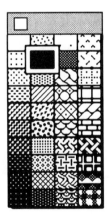

HYPERCARD HINTS

Below is a listing of some generally useful facts and shortcuts that we have found particularly helpful in interacting with HyperCard. We present them here, divided into two groups, so that you can use this list as a quick reference source. Each of the hints in the first group describes how to use the keyboard to accomplish directly a common HyperCard operation. The second group contains "What to do if..." hints that describe common HyperCard mishaps and their solutions.

Type the following key (or combination of keys) to perform the operation described. When a combination of keys is listed, press all keys at once. In combinations involving mouse clicks, the related keys should be depressed and held down while the mouse button is pressed.

Key Equivalents

KEY(S)	OPERATIONS
⌘ and Q	quit HyperCard
⌘ and H	go Home
⌘ and space bar	show/hide menuBar
⌘ and M	show/hide Message box
⌘ and B	show/cover current background
⌘ and X	cut selected item
⌘ and C	copy selected item
⌘ and V	paste item
⌘ and 1	go first
⌘ and 2	go prev
⌘ and 3	go next
⌘ and 4	go last
Return or Enter (from Message box)	send a message
Return or Enter (from Dialog box)	respond using default response for ("OK")
option and return	types ¬ for breaking Hyper-Talk command across more than one line
double-click	to open an object's Info... dialog box
shift and double-click (from Button or Field tool)	to open a button or field script
shift and menu-select Info... (from Objects menu)	to open any object's script

When Things Go Wrong (1)

- If you are unsure as to which copy of a stack is the current stack . . . select Stack Info... from the Objects menu.

- *If you click on a button* and get no response . . . it is likely that the Browse tool is not selected.

- *If a field, button, or graphic is not visible* . . . check to see if you are in background mode.

- *If a menu command is not available* . . . check to see that your user level is set correctly.

- *If an entire menu is not available* . . . see if a Paint tool is selected.

- *If you want to paste or create* a new first card for a stack ... create or paste the new card after the current first card, then delete (or cut and paste) the former first card.

- *If you want to move a field and its contents from one card to another* ... copy or cut the field using the Field tool, navigate your way to the card onto which you want to place the field, then hold down the shift key while selecting "Paste Field" from the Edit menu.

HYPERTALK

The following is a summary of the HyperTalk vocabulary items (messages, operators, commands, functions, properties, constants, keywords, and tool names) that are described in the text and/or used in the Æ stacks. For each vocabulary item, a brief description and example of its use from one of the Æ stacks is provided. After the vocabulary listing, a few additional hints are provided that are specific to HyperTalk programming.

ITEM	TYPE	DESCRIPTION/EXAMPLE
&	operator	concatenates two strings together *EX:* put "Total balance = $" & totalSoFar into card field "Results"
&&	operator	concatenates two strings with an intervening space *EX:* put "Max balance =" & value && "For" into card field "Results"
*	operator	multiplies two numbers *EX:* put op1 * op2 into result
+	operator	adds two numbers *EX:* put op1 + op2 into result
-	operator	subtracts second number from the first *EX:* put op1 – op2 into result
/	operator	divides first number by second *EX:* put op1 / op2 into result
<	operator	returns true if first value is less than second, else false
<=	operator	returns true if first value is less than or equal to second, else false
>	operator	returns true if first value is greater than second, else false
>=	operator	returns true if first value is greater than or equal to second, else false
=	operator	returns true true if first value is equal to second, else false
<>	operator	returns true if first value is not equal to second, else false *EX:* if item 3 of thisLine <> 1000 then ...
add	command	adds a value to a container *EX:* **add** item 3 of line count or card field "Data" to totalSoFar

(continues)

Continued

ITEM	TYPE	DESCRIPTION/EXAMPLE
after	keyword	used with put to place information following what is in a container *EX:* put (item 1 of thisLine) && (item 3 of thisLine) & return **after** card field "Results"
and	operator	returns true if both expressions are true *EX:* (if field A contains 0) **and** (field B contains 0) then . . .
any	operator	returns an arbitrary constituent of some piece of information *EX:* put **any** line of field thisType into thisWord
answer	command	displays dialog box with up to three buttons and waits for user to click; stores response in "it" *EX:* **answer** "Enter data before calculating or sorting" with "OK"
answer file	command	displays standard Mac open-file dialog box from which you choose a file to open; stores response (full name of file) in "it" *EX:* **answer file** "Open which TM file?" of type TEXT
ask file	command	displays standard Mac save-file dialog box in which you specify a file to save; stores response (full name of file) in "it" *EX:* **ask file** "Save current TM as:" with CF
before	keyword	used with *put* to place information in front of what is in a container *EX:* put quotient mod 2 **before** result
browse	tool	the Browse tool *EX:* choose **browse** tool
button	tool	the Button tool *EX:* choose **button** tool
	keyword	used in variety of contexts to refer to any button *EX:* Send mouseUp to card button "Clear"
card	keyword	used in a variety of contexts to refer to any card *EX:* go to **card** id 24025
char	keyword	selects a group of characters *EX:* put **char** 1 of card field "Text Field" into tempChar
charToNum	function	returns the ASCII code of a single character *EX:* put **charToNum**(tempChar) into tempASCII
choose	command	selects a tool as if you had chosen it from the Tools menu *EX:* **choose** button tool
click	command	simulates a mouse click *EX:* **click** at 276,92
closeCard	message	sent to a card when it stops being the current card *EX:* on **closeCard**
closeField	message	sent to a field when the user hits Tab, Enter, or clicks outside of the field after it has been changed *EX:* on **closeField**
closeStack	message	sent to a stack when it stops being the current stack *EX:* on **closeStack**
contains	operator	returns true if first text value is found in second container *EX:* if direction **contains** "L" then . . .
cursor	property	a value indicating the shape of the current cursor *EX:* set the **cursor** to 4

ITEM	TYPE	DESCRIPTION/EXAMPLE
delete	command	removes specified chunk from a value *EX:* **delete** last char of line thisLine
div	operator	performs integer division (with no remainders) *EX:* put decimalValue **div** 2 into quotient
divide	command	calculates quotient *EX:* **divide** sum by num
do	command	executes a string or the contents of a container as a HyperTalk command *EX:* **do** card field "Text Field"
doMenu	command	executes a menu item from within a script *EX:* **doMenu** "Quit HyperCard"
drag	command	simulates the dragging of the mouse *EX:* **drag** from 14,64 to 280,300
empty	constant	the empty string *EX:* if card field "Data" is **empty** . . .
end	keyword	ends all message handlers and functions *EX:* **end** mouseUp
exit	command	leaves a handler before its physical end is reached *EX:* if ("a" is not in thisLine) and ("an" is not in thisLine) then **exit** artCheck
false	constant	boolean value *EX:* put **false** into justEquals
field	keyword	used in a variety of contexts to refer to any field *EX:* put empty into card **field** "Results"
	tool	the Field tool *EX:* choose **field** tool
get	command	retrieves the value of an expression or property; places result in "it" *EX:* **get** the short name of the target
global	command	identifies variables as accessible to more than one handler *EX:* **global** whichField
go	command	changes the current card and/or stack *EX:* **go** to stack "Æ Home"
hide	command	removes specified object from view *EX:* **hide** card field "helper"
hilite	property	true if a button is highlighted, else false *EX:* set **hilite** of button counter to true
home	keyword	refers to first card of HyperCard's Home Stack *EX:* go **home**
id	property	system-assigned identifier for an object *EX:* set the name of background button **id** 11 to "Halt"
idle	message	sent to a card when no other messages are being processed *EX:* on **idle**
if	keyword	indicates one of HyperTalk's conditional statement forms *EX:* **if** item 3 of this line > 1000 then . . .

(continues)

Continued

ITEM	TYPE	DESCRIPTION/EXAMPLE
into	keyword	used with *put* to replace the contents of a container *EX*: put empty **into** card field "Results"
is in	operator	true if first argument is found in the second; else false *EX*: if (char 1 of word *it* of thisLine **is in** vowels) then . . .
is not in	operator	logical opposite of "is in" *EX*: if ("a" **is not in** thisLine) then . . .
it	keyword	container used to store results of many commands *EX*: if **it** is empty then . . .
item	keyword	text separated by a comma from other text *EX*: add **item** 3 of line count of card field "Data" to totalSoFar
length	function	returns the number of characters in a string *EX*: add (the **length** of keywords + 1) to spot
line	keyword	used in a variety of contexts to refer to a line in a field *EX*: put **line** 2 of card field 1 into **line** 1 of card field 1
	tool	the line Paint tool *EX*: choose line **tool**
location	property	the screen coordinates of an object *EX*: put the **location** of background button "Tape Marker" into arrowLoc
lockScreen	property	when true, navigation effects are not seen on screen *EX*: set **lockScreen** to true
lockText	property	when true, a field cannot be typed into (but can be clicked on) *EX*: set the **lockText** of the target to true
message box	keyword	the Message box *EX*: show **message box**
mod	operator	calculates the remainder of an integer division operation *EX*: put decimalValue **mod** 2 into result
mouseClick	function	true if the mouse has been clicked since current handler began *EX*: if the **mouseClick** then . . .
mouseDown	message	sent to an object to indicate mouse was depressed within its boundaries *EX*: on **mouseDown**
mouseEnter	message	sent to an object to indicate mouse has entered its boundaries *EX*: on **mouseEnter**
mouseLeave	message	sent to an object to indicate mouse has exited its boundaries *EX*: on **mouseLeave**
mouseLoc	function	returns current horizontal and vertical coordinates of mouse's location *EX*: if (item 1 of the **mouseLoc** > 188) . . .
mouseUp	message	sent to an object to indicate mouse was released within its boundaries *EX*: on **mouseUp**
name	property	user-assigned name of a stack object *EX*: set the **name** of background button id 11 to "Start"
next	keyword	points to the next card in the current stack *EX*: go **next**
next repeat	command	branches around statements within a repeat loop and continues iterations *EX*: if line i of field "Vocabulary" is not in field "Patient" then **next repeat**

ITEM	TYPE	DESCRIPTION/EXAMPLE
not	operator	logical negation *EX*: set the visible of card field "helper" to **not** (the visible of card field "helper")
number	property	the system-maintained level number of each stack object *EX*: put the **number** of the target into TempGate
	function	returns the count of the expression provided *EX*: put the **number** of lines of card field "Data" into num
numToChar	function	returns the character whose ASCII equivalent is provided *EX*: put **numToChar** (charToNum (char 1 of thisLine)—32) into char 1 of thisLine
offset	function	the position of one string in another *EX*: put **offset**(keyword, field "Patient") into spot
open File	command	prepares an external file for use by a stack *EX*: **open file** "binary data"
openCard	message	sent to a card when it becomes the current card *EX*: on **openCard**
openStack	message	sent to a stack when it becomes the current stack *EX*: on **openStack**
or	operator	logical disjunction *EX*: repeat until (ruleNumber > 0) **or** (lineNumber > 50)
pass	command	after intercepting a message, **pass** sends the message up the object hierarchy *EX*: **pass** put
pencil	tool	the pencil Paint tool *EX*: choose **pencil** tool
pop card	command	makes the most recently "pushed" card the current one *EX*: **pop card**
previous	keyword	points to previous card in the current stack *EX*: go **previous**
push card	command	saves the current card's id for later retrieval via "pop card" *EX*: **push card**
put	command	stores information in a specified location *EX*: **put** 3 into whichField
random	function	returns a random integer in a specified range *EX*: put the **random** of 4 into formNumber
read from file	command	reads characters from a previously opened external file *EX*: **read from file** "binary data" for 8
repeat	keyword	control structure for expressing iteration *EX*: **repeat** with counter = 1 to the number of card buttons
return	constant	name given to the Return keyboard character *EX*: put "Accounts with large balances (> $1000):" & **return** after card field "Results"
	command	used in function handlers to specify the final calculated value *EX*: **return** where

(continues)

Continued

ITEM	TYPE	DESCRIPTION/EXAMPLE
scroll	property	property of scrolling field expressing the amount the field is scrolled from the top *EX*: set the **scroll** of the card field "Results" to 0
select	tool	the select Paint tool *EX*: choose **select** tool
send	command	directs a specified message to a specified object *EX*: **send** mouseUp to background button "Clear"
set	command	assigns a value to an object property *EX*: **set** userLevel to 5
show	command	makes the specified object visible *EX*: **show** menuBar
target	function	returns the object that was the original recipient of the current message *EX*: get the short name of the **target**
then	keyword	used with **if** control structure *EX*: if (field A contains 0) and (field B contains 0) **then** put 0 into field R
true	constant	boolean value *EX*: put **true** into justEquals
userLevel	property	values 1–5 correspond to access levels browsing-scripting *EX*: set **userLevel** to 1
value	function	determines the value of an expression stored in a container *EX*: put the **value** of item 2 of field "thisCell" into field "newCell"
visible	property	determines whether or not an object is seen on the screen *EX*: set **visible** of card field "helper" to false
word	keyword	any string of characters with no intervening blanks *EX*: put **word** 2 of line tempGate of field "GATES" into A
write to file	command	writes text to a previously opened external file *EX*: **write** makeBinary(tempASCII) **to** file "binary data"

When Things Go Wrong (2)

- If you get an error message such as "Never heard of background field named X" . . . it is likely that you left the word "card" out of a script. Remember, HyperTalk assumes a field is in the background unless it is explicitly referred to as a card field.

- If you get an error message such as "Never heard of card button named Y" . . . it is likely that you left the word *background* out of a script. Remember, HyperTalk assumes a button is on the card unless it is explicitly referred to as a background button.

A.3   TROUBLESHOOTER'S GUIDE

This final section of the appendix should be regarded as the last place to look before calling the repairperson (or your instructor, or—worse still—the authors!). In it we provide guidelines for avoiding specific problems with individual Æ stacks. We have, to be sure, done our best to anticipate and compensate for such problems. Given, though, the interactive nature of many of the stacks, and the freedom and access that HyperCard affords its more advanced users (authors and scriptors), we could not program around every situation that might arise. For each Æ stack (in chronological order) that warrants it, we describe potential problems, their causes, and simple solutions.

We start by emphasizing a general point made earlier. All of the second edition Æ stacks have been written to run under HyperCard 2.1 (actually, they will run in version "2.anything" of HyperCard). They will not run in HyperCard "1.anything." Indeed, if you try to open one of the Æ stacks using an older version of HyperCard you will get a message indicating that the "New file format requires new version of HyperCard." If you have more than one version of HyperCard available, just make sure you are using some version 2 when you are using the Æ stacks.

- **Initialize and use an extra floppy disk** to serve as backup storage for any of the stacks that you will be using extensively and/or modifying. When asked in the lab exercises to "Save a Copy..." of a stack, do so on your storage disk. Do the same for homework and project stacks.

- **Starter Stack:** The stacks on the next to last card denoted with asterisks are *not* included with the Æ stacks. They are provided as part of the standard HyperCard package. If you click on any of these buttons you will be asked, for example, "Where is Stack Ideas?" You could then search for the disk containing Stack Ideas, or simply "Cancel" the search and return to the Starter Stack.

- **Disk Labels:** Labels cannot be printed (in fact, nothing from the disks can be printed) until (1) your Macintosh is connected physically to a printer; and (2) the Chooser Desk Accessory has been run. If you try to print you may get a system error message, but no other damage will result.

- **High-Priced Spread:** This stack produces an error message (intentionally) when it detects an ill-formed formula (one referencing a nonexistent cell, containing an unrecognized operator, or containing a nonnumeric value). It does not, though, protect from formula referencing cells that in turn contain non-numeric values. If you get an error message such as "abc is not the right type for +," just click "Cancel" and either change the cell containing "abc" or revise the formula that references it.

- **No Account:** The stack will function improperly (although it won't indicate an error) if commas, rather than spaces, are used to separate values in the Data field. Also, every data line must end with a Return.

- **Howard Stone:** A Return character entered into the Text field is treated as any other character—it is translated. Use the Enter key to initiate translation. In the lab exercise that requires the "do" command, if a non-HyperTalk command is entered for translation, a message indicating that the text is "Not a HyperTalk command" will appear. Click "OK" to continue.

- **Apple MacPippin:** The stack detects and reports three errors: Unrecognized Pippin Command, Illegal Address in Instruction (addresses must be numeric), and Illegal Reference in Instruction (addresses must contain only numeric information). Error messages of the form "Can't understand arguments to command ADD" may also be produced. All such errors are the result of not properly setting the values of program variables prior to running a Pippin program.

- **Logg-O:** Do not try to set the values for pins in the midst of creating a gate. Make all connections first (you have no choice), and then set pin values. Note that if a pin is the output for two gates, its value will ultimately be that dictated by the last gate added to the circuit.

- **ITM:** It is up to you to format your TM rules. The lines on the screen are merely graphic guidelines. They do not help the program to distinguish values in rules. Each rule must be on a separate line (ending in a Return) and the values on a line must be separated by spaces.

- **Hype-KU:** Be careful in editing the stack's forms and vocabulary. Each form and each vocabulary item requires its own line (ending with a Return). You may want to resize these fields if longer forms are developed.

- **ÆTM:** Remember the guest id and pin numbers ("XXX" and "0000") or it will be difficult to move beyond the first card of the stack. Actually, it will be difficult to do anything in HyperCard if you do not log on properly.

INDEX